MRS. LINCOLN

AND

MRS. KECKLY

The Remarkable Story

of the Friendship

Between a First Lady

and a Former Slave

BROADWAY BOOKS NEW YORK

MRS. LINCOLN

AND

MRS. KECKLY

Jennifer Fleischner

A hardcover edition of this book was published in 2003 by Broadway Books.

PRINTED IN THE UNITED STATES OF AMERICA

BROADWAY BOOKS and its logo, a letter B bisected on the diagonal,
are trademarks of Random House, Inc.

Visit our website at www.broadwaybooks.com

First trade paperback edition published 2004

Book design by Dana Leigh Treglia

Cataloging-in-Publication Data is on file with the Library of Congress.

ISBN 0-7679-0259-9

5   7   9   10   8   6   4

To my parents,

Ruth and Irwin Fleischner

Mary Lincoln.

&

Elizabeth Keckley

TERRITORIAL EXPANSION and SLAVERY, 1819–1854

Free States and Territories

Slave States and Territories, 1820

Admitted as Slave State, 1845

Open to Slavery by the Compromise of 1850

Open to Slavery by the Kansas-Nebraska Act of 1854

(Boundaries as of 1854)

CANADA

Maine
New Hampshire
Massachusetts
R.I.
Vt.
New York
Connecticut
New Jersey
Pennsylvania
Delaware
Md.
Virginia
N. Carolina
S. Carolina
Georgia
Florida

Atlantic Ocean

Great Lakes

Mich.
Ohio
Ind.
Illinois
Wisconsin
Iowa
Minnesota Territory

Kentucky
Tennessee
Ala.
Miss.
Louisiana
Arkansas
Missouri

Indian Territory
Texas

Kansas Territory
Nebraska Territory
Utah Territory
New Mexico Territory
Oregon Territory
Washington Territory
California

Gulf of Mexico

MEXICO

Pacific Ocean

0 Miles   200   400   600
0 Kilometers   600

Mrs. Lincoln

and

Mrs. Keckly

Prologue

*O*n a mild Friday morning in September 1867, two well-dressed, middle-aged women sat on a bench in New York City's Union Square Park, discussing money.

They were a curious pair. One was white; the other was not. The white woman was dressed in deep mourning, with her face hidden behind a heavy veil of black crepe. She was short and heavy-set and looked to be excited or agitated. When she spoke, which she did rapidly and almost steadily, she was unable to sit still, and she glanced around her frequently, as if checking to see that no one could overhear. But whenever she fell silent, her body seemed to slacken, her shoulders sink, and an air of despondency would come over her. She gave the appearance of being very much alone, despite the presence of her interested companion.

The second woman was also a fascinating study. She sat very still, listening, her back straight, her hands in her lap. Her face was handsome, with deep-set eyes, a firm mouth, strong nose, and a complexion that suggested she was of a mixed-race background. She wore her dark hair coiled in a braid on her head, and she was dressed as elegantly, though less richly and elaborately, than the woman beside her. At first glance, one would think her demeanor proud, even haughty. But a longer look would find in her composure the habit of waiting—silent, watchful, patient. She had the regal bearing of one who might have been a queen, but in fact, she was a mulatta who had been a slave.

The first woman was Mary Todd Lincoln, the daughter of a wealthy Kentucky slaveholder, who had become a President's wife by throwing in her lot with the driven, self-schooled son of a poor white farmer. The second was Elizabeth Keckly, the illegitimate daughter of her Virginia master and his slave, who had bought her freedom and gone to Washington, where she had become the dressmaker and confidante to the President's aristocratic wife. At their first meeting, the day after Abraham Lincoln's first inauguration, they had had to negotiate a fair price for Lizzy's services. Now they were talking money again, only this time they were devising a moneymaking scheme intended to help them both, though it was Mary's debts from overspending and her anxiety about poverty that spurred them on.

One might say they had changed places. At forty-nine, the former slave was a successful Washington businesswoman, but her companion, who would be forty-nine in December, was a traumatized, debt-ridden widow, living with her youngest surviving son in a genteel hotel in Chicago. Lizzy had continued to sew for Mary, who would even now accept only work done by Lizzy's own hand, but the two had hardly seen one another for two years. Then one day in March, a determined Mary Lincoln wrote a letter to her friend: "Now, Lizzie, I want to ask a favor of you. It is imperative that I should do something for my relief, and I want you to meet me in New York."[1]

As they sat near the majestic equestrian statue of George Washington that dominated one end of the park, their heads inclined together in confidential conversation, the two women focused on the mundane details of what they intended to accomplish. And although their interests were decidedly mercantile, the conversation itself was a type of quiet revolution that Washington scarcely could have imagined. That two *women* should be devising a commercial transaction without the knowledge of male relatives or guardians was already a somewhat bold undertaking. But that one of them was a President's widow and the other a woman of African descent and a former *slave* was indeed a test of the possibilities of citizenship in the nation. Four generations earlier, many Americans believed that human enslavement was incompatible with their founding ideals of equality, liberty, and happiness for all, but only north of the Mason-Dixon line, the border between Maryland and Pennsylvania, was slavery abolished in their time. It took a war between the states—after decades of westward expansion had made slavery an explosive issue, as two million square miles west of the Mississippi had to be allotted to Northern freedom or Southern slavery—to resolve the tragic contradiction inherent in the founding of the republic. To be sure, the end of slavery exposed fresh contradictions: if one asked her, the freedwoman Lizzy would have said that she felt less kinship with the Irish nursemaids who sat chatting nearby while their young charges played than with the lavishly attired President's widow by her side. And the widow would have said the same.

With retailers beginning to cram into the basements and parlor floors of the mansions and brownstones on the square and boardinghouses and hotels moving in, Union Square was slightly past its prime as the prestigious residential center of the city. Money was migrating northward: the wealthy were moving to Madison Square and Gramercy Park and developers were eyeing upper Manhattan and beyond. Vast emporiums and mansions rose along northern Fifth Avenue and would soon pass 52nd Street, where the abortionist Madame Restell had daringly built her "palace" in 1862. But Union Square was familiar territory for Mary Lincoln, who in her own heyday—her proud, expansive early days as "Mrs. President"—had bustled in and out of the fancy stores that lined the west side of lower Broadway in an exultation of "shopping" (then a relatively new verb), spending the $20,000 appropriation that Congress had granted to refurbish the shabby White House. Custom-made carpets, damask draperies, ornate furniture, and monogrammed china were ordered, packed, and sent to her new home in Washington. She also picked up several costly black point lace and camel's hair and cashmere shawls, all exceedingly fashionable. Trailed by reporters, the lady made news with her high-flying tastes and lavish spending.

Those days were over. And after all that had happened, it was Lizzy Keckly who had proven herself to be Mary Lincoln's closest, most durable confidante from her Washington days. "I consider you my best living friend," Mary would write to her; and at the time, it was true, for there was no one else who would do what Mary was asking. Resourceful and energetic, imperious and needy, Mary had exhausted all the white people whose aid she could command or cajole. Yet she could be a shrewd assessor of character (that is, when vanity did not get in her way), and over the years she had come to appreciate Lizzy's gifts; she knew that she could count on Lizzy to be discreet and to manage delicate situations, especially those involving well-heeled white folks. The plan to raise funds that Mary proposed to Lizzy was simple: they were to enlist a Broadway broker to sell off her old clothes and jewelry. Surely, there were many who would pay to own a little something that Mrs. Lincoln herself had worn. In summoning Lizzy, Mary Lincoln anticipated having the benefit of not only her companion's sound advice and comforting approval, but also her assistance in carrying out the idea.[2]

As mistress of the White House, Mary Lincoln had used the royal "we," and the gentlemen who frequented her White House salon nicknamed her "La Reine." Publicly, she liked the title "Mrs. President." She reveled in the creation of her image, born in the columns of the daily newspapers that rolled off the steam presses in unprecedented numbers, midwifed by the special correspondents who, reporting on Mrs. Lincoln's comings and goings, telegraphed their dispatches to papers throughout the land. One revolution in technology—the cheap and endlessly reproducible photograph—made it possible to see what she looked like in a variety of attitudes and poses. This was the first generation of photojournalism, the Lincolns the first consistently photographed Presidential couple, and the Civil War the first photographed war. This public visibility was Mary Lincoln's making; it also contributed to her eventual downfall.

Elizabeth Keckly was a "first" too: part of the first generation of post-Emancipation black Americans, an immigrant from a world of bondage into the promised land of freedom. Lizzy was Mary's dressmaker, confidante, and mainstay during the difficult years that the Lincolns occupied the White House and the early years of Mary's widowhood. But she had already been established as *the* seamstress to the Washington elite when she was first hired by Mary Lincoln to make sixteen dresses. As one Washington correspondent reported, "Stately carriages stand before her door, whose haughty owners sit before Lizzie docile as lambs while she tells them what to wear."[3] For Mary Lincoln, viewed by capital insiders as a parvenu outsider from the hinterlands out west, securing Madame Keckly's services was the social equivalent of joining the right club. Ironically, during the winter of 1860–61, while Mary was dreaming of all the outfits she would need in the White House and the Southern states began seceding from the Union, it was Mrs. Varina Davis, wife of Mississippi Senator Jefferson Davis, the future President of the Confederate States of America, who was Lizzy's best Washington client.

Nor did Lizzy underestimate her connections. As a "colored woman" close to power, she used her position not only to advance herself, but to influence the Lincolns' attitudes toward the recently freed slaves who were pouring across Union lines and into Washington during the war. Self-made and self-reliant, she too sat for her studio portrait, as was the custom of the day. It shows an erect, dignified, and self-contained woman, wearing a richly wrought silk dress with a brooch at her throat and matching earrings. Her hands are graceful, shapely, and strong.

When I began this project, I knew that I wanted to restore Elizabeth Keckly to her place in history, to give voice to her life and story. I also wanted to give a fuller, truer picture of Mary Lincoln, and this I believed I could do by recognizing her relationship with Lizzy. For it seems obvious to me that we can hardly understand the way the Southern-born Mary Lincoln experienced her world without registering the shaping presence of the various black women in her life—from the slave women she loved as a girl, who virtually raised her, to the freedwoman she turned to during the crisis-ridden 1860s, when America found itself embroiled in civil war and Mary's private world was falling apart. Indeed, a niece of Mary Lincoln's would point to her aunt's early dependence on her "black mammy" to explain the way she turned so naturally to Elizabeth Keckly. Nor can we understand the mixed-race Elizabeth Keckly without exploring her "mixed" life, moving between opposing worlds that had been falsely, and tragically, designated "black" and "white."[4]

The more deeply I became involved in their lives, the more fascinated I became by the dynamic of their "friendship"—their term for their relationship. But I was troubled by a too easy use of the word. What kind of friendship was it, after all, when the black woman who was paid for her time deferred to the white woman who, for her part, turned to her "friend" out of a need most often triggered whenever she felt betrayed and abandoned by the white world? How could so asymmetrical a relationship based on such self-interested interdependence be what any of us would regard as a friendship? Yet there is no other word that conveys the warmth, understanding, and intimacy of their connection. And although it might resemble, it differed radically from the intimate, interracial relationships they had as girls and young women living under slavery. Lizzy's freedom made her Mary's partner in creating the terms of the relationship. Had Elizabeth Keckly been Mary Lincoln's slave, neither woman would have addressed the other as "friend."[5]

Still, slavery was an important bond. Intelligent, ambitious Southern women from slavery households, Mary Lincoln and Elizabeth Keckly recognized in one another a strange kinship of contradictions, fraught with mixed emotions. Theirs was a worldview shaped by slavery, where black and white lives were inextricably mixed in every way. For those antebellum Southerners who used the popular phrase "the family, white and black" to refer to the extended households in which they grew up, the phrase had a literal meaning, even if that meaning was rarely openly acknowledged. They *were* family—in every sense of the word. Sex between (mostly) masters and slave women had created a population of slaves that had become visibly whiter. Fathers owned their children; sisters slaved for their half-brothers. The frenzied rhetoric against "mongrels," "mutations," and "miscegenation" (a term coined in 1863, the year of the Emancipation Proclamation) simply underlined the fact. Indeed, although I was surprised, I was not shocked to learn that Elizabeth Keckly and Mary Lincoln were related by marriage: a cousin of the Burwell family who owned Lizzy had married a Todd, a distant relation of Mary's. Still, if Mary and Lizzy knew about this connection, they would not have chatted about it over tea.[6]

Then, too, their relationship, which bridged a revolutionary period in race relations that began before and extended past the emancipation of four million black slaves and the abolition of slavery, was remarkable for the degree to which it flew in the face of conventional behavior of the day. It was a highly visible companionship in an age when interracial friendships were uncommon, and it was noted not only privately by White House observers but also publicly in the newspapers. Moreover, the Elizabeth Keckly whom Mary Lincoln considered a friend was no "faithful mammy," the idealized maternal center of the slavery household. Pragmatic, clear-minded, and upwardly mobile, Mrs. Keckly brought qualities to the friendship that extended far beyond comforting familiarity. Self-made and self-sufficient, she inspired the tormented Mary's affection, respect, and trust.

There are two other restorations that warrant mentioning, which result from my wish to be true to these women's own representations of themselves. The first time I saw Elizabeth Keckly's full signature, on an application for a war pension after her son's death in the Battle of Wilson's Creek, I was thrilled. It's not that I hadn't expected to see her signature there, because I did, but that there is something about a person's signature that seems to bring that person to life. I knew that she'd held the paper I now held, leaned over it, and wrote her name. It was as if I could feel her presence. But then, I noticed that she spelled her name differently from the way it appears in her published memoir and in the history books. She spelled it "Keckly," not "Keckley," as I had always seen it. I checked against her signature elsewhere, thinking that perhaps the pension signature was smudged or that she varied the spelling. But she never did. I also noticed that when she signed her first name she wrote "Lizzy," not "Lizzie," as Mary Lincoln spelled it. So, in writing this book I decided that if I was to restore Elizabeth Keckly's "voice" I must also restore her name, as she knew it: Elizabeth Keckly, Lizzy Keckly.

I have also done something like this for Mary Lincoln, who dropped the Todd after her marriage and never used it when signing her name. In my book she is referred to as Mary Lincoln.

CHAPTER ONE

$\mathcal{A}$s Mr. and Mrs. Robert Smith Todd looked forward to the birth of their fourth child in 1818, they were likely hoping for a boy. Two little girls— five-year-old Elizabeth and nearly three-year-old Frances—and one boy, one-and-a-half-year-old Levi, were already running around the yard on Short Street at the center of town and up the hill to their widowed Grandma Parker's house next door. By December, as her time neared, the children's twenty-four-year-old mother, Eliza Parker Todd, had retreated to her bedroom on the second floor of the nine-room house, leaving them to be watched by their slave mammy. The Widow Parker, who had given the young Todds the lower part of her double lot as a wedding gift, probably helped supervise the household slaves, among them three of her own whom she had loaned to her daughter: a young girl, a woman in her twenties, and an older woman. The sweet-natured Eliza admitted when she first married at eighteen that she had no idea housekeeping "was attended with so much trouble." Indeed, six months into her marriage, while the young couple were still living with the Widow Parker waiting for their house to be built, she had written, perhaps teasingly, to her maternal grandfather, "It really is almost enough to deter girls from getting married." In any event, she concluded, "it would never do for me to go far from Mama as I shall stand so much in need of her instruction."[1]

Her husband, a second cousin whom she'd known virtually all her life growing up in Lexington, would not have asked her to move anyway. Robert Smith Todd had his own parental ties to Lexington, Kentucky, in the shape of a patriarchal Todd tradition of local power and influence. Well-connected and trained as a lawyer, twenty-seven-year-old Robert was already launched upon hectic political and business careers, apparently determined, if not absolutely destined, to follow in his father's and uncles' footsteps. His concerns kept him from home for long periods elsewhere—in Frankfort, thirty miles to the west, where he served as clerk in the Kentucky House of Representatives, and at other times almost eight hundred miles south in New Orleans on buying trips for his struggling wholesale/retail firm. So Robert Todd may not have minded the constant presence of a mother-in-law in the house. Later, he would come to depend on it.

The new baby, another girl, arrived on a cold Sunday, December 13, 1818. Her parents named her Mary Ann, after her mother's only sister. Like other well-to-do Kentucky women of her day, Eliza, having survived this infant's birth, would have breast-fed her daughter for several weeks or more before handing her over to a wet nurse, most likely a slave. After recovering from the birth, Eliza would have enjoyed returning to some of Lexington's social and cultural activities: paying and receiving morning calls, for which Lexington ladies dressed formally in silks and satins; taking afternoon drives in the Todds' Lexington-built carriage; and visiting the public library, which was open every afternoon except Sunday in a building on the corner of the town square. More likely, she looked forward to visiting Mrs. Plimpton's millinery in Mr. Plimpton's store, at Main and Main Cross Street; attending music concerts in the public rooms of the town's many taverns; and gathering with her neighbors for the thrilling lottery drawings, also held in the taverns, which were the town's favorite means of raising money for schools and churches. There were always plenty of parties and picnics and frequent celebrations honoring a steady parade of patriots and politicians. When little Mary Ann was almost seven months, Eliza may have stood outside Postlethwait's Tavern on July 3, waving a handkerchief as salutes were fired to honor President Monroe and General Jackson, who beamed acknowledgment to the assembled crowd. Later in July she might have attended the university's Commencement Ball, for which gentlemen could get tickets at Postlethwait's but ladies had to apply to the ball's managers.

There would not have been much for her to do at home. Aunt Chaney, one of the family slaves, did all the cooking and had absolute charge of the kitchen; when the children got on her nerves, she banged the pots and kettles and ordered them out. It was Chaney who baked the memorable beaten biscuits and corn bread, whose recipes ("jes' a pinch—jes' a bit more") the future Mary Lincoln would one day try to record in a notebook for the benefit of her Irish serving girl in Springfield. Aunt Chaney considered it criminal—and not a bit surprising—that "the po' white trash Irish" didn't know how to make good corn bread. Equally chauvinistic Nelson drove the family carriage, served in the dining room, and did the marketing across the way at the tradesmen's stalls in the Main Street market house, next to the courthouse. Female slaves aired and made the beds, carried the water, started the fires, washed and hung out the clothes, swept, dusted, scrubbed, and polished in every room in the house. Another slave tended the garden. And although Mrs. Todd did her own mending and trimmed her own hats, the French swisses and sheer muslins that her husband brought back from New Orleans all went to a sewing woman, possibly a local woman or a slave. Above all, there was the children's Mammy Sally. She loved "her" Todd children as if they were her own—at least, according to the Todds.[2]

Lexington sits in the region of Kentucky known as the Bluegrass, named for the bluish tint of the wind-rippled long-stemmed grass whose seeds were sown in the nineteenth century. The Bluegrass covers a circular area of roughly eight thousand square miles at the heart of the state. With its long growing season, temperate climate, plentiful rainfall, and limestone-laden, phosphate-rich soil, this section of Kentucky seemed like an Eden to early visitors—or, in the language of a nineteenth-century gazetteer writing for Easterners considering emigration, "The Garden . . . of the world." Not satisfied with the idea of Kentucky as Paradise, one Western preacher reckoned that heaven was a "Kaintuck of a place." But travelers reserved their most extravagant praise for the "small portion of highly beautiful land" directly surrounding Lexington, the two thousand square miles of the Inner Bluegrass. "The country around Lexington," wrote one Pennsylvanian, "for many miles in every direction is equal in beauty and fertility to anything the imagination can paint." When an eastern Kentuckian dies, it is said, he wants to go to Lexington.[3]

With a grid layout reminding visitors of stately Philadelphia, Lexington in 1818 was a center of culture and refinement, known as "the Athens of the West" and noted not only for its girls and boys academies but also for Transylvania University, the first university in the Western United States, founded in 1780. Already it boasted a leading law school, where the young Henry Clay was a professor; more famous still was the medical school, with an extraordinary library of rare and valuable works that were bought in Europe by the school's charismatic Dr. Charles Caldwell, who also gave regular lectures abroad.

Under the circumstances, Robert Smith and Eliza Todd could have been forgiven for thinking themselves among the "first people" in the land, despite their location west of the Alleghenies. On both sides of the Todd-Parker union there were Revolutionary War heroes: generals and majors and Eliza Parker's great-grandmother, who rode out to the camp at Valley Forge in the winter of '77 with provisions for her husband, Captain Andrew Porter, and was said to have impressed Washington with her devotion.

Indeed, the Todds could have been forgiven for thinking themselves at the center of their universe, for they could boast of being a vital part of a wide network of leading local families, beginning with their Porter and Parker cousins and extending to their Kentucky kin by marriage, which would in time include the prestigious Shelbys, Breckenridges, Wickliffes, McDowells, Bullocks, Woodleys, Brents, Didlakes, "and so on and on," as the Lexington *Herald* put it. Even the nation's heroine, the stalwart Dolley Madison, who, four years earlier, standing in the charred and gutted ruins of the White House, had announced, "We shall rebuild . . . the enemy cannot frighten a free people," had been married to a Todd before a Madison. Such connections made a difference in a world where (as one lady wrote) "we claim our relations to the forty-fifth cousin." Even the Almighty was bound to be impressed: as Abraham Lincoln quipped on the family's changing their name from Tod to Todd, one "d" was good enough for God, but not the Todds.[4]

Perhaps the Todds were justified if they were inclined to consider Lexington their particular contribution to the American West. Their neighbor and Robert's political mentor Congressman Henry Clay (the future senator and frequent presidential candidate) may have become Lexington's most famous and influential resident, but by the time he arrived in 1797, an eager young lawyer on the make, the Todds had already helped build Lexington into the town where ambitious men like Clay aimed to be.

"Start early and git down to Caintuck," wrote William Calk in his diary on April 20, 1775. Soon afterward, soldiers encamped in a wilderness clearing at McConnell Springs in central northern Kentucky decided to give to their fledgling settlement the name of the town in far-off Massachusetts where, on April 19, minutemen had exchanged the first shots of the Revolution with British soldiers. Among the party of soldiers was said to have been the nineteen-year-old Pennsylvania-born Levi Todd. With his two older brothers, John and Robert, Levi helped found a Kentucky dynasty that would shape his granddaughter Mary Todd's childhood, permeating her earliest sense of identity and place.[5]

Yet when Mary Ann Todd was born, Lexington was barely a generation—and not many miles—from its frontier days. Six years earlier, above the mouth of the Green River in northwestern Kentucky, three Indians attacked a white family, killing the elderly father and wounding his son. The then-single Robert Smith Todd gave a friend a matter-of-fact report: "It appears that there was a Quarrel between this young man and one of the Indians because he had beat him shooting, and no doubt had given him some provocation, one of the Indians was killed in the encounter which no doubt saved the lives of all the family."[6] If his daughter Mary ever fantasized about transforming a backwoodsman and Indian fighter into a gentleman, she no doubt drew on her hometown for models.

Inheritors of a spirit of rebellion, the Todds were descended from Scottish Covenanters who fought against England's king and Church, then found refuge in northern Ireland before immigrating to Montgomery Country, Pennsylvania, in 1737. These immigrants, David and Hannah Todd, sent three of their sons to be educated at the Virginia school run by the boys' eminent uncle, the Presbyterian Reverend John Todd. In 1778, through their uncle's friendship with Virginia Governor Patrick Henry, the Todd sons were commissioned to fight under General George Rogers Clark to secure the conquest of the Illinois territory. Afterward, Henry appointed the oldest son, John, the first civil governor of Illinois.

But it was Kentucky that promised most fair, a region where whites and Indians clashed bitterly over the area's unsurpassed hunting grounds. A decade earlier, older Indian leaders' efforts to reach accommodation with pioneers had faltered, and an enraged young Cherokee leader named Dragging Canoe had warned Daniel Boone that white settlers would find Kentucky "a dark and bloody land." Anglo-American expansion during the 1770s unified Indian militants, to whom white settlers were little more than invading colonizers who razed their villages and burned their corn. Indian raids on white settlements grew bloody and fierce; hundreds of Kentuckians were captured or killed and thousands of their horses stolen. During the Revolution, the British spurred the Indians on.

Mary and her siblings grew up hearing tales of the frontier exploits of her grandfather and great-uncles, especially her legendary uncle, Illinois Governor John Todd, who, as Colonel Todd, was second in military rank on the frontier only to General Clark. On August 19, 1782, ten months after the British surrender at Yorktown, Colonel Todd led 182 Kentuckians against the combined forces, almost one thousand strong, of Ohio Indian Nations warriors and British soldiers in the Battle of Blue Licks, outside Lexington. When a third of the Kentucky force was killed that day, compared with three killed and four slightly wounded of the British and Indian force, John Todd lay among the dead. Adding luster was John's legendary wealth: he had owned twenty thousand acres, and when he died his only child, a daughter, became one of the wealthiest people in Kentucky. It was also Uncle John Todd, as Mary knew, who had a Kentucky county named after him.[7]

Meanwhile, Mary's grandfather, John's younger brother General Levi Todd, had been sowing his own fortune in Lexington and surrounding Fayette County. In 1781, he became one of the first purchasers of Lexington's half-acre lots, with an additional five acres for crops, which were laid out on a grid plan in the original 710-acre town. Then, after the war ended, Levi, like other veterans holding warrants for land west of the Alleghenies, moved in to settle his claims. Using warrants and purchase rights, he built an estate of seven thousand acres in Fayette and Franklin Counties.

By 1790, the earliest wave of Lexington residents had transformed their corner of Kentucky from a handful of log huts outside Colonel John Todd's stockade—with forty-seven inhabitants, mostly bachelors in frontier dress, who lived off the buffalo, deer, turkey, and geese they shot and were menaced by Shawnees and other Ohio Indians—into a bustling commercial and intellectual center of 843 residents. They slashed and burned away the thick-quilled canebrakes, which grew in dense clusters and could reach twenty feet high, and began planting pastures and fields. They divvied up town lots, designated ground for a cemetery and "a house of worship," and erected a court-house, a jail, and a schoolhouse. Town fathers made attendance at the log schoolhouse mandatory for Lexington boys to keep them from wandering where Indians might capture them. Levi Todd wrote to his parents in Pennsylvania to join him in Kentucky, where, with his new wife, Jane Briggs, whom he had married in 1779 in the fort at St. Asaph's in Lincoln County, he had begun a family. Also contributing to the end-of-century population boom were Mary Ann's maternal grandparents. Major Robert Parker was a Pennsylvania cousin of the Todds, and his bride, the spirited Elizabeth Porter, was the daughter of General Andrew and Elizabeth Porter. They arrived in 1790, having set out from Pennsylvania on horseback the day after their wedding.[8]

For ambitious men moving west at the end of the eighteenth century, Kentucky was an open field. Cheap land and opportunity attracted thousands of migrants, and the tendency of the laws encouraged enormous land claims for wealthier men like the Todd brothers. Later immigrants came down the Ohio River in flatboats, then overland on the Buffalo Trace into the interior, or made their way slowly from Cumberland Gap across the narrow Wilderness Road (cut through in twenty-two days in the spring of 1792 by woodcutters paid with the donations of 104 subscribers, among them Robert Todd, Robert Breckinridge, Governor Shelby, and Levi Todd, who gave $12). Still others sent their slaves ahead to take the risks and burdens of frontier settling for them; these included North Carolina merchant Thomas Hart, the future father-in-law of Henry Clay, who joined in a land speculation company and, from the comfort of his home in Hillsborough, fretted about "send[ing] a parcel of poor slaves where I dare not go myself." In the 1790s, Kentucky's population tripled, reaching 220,955 in 1800. Meanwhile, the slave population quadrupled, totaling 40,343 in the state, their numbers concentrated in the plantation-rich Bluegrass; soon, that number would be one-third of the population of Lexington and the Inner Bluegrass.[9]

The Bluegrass, with Lexington at its heart, generated fabulous wealth for its first-generation white families. Realizing that hemp, not tobacco, was going to be their region's pot of gold—its long, fine fibers made the ropes and bags that tied up the South's cotton bales—planters had slaves lay out their fields with the valuable crop. Lexington merchants branched out into manufacturing, opening the rope walks and bagging factories (by 1820, this workforce was 98 percent slave labor) that would make many of them very rich men, among them John Wesley Hunt, who became the first millionaire in the

West. Meanwhile, land speculation in the late eighteenth century had made Lexington a boomtown for lawyers, who got rich adjudicating countless over-lapping land claims and litigating the property suits and countersuits that sprang up as fast as weeds. It was what had drawn the lawyer Henry Clay from Virginia. As clerk of Fayette County, Mary's grandfather Levi Todd earned fees whenever property changed hands, which was often. He also made money as an attorney and land surveyor, preferring these to farming.[10]

In addition to riches, there were also republican ideals to inspire these im-migrants. To be sure, Kentucky was a mecca for Virginians "burdened down by worn-out lands, excess sons, and unprofitable slaves," and many, including Levi Todd, saw Kentucky as a place to re-create and regenerate the colonial Virginia Piedmont and Tidewater cultures, which in their view had grown stagnant and stale. Already, Virginia had become the Old World, corrupt and degenerate, and Kentucky the promising New. As Levi wrote to an Eastern friend, "If the citizens of the Eastern waters do not corrupt our principles, we shall, I believe, be a free and happy people. Kentucky will be an asylum for liberty." Mary's black mammy, Aunt Sally, who marked the Todd fence with a secret sign to runaways that they might stop for food and rest before con-tinuing north to the Ohio River and freedom, may have taken a different view.[11]

As an adult, Mary Todd would draw fire for vulgar crassness and grasping materialism, yet she was also praised for her elegance, charm, wit, and intel-ligence. Such qualities were come by honestly, as the Lexington she inherited from her grandparents and parents was rich in both. By the time Mary arrived on the Lexington scene, forty years of intensive, focused commercialism and gentrification had established a standard of living that, for people like the Todds, had become a matter of pride, value, and identity. Despite the town's inland location, which made moving goods in and out an arduous task and tended to inflate prices, by the turn of the century dozens of stores and ordi-naries lined the commercial grid of Main Cross and Mulberry Street running north-south and Main and Short Street at the center of town. Tradesmen's stalls filled the Main Street market house, a brick structure with sixteen pil-lars that had been erected on the site of Colonel John Todd's fort. They catered to a rising bourgeois class ready to ride full tilt into the gratifications of conspicuous consumption. "What a pleasure we have in raking it in and spending it with our friends," proclaimed Thomas Hart, the merchant-manufacturer originally from North Carolina. Already by 1807, the year Levi Todd died, while Easterners nursed visions of Kentucky as a wilderness over-run by savages and bears, one could buy fancy silver pieces from one of several Lexington silversmiths, among them the renowned Asa Blanchard, whose shop at the corner of Short and Mill Streets featured the beautiful English-style gold and silver pieces that established him as one of the country's leading silversmiths. Fashion-conscious Lexington wives and daughters, earning their reputation for extravagant dress, bought imported French heeled shoes and paisley shawls (a particular favorite of the future Mary Lincoln) and took home yards of European tamboured and jaconet muslins, dimities, and nankeens to be stitched into the latest design. Rising men, bursting with accomplishment, kept architects, carpenters, brickmakers, bricklayers, and stonemasons busy constructing public buildings and elegant homes, with design details testifying to their owners' individuality and self-worth, like the octagonal study lit by a skylight at Henry Clay's 600-acre Ashland, based on Benjamin Latrobe's design, and the Greek Revival doorway Robert Smith Todd would add when his family moved to his second, larger, more impressive house on Main. The "expense of furnishing and keeping so large a house clean" was no small thing, as the mother of Brutus Junius Clay, Henry's younger cousin, warned her son before he built his elaborate brick Federal and Greek Revival house in nearby Bourbon County: "It gets mouldy, spider webs, moths in the carpets." But big houses were an expression of self, and Brutus had his mansion, Auvergne, built.[12]

Mary's parents, second-generation Lexingtonians, were raised at the center of this world of heady exuberance and high expectation. Robert Smith Todd was born February 25, 1791, at his family's country villa on the 235-acre estate his father had built about two miles east of town on the Richmond Pike, just past where Henry Clay would construct his own plantation. Named Ellerslie after the Todd ancestral Scottish village, the villa was the kind of oxymoron—the new ancestral home—beloved of American gentry. Like the Virginia estates after which these end-of-the-century homes were modeled, Ellerslie was a twenty-room brick Georgian mansion set in elegant grounds laid out with formal gardens, orchards, meadows, fields, pastures, and numerous outbuildings. It took nearly thirty slaves to work the Ellerslie fields and manage the livestock, polish the silver, wipe the china, change the numerous beds, and dust the library's leather-bound books. There Robert Todd grew up surrounded by a large and noisy family as the seventh of Levi and Jane Brigg's eleven children, to which would be added a half-brother when his mother died and Levi remarried.

Much less is known about Mary's mother, Eliza Parker. She was born in 1794 and spent most of her girlhood in the brick house on Short Street up the hill from the house she would live in as a young wife and mother. Her father, Robert Parker, was a prominent surveyor, merchant, and miller who served briefly as clerk of Lexington's governing body. He died in 1800, when Eliza was six, leaving his "lands, slaves, etc. to wife, remainder to children equally," with instructions to provide his four boys and two girls with as good an education "as my estate and other circumstances will admit of."[13] His widow sold their place in the country and moved into the center of town, where she had the new house built on Short Street. There, with the help of six slaves, she raised her six children, and then, after they were grown, carried on by outliving her husband by forty-nine years. Known to all as the Widow Parker, she was a dominant force in the lives of her children and grandchildren.

It is from the Todds that Mary was said to have inherited her taste for material comforts and modern living. Her grandfather Levi Todd, a portly five feet eight inches tall, set the pace in fashionable consumption when in 1800 he became one of only two people in the county (along with Major James Russell) to own a four-wheeled carriage. (By his granddaughter's day, one could count more four-wheeled carriages in Lexington than in any American town of its size.) Her father, Robert Smith Todd, clearly enjoyed his fine clothes, private carriage, rare brandies, and the "famous" mint juleps Nelson mixed for his guests; these concoctions of whiskey, sugar, ice, a bit of water, and sprigs of fresh mint were considered to have medicinal value. A little girl growing up in this world would learn to consider fashionable dress, pianos, carriages, rugs, double parlors furnished with mahogany furniture and hung with a sample of Lexington portrait painter Matthew Jouett's work, good schools for the children, a country estate, and regular restorative trips to nearby springs a natural part of everyday living.[14]

As for manners and habits of mind, the turn-of-the-century Bluegrass squire modeled his behavior, as he modeled his estate, on that of the gentry of Piedmont and Tidewater Virginia, meaning that horse racing, foxhunting, dancing, billiards, and cards—accompanied by whiskey—were the entertainments of choice. To this, the proud Bluegrass man added an elaborately developed code of honor that allowed for duels and other, less formal means for violently settling disputes. In the town streets, visible from the rooms where the young people took dancing lessons and the ladies afternoon tea, was enacted a level of public violence that frontier living had rendered the norm. Scuffles and fistfights were common. Like Scottish highlanders, Bluegrass gentlemen carried dirks (short daggers) in their vests, which, when provoked, they used readily and openly. Students at Transylvania University were formally forbidden to bring their dirks, knives, or swords into any of the school's buildings, not just the chapel. Assailants were tried for murder, but persuasive claims of self-defense and a sympathizing public often led to acquittals. Among themselves women like Mrs. Susan Corlis commented on the lamentable ways of men. "What a pity it is they have not more command of their passions and use the knife & dagger so freely," she wrote her daughter.[15] Such an environment would seem fertile ground for outsize feelings to take root; visitors frequently commented on the Kentuckian habit of exaggeration and overstatement. Here, too, cultivating enemies was as natural as maintaining friends, and making mental lists of those who had failed one a form of comfort as reassuring, in its way, as calling to mind those who had proven true.

Twenty-one-year-old Robert Todd and eighteen-year-old Eliza Parker married in Grandma Parker's parlor on November 13, 1812, while Robert was home on sick leave from the War of 1812, the battle against Great Britain mostly over the unsettled land in the West. The fact that they were second cousins, sharing a great-grandfather, simply made their kin-minded families that much happier at this affirmation of family pride. They were said to have begun courting early, as early perhaps as Robert's college days at Transylvania University, just two blocks from the Parker house, which he entered when he was fourteen. After graduation, he set out to study law.

To become a lawyer, a young man of that day had to "read" with an established lawyer. Or, as one St. Louis man advised his nephew, whom he had sent to Lexington for his education, you must "court the company of men of learning, sober, sedate and respectable characters. . . . You will not only gain information from them but respectability and influence." As the uncle more urgently advised, "Try and become acquainted with Mr. Clay, or some eminent lawyer in that state." For Robert Todd, already a member of the court, such introductions were easy, and plum legal apprenticeships dropped into his ready hand. From there, it was but a short step into politics.[16]

Handsome and nearly six feet tall, with blue eyes, light brown hair, a strong neck, and a ruddy complexion, Robert was courtly, industrious, and personable. He was also energetic to the point of nervousness, and he propelled himself into the role of Robert Smith Todd, Esq., with characteristic verve. Elected at twenty-three as clerk in the Kentucky House of Representatives in Frankfort, where he served continuously until declining to run again in 1835, a three-term assemblyman for Fayette County in the Kentucky House of Representatives and three-term state senator (also in Frankfort), he also served in Lexington as councilman, then magistrate, and then sheriff. Besides which, he was an officer in the local Masonic lodge. Then, too, over the years, patronage appointments were sent his way. With a cousin's help, Robert got a clerkship in the Lexington branch of the Bank of Kentucky; by 1835 he was the branch president. He also was made a judge in the Fayette County Court; judgeships, like bank positions, were political and highly charged, especially during the court crisis of the 1820s, when Kentucky legislators and courts battled over jurisdiction of state banking and financial policy.

Meanwhile, Eliza had been having their children at the customary interval of one about every two years. First born was daughter Elizabeth in 1813, one year after their marriage, followed by Frances in 1816, Levi in 1817, Mary Ann in 1818, Robert in 1821, Ann in 1824, and George in 1825.[17] Much like Robert's transit toward male adulthood, Eliza's formal preparations for her destiny as wife and mother had been typical of middle-class girls of her age: a few years most likely at Mrs. Beck's Lexington Female Academy, where she took lessons in reading, composition, grammar, arithmetic, letter writing, and, for an additional fee, knitting, painting, embroidery, and sewing. For this, her mother would have paid $150 a year. Little wonder Eliza felt herself "so much in need of [Mama's] instruction" when she married at eighteen.

Unfortunately, the expansion of Robert and Eliza's family coincided with their town's slow decline. The successful trip of the steamer *New Orleans* in 1811, which had sealed Lexington's fate as an inland town unable to compete with the river cities of Louisville and Cincinnati, and a postwar depression made emulating their parents' lives, especially as they shared their consumerist values, an ongoing struggle. Similarly, in the next generation, their daughter Mary Todd would grow up cultivating expensive tastes she would not always be able to afford.

As the family grew, Robert found he needed more money. In 1817, the family estate, Ellerslie, was sold and Robert went into his first business partnership. With fellow veteran Bird Smith, he opened Smith and Todd, an "Extensive Grocery Establishment," at Cheapside. Advertising that a member of the firm would personally attend foreign markets to bring customers the best articles at the lowest prices, Robert made long buying trips to New Orleans for barrels of cognac and Jamaica spirits, casks of Medeira and Malaga wine, sherry, Irish whiskey, Holland gin, clarets and ports they stocked alongside local whiskey, brandy, groceries, glassware, chewing tobacco, and thousands of pounds of "good hog lard." The timing of the new enterprise was imperfect, however; the bank panic of 1819 led to a nationwide depression, and by 1821, Smith and Todd were out of business. One year later, what was already a difficult time for the Todds grew worse. In 1822, they lost their toddler, Robert Parker, who died at only fourteen months.[18]

As an adult, Mary was fated to outlive a murdered husband and three of her four children. Eventually, her losses destroyed her. Who knows what effect the death of this baby brother had on Mary, then only three years old, or what seed of vulnerability it planted? It may be that the surviving Todd children did not suffer greatly at the loss of their brother. But if they did not pine for their mother's attention—for not only would Eliza have retreated into mourning, but as long as her children knew her she was preoccupied with a new pregnancy, lying-in, or latest newborn—and if they did not suffer from their father's long absences and his grief, they would have been highly unusual children. And if the oldest girl, Elizabeth, held her little sister Mary to soothe her wounded spirit while their mother nursed sister Ann (whose arrival had also deprived Mary Ann of her full name), it filled a hole in the lives of both small girls and was the first stage in a lifelong bond that was arguably Mary's most durable in a life not given to—or *given*—long-lived relationships. Mammy Sally negotiated among the competing demands of five small children while their mother was upstairs anxiously awaiting the birth of her final child. When Mary ran into the shelter of Sally's arms, it was the origin of her reliance on the competency and comfort of a black female servant.

It was this last birth that dealt the ringing blow of loss that changed everything for Mary and her siblings. That last child—a boy named after George Rogers Clark, the Western commander of General Todd and his brothers—

came into the world in 1825 while most of Lexington was celebrating Independence Day at a picnic at Fowler's Garden, just beyond the town's limits. Both were memorable events. At the picnic, roast pig and beef dripped from spits and whiskey poured from open buckets and kegs. At night, there was an "elegant dinner and dancing," as the *Kentucky Gazette* would report, where Mr. Henry Clay, Major General Winfield Scott, and other distinguished guests toasted "the memory of General George Washington." General Scott gallantly saluted the "Ladies of the Western Country—the rose is not less lovely, nor its fragrance less delightful, because it blossoms in the wilderness."[19] Since mid-May, when General Lafayette's triumphal return tour to the United States had passed through Lexington, there had been weeks of revolutionary fervor, and the Todds may have been thinking of military processions and revolutionary cockades when it came time to name their newest son.

But within hours of giving birth, Eliza developed a fever. Normal births were still women's work, and it is unlikely that any outsider except a midwife, possibly Harriet Leuba, the watchmaker's wife who lived down the street, was in attendance. But doctors, if available, were called for difficult cases, and Robert sent for the best the town had to offer. With a medical school nearby—a rare boon for any town, especially a Western one—he could call in specialists, and he may have called in as many as three: his friend Dr. Elisha Warfield, once professor of surgery and obstetrics at Transylvania Medical School; Dr. Benjamin Dudley, a popular professor of anatomy and surgery; and Dr. William Richardson, not as liked or respected as his colleagues but a well-known specialist in midwifery and women's diseases. Their efforts, however, failed.

Years later, Dr. Lunsford Yandell recalled that when he started studying medicine at Transylvania in the 1820s, his doctor father put William Buchan's *Domestic Medicine* in his hand and remarked, "Every student ought to learn enough of the practice, at the outset, to place him on an equality with the old women of the country." Harriet Leuba probably knew how to make "salves, syrups, pills, teas, and ointments, how to prepare an oil emulsion . . . how to poultice wounds, dress burns, treat dysentery, sore throat, frostbite, measles, colic, [whooping cough] . . . how to lance an abscessed breast, apply a 'blister,' . . . induce vomiting, assuage bleeding, reduce swelling, and relieve a toothache, as well as deliver babies." Every mistress's commonplace book contained folk recipes for ointments and remedies, like Mary Burwell's recipe "for the Dysentery," a mixture of vinegar and salts in a gallon of water, taken "in a tumbler of cold water." But neither the midwives, who generally delivered the town's babies, nor their competitors, the medical experts who were called in emergencies, knew what to do for the hemorrhages, convulsions, toxemias, and puerperal infections (the major cause of childbirth deaths) that killed about one new mother for every two hundred live births.[20]

Given their fees and status, the doctors used more dramatic measures to try to save their patients. Yet, as one historian notes, the therapies they might have tried on Eliza—calomel (a mercurial compound) to induce violent purging, laudanum (a liquid opiate) to reduce cramping, and bloodletting (as much as 40 ounces, or until the patient was nauseous)—would have done little for the dying woman "except perhaps to make her feel worse." When morning came thirty-one-year-old Eliza Parker Todd was dead, probably of a puerperal fever caused by an invasion of bacteria into the uterine cavity.[21]

When the children were brought in to say good-bye after their mother's body had been washed and laid out, they would have been too frightened and bewildered to hear the words of consolation that no doubt were being offered all around. They had recently lost their little brother; here was death again. Someone took the new baby and gave him to a wet nurse, for he would survive. The stricken widower sent out a printed funeral notice, inviting mourners to "his residence on Short Street this evening at 4 o'clock, July 6, 1825." Notices were necessary because the town's two newspapers were published only twice a week, and funerals and other occasions could be over before the next editions were out. As he handled the arrangements, Robert likely recalled how his own father was left with eleven children to raise after the death of his wife. Certainly he was wondering how in the world he was going to take care of his own six small children.

An unmarried aunt on their mother's side, Ann Maria Parker, moved in from next door to manage the house; one of Robert's sisters, Eliza Todd Carr, who had a family in nearby Walnut Hills, helped as much as she could. Grandmother Parker frequently came down the hill or had the children sent up to her. Now almost twelve, Elizabeth stepped further into the mothering role she had always played toward her younger siblings, especially her sisters. Serious and devoted, she may have felt it her responsibility to look after the others, although she was still a child herself and no doubt deeply unhappy.

Then there were the slaves—like family, the children would have thought—and they were surely a source of consolation. The usually irritable Aunt Chaney may have let the older girls help her in the kitchen when August arrived and it was time to put up the butter and get the pickling done for the winter. Perhaps she even spoke gently and gave the children treats. The formidable Nelson may have taken them for carriage rides into the country, letting the children stop to gather flowers to bring home or for the girls to put in their hair, a stylish fancy Mary would always love. Mary would also always enjoy carriage rides, perhaps for the privacy and intimacy they provided for conversation or for their soothing and liberating motion and stir.

But it was Aunt Sally who would have comforted them at night, when frightening shadows crossed the bedroom walls. As she helped them into bed after they had recited their prayers, she may have told them how the ghosts of loved ones often come back to help and protect you; they also gave you counsel and sometimes even showed the way to hidden treasure. It may have been that during one of these nightly visits Sally shared with the lonely children the slave's prayer for protection, which Mary invoked one day when she was at the Carrs with her siblings and cousins. While they were playing, a group of friendly Indians in blankets and feathers walked by, sending the terrified children scattering to find hiding places. Only Mary could not find a safe place to hide. She panicked and ran to the middle of the room, where she stood and cried out, "Hide me, oh, my Savior, hide." And if Mary had a nightmare about her father dying too, a natural fear under the circumstances, it was probably her Aunt Sally who hushed her back to sleep, while she clutched one of her beloved dolls to her chest.[22]

"A jewel of a black mammy": this is how a cousin who grew up with the Todds remembered Aunt Sally; "she alternately spoiled and scolded the children, but they loved her and never rebelled against her authority." Aunt Sally liked to attend the "white folks'" church, McChord's Presbyterian on Market Street, where Robert was a trustee and Mary attended Sunday school. She sat in the second gallery—the only place blacks were allowed to sit—and kept her eye on the Todd children lining Pew 15. They evidently watched her, too, as once Mary teased Sally about napping during the sermon.[23]

Walking to and from church or school, one could see the landmarks of Lexington's lucrative slave business, inevitably casting a shadow over the affection between the white children and the Todd slaves. In the market square, visible from their house, black slaves were auctioned. One lot eastward, adjacent to the market, was the courthouse yard, where in the northeast corner stood a slave whipping post "of black locust, one foot in diameter, ten feet high and sunk two and a half feet in the ground." A little farther east, at Mulberry and Short Street, two blocks from the courthouse, stood the stately brick jail, looking more like a private home. Known as Megowan's after the jailer Thomas B. Megowan, it was where slaves—and kidnapped free blacks—were held, dressed up for market, and sold. (Megowan was also a hotelier—perversely, a related line of work.)[24]

Lexington would not become a center of the slave trade until the 1840s and 1850s, by which time the once-prestigious Lexington Theater was leased to slave trader Lewis G. Robards, who turned it into the largest slave jail in the West, with a second-floor set of apartments featuring his choicest stock of mulatto slaves. But by Mary's childhood, coffles of slaves were already being driven through the eighty-two-and-a-half-feet-wide Main Street, headed for the Mississippi flatboats bound for slave markets in Natchez and New Orleans, loaded with Kentucky slaves chained together on the decks to prevent their escape. The slaves were marched through town, where they could not be missed, "manacled together, two abreast, all connected by supporting *a heavy iron chain*, which extended the whole length of the line," according to the Lexington *Western Luminary*. Traders occasionally staged grotesque parades, like the trader in 1822 who gave the first pair of slaves violins to play, the second cockaded hats to wear, and the slave in the center, his upraised hands in chains, an American flag to wave overhead. Surrounded by such sights as these, whereas indoors, there was one's mammy to dry one's tears, a slaveholding child learned to tolerate the queasy mix of familial intimacy and paternalism with the racism and raw commercialism that defined slave ownership. This, or reject outright a fundamental pillar of one's own culture.[25]

After Eliza died, Robert Todd characteristically turned to activity for solace and relief: for the next six months, he threw himself into work and society in Frankfort, leaving his six children (ranging from a few days to twelve years in age) in the care of female relatives and slaves. Unwittingly, Robert compounded their loss, for if losing their mother hit with a sudden force, losing their father as a direct consequence submerged the children in the prolonged misery of his seeming neglect and rejection. If their mother's death felt like abandonment, their father's withdrawal added to their burden of fear and guilt.

The children's anxieties must have been further roused when a neighbor carried gossip back to Lexington from Frankfort. It explained why their father was so much away and why, even when he was at home, he seemed so unsettled and distracted. There is evidence that Robert was telling himself that his new mission in Frankfort was being undertaken for his "young folks" at home, and it might even have been mostly true.[26] Yet not everyone approved when they heard that within six months of Eliza's death he was already courting a second wife.

In fact, by early fall, he had settled on his choice, and it only remained to propose and persuade her. Robert had met Miss Elizabeth L. Humphreys of Frankfort during one of the previous winter legislative sessions. Since then, he had probably seen her, or one or another of her high-powered relatives, several times at least. Her father, Dr. Alexander Humphreys, who had died in 1802, had come from a prominent family in Virginia. But it was her impeccably turned-out mother who ruled Frankfort society in inimitable style. The Kentucky capital's grand old lady, Mary Brown Humphreys was admired widely for her intelligence, virtue, and taste, which her reputation for reading Voltaire in French did nothing to compromise. Hers was the family that Robert was bound to know: of Mrs. Humphreys's four brothers, two taught medicine at Transylvania University (in 1802–3 Samuel Brown introduced the smallpox vaccination in the region) and two others represented Louisiana and Kentucky in the U.S. Senate. The Louisiana Senator James Brown was married to the sister of Henry Clay's wife, another link to Robert's circle.

Robert was said to have courted his first wife "like a house afire." Elizabeth Humphreys he courted like a lawyer who had himself as a client. Apparently, the couple had an understanding by January 1826 ("a contract," as Robert called it), for when Robert returned to Frankfort on the thirteenth, after a brief absence on business, he was expecting to be able to fix a wedding date. He arrived instead to find that Elizabeth had left for a long visit to New Orleans. "I returned home [to Lexington] with a wounded spirit," he wrote her. "The apprehension that you had left home under the idea that I had been *neglectfull* or had failed to exhibit that interest in whatever concerned you which from my professions, might and ought to have been expected, for the first time crossed me and gave much pain." It was the beginning of a rather fretful courtship. Anxious to pin Elizabeth down, Robert pressed his suit in a stream of letters, urging her repeatedly to set a date. Her letters were not nearly as numerous. Three scheduled deliveries of mail a week came by stage to the Lexington Post Office, which was run by Postmaster Joseph Ficklin, but when Nelson went to pick up the family's mail, paying cash for each letter depending on its weight and the distance it came, he often returned without a letter from her. If she was "training" Robert, punishing him for the times he broke engagements with her for business trips or for when unexpected houseguests came to Lexington, she was only giving him a taste of what to expect as, for ten months, she held him at bay. All the while, she could look upon the miniature of him, painted by Jouett, that her suitor had sent her, to console—or aggravate—her when the original did not appear.[27]

One can see why it was said that Mary took after her father temperamentally, for what comes across in Robert's letters (Elizabeth's side of the correspondence has disappeared) is his impatience, even pique, when Elizabeth does not comply with his single-minded designs. "When we came to a contract," he wrote her in February, "you claimed a respite for its performance, and no period was fixed on for that purpose; I will not repeat to you the circumstances under which, & the motives which induced me to make you my proposal, at the period I did." His obvious hurry to wed, if it did not outright offend her, presented a problem of etiquette, especially for the proper daughter of the proper Mary Humphreys, and he urged her "to consult your convenience and pleasure on the subject, and . . . select a period which will be convenient to you, and will conform to what you may deem a proper regard to public opinion as regards us both, as to the time when our views may be carried into effect—Would not some day of the month of June suit you, and both of us?" Two pages later his barely hidden impatience erupted into irritability, and he accused her of hiding something from him. Has she heard any unpleasant stories about him, "idle speculations," he wanted to know? "I am afraid your *total silence* of which I think I have some little cause to complain, has proceeded from considerations of this kind—and may I not infer a want of confidence?"[28]

Even putting aside the matter of propriety, Miss Humphreys could have had other reasons to hesitate. For one thing, a thirty-five-year-old widower with six small children who presented himself as longing for a time "when my domestic circle will be complete; and when worn down by the cares & perplexities of the world, [I] can retire into the sanctuary of that circle," was no ideal catch for a single woman, even if she were already in her mid-twenties and dangerously close to spinsterhood. By the 1820s, young women could read novels and poetry instructing them in the language of romance and the promises of ideal love. How would any self-respecting woman respond to being pursued by a middle-aged widower who, with frank and unromantic self-absorption, presented her with a job? "I hope it is not necessary to tell you, that my situation is irksome and uncomfortable . . . and in truth, I feel more unsettled and afloat than I have ever done before—A Sun is wanting to complete the System of which I compose a part." It could not have helped when he added that he could not "descend to flattery" because of her "intelligence."[29]

There is something almost touching in Robert's desperation. And yet, even while being taken up by the melodrama of his own feelings, he did recognize that a single woman almost ten years his junior might want something more than to become his family's "Sun"; she might want children of her own, for instance. "My ideas of the felicity and duties of matrimonial relation may perhaps be of a sublimated character, but if so, I would imagine would not the less enable me to enjoy or dispense them, or to discharge the duties incident to that relation." And he anticipated another objection; that, given the number of his dependents and difficulties in business, he could not support her in the style to which she was accustomed or supply her with all that was "necessary for our comfort & happiness." However, were he not able to do so, he told her, he would "never have proposed a change of the situation where you now enjoy it."[30]

So it went, back and forth. In September, his friend Robert Wickcliffe, whose wife had died five months before Eliza, married Robert's first cousin, the widow Mary Owen Russell (Colonel John Todd's daughter). This was social sanction enough, and seizing his advantage, Robert wrote, "It was believed that he and myself were to have been married on the same day—he has taken the start of me, but I hope only a few days."[31]

Finally, Robert could stop writing. The couple were married in Frankfort on Wednesday, November 1, 1826. None of his family attended, "under the circumstances," a reference unclear in its meaning but in any event not promising.[32] A week later they returned to Lexington as husband and wife. Presumably, Robert was all relief that he had finally secured the Sun for the center of his family's solar system. Little did he suspect how chilling this sun's effect would be.

CHAPTER TWO

On a day in February 1818, Colonel Armistead Burwell of Dinwiddie County, Virginia, realized an increase in his personal property. Slight and unpromising as it first appeared and of no immediate benefit (in fact, quite the opposite), the tiny bundle represented a slaveholder's investment. The thoughtful, well-respected forty-one-year-old colonel (a veteran of the War of 1812 and former justice of the county court) relied on the planter's wisdom that "If a farmer is able to feed and maintain his slaves, their increase in value may double the whole of his capital originally invested in farming." Or, as another Virginian, Thomas Jefferson, had figured, "A child raised every 2. years is of more profit than the crop of the best laboring man." With no more than fifteen adult slaves to work in his house and his fields (one thousand acres on Sappony Creek, just southwest of Dinwiddie Courthouse, below Petersburg) and no means to buy more, Burwell's real wealth lay in the fertility of his female slaves.[1]

That day in February, the Burwell family's house

slave, Mammy Aggy, whose full name was Agnes Hobbs, had given birth to a baby girl. It was the first Burwell slave birth since May, when Aggy's sister Charlotte, who was Mrs. Burwell's personal maid, bore her second child and another slave, Sally, had her third. For this year, there was only one more slave pregnancy in sight (the cook, Mary, was in her fourth month with her third child). Of the five slave women of childbearing age, Aggy had been the least productive; already in her twenties, this was her first child.[2]

Still, even Armistead Burwell (pronounced Burl) would have had to admit that Aggy had always been "worth her salt," a favorite phrase of his. She was one of the family's most loyal and valuable slaves, beloved nurse to Armistead and Mary Burwell's children (eleven surviving out of thirteen, one born at least every other year) and seamstress for the entire household. Armistead had known Aggy all her life and practically all of his: Aggy, Charlotte, and their brothers had been born slaves into his parents' household during the last decade of the eighteenth century. Armistead, born in 1777, was already in his teens when Aggy was an infant in his boyhood home. She and her family were part of his inheritance.

In many ways, Aggy was a "privileged" slave; certainly her master and mistress would have thought so. She knew how to read and write, although law forbade slaves to be educated. And the Burwells had let her marry; her husband, George Pleasant Hobbs, was a literate, energetic man who lived with his owner, not far from the Burwell farm. With evident pride, Aggy named her daughter Elizabeth Hobbs, bestowing on the infant her husband's family name, a sign of autonomy in a slave and in striking contrast to her mistress's hasty notation in her commonplace book, a sort of housewife's diary, in which she copied recipes and inventoried household supplies, including slaves: "Lizzy—child of Aggy/Feby 1818." Aggy and George were an "abroad" marriage, but the couple were determined to be a family, and George was devoted to his wife and her child, even though he knew she was not his. Aggy could not have looked on her infant's fair face, fairer even than her own, without noticing its difference from the dark skin of her husband.

The full story of Armistead Burwell and Agnes Hobbs's relationship will likely never be known: whether he raped her against her furious resistance or she acquiesced; whether he was afflicted by feelings for her or used her coldly; whether she thought him better than other white men or hated him more purely. But it is certain that at least once, late in the planting season in the spring of 1817, when Armistead's wife was in her second trimester carrying the couple's tenth child, Armistead sought to have Aggy alone—in a field, in the woods, in the slave quarters, in the Big House—and she had no choice.[3]

We can only imagine what Aggy felt when she was shown her daughter for the first time by whoever assisted with the birth (the mistress may well have called in a doctor or midwife for the valued mammy). One day, she would tell her daughter who her real father was, but that was to be put off as long as possible. Yet if Agnes was like other slave mothers, it was not only her daughter's parentage that weighed on her mind. Many women spoke of their grief at giving birth to a child who was doomed to be a slave for life. Aggy would have heard of slave women who tried different plants and vegetable poisons to induce miscarriages; it was said that "tansy, rue, roots and seed of the cotton plant, pennyroyal, cedar berries and camphor" could bring about abortions.[4] Most desperate of all were the mothers who smothered their infants rather than see them grow up slaves or sold. Even the presence of a husband was little solace and less protection. There were weddings for slaves, performed by other slaves, masters, and preachers, at the end of which a broom was held about a foot off the floor for the bride and groom to jump over; if they touched it, it meant trouble down the way. But there were no papers, no legal documents, and because slave families did not legally exist, a parent, spouse, or child could be sold away at any time. It was the rare, lucky slave mother who had all her children nearby.

Having a girl brought a deeper misery to a slave mother. "When they told me my new-born babe was a girl, my heart was heavier than before," wrote a former North Carolina slave, Harriet Jacobs, after she escaped to the North. "Slavery is terrible for men; but it is far more terrible for women." Twelve years later, Aggy may have added inches to the hem of Lizzy's dress, as did the mother of a Georgia slave named Lucy McCullough, but she would have done so knowing that there was little she could do to protect her daughter from the kind of sexual exploitation she herself knew all too well.[5]

When Aggy resumed her daily chores, which she would have done as soon as she was able, she may have been permitted to keep Lizzy with her in the Big House, where Fanny, the Burwells' four-year-old daughter, seems to have made Lizzy her special pet (when they were in their twenties, the two would be comfortable enough to exchange gossip about the family and tease another). But if Aggy could not bring her baby into the house, she would have left her in the care of an older slave woman or, more likely, one of the older slave children, who would have looked after little Lizzy in a group with the six other slave children under six years old whose mothers were owned by Armistead. As a child, Lizzy Hobbs would have drawn on the comforting familiarity of this extended slave family, which included the slave women who had grown up with her mother and now shared the burdens of raising each other's children: Charlotte, Sally, Lucy, Annabella, and Mary (only Mary seems not to have been a Burwell slave child; the others may have been sisters or otherwise related). Of their twenty-one children, born between 1812 and 1828, the closest in age to Lizzy were her playmates in the slave quarters, where slave children, barefoot and dirty, could be heard shrieking with pleasure at games of jump rope, ball, marbles, horseshoes, and hide-and-seek. In their midst, one could also see the small, shining faces of running white children, the overseer's or master's legitimate offspring, who played with the slave children until all grew too old for such games. It is not known how many of the slave children, apart from Lizzy, were the white children's half-brothers and -sisters.[6]

While there would have been whispers in the slave quarters about the white parentage of the mixed-race children, an open secret on plantations, Burwell slave children could also hear stories about their slave ancestors, going back to early colonial days. It was a Burwell family boast that the "Burwell slaves" came down with the family through generations, from the early eighteenth century, when the colonial Burwells amassed their vast landholdings in southeastern Virginia and stocked their grand estates with new purchases from African slave importers. Unlike other families, the colonial Burwells followed the inheritance practice of entail, in which all property, including slaves, went to whichever male inherited the land. This meant that slaves were not sold away from the land, as in many plantation families. And although a father might give a slave or two as a gift to a daughter or grandchild (mulatto children were preferred as domestics), he generally passed his slaves to his sons, with most going to the eldest.[7]

Lizzy's father was the only son of the six children of John and Anne Powell Burwell. John Burwell died at forty-two in 1788, at which time eleven-year-old Armistead stood to inherit not only his father's property, an estate called Stoneland, but also the descendants of slaves that John may have inherited from *his* father (although, as the second son of a third son, John inherited less than other Burwells, and Armistead was poorer than many of his cousins). It would have been a source of pride to the Burwell slaves to be able to trace their ancestors back generations—if only to the port markets of Virginia. There, at the height of the slave trade in the 1720s and 1730s, men like Armistead's great-grandfather Lewis Burwell III bought Africans by the dozens for his plantation. The earliest of the Burwell slaves were primarily from the West African coast, from northern Senegambia down to present-day Angola, although some may have come from the more inland region of the Niger Delta. They were farmers, merchants, craftsmen, hunters, and fishermen. By the nineteenth century, few oral histories went back as far as Africa, but some antebellum Burwell slaves could tell family stories extending back to Lewis III's day.[8] Being in possession of family memories, even those embittered by denigration and hardship, meant much to people who were permitted to possess little else. This no doubt contributed to Agnes's sense of self-possession, as she proceeded from giving her daughter her husband's name to teaching her survival skills of all kinds.

Dinwiddie County is anchored at the north by Petersburg, which at the time was Virginia's third-largest town, where men made money in tobacco factories, mills, and stores and spent it at the racetracks, cockfights, taverns, and theaters. Melodramas and farces were performed nightly during the racing season, not to mention such spectaculars as the one by the tightrope walker Mr. Church, who lured his audiences with a promise to "conclude" his performances "with A SPANISH FANDANGO, danced blindfolded over thirteen eggs." Named for a lieutenant governor of colonial Virginia, Dinwiddie was settled by descendants of English colonists, including numerous Burwells, who moved their households and slaves inland from their plantations near the Chesapeake. By the late eighteenth century, caravans of carriages and wagons could be seen snaking their way westward across miles over rough roads, many of them little more than trails, to settle in the area. With the white women and children crowded into the carriages and wagons in the front, white men followed, riding on horseback alongside columns of footsore black men, women, and children who were expected to walk the entire way. Bringing up the rear were cattle, sheep, and wooden carts groaning under their loads of furniture and household goods.[9]

It took about a week to travel the hundred-mile journey west and south deep into the Piedmont region where Armistead's grandfather first settled. The magical beauty of the countryside—where, from March to November, wild flowers blossomed in profusion and, during the summer, butterflies filled the air—could delight the white family, but nature's beauties would have had a different effect on worn-out slaves. One Virginia slave described his resentment at the "freedom of nature," which seemed to mock him in his captivity; he found a measure of revenge by picking up a stick and striking at the flowering bushes that bounded him on either side as he walked, "taking delight in smashing down particularly those in bloom." It was not only the walking that wore down the slaves, but lack of sleep. At night, while the skies flickered with fireflies like shooting stars and the white family slept, the overseer might wake the slaves for a head count.[10]

Those who stopped in the Piedmont, like Armistead Burwell's family, erected dignified mansions on the highest points of their land (modeled on English estates) and surrounded them with apple and peach orchards, vegetable gardens, landscaped gardens, ponds, streams, and meadows. Smaller buildings radiated out: behind the Big House would be a cook house, with a copper pot for boiling and an oven; beyond that, a smokehouse, dairy, stables, tobacco houses, corn barns, a grain mill, and then the clustered wood or log cabins of the slave quarters, with their small garden plots and poultry yards. Such a layout made it possible for Letitia Burwell, one of the many Burwell cousins, to look back on her childhood and write, "Confined exclusively to a Virginia plantation, I believed the world one vast plantation bounded by Negro quarters."[11]

But Virginia plantations were vast only in a child's imagination; in comparison to the plantations of the Deep South, which might stretch for miles and miles, Virginia's plantations were small. Most likely, Letitia's sense of boundedness by the black quarters was the product of this smallness, for while enslaved black laborers on a Mississippi or Alabama plantation could live far removed from the white family in the Big House, slave and master on the small Virginia estates lived and worked side by side. Moreover, beginning in the late eighteenth century, black slaves in Dinwiddie consistently outnumbered free white persons, another contributing factor to Letitia's perception of living in a world surrounded by "Negro quarters."

In Petersburg, where Lizzy would be taken to live in the early 1840s as the slave of one of Armistead's married daughters, over half the population was black, of which two-thirds were enslaved and one-third free, an unusually high proportion of free blacks in a Southern town. There were several reasons for this: following the Revolution, libertarian beliefs as well as the breaking up of immense colonial estates encouraged slaveholders to free significant numbers of slaves; also influenced by the spirit of the Revolution, many slaves sought their own freedom in lawsuits, flight, or self-purchase from their owners; and free black émigrés from Saint Domingue began arriving by the hundreds beginning in 1791, following the Haitian revolt. As can be imagined, white Petersburg was not especially welcoming. "With such a population we are forever on the Watch," Petersburg officials wrote about the ratio of blacks to whites in 1805, pointing to what had happened in Saint Domingue, where whites were finally forced out two years earlier. To limit the growth of a free black population, the Virginia General Assembly passed an 1806 law requiring newly freed slaves to leave the state within a year. As anticipated, the expulsion law virtually halted slave manumission. Even so, during the first three decades of the nineteenth century, black and white Southerners could and did fraternize more readily than in later years, when calls for slavery's immediate abolition roused white Southerners to defend slavery and their prerogatives as white people as never before.[12]

As a young girl, Lizzy shared an intimate geographical and psychological landscape with her white family, beginning in the Burwell house on Sappony Creek and then in the series of houses, often smaller and in various towns, that they eventually moved to. Like other household members, black and white, she toted baskets and bundles, ran errands and paid calls, passing to and fro among county farms or among town shops and houses, depending on where she was taken to live. In Dinwiddie County, in the time she was born, black and white, young and old could be seen in the narrow lanes and footpaths linking houses, barns, orchards, and fields. By then, after years of tobacco growing had depleted the soil, planted fields alternated with acres of exhausted farmland; "old fields" of yellow, coarse, sandy soil were left to revert to woods to regain their fertility. Covered with broom-sedge and pine trees of varying heights, depending on their age, these woods gave off a slightly balsamic scent.

Despite the county's proximity to the hubbub of Petersburg and the periodic excitement in Dinwiddie Courthouse during court sessions—when scores of circuit attorneys, jurors, magistrates, witnesses, and curious spectators transformed the square into a raucous scene of neighing horses, barking dogs, hustling peddlers, and bellowing planters, many just come from a drink of stout or spirits at the Dinwiddie Tavern—public roads through Dinwiddie were few and far apart. Before the railroads were built in the 1830s, people and goods were moved along the rivers and canals or over rutted dirt or noisy plank roads at only three or four miles an hour. The roads were so bad that, as Fanny Trollope, the novelist's mother, reported, it took some skill to balance oneself in a stagecoach to avoid being thrown about like potatoes in a wheelbarrow. May and October were the most popular times to travel, when the roads were best and one was least likely to be mired in mud or choked by dust. It was a good solid day's travel to cover the twenty-six-mile round-trip on the Stage Road between Dinwiddie Courthouse and Petersburg. This is why when Fanny Burwell, one of the Burwells' four daughters, needed two Bristol boards, a bottle of varnish, a varnish brush, and writing paper, she wrote her youngest brother, William, who was working in Petersburg, and asked him to send them to her rather than send someone from home or make a special trip herself. William sent them "by Adam," probably a trusted slave.[13]

If one theme emerges in Armistead Burwell's life, it is the constant struggle to make ends meet. One of his daughters-in-law complained with a certain degree of frustration that the Burwells were indecisive and unable to seize opportunities; in a more kindly vein, a Burwell descendent at a family reunion in 1870 claimed he could recognize a relative by "the hospitality and improvidences of the family." Some of Armistead's troubles may have come from failures of judgment or nerve; he seems to have been somewhat passive in his dealings, a man inclined to avoid trouble and blame, if he could. But he was hardly alone in the tenuous state of his fortunes. Times were hard. The bank panic in 1819, which eventually drove Kentuckian Robert Smith Todd out of business, closed banks all over Virginia, bankrupting many of its citizens. Crop failures from poor harvests and overcropped, exhausted soil devastated local farmers, including Thomas Jefferson, whose hopes of surmounting his debts ended once and for all. Recovery in the depressed 1820s was difficult. Armistead (like Robert Todd) was one of those whose fortunes collapsed. Unable to maintain his Sappony Creek property, he sold it to a relative for $1,000; he seems to have sold other property as well and moved his family several times. Then, in 1822, in a decision that necessitated a sacrifice of pride, he accepted an appointment as steward at Hampden-Sydney College, in Prince Edward County, seventy miles southwest of Richmond. The college trustees recorded in their minutes their view that Armistead was "moral, kind, and affectionate, one whose example would never prove detrimental, whose advice might often be beneficial"; they elected him to the post over several other gentlemen, probably similarly distressed Virginians. Thus, at the age of forty-five, Armistead sold off his livestock, packed up his household, and moved west to south-central Virginia to make a fresh start.[14]

It was not the first time that Armistead had to alter his plans because of the pressures of supporting a family. He had been thrust into a position of responsibility upon his father's untimely death when he was only a young teenager and was left to run the property with his mother, Ann. At that time, weighed down by John Burwell's debts and owning too few slaves to manage on their own, the family relied on the help of fifteen slaves who were loaned or given to them as gifts by a cousin, Lewis Burwell, and by Ann's father. With five unmarried sisters in the picture, Armistead apparently could not go to college. This gap in his education stands out in a family that valued learning; the colonial Burwells sent three generations of men to William and Mary and all of Armistead's sons attended Hampden-Sydney, where their father worked supplying students with meals and firewood for a monthly fee.

Before leaving Dinwiddie for his new job, Armistead would have taken stock of the wisdom of keeping his slaves, weighing the value of their labor and his actual need for them against their value in cash on the open market and the size of his debts. As a college steward, he would need slaves to slaughter hogs, milk cows, garden, cook and serve food, haul wood, clean, do laundry, and look after the children, but he surely would not need hands for field work. It is likely he sold off some laborers; the booming market for slave labor in the Lower South was a lucrative way for Virginia and Maryland slaveholders to be rid of excess slaves. (He may have already lost one slave without profit in the midst of the financial panic, if he was the same Sappony Creek master who advertised for the return of his runaway thirty-year-old slave in the *Petersburg Intelligencer* in 1819. Slaves knew that financial ruin to their master meant they might be sold, and many fled before that could happen.)[15]

Once he had settled his affairs, it simply remained for Armistead to force the rest of his slave household to move. This included Aggy and Lizzy's extended family, but not George, who had to remain in Dinwiddie with his master. As was typical of such long-distance arrangements, he was permitted to visit his family only twice a year, at Christmas and Easter. "I did not know much of my father," Lizzy later explained matter-of-factly, "for he was the slave of another man."[16]

Founded in 1776 with the democratic mission to make a liberal education available "to every family in Virginia" regardless of religious faith, the Presbyterian-affiliated Hampden-Sydney attracted the sons of families who lived far from the more aristocratic Episcopal College of William and Mary, the nation's oldest college, located in Williamsburg. When Armistead arrived in the fall of 1822, Hampden-Sydney was launched on a project of innovative reform under its new president, a professor of chemistry and natural philosophy, Jonathan P. Cushing. A graduate of Dartmouth College, Cushing—consumptive, dark-haired, and pencil-mustached—pushed to modernize and secularize education at Hampden-Sydney. He had faculty teach in their own fields only, not all subjects across the board, as had been the practice. He separated the theological school from the liberal arts college and encouraged the notion of the ideal graduate as an all-around, active man of letters. "We want men of refined minds in our country residences," declaimed a young alumnus before the Hampden-Sydney Literary and Philosophical Society. "We want accomplished writers, we want men of elegant leisure (only the rich are privileged to this), we want more than all a number of political men who are not lawyers."[17]

The Burwells moved into a small brick building adjoining the two-story brick Common Hall, where students took their meals for $10 per month. This, plus the extra deposit for wood, constituted Armistead's income, tying his earnings to the size of the student population. During the College's peak years, 1823–24, 140 students were enrolled, and unless they made arrangements to take their meals with a local family or at a local tavern, they came at the ringing of the steward's bell to eat together in the dining hall. It was Armistead's slaves, under the direction of his wife and the cook Aunt Mary, who did all the work necessary to make the meals; his slaves, probably the older children and young women, served them to the hungry students. A number of rules governed student behavior in the dining hall: students were forbidden to enter until the ringing of the bell; they were forbidden to carry utensils or food from the Commons unless given express permission by the steward; those who wasted food or damaged furniture had to compensate the steward; and students were "forbidden to molest or abuse servants waiting on tables."[18]

Armistead's were not the only slaves serving the campus. Students were allowed to bring their own slaves to school as personal servants; otherwise, they could hire them by the term from local slaveholders. Some of the slave earnings went to pay the salary of the pastor of the College Church, whose services were attended by students, faculty, local people, and slaves. In keeping with the college's reforming spirit, a new pastor, the Reverend J. D. Paxton, arrived the year after Burwell and two years after Cushing. He presided over the college's services in the new brick church, preaching to free and slave alike; a slaveholding man, he took special pride in preaching directly to the slaves on the importance of faith.

Armistead would have appreciated Paxton's teachings, especially if they resulted in his slaves learning to be patient and obedient. Like other Virginia slaveholders, Armistead had emancipationist leanings; however, the legal obstacles to freeing slaves and his perpetual need for income made it unlikely that he ever liberated any of his own. Yet the Reverend Paxton soon set an example against which Armistead may have privately measured himself. During his term at Hampden-Sydney, Paxton underwent a crisis of conscience, which led him to feel that he could not justify living off slaves while doing so little for their moral instruction. Soon, following the call of the American Colonization Society, founded in 1816 with the Kentuckian Henry Clay at its head to resettle freed blacks in Africa, he and his wife freed their slaves and arranged to have them sent to the African colony of Liberia (the first shipload of black emigrants had left from New York City for Liberia in 1820). Then he sold his house and land at an enormous loss and left Virginia for the North.[19]

The year after their arrival at Hampden-Sydney, Mary Burwell gave birth to the Burwells' last child, a daughter named Elizabeth Margaret. With four other children under age ten, Mary decided it would be expedient to use Aggy's daughter to look after her infant and save Aggy herself for other chores. Lizzy was five years old when she was taken to live in the Burwells' house to look after the new baby. In keeping with the family tradition of giving mulatto girls and women as gifts to their daughters, the Burwells promised Lizzy that if she were good and rocked the cradle so that the baby didn't cry and kept the flies from the baby's face, she would be Miss Elizabeth's "little maid." She probably slept on a straw pallet next to the baby's crib, to be available should the baby wake crying in the night.

Even though it meant leaving her mother's cabin, Lizzy was proud of her new position, and she worked as hard as she could at her chores: sweeping the yard, collecting greens from the garden and pulling up weeds, gathering eggs, sweeping the hearth, dusting and performing other light household chores, and knitting socks. She was especially pleased with the white apron she was given to wear over her short dress, an added distinction. Unlike the other slave children, who spent their days playing out of doors, her long hair was combed and plaited and her hands and feet were clean.[20]

It was Aggy who taught her daughter the skill that would save her: sewing. She may have started Lizzy off as young as three stitching bits of calico for a patchwork quilt, using easier long, straight stitches, and then instructed her by the time she was six in the mysteries of putting together a shirt (cutting and fitting were skills to learn later). Aggy also taught Lizzy how to spin and weave. The Burwell girls would have learned how to sew too, for they were expected to know how to mend, hem, and alter clothing. Yet, because sewing for money was considered a disgrace for a white woman and mending was such tedious work (especially if it was a brother's shirt), most young girls preferred spending their time embroidering, doing fancy lace work, or painting on velvet (popular in the 1820s). Clothing was still made at home; often, the mistress gave the patterns to the slaves, and the slaves would make the clothes. The slaves' clothing, made of coarser fabrics, was often fitted right onto the body so as not to waste any cloth. Most likely, Aggy sewed for the white folks during the day and for the slaves at night.[21]

When she was in her forties, Lizzy remembered the baby Elizabeth as "a sweet, black-eyed baby . . . my earliest and fondest pet," although she "grew into a self-willed girl . . . and was the cause of much trouble to me." Trouble came earlier than that, however, when Lizzy was still five and just learning to mind the baby. One day, left alone with her charge, Lizzy accidentally tipped the cradle too far and tiny Elizabeth tumbled out onto the floor. Frightened and confused, Lizzy cried out for help, then, seeing the fire shovel, she grabbed it and tried to scoop up the baby. When her mistress saw what was happening, she told Lizzy to let the child alone and then ordered her to be taken outside and whipped for her carelessness. Whoever followed the mistress's orders did not spare the five-year-old at all, but lashed her severely. Lizzy had never been whipped before, and she would never forget it. It must have been a vivid reminder of her place in the Burwell family should she ever—because she was pretty, smart, and eager to please and because they could be appreciative and kind—be beguiled into forgetting.[22]

Working in the main house often brought with it a better diet, better clothing, and exposure to opportunities for personal improvement, for literacy or for travel as a maid or valet, unavailable to the field slave. But being a household slave—a "slave in the middle," it has been called—was at best a mixed blessing. The domestic who worked and lived with the master's family had to learn to mediate between the worlds of the Big House and the slave quarters, a sometimes dispiriting and isolating task. In the daily give-and-take with the master's family, there was "bred affection and warmth . . . [but] also violence and hatred, often . . . all at once, according to circumstances, moods and momentary passions," making the slave's life a high-wire act of forced intimacy, indirect power, and hidden danger in equal measure. For a mixed-race slave like Lizzy, the contradictions were starker, the tensions perhaps more fraught.[23]

Judging from photographs of her as an adult, one imagines that as a child Lizzy presented to the world a grave face and dark, serious eyes lit with intelligence and perception. From early on, she learned to fend off her sadness with work and a determined, busy self-reliance. These were qualities that might serve as a counterweight to the lethal burden slavery laid on the body and mind of a developing child, what Frederick Douglass called the "soul-killing effects of slavery." Yet, along with her fair skin and features—the deep-set eyes, strong brow, and prominent nose visible in Burwell family photographs and portraits—they also might have earned her Mary Burwell's resentment and made her the vulnerable target of Mary's displaced rage.

The slaves remembered their mistress, Mrs. Burwell, as a "hard task-master" impossible to please; even her own daughters admitted that she was a severe mistress. In 1800, at age sixteen, Mary Cole Turnbull left her father's large plantation, with slaveholdings more than twice the size of her future husband's, to marry Armistead Burwell. A pious woman, she was educated enough to write a good letter, though not nearly as educated or sure of herself as her daughters would be. Nervous and sensitive, she was quick to feel social slights and was often worried about money. On a long visit to a married daughter in Petersburg in 1842, she felt not "on an equality with those that I . . . come in contact with I tell you it is not agreeable to be where money carries the day."[24] Protective of her children, she bristled when she thought that her Petersburg-educated daughter-in-law, who was married to her eldest son, was arrogantly dismissive of the child of another son. Yet even without her insecurities, it is no great mystery why the sight of her husband's bastard mulatto child, like the daily presence of that child's mother, whom some of her own daughters looked to as a second mother, should be a constant source of aggravation.

Mary Burwell had a less antagonistic relationship with Charlotte, Aggy's sister, who was her personal maid, although it was characterized by negotiations for power. When Mary punished her, Charlotte made certain her mistress knew she was unhappy and insulted. Once, this worked so against

Mary's own comfort that she promised Charlotte that if she would only look cheerful she would let her go to church on Sunday and would lend her a silk dress to wear—"two extravagant promises." Two weeks after that Sunday, realizing that she didn't have a good dress to wear to a neighbor's gathering and that her best silk was with Charlotte, Mary asked to borrow it back. Charlotte no doubt felt a certain triumph. Yet she spent her life doing what Mrs. Burwell ordered and regularly scrubbed floors, washed clothes, and occasionally milked cows on command. Mary trained Charlotte's three daughters, Amy, Hannah, and Lucy, as housemaids, and she always took a particular interest in them. Years later, when she was an incomeless widow and was considering selling the girls or hiring them away, she did what she could to keep them together. She would take no such pains with Lizzy and Aggy.

Her husband's feelings toward Aggy and Lizzy were equally vexed. Indeed, it was out of some mix of feelings—perhaps guilt, perhaps self-justification—that he decided, a few years after coming to Hampden-Sydney, to "reward" Agnes by making arrangements with George's master for her husband to come live with her at the college. Lizzy was about seven years old, and she remembered how the promise lightened her mother's spirits and replaced the look of weary exhaustion she habitually wore with a smile of anticipation and pleasure.

But the pleasure was short-lived. George's master decided to move to Tennessee and take George with him. By that time, the population at the college had dipped so low that Armistead would not have had the money to buy him, had this been an option. "He was a kind master in some things," Lizzy would recall, "and as gently as possible informed my parents that they must part." The little time that Lizzy had with her slave father made a lifelong impression on her, for George was loving and affectionate, called her his "little Lizzy," and liked to say that he couldn't decide whom he loved best, his daughter or his wife. With evident pride, he urged Lizzy to be not only a good girl but also a good scholar, to "learn her book," giving her a clear message to strive to make more of herself than anyone would expect; to the end of her life, Lizzy spoke of her regret that she had not been better educated. She undoubtedly drew strength from her few memories of her father. George had wanted to be a strong husband and father: more than six years after he was forced to separate from his family, he still dreamed of being able to hire himself out so that he could raise the $120 a year he needed to buy his own time from his master and come back to Virginia for his family.[25]

According to Lizzy, George's departure blasted her mother's hopes for happiness. And her master's attempted kindness—if that is what it was—made things even worse with their mistress. Mary Burwell flung at her "rival" the hopeless denigration of her position. Stop "putting on airs," she told Agnes when she saw her weeping. "Your husband is not the only slave that has been sold from his family, and you are not the only one that has had to part. There are plenty more men about here, and if you want a husband so badly, stop your crying and go find another."[26] Agnes continued to do her duty and to smile lovingly at Mary Burwell's children and grandchildren for thirty years more, but she grew hard with an implacable hatred against her mistress. Thus she also taught her daughter how to hate.

Mary Burwell was likely to have been more reticent with her own daughters about her feelings toward their mammy and their father. No mistress wanted to expose herself to an open discussion of her husband's infidelity. "Like the patriarchs of old," Southern diarist Mary Boykin Chesnut famously observed, "our men live in one house with their wives and concubines, and the mulattoes one sees in every family exactly resemble the white children—and every lady tells you who is the father of all the mulatto children in everybody's household, but those in her own she seems to think drop from the clouds, or pretends to think so."[27] Living silently with the knowledge of her husband's sexual encounters with slave women, hiding whatever jealousy, anger, or shame she might feel, the typical Southern wife protected herself by the fragile fiction of racial superiority. She would have been taught that male lust was a fact of life, and that although it was wrong for a Southern husband to have sex with another white woman, sex with black women fell outside the social category of adultery. Besides, as she and everyone knew, the black woman was an oversexed and lascivious creature.

Intercourse between white men and black slave women was almost expected, even culturally accepted, as long as it was publicly denied. Laws against interracial sex and marriage had existed since colonial days, the earliest going into effect in Virginia and Maryland in the 1660s. There was some perplexity as to what should be forbidden: at first, Maryland outlawed only interracial marriage and Virginia outlawed only interracial sex, though by the end of the century, both acts were illegal in the colonies. At the same time, Virginia legislators dropped their earlier ban on interracial sex between white men and black women, reserving punishment for illicitly coupling black men and white women only. Meanwhile, to make sure that the "abominable mixture and spurious issue which hereafter may encrease in this dominion" were considered black, the colonials broke with the tradition of English common law, which held that the status of the child followed that of the father, and declared that the mulatto children followed the condition of the mother, whether slave or free.[28]

By the nineteenth century, laws against interracial marriage were strictly enforced, and by the 1840s ethnologists were publishing studies warning about the evils of the "mulatto breed." In a pamphlet entitled *Two Lectures on the Natural History of the Caucasian and Negro Races*, the ethnologist V. Josiah Nott identified the mixed-race woman as "particularly delicate, and subject to a variety of chronic diseases . . . bad breeders and bad nurses—many do not conceive—most are subject to abortions." One prominent Mississippian declared, "Hybridism is heinous. Impurity of races is against the law of nature. Mulattoes are monsters."[29]

There were other lessons for Lizzy to learn about the world and her proscribed place in it. Most of all, she would have seen how much depended on the fortunes of her master. After Jefferson's "Academical Village," the University of Virginia, opened in Charlottesville in 1825, enrollment at Hampden-Sydney fell to eighty-four students and the trustees recommended lowering the board to $9, an enormous loss of income for Armistead. To make up lost income and to economize, he decided to sell one of the slave children he owned. At the time, a healthy young child might bring in $400 or more, money Armistead sorely needed; he had just bought his hogs for the winter and could not pay for them. Up until the very last morning, when the slave trader from Petersburg arrived, he tried to keep his plan from his slaves, a measure no doubt designed to avoid annoying fuss.

He may have decided to sell the cook Aunt Mary's three-year-old, as Mary had more children than the other women. Joe was the fifth of her eight children; maybe Armistead thought she could spare him. On the morning of the sale, he told Mary to clean Joe up and dress him in his Sunday best and send him over to his house. The slave quarters stood near the smokehouse and the new one-story, two-room kitchen, where Mary cooked, which was across the yard from the steward's house. Feeling uneasy, she did as she was told. The other slaves may have watched in silence or turned away slowly, pretending not to see. At least for now, they were spared.

Armistead placed Joe in a scale and weighed him, then sold him by the pound to the trader, who, after settling Joe in his wagon, quickly drove off.

Mary saw what was happening and pleaded with Armistead not to sell her son; he quieted her by telling her that Joe was only going to town in the wagon and would be back the next morning. When Joe did not return the next day, Mary knew it was over. Yet, even in her despair, she was too angry to acquiesce to Armistead's explicit demands that she hide her intense grief for the loss of her son behind a cheerful face and manner. One day, fed up with Mary's sorrowful, accusing face, Armistead had her whipped. He was not unique in punishing a slave who seemed miserable or malcontent. In response, slaves learned the advantage of wearing a mask, but they also understood the potential power in letting it drop.

Lizzy was seven when Joe was sold, and it terrified her, for she thought she could be next. She was also haunted by Mary's agony. Her master used to tell her repeatedly that she "would never be worth her salt," an implicit threat that he could sell her if he chose. She had every reason to believe him; she would see her father taken away, too. Anxious to prove herself, she worked as hard as she could. If she ever benefited from being Armistead's child with an occasional kindness or privilege, such as learning to read and write, in the end she knew she was her mother's child, fated to follow her condition, not her white father's.[30]

And she had every reason to assume that one day Armistead would turn the full force of his anger upon her. At least this might have been the lesson she learned when, one day, her mother discovered the body of one of her brothers (Lizzy's uncle) dangling from a tree by the stream, where she had gone to fill a bucket of water. They would learn that he had hanged himself when he could not find the new pair of plow lines that Armistead had given him to replace the missing first pair. Armistead had warned him that should he lose these, he would be severely punished. Later, they would find out that they had been stolen, but by then it did not matter; apparently, Lizzy's uncle chose to hang himself rather than "be punished the way Col. Burwell punished his servants. Slavery had its dark side as well as its bright side." These are Elizabeth Keckly's words.[31]

CHAPTER THREE

Whatever Robert Smith Todd told his household to prepare them to welcome his new bride into the domestic circle, it did not work. Grandma Parker, setting herself against the woman she saw as her daughter's replacement, did nothing to hide her steely resentment. Then, too, she may have seen Mrs. Humphreys, the bride's mother, as a rival grandmother. It took Mary only one visit to her worldly, elegant, exotic, new grandmother in Frankfort, where she attended a ball with Mrs. Humphreys and watched her lead the grand march arrayed in a splendid satin gown and French lace cap, for her to declare, at the age of ten, "If I can only be, when I am grown up, just like Grandma Humphreys, I will be perfectly satisfied with myself." Grandma Parker, although beloved by Mary, had the misfortune of being too familiar to inspire such worship.[1]

There was also trouble belowstairs following the newcomer's arrival. The new Mrs. Todd did not come alone, but with a small number of her mother's slaves, whose presence made the Todd

45

slaves feel the need to guard their turf. Mammy Sally openly resented Judy, the young slave nurse whom Mrs. Humphreys had sent with her daughter to take over some of the child care. Sally never trusted Judy with a baby or a sick child, evidently preferring to do twice the work. The two women did take turns going to church and watching the littlest children at home, but on her church Sundays Sally would return determined to scold Judy for neglecting her duties. Another of Mrs. Todd's slaves, Mary Jane, was too young to be a threat. But Jane Sanders, a slave woman whom Mrs. Humphreys had "brought up and trained" and who was charged to help run the household and serve in the dining room, may have stepped on Nelson's or Chaney's toes.

Yet if the children's grandmother and mammy were not to be won over, the children might have been, even if they were bound to feel embittered toward any stepmother who came between them and their father. Kindness, patience, and love might have won their affection. Betsey Todd was elegant and educated, calm and competent (she could manage her own country estate, Buena Vista, near Frankfort), but she was not playful and she was not warm, and she seems to have done little to accommodate the children. An exacting mother who held to the strictest views about proper manners and dress had raised *her*, and she tried to impose the same order on her new charges. Or she may have considered the Todds not quite up to snuff. She informed the girls that it took seven generations to make a lady, leaving them perhaps to feel that they were six generations short. The noise, the dirt, the squabbles, the tears of the children—these were not tolerable, because the children were not hers.

That soon changed when the new Mr. and Mrs. Todd began having their own children, as Robert had promised Betsey they would. Many couples during this time practiced several methods of birth control: withdrawal, douching, and separate bedrooms.[2] But the Todds, evidently, did none of this. Their first child arrived a year after the marriage and was named Robert Smith, but he died after only a few days (after this second death of a son named Robert, the father ceased naming sons after himself). Eight children followed in regular succession: Margaret in 1828, Samuel in 1830, David in 1832, Martha in 1833, Emilie in 1836, Alexander in 1839, Elodie in 1840, and Katherine in 1841, when Betsey was in her forties.

These children were effectively Robert's second family, but they were Betsey's first, and Mary and her siblings were made to feel this distinction. They were often sent to visit their Aunt Eliza Carr, Robert's sister, who lived with her family at Walnut Hills, seven miles southeast of Lexington. The first Todd children spent long stretches of time there, where they had another aunt and uncle, the Reverend Robert and Hannah Todd Stuart, and cousins to play with. These were certainly happy visits, when the cousins picked walnuts and chestnuts and went on merry picnics; in the winter they took sleigh rides in the straw-filled wagons, to which runners had been attached, and afterward roasted apples and popped corn in the huge open fireplace. Yet the subtext of these visits was to get the children out of "Ma's" way and, with each successive child, to make room for the second family. Years later, Mary recalled these visits, describing her Walnut Hill cousins as being "so kind to me in my desolate childhood."[3]

Naturally, it was the mistress of the house who set the day-to-day rhythms and tone in the Todd household. Because of her many pregnancies, Betsey's own health was delicate, and she was generally in no condition, even were she so inclined, to mind the first six Todd children, not to mention the eight that followed. When she wasn't entertaining, she rested in her room and sat in her parlor, reading or knitting, for she liked to keep busy. She required much nursing herself and a household of slaves to keep things going.

Robert was a solicitous husband. It was for Betsey's health that the family took trips to Orchard Springs, a fashionable resort where they sometimes met her brother's family from New Orleans. It must have been a relief to Robert, caught between his wife and first children, that Mary and her sisters (her brothers sometimes chose to stay home) loved these visits to the springs, where fashionable ladies and gentlemen from all over the South took the waters, paraded about, and socialized with gusto. One could learn much about society in such places, and a girl with Mary's aspiring tastes would have fairly glowed to be included. In summer, the family also escaped the heat by going to Betsey's Buena Vista. These may have been the family's happiest times, when the children could roam away from the crowded house into the woods and fields.

As for Robert, having settled his domestic affairs, he immersed himself in a new business—a retail partnership, Oldham, Todd and Company—which meant biannual trips to New Orleans. He was also needed regularly at the company's cotton manufactory north of Lexington, and his unabated political ambitions were still centered in Frankfort. He was doing what he needed to do, earning money to support his ever-expanding family, but his travels left

Eliza's children pretty much to their stepmother's mercy, and the children suffered deeply for it.

Mary was almost eight when her father brought her stepmother home. When they were introduced, the new Mrs. Todd would have found herself gazing down into a round face that looked much like her husband's, with wide-set, clear blue eyes and long lashes, set off by chestnut hair with glints of gold. She would have quickly discovered how bright and engaging little Mary was when she spoke to her. But it was only a matter of time before trouble came. By all accounts, Mary was a moody child, temperamentally like her father but more volatile: a "bundle of nervous activity," given to shifts so rapid, frequent, and extreme that her cousin Margaret Stuart described her at the time as "having an emotional temperament much like an April day, sunning all over with laughter one moment, the next crying as though her heart would break." To someone with her stepmother's proper upbringing, Mary presented a difficult challenge. For when it came time to tell Mary no, the new Mrs. Todd encountered a feisty little girl who threw tantrums and fought back. It may have been Mary's mouth—her inability to suppress her feelings or check her tongue—that most upset the conventional Mrs. Todd. Mary's sisters thought that Betsey Todd was harder on Mary than on the others; but it was Mary who consistently violated the precept that children were to be seen and not heard.[4]

According to family tradition, one notorious encounter concerned Mary's desire, at age ten, to wear a grown-up skirt to church, which at the time meant having a bustle, generally made of padding, in the back. Mary may have seen the most fashionable of them at Grandma Humphreys's ball in Frankfort that year or in the pages of the popular women's magazine *Godey's Lady's Book*. But little girls were not permitted to wear such grown-up styles (which also included wearing gigot, or leg-of-mutton sleeves, and longer skirts over petticoats, not ankle-length pantalettes, or drawers). Naturally, the taboo made wearing a bustle all the more tantalizing and desirable.[5]

Mary knew that her stepmother would never permit her to wear one anywhere, not to mention church, so asking permission was out of the question. Instead, she simply decided that she and her cousin Elizabeth Humphreys, Betsey's niece, who shared Mary's room while attending school in Lexington, were going to make their own bustles for the next Sunday. According to the story family members told, the girls secretly gathered willow branches from a neighbor's yard, and Mary directed her cousin in constructing the necessary bustle for their narrow muslin skirts. They hid all evidence of their labors in their room, awaiting Sunday morning.

Even as a young child, Mary displayed a flair for fashion, and she enjoyed sewing clothes for her dolls. Light sewing and embroidery were genteel female accomplishments, learned at home and in school. Fashion-conscious women could update last year's creations without returning to their dressmaker and milliner by retrimming their own dresses and hats. But Mary, apparently, knew how to cut and sew dresses in full, the only Todd girl who could. Where she would have learned this is not clear, as her stepmother was no seamstress and her schools did not teach sewing at this level. If, as is possible, she learned to sew from a slave woman, it would have been an early type of the collaboration she would have with Elizabeth Keckly. In any event, Mary's sewing talents stood out in her family, and she was probably given her own sewing kit with needles, scissors, thimble, and emery bag (for holding the powdered, abrasive emery, used to keep needles clean), an important gift in a young girl's life.

That particular Sunday morning, Mary was already dressed in her restyled skirt and out in the street when Mrs. Todd caught the slower Elizabeth in the doorway. "What frights" you are, Mrs. Todd scolded, and forced them back into the house to change. Elizabeth submitted quietly, but Mary, as if mortally offended, "burst into a flood of angry tears. She thought they were badly treated and freely said so." Mary did change but remained angry, and it was not made right between the two until Mr. Todd returned from New Orleans with some sheer pink muslin and Mrs. Todd allowed Mary to direct the sewing woman how to make their dresses.[6]

If this was a persistent dynamic in the house—that is, if Mary and her stepmother frequently found themselves at odds until the return of Mr. Todd, bearing gifts, helped to salve at least the child's wounded feelings—then it may explain why Mary would remain so susceptible to the emotional comfort of expensive, pretty things, associated as they were with her father's love. She would also have learned, in this case at least, the pleasurable sense of power to be had in giving directions to a dressmaker whose job it was to listen exclusively to you.

With her stepmother's antagonism and her father's absence, Mary's attachments to other women took on an importance they might not have had otherwise. She was close to her Grandma Parker, who gave Mary and her sisters small sums of money for their clothing and living expenses when they were older. Yet when Mary's cousin Elizabeth wrote down her memories of the years she lived with the Todds, she unwittingly presented a portrait of Mary as being closer to Mammy Sally than to any other adult. During these years, Sally was Mary Todd's maternal haven, her most consistent adult caretaker. Sally had nursed her before her mother's death and remained loyal in her affections after her mother died, and her relatively uninterrupted presence would have consoled the little girl in the midst of the emotional chaos in which she seems to have lived.

All her life Mary would find it difficult to tolerate separations from an ever-shifting stream of friends and relatives whose lives flowed through hers. Her need for companionship was great and she loved with warmth and passion, but she pushed people away as suddenly and ferociously as she pulled them toward her—as suddenly and ferociously as death, or as a stepmother who sweeps away an old family for a new one. Separations from loved ones felt like death. And deaths (and there would be so many) felt like the end of the world, the end of her. When, later in her life, in the wake of death and given over to wild despair, she turned to Elizabeth Keckly, Mary was acting on one of her deepest emotional experiences, returning to a sustaining source of her early life.

For the important thing about Mammy Sally was that she stayed, and she stayed even when one tested her. This is what Mary's many practical jokes against her seem meant to restage and prove. When Mary salted her coffee, Sally took it in stride, offering Mary rituals of forgiveness, which the girl desperately craved. For example, Sally told the children that jaybirds went to hell every Friday night to report to the devil all the bad things the children had done during the previous week. According to Sally, the disparaging high note of the jay communicated secrets: "Mary hid Mammy's slippers when po' old Mammy was tryin' to res' her foots in the garden after lopin' 'roun' all day after bad chil'en"; or "Ann hollered when Mammy curled her hair." Mary, seeking to tease Sally and play out the game, liked to challenge the bird. She would stand before it, chanting at the top of her lungs: "Howdy, Mr. Jay. You are a tell-tale-tell/You play the spy each day, then carry tales to hell." When the bird cawed back at the little girl making all the noise, she would run shrieking to Sally for protection.[7] From this Mary learned that a girl could be bad, bold, impudent, and busting with back talk, but still find forgiveness and protection from her maternal figure. Her experience with her stepmother taught her the opposite.

The mammy's relationship with the master's children demonstrates the degree to which Southern children were raised in a culturally mixed world, where customs and beliefs were exchanged between black slaves and white slaveholders. On Sundays in the galleries of McChord's Church, Sally listened to the Todd family preacher, but the rest of the time she was a one-woman African American church to the Todd children, a fount of folk wisdom and tales. She told Mary about "ole Satan," who had horns "just like that old male cow animal out at your Uncle Stuart's house in the country." From Sally, Mary also learned the significant fact that Satan's tail was "neat but not gaudy as the devil said when he painted his tail green." And she listened intently to Sally's renderings of the popular slave stories about Brer Rabbit, whose life was a perpetual state of war but who survived by his ability to outwit the stronger, bigger Mr. Fox. These tales would have delighted the powerless child, bound to the rule of an arbitrary stepmother. A child could learn not only survival skills from the trickster Rabbit, but also how to get revenge. Be polite to Fox as he is to you, one oft-told tale advised, and answer his cheery "Good mornin', Br'er Rabbit" in kind, even though you suspect he is plotting to eat you; for then, when he says "I'm goin' to ketch you," you can tempt him with something better: for instance, "a man house where he got a penful of pretty little pig," when you know that when Mr. Fox goes to the house, smacking his lips in hungry anticipation, he will find a pen filled not with pigs, but hounds who chase and kill him.[8] One can suppose that nothing could have pleased Mary more than to imagine being rid of her wicked stepmother in some such way.

And it was Sally, not her stepmother, who was the source of the hands-on care vital to carrying children through accidents and illness, an especially difficult task in an age when birth, sickness, and death were managed at home. During the lethal cholera epidemic in the summer of 1833, there were not enough coffins in Lexington for the 502 people who died; people hauled trunks and boxes out of their attics to bury their dead in, while the bodies of slaves and poorer people were dumped in trenches spread with lime. The children were forbidden to eat fruits or vegetables, which were thought to carry disease, and were kept to a diet of biscuits, eggs, boiled milk, and water. Hungry, but mostly wanting something different, Mary ate some forbidden mulberries. Aunt Chaney caught her, and there was a panic. Her stepmother sent for the doctor, but it was Sally who took charge of Mary, practically holding her nose for her and forcing her to take ipecac, a medicine given for all family emergencies.[9]

In the Southern household, the master's children and their slaves could even share a secret world, apart from and unknown to the children's parents. This was true in Mary's case. One day, when she asked Sally about a knocking outside, Sally told her and cousin Elizabeth that it was a runaway slave, and she showed them the mark she made on the fence to signal to runaways that they could stop here for food. These were fugitives bound for the Ohio River, where they could cross from Kentucky into Ohio free territory. Mary knew that helping slaves was illegal, but out of loyalty to her mammy, she offered to bring the corn bread and bacon to the runaway herself. Sally, however, would not let her. "He would hide from you like a rabbit," Sally explained; "nothing but a black hand reaching out to him" can help him.[10]

The tenderhearted girls were thrilled to know Sally's secret and told no one. Nor did they question Sally's complicity with the runaways. When the children heard stories about cruel masters they readily sympathized with the runaway slaves. They were, therefore, horrified when, in 1834, the newspapers reported the story of a burning house in New Orleans, where firefighters discovered slaves chained in the attic. The indignation of the press was their own, and the fact that the sheriff and his officers needed to intervene to keep the populace from tearing down the house affirmed their sense of horror. There were even horrors closer to home. In Lexington, six slaves were known to have died at the hands of the vicious Caroline Turner, the Boston-born wife of Judge Fielding C. Turner. But it was only after she picked up a small boy she was beating and hurled him out of a second-story window, crippling him for life, that Caroline Turner faced criminal prosecution. To avoid a trial, her husband had her committed to the Lunatic Asylum, which had opened in 1824. However, Mrs. Turner demanded a trial, and Robert Todd was among those impaneled to inquire into her "state of mind." Apparently, she knew what she was about, for she was released before the trial began. Caroline Turner finally met her just end in 1844: she was flogging a slave named Robert, when he broke the chains holding him to the wall, grabbed her throat, and strangled her.[11]

Charges of cruelty also touched Mary's family. As a young man, her brother Levi may have beaten two slaves so badly that one had regular nosebleeds and the other's face was badly scarred—at least, that is what Betsey

Todd hinted when, years later, after Robert's death, Levi and his siblings sued her over the value of their father's estate, including his slaves. In this suit, George, who thoroughly despised his stepmother, accused Mrs. Todd of ill-treating the Todd slaves—clothing them badly, not giving them bedclothes—a charge she denied. We do not know what Mary thought of these charges, or even if they were true, although this kind of brutality was common enough. Indeed, such things might never have been mentioned were it not for the inheritance lawsuit; at stake for the deponents was not the condition of the slaves, but the diminution of their value if they had been abused.[12]

The violence of slavery was inescapable, and slaves like Sally and Agnes Hobbs, who chose not to try to escape, needed ways to survive enslavement with dignity and self-respect. To help others resist or flee while submitting to their own situation would not have been unusual for slaves of Sally's and Aggy's position. Telling subversive stories to the master's children would have been another outlet for suppressed feelings. For, surely, that penful of pretty little pigs that turn into hounds and kill the more powerful Mr. (or Master) Fox suggests a metamorphosis into avengers of penned-up slaves. It also seems likely that when Sally called Mary a "limb of Satan" for putting salt in her coffee, she was using a kind of double language, an African American rhetorical tradition of "signifying." As the offspring of the master, Mary was a "limb of Satan" indeed, although Sally would never have said so directly; the fact that this became a standing joke among the Todd children says much about her success at indirection. Still, children, like spies, will uncover most adult secrets, and there is reason to think that Mary understood how to decode Sally's tales. In her early teens, poised on the brink of entering into the grown-up and, therefore, *white* world, Mary told her cousin Elizabeth that she was going to tell Sally that she really liked "biggoty Mr. Fox better than Br'er Rabbit."[13] In other words, she preferred the master to the weaker slave.

Kentuckians routinely claimed that Kentucky slaves were better treated than slaves in any other state and, as far as they were concerned, their relatively lenient slave laws proved it. Kentucky slave laws were in fact less draconian than those in the other slave states; for instance, there was never a law against slave literacy, although the popular view was strongly against it. Of the slaveholding states, Kentucky had the most vocal and enduring antislavery movement, centered in the Bluegrass, involving Todd neighbors and family friends. Yet a slave who was caught on the streets after 7:00 P.M., when the watch-bell rang their curfew, could be lawfully given thirty-five lashes.[14]

Even then, the chaotic world of slavery politics divided Mary's extended family circle against itself, a foreshadowing of what was to come, when the Civil War would literally sunder her family along Union-Secessionist lines. In 1828, slave-dependent Lexington became the center of a violent battle over slavery when a bill was introduced into the Kentucky legislature to prohibit the importation of slaves into the state, except for those owned by people moving there. Then, the following year, the Kentucky Colonization Society was organized in Lexington to resettle freed slaves in Africa, thereby formalizing the growing split between local proslavery and antislavery camps and generating news articles, pamphlets, and speeches.

That year, Mary's cousin Charles Wickcliffe, who was the son of her father's friend and the brother of Mary's friends Mary and Margaret, shot and killed Thomas R. Benning, the editor of the *Kentucky Gazette*, for publishing an attack against his father for his proslavery activism as Fayette County's state senator. Wickcliffe was acquitted of murder in a trial in which he was defended by his father's and Robert Todd's friend, the town's leading lawyer Henry Clay, who also happened to be one of the founding members of the Kentucky Colonization Society. But the bad blood did not end there. The new *Gazette* editor, George J. Trotter, infuriated by the acquittal, challenged young Wickcliffe to a duel. Pistols were fired at eight feet (not the usual twenty paces), and when it was over, Wickcliffe lay dead with a bullet in his chest.

Passions were further inflamed by a series of antislavery articles written by Colonization Society member Robert J. Breckinridge, another Todd friend. To assuage white fears about black unrest, Henry Clay, in his founding address to the Society early in 1830, had envisioned the two races "separated . . . in distinct and distant countries" after the emancipation of the slaves. But any talk of emancipation stirred up the specter of a large population of free blacks in their midst, no matter the promise of colonization to another country. The same year that Mary read about the slaves chained in the burning house in New Orleans she would have heard the young minister in her family's church deliver a dire prediction that Kentucky blacks would soon outnumber whites; when they did, he told his congregation, "they would overcome every obstacle, and the scenes" of Saint Domingue, where a bloody slave insurrection ended French rule, "would be acted over again in the state with 'Tenfold horrors.' " Even more frightening was the reaction of the black worshipers in the "overflowing" galleries, who, according to Mary's cousin Margaretta Brown, "expressed their approbation by every token that they dared display."[15] Among those listening was very likely Mammy Sally.

By the time Mary was eleven, the year the Kentucky Colonization Society was forming, Lexington found itself in the grip of the fear of slave rebellion, the fateful companion to the indulgence of holding people as slaves. In 1829, slaves bound for market attacked three Lexington traders, killing two of them. Seven of the slaves were hanged, but tensions remained high. Congregations of slaves made Lexington whites nervous. In February 1831, an itinerant schoolmaster decided to hold a dance for slaves in his school on the outskirts of town. A white patrol was alerted and, falling upon the school, shot and killed one of the slaves who ran out and wounded several others. After that, more displays of force and discipline were deemed necessary. On August 13, four local slaves accused of arson were publicly hanged in the yard of Megowan's jail, a few blocks east of the Todd home, before a crowd estimated at between five and ten thousand. Their bodies were left hanging as an example for four days, until the stench drove the authorities to remove them. A week later, in Virginia, a group of slaves, at most numbering fifty or sixty mounted insurgents, rode through eleven farms murdering fifty-seven to sixty white men, women, and children. All of the black rebels involved in the Nat Turner massacre were either killed or captured; nineteen of them, including Turner, went to the gallows.[16]

Even though they were slaveholders, Mary's family had long evinced antislavery leanings. Indeed, Kentucky might have entered the union a free state had Colonel John Todd prevailed when he introduced into the Virginia legislature in 1777 bills for the emancipation of slaves in Kentucky County. On her stepmother's side, Humphreys family members had wanted to outlaw slavery in Kentucky's first constitution. Her Grandma Humphreys and Grandma Parker both left wills emancipating their slaves, Mrs. Humphreys in 1836 and Mrs. Parker in 1850. And when he ran for state senate in 1840, proslavery Democrats would paint Robert Todd the "Emancipation Candidate" because of this history of emancipation sympathies and the abolitionist leanings of his business partner. Todd would reject this label, pointing out, "Were I an abolitionist or an emancipator in principle, I would not hold a slave." Despite his disavowal, a heritage was there for Mary to draw on in the years ahead, when the politician she married drew similar attacks from proslavery Democratic opponents.[17]

Mary made of her conflicting experiences of slavery what she could. Shaped by her loyalty to her father, her affection for her family's slaves, and, perhaps, her identification with slaves who, as silenced outcasts, might have stirred her sympathies as a rejected child, she tried to come to terms with the institution of slavery. In 1833, when the nonimportation act became law, Mary sided with the conservative emancipationist Whigs, led by her father's friends Breckinridge and Clay, who saw banning the importation of slaves into Kentucky as a step toward gradual emancipation and colonization, leading to the eventual decline of slavery. At fifteen, she may not have appreciated the men's commercial interests in the law: their belief that forbidding imports would increase the value of existing slaves by limiting their numbers and keeping out rebellious or otherwise difficult slaves from other states. Her arguments against the slave trade were more personal. Mary told her cousin Elizabeth that it was wrong to sell human beings, and that her father would never sell Aunt Chaney or Mammy; they were like family, and it would break her heart. That same year, Mary also may have heard rumors about the slave family ties of the Wickcliffes, her friends and cousins by marriage. In 1833, when a shipload of Kentucky slaves set sail for Liberia in the *Ajax*, on board were Alfred and his mother, Milly, a slave raised by Mary Todd Russell Wickcliffe. Everyone knew that Alfred was Mrs. Wickcliffe's grandson by her son, John, who had since died.[18]

The small but visible presence of free blacks in Lexington—221 people in 1830 out of a total population of 6,026 (or 3.67 percent)—a population midway between enslaved blacks and free whites, provided Mary with other occasions to contemplate the bizarre entanglements of slavery.[19] They would never have socialized together, but most free blacks worked for their white neighbors, and Mary knew many by sight and some by name.

She probably knew the barber Samuel A. Oldham, who ran a well-advertised "toilette salon" in the Cheapside market, selling wigs and false whiskers of various colors. (Most barbers were black, as being a barber was considered beneath whites.) A prosperous man, he served as an attorney executing deeds and wills for his fellow free blacks who could not read or write, frequently providing surety for other, poorer free blacks seeking to purchase the freedom of family members. Freed in 1826 by his master, James Harper, by 1830 Oldham had saved enough money to purchase his wife, Daphney, and her two children from *her* master. Over twenty years later he was still purchasing family: in 1857, Oldham and his son-in-law, the husband of his daughter Fanny, paid $400 to buy Fanny in order to "carry her out of the state to emancipate her."[20]

In these years of Mary's political education at the feet of her father and his friends, there was no other subject as central to them as slavery. Slavery was at the foundation of their very way of life: touch that, and one touched the heart and soul of the South. The expansion of slavery into the territories, the infrastructure of the domestic slave trade, the morality of slavery, the natural condition and relation of the races—these were topics she would have heard discussed regularly by the adults around her. Nor were these discussions abstract, about people and events far away. It was a political household, filled with political men, and to be a Todd was to be exposed to political controversy from an early age. All of the Todd children grew up listening to their father and his dinner guests exchanging news and opinions about the vexing questions of the day over their dessert. Lexington was an important stopover for campaigning politicians, ambitious businessmen, intellectual travelers, and all sorts of opportunity hunters heading west, and enough of them found their way to the convivial Mr. Todd's dining room to furnish an alert child who kept her ears open a thorough education in current events.

For Mary, the clever "daddy's girl" who adored her father and longed to please him, politics was like the mother's milk she missed. One can see her sitting at his table, eyes wide and sparkling, proud to follow the conversation. Flirting and dressing up were tried and true methods of winning the affections of her father, and Mary did both. But identifying with her father's interests and opinions was a way to hang on to him psychologically when he was not there, to have him as a part of herself. So it was natural that she should be the family's "tomboy," and even more natural, given her intelligence and ambition, that she should become the bookish and politically engaged girl that everyone would remember.

Mary's earliest political ambitions were tied to her father's success before they were tied to her husband's. In 1832, when she was twelve, she is supposed to have "begged" Robert Todd to run for President because she wanted to live in the White House (*sans* stepmother, no doubt); only when her father demurred did she give her full support to his favorite, Mr. Clay, who was about to make his second run for the office. It is said that she told Clay of *her* political plans one day when she rode out to Ashland to have him admire her new pony. "Mr. Clay, my father says you will be the next President of the United States," she announced to Clay and his guests, whose dinner her entrance had interrupted. "I wish I could go to Washington and live in the White House." "Well, if I am ever President," he gallantly told his interrupter, not the last man to forgive Mary her rudeness after being charmed by her coquettish flattery, "I shall expect Mary Todd to be one of my first guests." For Mary, politics was already an all-consuming affair of the heart. When the Democrat President Jackson, Clay's rival, made a campaign swing through Lexington in 1832, one of Mary's young pro-Jackson friends with whom she was debating declared, "Andrew Jackson . . . is better looking than Henry Clay and your father both rolled into one." Mary became so angry that she did not speak to her friend for years. When her friends talked about the men they expected to marry, Mary said her husband would be President of the United States.[21]

Mary's first year at school, when she was not quite eight, coincided with Betsey Todd's arrival—a not surprising synchronism, given that the age a child was sent to school was left up to the parents, and also given that the other option was to have her tutored at home, as several of Betsey's children were. Along with cousin Elizabeth, Mary became a pupil of the highly respected Mr. John Ward, an Episcopal minister originally from Connecticut, whose school was on the corner of Market and Second Street, only two blocks from the Todd house. The regimen for Mr. Ward's pupils was strict but wholesome, requiring early-morning recitations; and on school mornings, whether it was light or dark, Mary and Elizabeth got out of bed and hurried the short distance to school together. Mary may have enjoyed these prebreakfast presentations, for with her good memory and pleasure in performance she did well at them. Their homeward walks were more leisurely, and they often stopped at Mathurin Giron's confectionery, where they could get delicate sweets and watch spectacular cakes being decorated with spun sugar roses or little sugar cupids. At night, the girls studied together. Elizabeth, apparently the slower reader, would still be reading through her books while Mary was already knitting the socks required of each girl every night.[22]

Other Lexington academies were beginning to be thought overrated, but Parson Ward's was considered first-rate. Townspeople seemed to agree with Dr. Lunsford Yandell, who boarded with the Wards during the 1820s along with his wife, Susan, and his two sisters, Mathilda and Martha; he approved of Mr. Ward's "very highly respectable mind, well imbued with sound science, affable, friendly, & of manners plain & unostentatious." All in all, Yandell adjudged Ward "a man equally qualified by nature and education for the most perfect of teachers—to superintend their [sic] studies of Mathilda & Martha."[23]

At Ward's, Mary would have been in a household that valued female intellectual accomplishment. Mr. Ward promoted coeducation long before it became the norm, and over one hundred boys and girls attended his school. Sarah Ward, a Lexington native, aided her husband, and even the serious Yandell was impressed by the fact that "her knowledge of the more solid & substantial branches of education is very superior; & what she wants in the more spurious & ornamental accomplishments she more than atones for in the acquaintance with Geography, Astronomy, History, etc." Then there was Ward's intellectual sister, "who lives with him [and] is also a lady of first-rate intelligence. She has visited Europe, & not without profiting greatly [from] higher opportunities for observation." Yandell was evidently taking notes, for about this time he declared that he "always wanted" a wife who could be "an *intellectual* companion"; accordingly, when he sat down to study his medicine at night, Susan read with him. She must have been an exceptionally politic wife, for when they both took French lessons, Yandell believed that she took them primarily "in obedience to my wishes."[24]

By the 1830s, *Godey's Lady's Book* was advising its middle-class readers that no woman was complete without the kind of "mental culture" acquired by study. So-called mental improvement was as valuable as property improvement, making public lectures, libraries, and schools for girls as well as boys key fixtures in American towns. In Lexington, married women and unmarried girls alike took lessons in French and attended the Transylvania doctors' lectures at the Lyceum. The Lexington public library was the largest in the West; literary and debating societies met regularly. One English traveler would observe that in Lexington "literature was the most common topic of conversation" in the parlors, if not the taverns.[25]

There was some debate over the purpose and depth of female learning. When she first arrived at Parson Ward's, Susan Yandell felt that "the University has given a tone to the manners of the place, & every one must affect to be more pleased with literature than anything else. . . . indeed I have become acquainted with some females of polished manners, and highly cultivated minds. I only wish to convey the idea that there are . . . places in the world, where women may be found, who are not always kneeling at the shrine of fashion and admiration." Yet in the genteel world of mental culture in which

Mary Todd was schooled, being literary *was* fashionable, as the English-woman Harriet Martineau acidly observed: "All American ladies are more or less literary: and some are so to excellent purpose: to the saving of their minds from vacuity. Readers are plentiful; thinkers are rare." Every woman was a linguist, Martineau continued; in truth, studying French was popular because it was chic to be able to drop French phrases into one's sentences.[26]

Mary continued at Ward's for six years, until she turned fourteen, an age when the formal education of many girls came to an end. At that point, any subsequent "mental improvement" was achieved under the tutelage of a mother or future husband, and Mary had neither at hand. The question of what to do with her arose.

By then the tide of influence in the Todd household flowed strongly in Betsey's direction and the number of Mary's allies was diminishing. First, in February, when Mrs. Todd was in her last trimester with her fourth child, Mary's oldest sister, Elizabeth, married Ninian Edwards, a student at Transylvania University, whose father was governor of Illinois. Elizabeth may have already been living with Aunt and Uncle Carr at Walnut Hills, where the ceremony took place, but certainly her marriage left Mrs. Todd without her services as the children's surrogate mother and Mary without her closest sibling relationship. Then in March, the baby was born, and a few months later the family moved to a larger house on Main Street (appropriately, a former inn), several not insignificant blocks out of range of the Widow Parker. The new Todd home was a double brick house with four chimneys, a stable and slave quarters out back, and a large formal garden with a stream at one end. A more suitable setting for the massive silver that the couple bought with money Betsey's uncle Dr. Samuel Brown had given them as a wedding gift, the new home was a statement about the family's new status. It also was a statement about Betsey's new position in the home, now that they were living where Mr. Todd's first wife had left no trace.[27]

Once settled in, the Todds contrived an unusual arrangement for fourteen-year-old Mary. On Monday mornings for the next four years, the uniformed Nelson drove Mary in the Todd carriage one and a half miles out the Richmond Pike to Madame Mentelle's boarding school, opposite Clay's Ashland, where she stayed until Friday afternoon, when Nelson returned in the carriage to pick her up and bring her home for the weekend. Knowing that other students went home every night, and that even Cousin Elizabeth remained living at the Todds, makes it hard to dismiss the idea that Mary was purposely being put out of the way. Fortunately, good results often come of bad intentions. The sixty-two-year-old Madame Mentelle was an extraordinary role model for a smart, vulnerable small-town girl. Madame Charlotte Victoire Le Clere Mentelle was born in Paris, the only child of a French physician who, determined to raise his daughter "as he would have done a man" (according to her obituary), had employed a method of child rearing that left "in her heart no pleasant memories of her childhood." As an example of his method, he was said to have once locked her in a closet with the body of "an acquaintance" to encourage her to get over her fear of death.[28]

With such experiments as these he succeeded in raising a fatalistic woman with a lively imagination; Madame Mentelle was also opinionated, eccentric, tough-minded, and intellectual. An active, large woman, Madame walked back and forth into town, reading and talking to herself, and played the fiddle at dances. Her political views were radical and potentially thrilling to a well-bred Southern girl. She took a dim view of the United States government and scoffed at "this constitution that does not speak of freedom, these men who appear to have noble thoughts"; considering the existence of "slavery and the tyranny of the Negroes, you will find this [talk of liberty] more ridiculous and more absurd than if one said nothing." And when one brought up this hypocrisy with Americans, they began babbling and you were left "listening to crazies who imagine themselves [to be] talking rationally."[29]

Her husband, Augustus Waldemare Mentelle, was equally fascinating. He had been a professor in the National and Royal Academy and historiographer to Louis XVI. Married in 1792, the Mentelles fled the massacres of revolutionary France and came to Ohio, where they were duped into a bad investment in a land speculation company. Dropping the "de" before Mentelle, they moved to Lexington, where by 1798 they announced in the *Kentucky Gazette* their availability "to teach young people of both sexes French language and dancing." Although Madame was convinced that Americans "will never be friendly to The European, or even more to the sensitive French," the Mentelles became a fixture in Lexington. After teaching French at Mrs. Beck's school, Madame Mentelle opened a school of her own, while her husband was a cashier at the bank where Robert Todd worked. Soon the Mentelles moved to a house on land donated by Mary's cousin, Mrs. Mary Russell (the soon-to-be Mrs. Mary Russell Wickcliffe). In the 1820s, they opened their boarding school in their home.

For $120 a year, including "Boarding, Washing, & Tuition," Madame Mentelle promised her "scholars" "a truly useful & 'Solid' English Education in all its branches," with French taught if desired. It was here that Mary recovered a measure of happiness, lost when her mother died, for here she was a popular, lively, star pupil. She learned to speak French fluently, had the lead in a French play, and honed her skills for mimicry and gossip as she strolled with her schoolmates down the Lilac Walk to the road. She also learned to dance with grace and skill, a pleasure she would later bring to the White House. At Mentelle's boarding school, girls could not have visitors, so to keep the children busy in the evenings, when they were more likely to grow homesick, Monsieur Mentelle played his violin while Madame Mentelle and her two daughters led the children around the floor through "Cotillions, Round and Hop Waltzes, Hornpipes, Galopades, Mohawks, Spanish, Polish, Scottish, Tyrolienne dances, and the Beautiful Circassion circle."[30]

There were quiet evenings at school when Mary must have felt sorry to be living as though exiled from her father's house, a mile and a half away. Yet if Mary ever grew despondent at being displaced from home, she may have told herself that she had it better than the others—especially the younger, difficult, unfortunate Ann, over whom the thought of such a triumph would have mattered. Ann was Mary's fiercest rival, if only by virtue of birth order and sex, although, as their oldest sister observed, the fact that they were temperamentally similar increased the intensity of the rivalry. In addition, with Elizabeth gone to Illinois with her new husband, Mary may not have felt protected at home. Frances was nice enough, but she was quiet, and she and Mary were not especially intimate (Frances and Ann seem to have been closer). There is no indication that she was close to her brothers, either; Levi may have been something of a bully, and the baby George, intelligent and intense, was essentially raised with their half-siblings. It was with calculated self-pity, but also with truth, that Mary would later tell Elizabeth Keckly that "my early home was truly at a *boarding* school."[31]

Ready for something new, eager for attention and approval, and longing for direction, like any newly sprung teenager, Mary absorbed what the Mentelles had to offer, especially Madame. Her lifelong love of all things French, her grace and pleasure at dancing, her genuine admiration for books and intellect, her theatricality, her fascination with royalty—these can be traced to the aristocratic and melodramatic Mentelles, who "could never allude to" their martyred King and Queen "without tears."[32]

Partly, what Mary loved about the Mentelles was what she thought she also found in her aristocratic, educated father. During the years that school was providing her with an arena of success, one could also find her exploring her father's library, which she could enter unseen from the garden and through the conservatory. It is easy to imagine her pleasure in the sanctuary of his room and the joy she must have felt in scanning the leather-bound volumes until the moment of choosing and pulling one book off the shelf. In her father's library, she could have read Shakespeare, Sterne, Pope, and Burns. From the evidence of her letters and others' observations, she grew up to be very well read. In a crowded household, reading was an escape, a chance to get as far away as imagination would go. Significantly, Mary's love of reading also gave her a way to attract attention, for she loved poetry most of all and enjoyed reciting it better than anything else. She "was forever reciting," at school and at home; no matter that "this was the cause of many a jest among her friends," as children do not enjoy watching other children show off.[33]

After four years at Madame Mentelle's, Mary moved back to the Todd house. It was the summer of 1836, and she was almost eighteen. There could not have been much room at home and certainly no privacy: nine children were scrambling for space and attention and another baby was expected in the fall; a Yankee tutor for the younger children was boarding with the family; and there were always overnight visitors coming and going. Then, in October, one month before the baby's birth, twenty-year-old Frances, who was unhappy at home, created more room by going to Springfield to live with Elizabeth and Ninian, at their suggestion. This left Mary even more bereft of allies and quite possibly also envious of her older sisters' escapes; so when Elizabeth invited Mary to come for a long visit in the summer of 1837, she readily accepted, staying in Springfield for three months. When she returned to Lexington she went back to Dr. Ward's, where, in addition to continuing her studies, she tutored younger children. It is evident that by then Mary was only waiting her turn to get out. Release came when, in May 1839, Frances married Dr. William S. Wallace in Springfield and Elizabeth wrote to Mary "to come out and make our home her home." ("She had a Step Mother," Elizabeth later matter-of-factly stated, "with whom she did not agree.") Mary moved into the newly vacated room in the Edward house. She was twenty-one and unmarried, but her move away from her childhood home was final. At the same time, she was also moving to a life outside a slave state, a difference she would note.[34]

Robert Smith Todd watched in dismay the unfolding pattern of escape from his wife. After Mary married a Springfield man in November 1842, Ann moved in with Frances. Then Ann married in October 1846, the same month that George, now in medical school, argued with his father to let him move into the Megowan Hotel. Robert, conceding, supported his son at McGowan's for the duration of his training.

Robert never was able to bridge the rift between his first family and his second. In letters to Ninian, one can sense his rueful sadness as he dwells on his indebtedness to his son-in-law and his failure at being able to give his daughters more "substantial evidence" of his love, beyond "words or mere professions." With each daughter's removal to Springfield, Robert quietly supplemented Grandma Parker's allowance to them with small gifts—of money for clothing, a set of knives and forks, and later some property. To Mary he would give a bit more, for she seems to have been his favorite, perhaps because he also loved the adoration reflected back at him. But money was tight—there were so many young children at home—and he fought off depression by becoming "deeply immersed" in work.[35]

Yet work was no solace. Looking back in 1841, the melancholy fifty-year-old man had begun to feel that he had stumbled in making his way. In business and politics, he "was made by his friends for him," he admitted to his son-in-law, but in the end it was they who had benefited, not he. Now, "after all the sacrifices he made for them to acquire fame"—sacrifices, he noted regretfully, of "Interest, and feeling"—he was left with a sense of failure.[36]

In contrast to the hyperactive manliness of his courtship letters, Robert's demeanor in the letters he wrote after his daughters moved away is doleful and a little hapless. Hoping to encourage them to visit, he hinted that things had changed at home: "circumstances have changed & we all change." However, things did not change, and a few years later Elizabeth explained that they all moved out because "circumstances rendered it unpleasant" for them "to remain in their father's house." In a culture of visiting, when relatives came and stayed for months on end (because traveling took so long and cost so much), the Todd daughters rarely returned to Lexington after they left. As to the limits of "Ma's" hospitality, Mary had this to say: "If she thought any of us, were on her hands again I believe she would be *worse* than ever."[37]

CHAPTER FOUR

*B*eing Armistead's daughter may have protected Lizzy Keckly from the auction block, since a man who sold his own blood into slavery was talked about in the worst terms. No one respected a man who put his own child up for sale, but it was a generous master who lent his own flesh and blood to a friend or relative who needed an extra hand but could not afford to purchase it. In 1832, the year Mary Todd was sent to boarding school to continue her education, Lizzy became, in her words, a "generous loan" to Armistead's eldest son, Robert, and his new bride. So continued *her* education—in what she called the "hardy school" of slavery.[1]

In 1830 Armistead Burwell left Hampden-Sydney, where dwindling student numbers had reduced his income, and moved his household back east to family property in Boydton, just north of the North Carolina border. There he returned to farming, intending to try his hand at growing tobacco. Meanwhile, the family circle was shrinking. The older boys—Robert, John, and Armistead—were out on their own; Benjamin stayed behind in college. Ann, his oldest daughter, had married Hugh Garland, a Hampden-Sydney professor of Greek. The couple moved with her parents to Boydton, where Garland, after a year studying law at University of Virginia, set himself up as a lawyer. That left Mary, who would marry Hugh's brother Landon the following year; sixteen-year-old Fanny; thirteen-year-old Charles; eleven-year-old William; and seven-year-old Elizabeth.

With the family no longer needing a baby nurse and Mammy Aggy still able to take care of the remaining children and keep up with the sewing, Armistead perhaps began to feel that Lizzy's services could be spared. He also may have believed that his home life would be easier with this mixed-race daughter farther away.

Lizzy was fourteen—the age at which Mary Todd was sent to Madame Mentelles—when Armistead lent her to his oldest son. Robert had been ordained as a Presbyterian minister and recently married. His wife, twenty-one-year-old Margaret Anna Robertson, was a well-born and educated woman from Petersburg, where the wedding was held. The couple took Lizzy with them to the coal-mining region of Chesterfield County, near Petersburg (to a town coincidently called Ellerslie, the same name as the Todd family estate), and they stayed there for three years. Robert presided over a small country church, Anna ran the house and gave birth to two children, and Lizzy, their only slave, "did the work of three servants."[2]

That is how Lizzy later put it, when resentfully describing her new position. Robert's salary was a pittance and Anna was almost always pregnant or nursing—contributing factors, no doubt, to her irritability, which she took out on Lizzy in persistent scolding and criticism. The oldest of seven children, descended from the eminent Spotswoods on their mother's side but left penniless when their parents died, and raised by their childless aunt and uncle, Anna Burwell had dreamed of a "first rate Education"; instead, after her uncle died, she had to begin teaching at eighteen to earn her living. She may well have been anxious to assert her authority over her only slave, especially Lizzy as she then was: barely eight years Anna's junior, proud, intelligent, strikingly beautiful, and, as Anna likely would have known, Robert's half-sister. For the insecure, anxiety-ridden Anna, Lizzy was a disaster.

The antipathy was mutual. Lizzy would look back on her sad-eyed mistress with disdain: she was "helpless. . . . morbidly sensitive, and imagined that I regarded her with contemptuous feelings because she was of poor parentage," which she probably did. To be a slave was bad enough, but to be a slave in a poor family was worse, a definite step down. Besides that, Lizzy was accustomed to a larger household, where "labor was divided and subdivided"; now she suddenly found herself expected to do whatever needed doing. There were loads of laundry, ironing, housecleaning, fireplace tending, cooking, serving, cutting, sewing, and mending clothes, baby nursing, poultry keeping, and vegetable growing—typical tasks of a small household. It was little consolation that Anna may have shared some of these chores with Lizzy—certainly some baking and cooking, light housekeeping and sewing—for that meant they were on top of each other all day long. Mostly Anna managed, and scolded, Lizzy.[3]

By all accounts it was a trying beginning. Robert's sister Fanny came for a visit, but did not want to return and Robert could not blame her. "It is hardly worth while to ask you to come down again this winter," Robert wrote her in 1834. "I cant promise you a more pleasant time than you had last, except a more comfortably fixed home & yard." There are signs that Anna did not get on with Robert's family either. Robert's mother complained that Anna held her children "too far superior to any others." The elder Mrs. Burwell also found Anna hard to live with: "I could not make this my home," she wrote Fanny during a visit, as Anna was always "anxious about trifles."[4] But it was Lizzy—the most vulnerable—who suffered the most. And it was Robert—whom Lizzy's mother helped raise and who, already sixteen when Lizzy was born, may have dandled her as a baby on his knee—who was caught between his wife and his slave.

Not long after his sister's visit, Robert began looking to escape the small town of Ellerslie and "find, if possible, a more inviting field of labour . . . [to] look out for a resting place, or rather—a working place, for there is no *rest* for the servants of God in this life," he concluded wearily. Release came one year later in the form of an offer from the Presbyterian Church in Hillsborough, North Carolina, and within months the family moved: Robert, a pregnant Anna, two-year-old Mary, one-year-old John, and Lizzy, who would soon turn eighteen.[5]

In nearly all respects Hillsborough was an improvement. Twelve miles west of Durham, Hillsborough was a hive of political and intellectual activity, and the Burwells, who were cultured and educated people—Anna was said to be able to recite *Paradise Lost* by heart and Robert was a companionable, scholarly man—must have been heartened. The seat of Orange County since 1754, in the central Piedmont region of North Carolina, Hillsborough bustled with lawyers, doctors, merchants, craftsmen, and tradesmen. Many of the county's professional class lived there, including Justice Frederick Nash and the eminent jurist Chief Justice Thomas Ruffin. It was a close-knit, settled community of Scots and Scotch-Irish immigrants, whose families successfully entered into businesses and marriages together. Although not as affluent as nearby Granville County, whose planter class looked down on the mix of professionals, merchants, farmers, and laborers, Orange County was prosperous, slaveholding territory. "All were slave holders," recalled John Bott Burwell, Robert and Anna's eldest son; if he was inaccurate as to fact, he was accurate as to attitudes, continuing that all "had plenty of labor always at their command. . . . If a man did not have a cook, he bought one." In fact, on average, not quite a third of Orange County whites were slaveholders, of whom over half owned fewer than four slaves; in all, under 33 percent of the county's population were slaves and about 3 percent were free blacks. In Hillsborough, Lizzy would become accustomed to seeing slaves with more mobility than she was used to, who were hired out for pay, had gatherings, and socialized regularly among the houses and local farms. And she was likely to encounter more free African Americans than she had before.[6]

The Burwells moved into a small, two-story frame house with bay windows and two rooms on each floor, on a corner lot within easy walking distance to the center of town. Built in 1821, the house stood in a cluster of trees on the top of a knoll. A green lawn sloped toward the street, which the children—there would be twelve little Burwells in all—loved to roll down and race back up. The Burwells would add onto the house to accommodate the girls' boarding school that Anna soon opened and put up additional outbuildings out back, including the freestanding "Brick room," originally used for music lessons, which is still there.

Anna also had a greenhouse and a garden around the house, planted with roses, hydrangeas, and other flowers, fruit trees, a meadow, and rows of vegetables, including beets, cabbages, radishes, greens, potatoes, and tomatoes, all the wonder and envy of her neighbors. Gardening was considered therapeutic for ailing nineteenth-century wives, making it a form of female exercise husbands and doctors endorsed. Thomas Ruffin recommended it as an activity to his wife, Anne Kirkland, who suffered frequent breakdowns (she, not incidentally, had married at fifteen and bore fourteen children). As he said, "There is nothing that contributes more to a sound body and a cheerful mind" as spending as much time as possible "in sowing seeds and training [your] flowers and admiring them." Gardening, even if one's slaves did most of the work, provided much-needed exercise and time out of the house. "Flowers are the source of my best earthly pleasures," Anna Burwell admitted in her diary.[7]

We do not know how Robert felt about moving to a town a good two days' journey from his larger family, but he was already well into his thirties, independent and free, and therefore likely to be relieved to be launched elsewhere. He was "a man of pleasant manners, very modest and unassuming," according to Thomas Ruffin's sister-in-law Phebe Kirkland, one of a large and prosperous Hillsborough family that attended Robert's church. Robert busied himself with ministering to his new flock, preaching his morning and evening Sunday sermons and starting up a "little class" for Bible study on Tuesday nights. At home, he was a retiring and scholarly man and eventually made the separate Brick room his study, with Anna's ambivalent comment "[I] trust it may be for the best." He let Anna rule in the house, and so completely that the "country man" who delivered butter, eggs, and vegetables referred to her as the "Widow Burwell," as he assumed she was one. Occasional trips to preach in nearby Bethany or New Bern and picnics with other husbands were his male refuge. As a rule, he did not expect much of life; one hears the resigned sigh emanating from his letters.[8]

Anna was different; her letters and diary are records of her struggle to get the better of her own unhappiness and disappointments. For the first two years in Hillsborough, she was often so "low spirited" at being "separated from beloved relatives and friends," that her cherished Aunt Bott, who regarded her as a daughter, had to remind her of her Presbyterian duty: "For the sake of the cause your husband is engaged in . . . Strive, my dear Anna, to do it cheerfully, and take up this cross. . . . Look to the bright side of the picture." Though she did her duty, making shell and wax flowers to sell at the church fair when she was nine months pregnant, visiting the sick and dying, attending Friday night meetings of the Ladies' Benevolent Society, arranging concerts for the girls who would be her pupils, Anna found cheerfulness elusive. Gloom and guilt were always more in reach. " 'Tis hard to cast our burdens on the Lord," she once wrote to her daughter Fanny, born in 1838, whom Lizzy would have looked after; "we seem to love to carry them ourselves."[9]

Her marriage was fretted with difficulty. Robert and Anna were different in temperament and sensibility: he was softhearted, buying the children a carriage when she would not, because of the expense; years later, at his infant granddaughter's funeral, when Robert was so upset that he could not read the service, Anna was stoical. To her daughter and confidante Fanny, Anna complained about "the lack of the Burwells' . . . *promptness* & *decision*." Everything hard, she felt, was left up to her. When it came to deciding what to do, her husband's "usual reply" was " 'I don't know' (three words that I wish had never been strung together)." Yet privately, in her diary, she grieved about his withdrawal from her. At thirty-five, she felt that "my sorest earthly trial" is "my husband's coldness of manner toward me . . . oh for the grace to bear it aright." Perhaps it was her fault, for if she could "love him more & think of him more," then such a grief there might not be. Wifehood had dashed some of her greater hopes.[10]

Moreover, Hillsborough never really became a happy place for her. Anna felt trapped there. " 'Tis really enough to give anyone the Blues to live in this mud hole—where you see nothing and hear nothing," she wrote to Fanny at age forty-five but seems to have felt continuously for twenty years. She had sent Fanny to New York City to study music, and one senses that Anna believed she was giving Fanny opportunities she herself had missed (even though what she wanted was for Fanny to return to Hillsborough to help teach at the school). Hillsborough society was confining, tedious. "I always feel constrained when I have invited company," she told her diary, "& somehow all the conversation is so trifling." Yet going out seemed to bring another sort of trial: I "never go out that I do not say something I ought not to," she agonized in a typical postmortem account of a visit.[11]

As for Lizzy, she *was* trapped—literally—in Hillsborough. For her, there had been no question of elected duty, but obedience to a master's will. When Armistead gave Lizzy to Robert, it was her second removal from her mother and home, the first being the time she was taken from her mother's cabin into the master's house. The memory of her slave father's sudden removal was still fresh (indeed, never to be forgotten). Having to go to North Carolina would have felt like banishment, like death.

Lizzy's efforts to rally herself did not work. Three years after moving to Hillsborough she felt as dejected as ever. "I love you all very dearly," she wrote her mother, "and shall, although I may never see you again, nor do I ever expect to. . . . however, it is said that a bad beginning makes a good ending, but I hardly expect to see that happy day at this place." Anna made winter trips to Petersburg to visit her family, and Lizzy may well have asked to be taken along. The Burwells had moved to a house called Mansfield on the James River, just south of Petersburg, and she would have hoped to see her family there. "Miss Anna is going to Petersburg next winter, but says she does not intend to take me," Lizzy wrote her mother; "what reason she has for leaving me I cannot tell. I have often wished that I lived where I knew I never could see you, for then would not have my hopes raised, and to be disappointed in this manner."[12] It tells us something about Lizzy's persistence of spirit that she could even *be* disappointed. Pity the child who had no hope.

In a household steeped in unhappiness, Anna and Lizzy were survivors: strong-willed, ultimately tough-minded, and clever. They had other things in common as well. They each endured bouts of depression, suffering the churning anxiety that springs from the misery of being far away from home and family. Moving to Hillsborough meant separation from all they knew, and each had sustained the kind of childhood losses that made later separations as painful as reopened wounds. Both expressed feelings of being unloved, unwanted. But instead of a bond, their similarities exacerbated all difficulties. More than anything, the sensitive Anna must have seen the limits that Lizzy's intelligence placed on her control over her. She could neither patronize Lizzy, nor bully her into giving her respect. A formidable figure in the lives of her family and pupils, Anna nevertheless felt threatened by Lizzy.[13]

Before Mary Lincoln, Anna Burwell was the most significant white woman in Lizzy's life, a life in which white women *were* significant. In some ways, Anna was Lizzy's most useful early training for handling Mary Lincoln, another smart, temperamental, and controlling white woman. To be sure, Anna's formative impact was not all negative, for Lizzy also absorbed the respect for learning and the lessons of discipline and self-reliance that Anna would impart to her students, and in the mournful, yet persevering voice of Lizzy's letters and memoir, echoes of the Presbyterian, morbid Anna come through.

More than anything else, Lizzy was at Anna's mercy, a desperate position; there was no large family of slaves to shield her. Nor could she, as she could in Washington, have a place of her own, away from her difficult mistress. And whereas it seems likely that Mrs. Mary Burwell deferred to Armistead, Anna, at nearly six feet tall, was far more forceful than her well-intentioned but passive husband. "During this time," Lizzy would recall, "my master was unusually kind to me; he was naturally a good-hearted man, but was influenced by his wife."[14]

"Money matters are at the bottom of all the trouble." Thus Anna concluded about the tensions at home, and so to help out and "do better," by early 1837 she began taking girls into her home to teach. In June, encouraged by some of Robert's congregants who wanted an alternative to the town's Episcopal Female Seminary, Anna took the bold step of placing a notice in the Hillsborough *Recorder* of her plan to open, "on the first of August, a female school, in which will be taught the usual branches of English education."[15]

It had been a tough spring. An influenza epidemic swept through Hillsborough, followed by cholera, which luckily, as it was said, killed "only" two children under two. In May, while nursing her third child (a daughter born the August before), Anna went three times a day to nurse the premature baby of a neighbor who was coughing up blood and too sick to nurse her child. In church, Robert preached on uncertainty and suffering. One "searching sermon," delivered at the end of July, two days before the opening of the school, was on the text "Lord, is it I?", the question the disciples ask in response to Christ's saying that one of them is to betray him.[16]

Anna Burwell's school was a family business, a necessary supplement to Robert's $400-a-year salary. Robert gave lessons, too (not surprisingly, he had the reputation of being more lenient than his wife), and when their daughters were older they, too, taught in the school. However, there was never any doubt that the children, like the slaves, were in Anna's charge.

Anna advertised her school's four-year course as one in which "great care is taken to teach the young Ladies to *think*, and to make them thorough scholars, and useful members of society." Her school's motto was "Not how much, but how well." She aimed to make her students, who "came mostly from North Carolina farming and professional families . . . from the rising middle class and elite," useful and even productive young women. Like Mary Todd's Madame Mentelle, Anna expected girls to be rational creatures.[17]

No doubt she was persuaded by her own experience—and perhaps the example of the local widow she hired to give music lessons at her school, whose husband had died, leaving her with debts and children, the usual combination—"that girls should have educations to qualify themselves to help themselves." As she privately told Fanny, "I never found any one got rich by *expectations*" of marriage or inheritance. Such feminist goals are impressive even today, and they certainly went against cultural expectations for women of the time. Aunt Bott, who knew her niece well, suspected that Anna "talk[ed] too much" and wrote her that "you must remember how young you are, and that humility is a sweet and becoming grace to a young woman."[18] To teach girls to think was a bold stroke when rote memorization was far more common a method of instruction and thinking and expressing opinions were not among the usual desired female attributes. A woman who thought and wrote this way would have been both admired and feared.

Terms began in August and January, although students were dropped off unexpectedly at any time in any manner. One man pulled up to Anna's window in a buggy and told her, " 'I want to leave my load with you.' By his side was seated a girl or rather a young woman . . . but I little dreamt she was the *load* as she turned out to be." But Anna was up to any challenge: "I'll report her improvement which I flatter myself will be perceptible in a short time— at any rate her hair is to be cleansed & oiled instead of wet—& her clothes made to fit her."[19]

A June 14, 1838, advertisement listed the school's curriculum and terms: English Studies, $17.50; French (taught by a native), $15.00; Music, $25.00; Drawing & Painting, $10.00. One of the few female academies in North Carolina, Mrs. Burwell's school was a source of community pride. Hillsborough praised Mrs. Burwell's "Latin & French" and her rigorous "female school." "Mrs. Burwell's method of teaching is highly approved. Mr. B. is an excellent Pastor, gives general satisfaction," wrote Jane Clancy to Polly Burke, the governor's only child, who used to run a Presbyterian school nearby and was now in Alabama. "Children have every advantage here, now," boasted the doctor's wife, Mrs. Anne Webb, describing Mrs. Burwell's school. Members of the Presbyterian Session and the Ladies' Benevolent Society contributed to renovations to enlarge the house, but Dr. Webb personally underwrote construction of the Brick room, and the Webbs' daughter Mary was Mrs. Burwell's first full-time pupil and first graduate.[20]

At a time when notions of female gentility scorned the idea that a lady should do housework, Mrs. Burwell's students were expected to make their own bed, help wash their own dishes, and sew. Wrote one of her pupils, fourteen-year-old Susan Murphy, to her mother: "Mrs. Burwell is very particular with everything we wash up the dishes if we choose to if not we need not to we have to make up our bed and fold up our night gown very neatly every morning if we don't do it we will get a errors mark. When we get up from the table we have to set back our chair our food is very common we have for supper light bread and butter and for breakfast nearly the same we are just like a family we talk to just like we would our mother every night she goes in our room and kiss us all we girls kiss another every night before we go to sleep." Anna's maternal presence could not allay homesickness, however. In a desperate postscript, Susan cries out, "I never wanted to see home so in my life I cannot stay here any longer than next winter . . . if [Pa] don't send for me I will go in the *stage* for I cannot stand it I must go home if I have to walk."[21]

It may have been something, or nothing, that was making Susan so blue. Boarding schools were not happy places, and a schoolmistress's nerves were easily frayed by noisy, high-spirited (or low-spirited) girls. It says much that fourteen-year-old Mary Todd preferred being sent off to boarding school to being kept at her stepmother's home.

In contrast to the students at Mrs. Burwell's, Lizzy served with no prospect of vacation or graduation: endless years of enslavement were stretched out before her. If, like Susan Murphy, Lizzy felt that she would do anything to get home, she still saw herself as only a slave and her only means of escape the hope of belonging to someone else. "Tell Miss Elizabeth," she wrote to her mother, "that I wish she would make haste and get married, for mistress says that I belong to her when she gets married."[22]

The daily routine in the parsonage was nonstop and exhausting, affording numerous occasions for Anna and Lizzy to clash. The household woke at six, at which hour Lizzy (and possibly another slave) roused the children, cleaned the parlor, and made the fires; meanwhile, Anna, on good days, assembled the children for their prebreakfast recitations (on bad days, she lay in bed until breakfast). At eight, Lizzy helped serve breakfast and then wash up; this would be repeated at dinner and supper. If Lizzy were the only household slave, she probably divided the rest of her time in looking after children, sewing, cleaning, and washing and ironing; if there were other hands by then, as seems likely, Lizzy might have spent much of the day in child care and sewing, for there was plenty to make and to mend to keep the household in clothes. Lizzy never specifically mentioned having to cook except once in 1842 in Virginia, when she filled in for some of the other slave women who were needed for planting corn.[23]

For her part, Anna split her time in teaching, overseeing the housekeeping, bill paying, shopping in town, "trading" with country men who drove their wagons up to the back porch to sell eggs, milk, and chickens, baking, putting up preserves, and directing the slaughtering of hogs. With much to worry her, including her own and everyone else's behavior, she was often drained and sometimes on the verge of tears. Following breakfast, she did housekeeping until eleven, then she dressed and taught in her room while

Robert took classes in his study. Piano and guitar lessons were conducted out back in the Brick room, at first by the needy widow who taught music at the school, later by one or two of the Burwell daughters or a niece. Dinner at two, then, as she told her daughter, "I have to do one little thing & another—from four to five all the girls sew in my room. They walk from five to six [or dance if the weather is poor], then comes supper & by that time I am *done over*." Yet there was more to do, for evenings were spent in Bible reading and catechism with the children or visiting neighbors. Letter writing got done, if at all, before bedtime. Marketing was reserved for Saturday, if possible, for her the most trying day of the week, when there was so much to do to get ready before the Sabbath and the children were all underfoot.[24]

Lizzy was held in Hillsborough for seven years, from 1835 through early 1842. By the time she returned to her family in Virginia (sent home with her old mistress, Mary Burwell), the household work under Anna had multiplied. There were now six Burwell children, ranging in age from a few months to nine years. There could be up to twenty boarders from August to December and January to June, and twenty more day students showing up on a given morning for classes. The house was filled with the chatter of children's voices, the scuffling of shoes, chairs scraping against floors. Many hands were needed to clothe, feed, and keep washed and clean all those children. It is unlikely that Lizzy was the only slave in the household by the time she left. The Burwells may not have owned others, but after opening their school they most certainly began their practice of hiring slaves, which they continued to do for at least the twenty years they ran the school.

How Anna supervised her slaves is revealed in her diary, and although the entries that survive cover the period after Lizzy left, they confirm what Lizzy would later say about her mistress's short temper and insecurities. Next to the children, Anna's major daily concerns were about her slaves. They were a vexation to her, a daily trial and test. Anna yelled if a slave did not "behave exactly right" or was "insolent" or "impertinent" or "negligent" (Anna's vocabulary, and the popular one used to describe slaves). There were also days when "nothing seemed to go right," as when it rained so hard that the water in the pump was muddied and the washing couldn't get done, or when the slaves got sick and couldn't work, or simply when a child "wanted . . . one way & I another." On days like this, Anna would despair, confiding to her diary at least once, "So all together I felt like giving up." It would have mattered little to Lizzy, or to anyone shut up with a mistress who snapped persistently, that Anna tormented herself about her inability to control her temper. "My besetting sin is hastiness of temper," she confessed in her diary. "Oh that I could conquer this besetting sin" of "fretfulness at my servants." Sitting alone night after night, she "resolved to continue to record my faults in the hope that it will make me more watchful." Frightened by her anger, the "sinful feeling" that would rise up in her throat, Anna believed it was a failure of faith that "tormented" her with "those horrible thoughts that sometimes almost craze me." And it was vanity and ambition that made her strive to have her way: "Oh that I could keep eternity & its realities in view & think & care less for this world."[25]

She was frequently falling out with one slave, Mary Ann, on whom she relied in the years immediately after Lizzy was sent home. Mary Ann was "very lazy and careless," "very insolent," and so on. Yet one day, when Mary Ann's husband, Mitchell, came to the Burwells and told them that he'd "run away from his master & now wants us to sell Mary Ann with him," they did not dismiss him out of hand. "I felt much troubled about it don't know what to do." One week later, "Mr. Burwell had to tell Mitchell he must go to his master from whom he has run off—a most painful trial to us all." Nine years later, when Mary Ann (now married to a slave, Alfred) was in labor all night, Anna was "agitated and distressed but everything turned out better than I expected," and she hired a woman "to nurse her & she is doing well."[26]

Then there was trouble with Hannah, possibly another loan from the Burwells, sent by the time Lizzy left. Hannah was the daughter of Lizzy's Aunt Charlotte and two years younger than her cousin. Hannah was sometimes so drunk that she could not work. Things came to a head one October when, as Anna described it, Hannah and her husband, Phillip, "got to fighting & greatly disturbed us, don't know how to manage the business." The next day, Hannah was "in great distress about her conduct"; three days later Anna recorded a "great disturbance on our lot when Phillip came for his things." After Phillip left, Hannah's drinking worsened, and by mid-December Anna determined to sell her. But Hannah came to her and "begged that we would allow Phillip to come back to try to see if she would not quit drink. This we consented to do." In January, Anna wrote Fanny that "Hannah has been sober as a Judge since Xmas & if she will only keep so, we shall be glad, but if she don't, to Richmond she goes."[27]

Not that one needed to go to Richmond or Petersburg to sell one's slaves.

In 1836, the Kirklands brought Chany and Sukey, "unruly and insolent" slaves, to the local slave dealer, George Laws, who got $884 for them in Alabama. Ads for slaves ran in the Hillsborough *Recorder*, like this one, which appeared June 9, 1837: "For Sale: A Likely Young Negro woman, with four likely boy children. Apply to the subscriber. John Phillips." But the threat of Richmond might have been more mortifying to Hannah, a palpable vision of being shipped to a filthy market to be prodded and auctioned off like cattle. Even though Anna never followed through on the threat, she did not hesitate to use it to terrify Hannah into obedience.[28]

If there was a slave woman Anna liked it was one they called Aunt Judy, the cook, who died in the house in 1851 (the 1850 census lists eleven slaves in their household). "It is pleasant to me to think of Judy," Anna wrote Aunt Bott. "I think I hardly ever met with so amiable a coloured person, she was so humble and gentle, and always in her place, doing her duties so silently."[29]

Anna's diary discloses the complexities of the daily interactions between mistress and slave. Surely, Anna's rituals of self-mortification occasionally softened her attitude toward Lizzy Hobbs. But what Lizzy took away from Hillsborough was a hardened memory of pain and denigration. Lizzy (unlike Hannah) was too self-contained to drink, but (unlike Aunt Judy) she was neither humble nor silent. She refused to accept Anna as her "legitimate" mistress and admitted to having resisted Anna's rule; she even felt justified in defying her. Anna's phrase to describe Lizzy arose no doubt from her experience of Lizzy's recalcitrance. No matter what, Anna used to say, "she is Lizzy yet too": neither easygoing nor pliable nor open to being molded by a mistress.[30] Blowups were inevitable, given the strong characters and frequently desperate moods of the two antagonists.

By the time Lizzy came to Hillsborough, slavery had taught her that although she must work hard *for* others, she could expect little *from* others. Nothing would happen in Hillsborough to improve her view, and much would happen to make it bleaker. The trouble started early on, during their first year there. "She whom I called mistress seemed to be desirous to wreak vengeance on me for something," Lizzy began her account of this episode in her life. It would have been difficult for Anna to overpower Lizzy herself, so she enlisted the aid of their next-door neighbor, William J. Bingham, principal of Hillsborough Academy. It was he, according to Lizzy, "a hard, cruel man, the village schoolmaster . . . a member of my young master's church, and . . . a frequent visitor to the parsonage," who "became her ready tool." Lizzy was probably hired out to Bingham by the Burwells (they always needed extra cash) and must have frequently run back and forth between the two houses to work. Anna, finding an ally in her neighbor and a more ready hand than her husband's, struck an agreement with Bingham that he would "flog" Lizzy to subdue her "stubborn pride."[31]

The son of a Presbyterian minister and schoolmaster, the austere thirty-three-year-old William James Bingham would have welcomed the Burwells into Hillsborough as fellow Presbyterian scholars and noncompetitors, for the Academy taught only boys. Although he would earn fame as a teacher and principal, teaching was not Bingham's first choice. He had planned to be a lawyer, but his schoolmaster father's sudden death in 1826 thrust him into the position of taking over his father's school, and he became the second in a family of three generations of eminent North Carolina educators, one among a number of Scotch-Irish Presbyterians who were promoting private education in the state.

Within Hillsborough's class structure, Anna Burwell and William Bingham were natural allies. The Burwells and Binghams occupied a social stratum below the wealthier slaveholding families of Hillsborough—the Kirklands, Strudwicks, Webbs, Ruffins, Smiths, Camerons—whom they essentially served. In small towns such divisions are conveyed in subtle ways: in a word, a glance, an invitation not offered. What social power the schoolmaster or mistress had was over others' children and all slaves.

Insecurity gave them a sharp eye for the stirrings of unrest. Proud or unruly children and slaves were intolerable, and Bingham had his experience suppressing both. In 1839, he put down a "rebellion" of armed students at his school, facing them with a drawn pistol; in 1831, after Nat Turner's uprising, Bingham, who inherited slaves from his father, was enlisted into one of the local patrols that were organized to protect white citizens against potentially rebellious slaves. (The parallel is more than just rhetorical, as slaveholders saw "slaves" and "children" as dependents in need of discipline and control, except that white children grew up, whereas slaves never did.)

Lizzy's description thirty years later of Bingham's brutality matches his reputation as an authoritarian schoolmaster. An intellectual elitist who elevated classical subjects over "the common English education" (and charged more for them), the athletic, sleek Mr. Bingham was remembered as a "Napoleon of schoolmasters"; one historian described him as "a stern disciplinarian who brooked no infraction of his academic rules nor of deportment." A former student describing Bingham drew a portrait of a sadist: "I never heard him stand and lecture boys. His theory was that the boy knew. When a boy ever missed declining a word, he thrashed him. He warmed him up, I tell you. He wasn't mad. He thrashed a boy, all the time looking nice and sweet like he was doing the nicest job he ever did in his life." The boys never did miss their lessons, the former student added. This was after the "rebellion," when Bingham quite specifically stated that there was "no room for *bad* boys" at his school. Indeed, there were "none but good and docile boys desired." Yet Bingham was said to be "solicitous" of his students: he regularly accepted boys who could not pay, even boarding them in his home, and he might offer to tutor a slow child.[32] Presumably, these were good boys.

Toward slaves Bingham's attitude could be contradictory. Ambivalent about slaveholding, he once considered freeing his slaves, but then reasoned that if he kept them, he could assure their humane treatment (this was after his beating of Lizzy). Yet it may be that the idea of blacks at liberty simply alarmed him. During the Christmas following the Turner rebellion, when he was in one of the patrols with orders to "shoot with mustard seed any Negroes" on the streets after the curfew bell had rung, Bingham was said to be particularly paranoid: "The boys say he walks backwards to & from school for fear a Negro might creep up behind him and knock him in the head," Alexander Kirkland reported. (Twenty-three-year-old Kirkland, a decidedly bad boy former student and Thomas Ruffin's brother-in-law, was in charge of Bingham's troop.) So conspiracy-minded was Bingham that when he offered a reward for a runaway slave, a woman named Cary, he added, "She is doubtless harbored by some villain in the neighborhood who is waiting for the reward of delivery. Five dollars will be given for the apprehension and delivery of Cary alone, or twenty-five dollars for Cary and her harborer."[33] Such double offers were rare in advertisements for runaways, even though fugitives were frequently "harbored" by secret allies.

Lizzy's flogging came one Saturday night in 1836. She was putting the Binghams' baby to bed, when Mr. Bingham asked her to follow him to "his study." He closed the door behind them and, with no explanation, ordered her to "take down [her] dress" because he was going to "whip" her. The sexual abuse implicit in whipping a female slave is clear. "Recollect, I was eighteen years of age," Lizzy wrote, "and yet this man coolly bade me take down my dress. I drew myself up, proudly, firmly and said: 'No, Mr. Bingham, I shall not take down my dress before you. Moreover, you shall not whip me unless you prove the stronger.' " Then she added: "Nobody has the right to whip me but my own master, and nobody shall do so if I can prevent it." In answer, Bingham grabbed a rope and leaped at her and tried to tie her hands. Lizzy fought him off as best she could, but he was "the stronger." After he succeeded in binding her wrists, he yanked down her dress and started whipping her with a rawhide. "Oh, God! I can still feel the torture now," she recalled thirty years later, "the terrible, excruciating agony of those moments." When Bingham finally released her, she stumbled home, her back a mass of bleeding welts.

She found the Burwells sitting together downstairs and confronted Robert; she wanted to know why he let Bingham flog her. " 'Go away,' he answered gruffly, 'do not bother me.' " But Lizzy persisted. "I *will* know why I have been flogged," she said. Suddenly, Robert stood up, seized his chair and knocked her down with it. Upstairs, perhaps, four-year-old Mary and two-year-old John lay in the dark, listening.

When Lizzy wrote about these events she was a successful dressmaker approaching fifty who felt compelled to show how she had struggled against her anger. It was neither Christian nor womanly to be angry, especially if one were not white. But angry she was. "I tried to smother my anger and forgive those who had been so cruel to me, but it was impossible. The next morning I was more calm, and I believe that I could then have forgiven everything for the sake of one kind word." (It was Sunday, when the family was in church, prayers on their lips.) Instead, the next Friday, Bingham again attacked her. This time, he was prepared with a "new rope and a new cowhide. I told him that I was ready to die, but that he could not conquer me." During their struggle, she bit into his finger. Enraged, he grabbed a stick and beat her with repeated blows, until he wore himself out. Their final battle took place the following Thursday. "As I stood bleeding before him, nearly exhausted with his efforts, he burst into tears, and declared that it would be a sin to beat me any more."

After Bingham's repentance, it was Robert who, according to Lizzy, egged on by his wife, took up the assault. One morning, he broke off the handle of an oak broom and tried to "conquer" her with it. By then, even Anna—at the time, pregnant or nursing daughter Ann—grew horrified at the sight of Lizzy's "bleeding form." Anna "fell to her knees and begged him to desist." But Robert's rage pushed him to make a final attempt to "subdue my proud, rebellious spirit." Only after another furious struggle did he relent, "and with an air of penitence" told her that "he should never strike me another blow; and faithfully he kept his word."[34]

Small Southern towns had many secrets, and everyone in them knew what they were. Circulation of gossip was as vital an activity as the circulation of blood to the body. Neighbors took tea together, converged at parties, saw one another at weekly prayer meetings and monthly concerts, passed by in streets, and met in the shops. In Hillsborough, friends were expected to supply one another with "wool," a term for gossip. Country men delivered news from back door to back door, along with milk, chickens, and eggs. Men traded tales in the courthouse or the bar at the Farmer's Hotel. Ultimately, letters kept distant relatives informed about local doings. The battle to break the Burwells' slave woman could not have gone unnoticed or undiscussed. This could be lucky for slaves, for in tight-knit towns, in contrast to more spread-out rural communities, talk could act as a check to a master's violence.[35]

However, in such matters, people generally minded their own business. And physical abuse was hardly news: "I burnt her with a hot iron on the left side of her face" a few days before she "went off," read one advertisement for a runaway named Bettey, who took her two children with her, one "mulatto," the other "black"; "I tried to make the letter M, and she kept a cloth over her head and face and a fly bonnet on her head, so as to cover the burn." "Breaking" a young slave who was considered "unmanageable" was common practice. In every region there were men known to be particularly good at it, and masters would send their unruly adolescent slaves to them for however long it took to break their spirits. Frederick Douglass, enslaved in Maryland, was sent to one such man—Mr. Covey, a poor farm-renter—who had a reputation for breaking young slaves.[36]

As Chief Justice in the state supreme court, Hillsborough's own Thomas Ruffin had reversed a lower court's ruling with a famous 1829 decision that a master could not be charged with battery against a slave. "The power of the master must be absolute to render submission to the slave perfect," Ruffin wrote; he continued, "I must freely confess my sense of the harshness of the proposition, I feel it as deeply as any man can. And as a principle of moral right, every person in his retirement must repudiate it. But in the actual condition of things, it must be so. There is no remedy. This discipline belongs to the state of slavery." Ruffin's distaste for his own judgment was genuine. Most law-abiding slaveholders preferred to deal with their slaves with what they saw as a beneficent paternalism rather than out-and-out violence. It was more in keeping with an affirming self-image, and easier on the conscience. For instance, Ruffin's son-in-law told him that after Ruffin's "valuable slave" Jesse turned up home again "intoxicated" after a Sunday off with "a boy of Judge Norwoods," he decided to forbid his slaves from visiting "the slaves over the [Eno] river at Judge Norwoods," who "were pretty much without a Master." Indeed, he forbade them to "visit *there*, or anywhere else but my permission."[37] But there was plenty of brutality in "the actual condition of things." Such a world of contradiction and uneasy self-deception was saturated in guilt, and it is no wonder that William Bingham and Anna and Robert Burwell were anxious souls.

Lizzy was frightened, angry, proud, and nobody's fool. After the beatings, she cried herself to sleep, but by day her eyes were dry, her face a mask. She had remained stubbornly silent during the whippings. She admits that she was sullen and "wayward" about her chores in the weeks following, but there was little else she could do to show the anger she felt or to exert her own force against the white people's brutal authority. Other slaves might do more; earlier that year, Lucy, one of the Ruffins' slaves, was suspected of setting fire to their house by stuffing lit coals in a rat hole in the dining room, an incident that may have heightened Anna's fear of Lizzy.[38]

By then, Lizzy may already have been thinking what she would later find the words to express, that "he who preached the love of Heaven, who glorified the precepts and examples of Christ, who expounded the Holy Scriptures Sabbath after Sabbath from the pulpit" was bent on laying her low. It is hard to imagine how she withstood listening to Robert preach week after week. Perhaps she sat there and prayed for the Lord to deliver her from her enemies or that they might be struck down, prayers familiar to slaves. When she could, she wrote letters to her mother, hinting at her distress.[39]

Anyone who has known small children and seen how quickly they take the impress of the world around them—molding themselves for survival, hardening themselves against hurt and humiliation—must believe Lizzy when she says that by the time she was four, "I had been taught to rely upon myself, and to prepare myself to render assistance to others." Using formal, generic language ("to prepare myself to render assistance to others") helped distance pain and preserve dignity. When she was older, Lizzy found a way to rationalize her childhood suffering: she said it was a valuable lesson in reality. "The lesson was not a bitter one . . . and the precepts that I then treasured and practiced I believe developed those principles of character which have enabled me to triumph over so many difficulties. Notwithstanding all the wrongs that slavery heaped upon me, I can bless it for one thing—youth's important lesson of self-reliance."[40]

This "self-reliance" is not the same as the American ideal of independence, or even the same as Anna Burwell's lessons of self-sufficiency. It referred to Lizzy's conscious awareness that there *was* no one for her to rely on but herself. Not even her mother could help her. Indeed, one of Lizzy's sources of sorrow was feeling "forgotten" by a mother who, for whatever reason, did not answer many of her daughter's letters. Who could blame Lizzy for turning abuse and injustice into a discipline and a duty, or for finding something redeeming in slavery, which had been her life? No one can dwell for long in utter darkness without finding some sustaining ray of light, some explanation that there was something good. In calling slavery "soul killing," Frederick Douglass conveyed the belief that the long struggle out of slavery would have to be a resurrection of "soul"—a reclaiming of identity. Indeed, it was Lizzy's ability to marshal such powerful psychological adaptations and to call on her energy and native intelligence that helped take her all the way to the White House.

During these years, Lizzy was developing the habit of mobility and the air of independence that would characterize her and make her, ironically, both invaluable and dangerous to whoever owned her. Her intelligence, her energy, and her dignified presence brought her notice among the black and white people in town and, as a result, the winter of 1837–38 proved a particularly busy time. Slave women as appealing as Lizzy were asked to be attendants or bridesmaids at white weddings ("maid" in its most literal sense), and between October and April she was asked to serve at six. This meant that, among other things, Lizzy was forming relationships outside the Burwell home. One can imagine that this fact both pleased and irritated Anna, whose pride of possession might have contended with her jealousy.

One of these weddings, about a week before Christmas, was that of Miss Ann Nash, one of four sisters, for whom Lizzy was a bridesmaid. Her wedding preparations were not to interfere with her work for Anna, so she had to do everything on her own time. "When the night came I was in quite a trouble," she reported to her mother. "I did not know whether my frock was clean or dirty; I only had a week's notice, and the body and sleeves to make, and only one hour a night to work on it, so you can see with these troubles to overcome, my chance was rather slim." Miss Susan Bingham was also married at Christmastime, and it is possible Lizzy served in that party, too. Then, toward the end of March, Lizzy was honored by a request to be "first attendant" at the "most respectable wedding" of all, but when the day came, she was too sick to go. "As usual with all my expectations, I was disappointed," she commented sadly.

Hillsborough also had its share of slave marriages; however, as no public records of these exist, one looks to letters for their occasional mention. Lizzy would have been invited to some of these, too. There was one at Christmas that year, as reported by Miss Taylor to Miss Burke: "a good marriage among the black ones this Christmas . . . Francis to one [of] Mrs. Whitted girls." As for Lizzy's request to her mother, "I wish you would send me a pretty frock this summer," it is good to imagine her feeling anything as normal and light-hearted as looking forward to times when she might dress up. And there is something touching about the way she told her Aunt Bella in a letter that she was so "particular" with her gift (a dress? a hat?) that she had "worn it only once."[41]

Yet such visibility no doubt contributed to exposing Lizzy to her greatest danger; by April 1838, she was hiding something more from her mother: "Although I could fill ten pages with my griefs and misfortunes; no tongue could express them as I feel. . . . Tell Miss Elizabeth that I wish she would make haste and get married, for mistress says that I belong to her when she gets married." Agnes may have guessed, might in fact have known, but it would not have been in her power to intervene, even if she were close by. It had happened to her and to other slave women she knew. When a slave girl reached puberty, she became an object of more than passing interest to the white men who knew her. Good-looking and twenty, Lizzy was fair game.[42]

Her "persecutor," as she would justly call him, was Bingham's old nemesis and Thomas Ruffin's brother-in-law, Alexander Kirkland. He had grown up in the stately brick house his father had built on the family's large farm, called Ayr Mount, which stood just over a mile east of town, but he probably now lived with his young family in a rented house in town near the family store. The Burwells' Lizzy could have come to his attention in any number of ways. His sisters were enthusiastic members of Robert's church, although he himself was notably less pious; his mother-in-law was the widow who taught music at Anna's school. He could easily have first spotted Lizzy in town and then recognized her when he saw her again or at one of the six weddings she attended that winter.

Born in 1807, Alexander McKenzie Kirkland was the second of two sons of Margaret Scott and William Kirkland, one of Hillsborough's most successful merchant-planters, who named his infant for his brother-in-law, the Northwest explorer Sir Alexander McKenzie. Charming and high-spirited as a boy, Alexander was the black sheep of the family. After taunting Bingham at Hillsborough Academy, the young troublemaker attended the university at Chapel Hill ten miles away, then was sent off (with other local boys) to a military school in Connecticut, from which he was temporarily dismissed for striking a fellow cadet. Upon graduating, he returned to Hillsborough, and after a few years of indecision, he chose business, like his father, and set himself up in a general merchandise store. Married to Anna McKenzie Cameron in January 1835, their first son was born the following year. It was in 1838, when Anna Kirkland was pregnant with their second child, that Alexander began taking Lizzy by force. In August, Anna gave birth to a boy; it was Alexander's last child with his wife. Sometime during the next year or two, Lizzy had Alexander Kirkland's third son.[43]

By the time Kirkland began preying on Lizzy, his business was failing. By 1839, he was deep in debt. He had moved his family back to Ayr Mount and sold "not only a slave named Polly and her three children, but also his right and interest in his father's estate" and in the property of his mother-in-law.[44]

At the same time, his scapegrace charms had dissipated; he was drinking heavily and was earning a reputation for violent outbursts. The year after he married, there had been a hunting accident, when he shot a Mr. Evans; an incident in which he "gave . . . some pretty severe blows in [the] face" to an "insolent" driver; and above all, some ugly behavior toward his pregnant, ill wife that led his usually adoring niece Catherine Ruffin to write to her mother, Kirkland's sister, "Of all the cowardly husbands I ever saw in my life, Uncle Alexander exceeds."[45]

By 1839, he was truly dissolute; on a visit to her aunts at Ayr Mount, Catherine sent her new husband a dismal report: "It grieves my heart to find uncle Alexander so altered; he has the appearance to me of a very intemperate man. He is fat and unnaturally flushed and is really stupid." The family also suspected that he was beating his wife, although Catherine, perhaps out of loyalty to Uncle Alexander, was relieved to find Anna acquiescent: "[Aunt] Alice thinks he is rough with Anna and I was glad to hear she bore it so meekly for she is a high-spirited woman and I was afraid would resent such treatment. He is living in perfect idleness and I do think idleness *is* the root of all evils."[46]

If one of those "evils" included sexually oppressing a slave woman, Catherine would never have admitted it. By then, Alexander Kirkland had undoubtedly been forcing Lizzy to have sex with him for at least a year. Thirty-one-year-old Kirkland was a giant of a man, six feet eight inches tall, and grown fat. Lizzy, eleven years younger than her assailant, could have been over a foot shorter and a fraction of his weight. When he came at her, he must have seemed monstrous.

It would be good to think that Kirkland's intensified drinking was in some measure connected to his relationship with Lizzy, some expression of his own bad conscience and misery. His deterioration coincided with the four years he abused her, but how, or whether, they were connected we may never know. By April 1842, Lizzy and her four-month-old were back in Virginia. In the meantime, Kirkland's condition must have continued to decline, as he was under medical care, but his death in May 1843 took his doctors and family by surprise. "He had no fever," Thomas Ruffin wrote Catherine, "nor, indeed, any particular disease known to his medical advisers; but his health gradually declined, & he finally ended his earthly career simply by the failure of an enfeebled & shattered constitution." His descendants argued that he died of cancer, but his biographer has suggested that it was the cumulative effects of alcohol that killed him. A week before his death, he had tried to put himself on a regimen to get better, "had even quit chewing tobacco at the request of the Dr. with a determined effort to try & get well." But by then it was too late, and he died with a "restless" mind, according to his brother John, who watched him in those final days: "He talked a great deal evidently greatly excited. He spoke frequently of dying, or repentance and hoped that God would forgive him & permit him to go to heaven. Occasionally his mind would waver & he would say that he did not know what he was saying. He prayed frequently that God would have mercy upon him."[47] His brother-in-law judged it for the best. "Poor Fellow!" Ruffin wrote. "He knew trouble early in life, & has encountered so many anxieties & distresses of different kinds, that for some years past, he has had few enjoyments. We trust he is better, much better off."[48] On his tombstone in the family cemetery at Ayr Mount is engraved the legend "Gone where the wicked cease from troubling and the weary are at rest."

It is impossible to know what Lizzy endured over those four years of abuse by Alexander Kirkland. Did she ever feel for Kirkland anything other than revulsion and hate? What were her feelings about herself? We do not know what her sexual experiences, if any, had been up until the time he claimed her.

Slave girls were taught to guard their virginity, or, as one slave mother warned her daughter, "Don't let nobody bother yo principle; 'cause dat wuz all yo' had." Raised as a house servant, inclined to identify herself with the "social graces, restraint, and morality of her mistress's class and culture," Lizzy would have suffered deeply the degradation of the use Kirkland made of her.[49] Like any girl who would ask her mother for a "pretty frock," she had dreams of finding a special someone, who would not have been Kirkland. She may have hoped to marry, like her mother, or at least to have her children (if she wanted them) with a man of her choosing. Given the stereotype of the oversexed black female, Lizzy would have been blamed for being loose, whereas Kirkland would have been looked upon as behaving regrettably, perhaps, even despicably—but not immorally. Neither Lizzy nor Kirkland (nor the minister and his wife) would have been outcast, for Lizzy's sexual violation fell well within the boundaries of convention and expectation.

Hillsborough, after all, was at the same time absorbing the horrifying spectacle of sexual abuse that was unfolding on Dr. James S. Smith's plantation. In 1839 Harriet, the twenty-year-old mulatto slave belonging to his daughter, Mary Ruffin Smith, had married a free-born mulatto named Reuben Day, and the couple had a son. But when Smith's two sons, Sidney and Frank, returned home from college at Chapel Hill, they ran off her husband so that they could have her for themselves. First Sidney, the lawyer, forced himself on her in her cabin, with her toddler son whimpering in the corner. Then Frank, the doctor, decided he wanted her. The two brothers came to blows over Harriet, with Frank finally getting his way and forcing Sidney out. Everyone knew what was going on, but no one interfered. A few years later, after Harriet gave birth to Frank's third daughter, the Smiths were said to have "pulled up stakes to get away from the glare of Hillsboro society and clacking tongues."[50] This may have been why the Burwells shipped Lizzy back to Virginia after the birth of her son.

Lizzy's sense of violation may be felt in her chilling observation "If my poor boy ever suffered any humiliating pangs on account of his birth, he could not blame his mother, for God knows that she did not wish to give him life." Such was the resentment that could easily taint the maternal feelings of any slave woman for her fair-skinned, master's child. Yet Lizzy *did* name her son George, after her slave father George Pleasant Hobbs, surely a sign of love for the child she did not want and attachment to the black father she knew loved her. If names are markers of identity, we can see George's contradictory burdens of identity in the fact that when he was a freed young man, he used his white father's last name, Kirkland. It may be that, like the slave woman Harriet's oldest daughter, Cornelia, who used her white father's name, Smith, and was proud of having "good blood" in her, "folks that counted for something—doctors, lawyers, judges, legislators. Aristocrats . . . going back seven generations," George took pride in his white ancestry.[51] In this, he would be different from his mother, who never used Burwell, *her* white father's name. *Her* name was still Elizabeth Hobbs, the surname of her slave father.

CHAPTER FIVE

Twenty-one-year-old Mary Todd could not have moved to Springfield at a better time. Her first visit, two summers earlier, would have been too soon, although at the time one could see the already brightening prospects for the future capital of Illinois. Indeed, that June, in 1837, Massachusetts Senator Daniel Webster, the great Whig orator and politician, had made the town a stop on his family's Western tour, and when he responded to a toast to his health with a speech that lasted an hour and a half, his listeners could not have been more delighted. The excitement peaked again a few weeks later, when all of Springfield turned out to celebrate Independence Day by watching the massive cornerstone of the future State House being maneuvered into place in the square. The fervent Edward D. Baker, a locally acclaimed orator, who with Mary's brother-in-law, Ninian Edwards, had campaigned alongside other Sangamon County legislators to make Springfield the capital, delivered the day's peroration from atop the buff-colored stone.

If Mary's first look at her sister's new home boded well, it was not until the summer of 1839, when she replaced the newly married Frances as the eligible Todd sister in the Edwards house, that Springfield officially became the new state capital and the kind of town that Mary Todd was used to and liked. In January, the governor had ordered the state officers to move by July 4 from Vandalia to Springfield. In no time, forty-three lawyers from twenty-one Illinois towns came to attend the courts in session. The hotels and taverns near the unfinished State House—the simple Globe Tavern, the magnificent new American House, Joel Johnson's even newer City Hotel, and Torrey's Temperance Hotel—began registering guests by the handful. With the legislature, state supreme court, and U.S. courts for Illinois convening at regular intervals and the politicians, lawyers, and businessmen converging on the square, the little world in which her sisters lived was especially interesting for the Todd daughter who was next in line to marry.[1]

Founded in 1821 near the winding Sangamon River three years after Illinois became a state, Springfield was barely past its frontier days when Mary Todd made it her home. Only eight years earlier it had been a raw prairie town of log cabins, unpaved streets (named Jefferson, Washington, Adams, and Monroe), a handful of dry goods and grocery stores, mail delivery once a week, and all of 850 inhabitants. There were few if any set social customs, and those that existed were simple; for example, a party of ladies wanting to entertain placed a lighted candle in the window as a signal that gentlemen were expected to call. Most of all, there was the endless-seeming prairie: in summer, an undulating sea of tall grasses and flowering weeds, festooned by countless wild strawberry vines; in winter, a barren brown expanse of dry grass, which easily caught fire. As one traveler noted, "The cultivated fields form a mere speck on the surface of the prairie."[2]

However, Springfield was centrally placed to catch the flow of westward migration, and by 1840 its population had nearly quadrupled to more than three thousand inhabitants. There were more farmers to break up more of the prairie, which yielded its secret treasure of soil so fertile that, as one newcomer wrote home to Scotland, "no manure is used for any kind of crop." In town, the newcomers put up homes, stores and shops, hotels and taverns, churches, schools, and a courthouse; they improved roads, although the town's streets remained unpaved, and they built badly needed bridges; as late as 1835 there were no bridges in Sangamon County, which meant waiting on the shores of swollen creeks for the waters to subside before crossing. They also had founded a Thespian Society, a Young Men's Lyceum (a debating society whose aim was self-improvement), a Colonization Society, a Temperance Society and a Juvenile Temperance Society, a Bible Society and a Female Bible Society, among other groups (thereby exemplifying Alexis de Tocqueville's remark on how much Americans liked organizing themselves into associations).[3]

Many of the people who moved to Illinois were educated, propertied, and professional Kentuckians, attracted by the cheap land to their west and the opportunities of a wide-open political arena; another sizable number came from faraway New England, with dreams of endless possibilities out west. In 1835, the Connecticut-born editor of the *Sangamo Journal* boasted that with the opening of a railroad service "our town will soon rival Lexington in population, wealth, and importance." Although this was a species of civic boosterism that might strike anyone coming from Lexington as absurd (Lexington was four times Springfield's size), it was, for a transplanted Yankee, a fine display of the "well-known" Kentucky bragging mixed with Western exaggeration, and probably appreciated.[4]

Not all of the Southerners who crossed over from Kentucky to Illinois found living in a free state compatible with their notions of business and social order. Many were slaveholders who counted slaves among their valuable property and were used to the service of slaves, and they often left home reluctantly, only after they had wrung dry the opportunities for advancement in their home counties. To be sure, the 1818 Illinois Constitution had consigned blacks to the condition of indentured servants, a nod to incoming slaveholders who wanted to make Illinois a slave state, and a loophole in the Northwest Ordinance of 1787, which banned slavery from the future states of Illinois, Indiana, Michigan, Wisconsin, and Ohio. When, in 1824, Illinois's slavery supporters lost in a historic referendum to legalize slavery in the state, they still managed to garner 42 percent of the electorate.[5]

The state's Southern-born population was a major attraction for migrating Kentuckians; nevertheless, there were those who continued on through Jacksonville, Illinois, and straight to slaveholding Palmyra, Missouri. According to one Kentucky Todd cousin who had moved to Jacksonville, "In nine cases out of ten they remark that if they could bring their Negroes here they would go no further."[6]

Eventually, the mix of Southern and Northern countrymen, plus an influx of German and Irish immigrants who replaced blacks as servants in wealthy homes, did encourage Illinois lawmakers to reach a compromise that may seem contradictory today, but made perfect sense to antislavery whites who did not want to live among a large population of free blacks. They outlawed slavery (the law was passed in 1848), but, like their neighbors in Indiana, they wrote into the state's constitution a ban on free black immigrants.[7]

Despite Springfield's rise, the Todd sisters, who had grown up with the refinements and self-regard of Lexington, must have wondered how they'd survive in this small prairie town. True, liberated from their stepmother's hostile rule, they probably enjoyed the freedom of manners and opportunities for adventure that a new Western town offered women as well as men. But although new sights and people were exciting, especially to Mary, the sisters were neither adventurers nor pioneers, and if Springfield seemed livable, it was because of the considerable cushion they had of Kentucky relatives and friends who already lived there. One could have joked that Springfield was the Western colony for restless Todds.

The Todd sisters, led by Elizabeth and surrounded by kith and kin, dwelled at the apex of Springfield society. At the beginning of the decade, Mary's uncle Dr. John Todd had the best house in town, a two-story frame. By decade's end, Elizabeth and Ninian had the most *important* house in town, a two-story brick on "quality hill," at the edge of town, where they entertained the Springfield elite. This included the state's leading Whig politicians, prominent among them Kentucky cousins: Mary's first cousin, tall and handsome John Todd Stuart, a lawyer and U.S. Congressman; the older, methodical Stephen T. Logan, a former circuit judge and three-times-elected Illinois legislator; and John J. Hardin of nearby Jacksonville, married to a Todd cousin, a three-term state legislator and future U.S. Congressman. They made their way to the Edwardses' Second Street house "on the hill," setting a social and political tone that could only have been familiar and affirming to the proud Whig daughter that Mary was.

Years later there were many to reminisce about the family's graciousness and hospitality; however, not everyone viewed the mystique of "the hill" with equanimity—"showy edifices, the principal expense of which seems to have been their decoration," wrote one passerby, obviously not a guest—or appreciated the "Todd-Stuart-Edwards" family's aristocratic ways, "with preacher

& priest—dogs servants &c," in the words of John T. Stuart's future son-in-law. (Elizabeth and Ninian Edwards and Frances and William Wallace worshiped at St. Paul's Episcopal Church, but Ninian's brother Benjamin, the Todds, Stuarts, and Lincolns joined the Presbyterian churches.) But no one then or later could deny the family's influence, and any young man or woman fresh in town with ambitions—political or marital—did well to seek an entrée into the Edwardses' elevated circle.[8]

Mary had ambitions both political and marital. For a woman, it was obvious that they would have to be combined, but this was a fate she never questioned. For Mary, politics and love were similar in their appeal: as with the novels she read, what fascinated her were the characters and the intrigue. All she could do at this stage in the game was keep her eye out for eligible men. It *was* a difficulty that the "considerable acquisition in our society of *marriagable gentlemen* unfortunately [often included] only 'birds of passage,' " Mary wrote in 1840 to one of her new friends, Mercy Ann Levering, about the politicians and lawyers who were temporarily lodged in town, as if handpicked for delivery into the Edwards parlor. Originally from Baltimore, Mercy had already proven Springfield's worth, her "fortune . . . made," in Mary's words: during the 1839–40 winter social season, on a long visit to her brother, one of the Edwardses' hill neighbors, she had met the New York–born, Princeton-educated lawyer James C. Conkling, a Springfield arrival of 1838, and they were now engaged. Still, as Mary philosophically continued, there were always "new recruits" to dance and flirt with, and as her "ever dear Merce" knew, Mary loved nothing better than "society" and parties, "brilliancy & *city like* doings . . . so much excitement, and this you have deemed necessary to my wellbeing: every day experience impresses me more fully with the belief." She then paused, self-conscious before her meeker, pious friend, who had advised her to turn from "earthly vanities" to "one higher than us all." Then continued: "I would such were not my nature, for mine I fancy is to be a quiet lot . . . in this dull world of reality tis best to dispel our delusive day dreams as soon as possible."[9]

By the time Mary wrote this in July 1840, no one in "the Coterie" (as Mary's "quality hill" friends styled themselves) could have read these lines without smiling. It was generally agreed that, as Conkling put it, "She is the very creature of excitement you know, and never enjoys herself more than when in society and surrounded by a company of merry friends." Then, too, Mary was not shy about her "day dreams," and at twenty-one was still saying what she had at fourteen, that "she was destined to be the wife of some future President. Said it in my presence in Springfield and Said it in Earnest," sister Elizabeth would recall, with not a little wonder. She was "the most ambitious woman I ever saw."[10]

Such focused ambition no doubt put pressure on the eligible young men who might be attracted to Mary Todd. No one seems to have left a record of her Lexington conquests, but the charming, vivacious, and quick-witted daughter of Robert Todd must have had suitors, local Bluegrass scions or Transylvania students, like the young Ninian who courted her sister. Years later Elizabeth would say that Mary saw no one to her liking among the men who called at her father's house (indeed, none of them went on to become President). To Mercy, Mary confessed in July 1840, "My beaux have *always* been *hard bargains*," by which she meant unsuitable or undesirable in some way.[11]

For a girl of her background, training, and culture, not to mention her high opinion of herself, to be twenty-two and not yet engaged may have been worrisome, and there is no question that Mary and her friends were all fixated on marriage—understandably so, as marriage was the goal of the women and the duty of the men. But if Mary felt like an "old maid," she never said so in writing. Besides, Mercy was her age and she was just engaged to Conkling, or "Jacob Faithful," as they called him. And there was her close friend Julia Jayne, the doctor's daughter, who was not only single but also shared her sense of fun. Most important for Mary's psychological well-being, there was no sign that her younger sister Ann was about to marry or that anyone thought other than that it was Mary's turn, after Elizabeth and Frances. Like the perfect family in a Jane Austen novel, the Todd sisters were marrying in the order most likely to promote sisterly affection.

It would be hard to imagine a social scene more suited to Mary, whose knowledge of society was, after all, limited to her family circles in Kentucky, Missouri, and Illinois. Rounds of parties, dances, levees, picnics, jaunts to neighboring towns, sewing societies, lectures, vocal concerts, a theatrical company, and the occasional traveling circus kept Mary and her friends busy. Meanwhile, they benefited from the fact that unmarried women in the West had more social latitude than their peers in the stuffier Eastern cities. In Mary's circle they entertained in pairs or groups, like her friends Miss Rodney and Miss Thornton, who hosted a summer "pic-nic," setting on a "velvet lawn" a table "loaded with a profusion of delicacies which our ladies know how to prepare so well" (so said "Jacob Faithful," writing to Mercy).[12]

There was also politics. The presidential election year of 1840, Mary's first full year in Springfield, brought women out onto the hustings for the first time in American politics. The Whig campaign for war hero General William Henry Harrison inspired an outpouring of support from women around the country, surprising and dismaying to the Democrats. Of course, women could not vote or run for office, but they could sing songs, attend meetings and conventions, and join in boisterous parades, riding floats, waving handkerchiefs and flags, and wearing sashes across their bosoms (noted by masculine admirers) blazoned with the candidates' names. A very few went further and gave speeches, and at least one woman, Lucy Kenney, produced a political pamphlet entitled *The Strongest of All Government Is That Which Is Most Free, An Address to the People of the United States*. For the young and flirtatious, the campaign was a boon, giving men ample opportunities to display, peacock-like, their leadership qualities and oratorical mettle, while the women could prove their ardent political devotion.[13]

Illinois, with its agrarian and Southern attitudes, might go Democratic, but Springfield, filled with free-labor, upwardly mobile, Northern-minded men, was a Whig stronghold, and the all-consuming campaign for Harrison and vice presidential candidate John Tyler ("Tippecanoe and Tyler Too," honoring Harrison's victory in 1811 over the Shawnee leader Tecumseh's brother at Tippecanoe Creek in the Indiana Territory) looked like a chance to break the Democrats' twelve-year hold on the presidency. To Mary and her friends, it must have looked like a chance for fun. "This fall I became quite a *politician*," Mary declared in December, "rather an unladylike profession, yet at such a *crisis*, whose heart could remain untouched while the energies of all were called in question?" Indeed, the mix of political and sexual energies was irresistible, and at least one Saturday evening at the office of the Whig *Sangamo Journal*, Conkling saw Mary and "some fifteen or twenty ladies . . . collected together to listen to the Tippecanoe Singing Club. It has become lately quite a place of resort, particularly when it is expected there will be any speeches. I had the honor of being called on myself that evening and made a few brief remarks."[14] Saturday nights were never better than this.

Elizabeth once suggested that Mary scared the Lexington bachelors away with her "witty, sarcastic speech that would cut deeper than she intended" and her "impulsive" feelings over which she had no control. In that way, Springfield was a chance to start fresh, and Mary's spirits were buoyant, liberated by the possibilities for remaking herself in a place where she was unknown. It would take time for her Springfield friends to see the mood swings that Lexington knew, although eventually they would have a saying among themselves to describe Mary: she "was always 'either in the garret or the cellar.' "¹⁵ Now, entering the front hall, she could put her best foot forward.

If timing is everything, then Mary Todd met Abraham Lincoln almost too soon. "I knew he was a rising Man," Elizabeth said of the period beginning in the winter of 1839–40, when Mary and Lincoln became acquainted, but "L[incoln] Could not hold a lengthy Conversation with a lady—not sufficiently Educated & Intelligent in the female line to do so." This was also Springfield's general assessment. As another local would say, "It seems to [me] that Mrs. Lincoln must have had prophetic insight to have chosen Lincoln, who was the most awkward & ungainly man in her train and totally lacking in polish."¹⁶ No naïf, Mary surely felt something of this, although when she left Springfield in June for a three-month visit to her uncle in Missouri, she was flattered and pleased to find herself on Lincoln's list of correspondents. Still, she might have been including Lincoln in her list that summer of "my beaux [who were] . . . *hard bargains.*"

However, just as Mary's move to Springfield coincided with its becoming the sort of town she might deem worthy, so she came in time to witness this ungainly, uncommon man emerge as the kind of leading light she was bound to notice. A woman with her ambitions and penetration would not have missed what others were seeing in Lincoln. At the start of the election year 1840, Lincoln was, in the words of a friend, "just emerging above the horizon."¹⁷ Toward its close, Mary could have easily thought, and she would not have been alone, Lincoln's potential was clear as the light of day.

Throughout the thrilling 1840 election year, Mary Todd could have watched Abraham Lincoln not only take charge of the law firm for his partner, her first cousin John Todd Stuart, who was at the time serving in Congress, but also assume a leading role in the Illinois Harrison campaign; and she would have heard, no doubt with gratification, of his increasing fame throughout the state as the best stump speaker for the Whig cause. At some point late in the year, Mary must have determined that here was the "rising Man" whose future, if not background, promised more than the other men "in her train." This included Stephen A. Douglas, the better-educated, worldlier, more quickly rising Democrat, who was Lincoln's political rival. Born in Vermont in 1813, Douglas had settled in Jacksonville, Illinois, at the age of twenty, and by 1840 had already become a leader in the Illinois Democratic Party. Only five feet four inches, he would be called by his contemporaries the "Little Giant."

That Mary Todd could charm when she wished is indisputable, her social graces being as much her father's legacy as her temper and uncertain moods. And she certainly did wish to charm when she settled into her sister's parlor, "in society and surrounded by a company of merry friends." The caustic remarks that wounded could also titillate and amuse when confided to an intimate third party. Even targets of her sarcasm acknowledged she was "a keen observer of human nature, an excellent judge of it, none better." Letters from this time reveal a satirical eye and a storyteller's flare. One would have maneuvered to sit next to her on the carriage ride home to gossip about the party and its guests. A young man who was about to marry looked "*becomingly* happy at the prospect of the change"; a gentleman in Missouri whom she met on a long visit "cannot brook the mention of my return [to Springfield], an agreeable lawyer & grandson of *Patrick Henry—what an honor!* Shall never survive it." Meanwhile, one of the Whig legislators whose name was most linked to Mary's during this time was Edwin Webb, "the *winning widower*." However, "*Mr. Webb*, a widower of modest merit . . . our *principal lion*," was out of the question, "there being a slight difference of some eighteen or twenty summers in our years, [which] would preclude the possibility of congeniality of feeling . . . [and] with his two *sweet little objections*."[18] Not surprisingly, raising stepchildren did not appeal.

Any woman who could talk about men like that could talk *to* men—even to men as awkward as Lincoln. As one friend remembered, she was "a bright, lively, plump little woman—a good talker, capable of making herself quite attractive to young gentlemen." She had a technique, she told Helen Edwards, the wife of Ninian's brother: "she read minds & committed much to memory to make herself agreeable."[19]

Clairvoyance and flattery were not the only weapons in her arsenal, although for many a professional, unattached man they would be enough. Her boldness and impulsiveness could be attractive as well. The spring after she arrived, a long season of rain made Springfield's unplanked streets avenues of mud, ideal for the hogs that ranged freely through town but forbidding to thinly shod ladies encumbered by long, voluminous skirts. Contemporary guidebooks advised a lady on how to "gracefully raise her dress a little about her ankle," folding it toward her right side with her right hand ("To raise the dress on both sides and with both hands is vulgar") in order to trip daintily over a sidewalk. But ladies were not advised on how to slog through mud. Typically restless, Mary persuaded Mercy to walk to the public square with her on wooden planks they threw down for a path. But when they wanted to return, they found that the planks were sunk deep in the mud. Mary—conventional Mercy refused—hitched a ride home in Ellis Hart's dray (a wagon used for hauling freight), an exploit that was celebrated by one of the young local doctors, who poeticized, "At length arrived at Edwards' gate/Hart back the usual way/And taking out the iron pin/He rolled her off the dray." Lincoln would remember this episode with amusement.[20]

It is not surprising that Mary attracted the notice of the aspiring, smart, eligible men who circulated among the legislature, courthouse, and the Edwardses'. She was new to town and pedigreed: not only a Todd, but an acquaintance of the great Whig hero Henry Clay. She was pleasingly flirtatious (had even flirted with Clay). True, she was no heiress—not with so many siblings and half-siblings—but her ability to make her own clothes, a seeming economy, made her more suited to most up-and-coming men anyway. And she was no beggar: her father gave her $120 a year for expenses, what it had cost to send her to Madame Mentelle's and more than enough to hire "female" help for a year, had she wanted it (the Edwardses had "colored servants" in the house, so she managed). And she was helped in her wardrobe by "presents" from her Grandmother Parker. Between these and the clothes she sewed herself, she was always carefully turned out. In a town whose ladies, one keen-eyed woman observed, did not achieve brilliancy, crowding the ballroom in the American Hotel "handsomely dressed, but not in the latest style," Mary's fashion sense, constrained by the limited stocks of Springfield's dry goods stores, could be kept more or less au courant by the pages of the popular magazine *Godey's Lady's Book*, and make its mark.

But, certainly, there was more. Better educated than most women, including her sisters, and genuinely interested and knowledgeable in politics, Mary Todd could hold her own in the kinds of conversation the leading Springfield men were having. Yes, she had "decided aristocratic pretensions" (as one of those men put it) and had demonstrated her contempt for a Springfield serenade performed in her honor by local musicians; but she *was* a Todd, after all. Also, she spoke French. But it soon became apparent that she was not such a snob as to dismiss her cousin John Stuart's law partner and political protégé—a lanky, sad-faced, thirty-year-old man whose idea of polite conversation was to "wade into a ballroom and speak aloud to some friend, 'How clean these women look!' "[21]

When Abraham Lincoln moved from the dead-end Illinois town of New Salem to Springfield in April 1837, a newly licensed lawyer, it was to become the law partner of the prominent Stuart. Moreover, he wore the laurel of having been one of the famous "Long Nine," the slate of legislators over six feet tall, all but one of them Whigs, who represented Sangamon County and brought Springfield the state capital, a campaign in which Lincoln's role was crucial.

Yet when he came to Springfield, Lincoln was, in the words of scholar Douglas L. Wilson, "in a mood of deep despondency." He was depressed by the debt he carried from a bankrupt New Salem storekeeping venture (which Lincoln and his partner, William Berry, called the "*National* debt") and by the fact that his horse and surveying equipment—his most recent reliable means of support—were attached in a lawsuit to collect the debt.

He moved in with a young merchant from a first-rank Kentucky family, Joshua Speed, who offered to share his large room and bed over his store with the sad-eyed stranger who he realized could not afford the "furnishings" for a single bed. He had trepidations about his "experiment" as a lawyer, as he told Speed. How would he fare in a pool with the top lawyers in the state? They were men who were better educated and better *bred* than he. This last became impressed upon him as he faltered before the portals of Springfield society. "This thing of living in Springfield is rather a dull business after all, at least it is so to me," he felt within weeks of his arrival. "I am quite as lonesome here as ever was anywhere in my life. I have been spoken to by but one woman since I've been here, and should not have been by her, if she could have avoided it. I've never been to church yet, nor probably shall not soon. I stay away because I am conscious I should not know how to behave myself."[22]

It was only six years before he wrote that letter that Abraham Lincoln had landed in the Illinois village of New Salem, in his own words, "a strange, friendless, uneducated, penniless boy, working on a flat boat—at ten dollars per month." Born in 1809 into a poor farming family in Kentucky, he received only about a year of formal school and had been a laborer his whole life. When he stepped off the flatboat in New Salem in 1831—six feet four, all legs and arms, bushy hair brushed up by his fingers, no shoes, homespun shirt, and coarse jeans that had shrunk up past his shins—his boorish appearance drew local comment (as one scholar put it, he looked like a rube "even on the frontier"). Fortunately in Lincoln's case, looks *were* deceiving, for as unschooled and unkempt as he surely was, when he began to talk, his "character at once seized observation and that only led to respect," in the words of the local schoolteacher.[23]

He knew already that he did not want to be a flatboat man for the rest of his life; or a store clerk, his first village job; or the New Salem postmaster that he later became (a political patronage appointment). Restless with ambition, he devoted the next several years to his self-education, a project he undertook with such deliberation that he virtually remade himself; "nothing with him was intuitive," his future law partner and biographer William H. Herndon would say. After a systematic study of standard English grammar and pronunciation (to erase his Hoosier twang), he began poring over books on mathematics, surveying, and law; at the same time, he was reading nearly constantly, mostly history, poetry, and newspapers. It is no overstatement to say that Lincoln was utterly self-taught, and by 1860, the year he was elected President, he was (Stuart would tell Herndon) "an Educated Man . . . though he dug it out himself." Yet it is also true that, at least in his young manhood, when he had nothing but his talents to recommend him, he was helped time and again in clear, practical ways, by friends who responded to the appeal of his fortitude, intellect, humor, earnestness, and melancholy. Although he was emotionally aloof and cold and given to bouts of isolating depression, Lincoln was also, in the words of a friend, "very fond of company, telling or hearing Stories told . . . Whitling pine boards and shingles, talking and laughing." And he was very tenderhearted toward the defenseless and weak, most readily animals and children, but also men and women who were vulnerable in some way—sick, dejected, exploited, or oppressed.[24]

John Todd Stuart was one of those who helped Lincoln make his way to Springfield. The men had met in 1832, when both were volunteers in the Black Hawk War, reinforcing federal troops against the final effort of the Sauk and Fox Indians to reclaim their land in northwest Illinois. Mustered in Illinois, they were discharged in Wisconsin less than three months later and rode home to Sangamon County together, sharing Stuart's horse, alternating riding and walking. Arriving two weeks before elections, they began campaigns for seats in the legislature; Stuart was up for reelection, but it was his friend's political debut, and the well-off and college-educated Stuart became Lincoln's political mentor, even though at twenty-three Lincoln was only two years younger. (To attend the legislature, Lincoln had to borrow money for a new suit.) From the start, Stuart liked Lincoln, and as they worked together as fellow legislators, liking quickly deepened to "respect and confidence." Soon Stuart was lending Lincoln law books, encouraging his unschooled protégé to pursue his dream of becoming a lawyer. New Salem friends "plagued" Lincoln for walking twenty miles to Springfield to borrow the books, "and he never denied it," they said. But it did impress them that he studied alone.[25]

They also noticed that he stayed away from women, at least eligible young women, for he was comfortable confiding in older, married women—maternal figures, it may be. Like Mary Todd, Lincoln had lost his mother, Nancy Hanks Lincoln, when he was small; she died when Abe was nine years old and his sister, Sarah, eleven. (Also like Mary, a baby brother had died when Abe was three.) He was profoundly lonely after his mother's death, left with a father, Thomas, who had no interest in his son's sensibility and intellect, unless they could be turned to clearing land, plowing, and planting. Fortunately, his father remarried within a year, and Lincoln's stepmother, Sarah Bush Johnston, a widow with three children, not only cleaned the children up and loved them, but also encouraged Abe to read as much as possible. She offered protection from the anti-intellectual disdain of his father, who considered his son's reading a sign of laziness and an excuse to avoid work. Lincoln was always closer to the women in his family, so when his sister died in childbirth when he was nineteen, her loss was another heartfelt blow.[26]

Backward with women his own age, Lincoln did fall in love during his New Salem years. Ann Rutledge was attractive, sweet-tempered, and smart but not highly educated, the daughter of one of the founders of the village. She returned his affections and they hoped to marry, but toward the end of the summer of 1835, a memorably hot and rainy season, she died from what may have been typhoid. Lincoln broke down, so consumed by grief, so "plunged in despair," that his friends feared for his sanity. "I never seen a man mourn for a companion more than he did for her," wrote Mrs. Elizabeth Abell, one of Lincoln's maternal confidantes. "He made a remark one day when it was raining that he could not bare [sic] the idea of its raining on her Grave." He stopped studying law and told at least one friend "he [often] felt like Committing Suicide." No one who knew him doubted this possibility, and he was watched over by several friends who tried to distract him from his gloom. His depression weighed on him for several months before he could recover his equilibrium and resume reading his law books. Afterward, when he had acquired the skills necessary to navigate Springfield society, he seemed less able to attach himself without ambivalence, as if he could not bear to risk another loss. He courted several women on and off with varying degrees of interest (his and theirs). Certainly, he became more adept at regulating his emotions, one notable exception being his feelings during his courtship of Mary Todd. That he never forgot Ann Rutledge, as some of his friends maintained, seems plausible, given his reaction to her death and his sincere and essentially unchanging nature. Like a subterranean stream, sadness ran deep and steadily through his being.[27]

If Lincoln's romantic history before Mary began in tragedy, it ended in farce. His next significant romantic attachment involved an educated Kentucky woman from a wealthy family, Mary S. Owens. They met in New Salem in 1833 when Mary was visiting Elizabeth Abell, her older married sister. Lincoln liked the fair-skinned, blue-eyed Mary, said she was "intellectual and agreeable," so after Mary left, her sister proposed to Lincoln that she would bring Mary back to Illinois "upon condition" that he would court her. Lincoln agreed, but when Mary Owens returned in 1836, after Ann's death, he was aghast at how she looked. Miss Owens, always "over-size . . . now appeared a fair match for Falstaff." These are Lincoln's words; by then, he had mastered the arts of satire and insult, in evidence in his political journalism of the time. In this letter written about Mary Owens in 1838 (a year after the fact) to another of his married lady confidantes, presumably an undersize woman, he satirizes her and his own predicament: "Now, when I beheld her, I could not for my life avoid thinking of my mother; and this not from withered features, for her skin was too full of fat, to permit its contracting in to wrinkles; but from her want of teeth, weather-beaten appearance in general, and from a kind of notion that ran in my head, that *nothing* could have commenced at the size of infancy, and reached her present bulk in less than thirtyfive or forty years; and in short, I was not all pleased with her. But what could I do?"[28]

As promised, he muddled on with his courtship, but spent most of his efforts persuading Mary to let him off the hook. Behind the satire lay Lincoln's self-consciousness. In May 1837, not a month after he moved to town, he reminded her that he was poor—a genuine sore point for Lincoln—and that he was "afraid you would not be satisfied [living in Springfield]. There is a great deal of flourishing about in carriages here, which it would be your doom to see without shareing in it." Then in August, he wrote her a long, contorted letter, which read, in part:

> I want in all cases to do right, and most particularly so, in all cases with women. I want, at this particular time, more than any thing else, to do right with you, and if I *knew* it would be doing right, as I rather suspect it would, to let you alone, I would do it. And for the purpose of making the matter as plain as possible, I now say, that you can now drop the subject, dismiss your thoughts (if you ever had any) from me forever, and leave this letter unanswered, without calling forth one accusing murmur from me. . . . Do not understand by this that I mean to cut your acquaintance. I mean no such thing. What I do wish, that our further acquaintance shall depend upon yourself. If such further acquaintance would contribute nothing to your happiness, I am sure it would not to mine. If you feel yourself in any degree bound to me, I am now willing to release you, provided you wish it; while, on the other hand, if I can be convinced that it will, in any considerable degree, add to your happiness. This indeed, is the whole question with me.[29]

Mary refused to release him, leaving Lincoln with no choice but to go through with his proposal, which he did in the fall. She rejected him, with the satisfaction of a woman who knows she is doing something thoroughly unexpected. Lincoln, in fact, was shocked: "At first I supposed it was an affection of modesty, which I thought but ill-become her, under the peculiar circumstances of her case . . . I tried it again and again, but with the same success, or rather want of success . . . I was mortified. . . . My vanity was deeply wounded . . . and to cap the whole, I then, for the first time, began to suspect that I was really a little in love with her."[30]

Miss Owens was clear about why she refused him: "I thought Mr. Lincoln was deficient in those little links which make up the great chain of a womans happiness . . . his training had been different from mine, hence there was not that congeniality which would have otherwise existed." For example, there was the time Lincoln failed to help her over a branch during a riding party, when the other men were solicitous of their partner's safety. Lincoln rode on ahead, "never looking back to see how I got along," later explaining that "he knew I was plenty smart to take care of myself." It would be hard to decide if this illustrates Lincoln's characteristic self-absorbed abstraction or a belief in women's equality (seeking reelection to the legislature in 1836, he had campaigned with the proposal that white women who pay taxes or bear arms be entitled to vote). In any event, it showed he was not quite up to the niceties of high-class social relations.[31]

According to Mary Todd's sister Frances, who was living with Elizabeth and Ninian in 1837 when Lincoln arrived in Springfield, her brother-in-law was "always talking of this Mr. Lincoln," but he did not bring him up to "the hill" as a guest until she asked to see him. "Yes, he took me out once or twice, but he was not much for society," Frances later explained. "He would go where they took him. . . . But he did not go much, as some of the other young men did." Other women were put in his way, but an outing or two was generally sufficient to reveal his insufficiencies in the courting line.[32]

Springfield presented Lincoln with a problem: in order to shine with genteel women, or at least not be eclipsed, he needed to learn the art of parlor flirtation. However, a man who favors the ancedote over the witty exchange, who is unable to do or say anything that runs against his feelings, is interested in building roads and canals, and wears ill-fitting, shabby clothes and isn't bothered by it, is probably unsuited to flirting.

There were men like Stuart, of genteel birth, who were comfortable in the male culture of the West, which could be raw and crude: telling off-color stories, cutting political deals, chewing tobacco, drinking whiskey, and, as militia men, as Stuart recounted, visiting the "the hoar houses—All went purely for fun—devilment—nothing Else." But Stuart was also tall and handsome and formally educated and could adopt a courtly manner perfectly pitched to the ladies in the Edwards circle. This was not so for Lincoln. He was a great favorite with men of all classes, a genial companion (he never drank, but he held his own telling hilarious stories). His preferred social circle was the group of young men, mostly aspiring lawyers, who gathered in the back of Speed's store, in front of the large fireplace, to discuss politics, religion, philosophy, and literature. But with women—specifically, marriageable women of the Todd class—he was generally flummoxed.[33]

He was painfully aware of this. It was one thing to read books on surveying and law—one could teach oneself a profession that way—but one could not teach oneself the language of polite society or master from reading, even Burns, Byron, and Shakespeare (whom he could recite), the genteel banter that "quality hill" women expected. Minus the fortune of growing up with women like this, one had to spend time with them learning their ways. Ambitious as he was, Lincoln must have wanted to engage the Edwards female circle; he already knew, and was accepted by, the men. Interestingly, his self-conscious awkwardness with women did not translate into his feeling unworthy of courting any woman he might choose. Of his own merits he seemed sure.

By the time he met Mary Todd in 1839, Lincoln had been accepted into Springfield. That year, he was elected a town trustee and chosen presidential elector by the first state Whig convention. In December he was one of the managers of a cotillion at the American House. The ball was in honor of the first legislative session to be held in Springfield, and it was one of the big social events of the year, with state legislators and the town's elite invited. It was also one of Mary Todd's first large parties in Springfield.

It is likely they had already met, or at least been pointed out to one another as members of Springfield's consortium of appropriate, marriageable people. Lincoln would naturally have wanted to meet this first cousin of his law partner. Then, too, he would have been intrigued, if not dazzled, by her proximity to Henry Clay, long his hero, his "beau ideal of a statesman." Mary, like Frances, would have heard her brother-in-law talking about this man Lincoln, and she could have seen him or read about him in the *Sangamo Journal* as one of the leaders at the Whig convention in October, whipping up enthusiasm for William Henry Harrison.

The ball was their first recorded encounter—the first, that is, that brought results. Lincoln, lethargic and standoffish, may have been taken by her liveliness and warmth. It was said that he was fascinated by her conversation, perhaps by her intelligence and bold, quick wit. She would have found something appealing in his sad face, a kindred lonely look she knew too well. They had common interests: their love of reciting poetry and their passionate support for the Whigs, the forerunners of the Republicans, who were pro–capitalist development and antislavery, in opposition to the Democratic commitment to slavery. Perhaps Lincoln shared with her some of his ambitions for the upcoming presidential campaign. There were mutual friends and acquaintances to discuss. Or he may have discovered early that she liked a good listener more than anything—which perhaps came as a relief.[34]

Then again, because balls are not for conversation they may have spoken hardly at all. Family tradition has it that he danced with her with ill success, eliciting a punning remark. But Lincoln did not dance, so he most likely watched her spinning about with others, a more advantageous position from which to appreciate her fascinations. Surely, dancing with her required more skill than he possessed. Already circulating was Herndon's story about the time he danced with Mary at a party and, in a misguided attempt at a compliment, told her that "she seemed to glide through the waltz with the ease of a serpent." To which she responded, "Mr. Herndon, comparison to a serpent is rather severe irony, especially to a newcomer."[35]

The story of the Lincolns' courtship and marriage is, at best, a morass of confusion. Conflicting testimony by friends and relatives—some said he jilted her at their wedding ceremony; others said he did not, that they were not even engaged—points to more than the usual faulty memories and historical ambiguities. It seems to strongly suggest that there was something off from the beginning. How could the people who knew them well and were around them, their family and friends, have given such different, indeed, incompatible eyewitness accounts? Mary actively contributed to the confusion. Years later, after her husband's assassination, growing alarmed at all the would-be biographers sniffing around the private corners of her marriage and publishing their findings, she began spinning counterversions—some rebuttals, some preemptive strikes. Fortunately, in his book *Honor's Voice: The Transformation of Abraham Lincoln*, Douglas L. Wilson disentangles the evidence to give a persuasive reconstruction of the chronology of their courtship.[36]

With the fancy excited by the December ball fed by the excitement of the presidential campaign, to which *all* of Lincoln's and Mary's friends were contributing their energies, emotions were no doubt running high, opening the way for feelings of love. Both arenas showed Mary to Lincoln at her best. Her effortless dancing, tidy figure, and lively demeanor distinguished her in a ballroom. Then, too, she was without question the most ardent, ambitious, shrewd, and well-connected lady Whig of Lincoln's acquaintance. Naturally, she drew comparison with Mary Owens, another smart, aristocratic Kentucky woman, but whose views on women and politics could be summed up in her own words: "Save me from a *political woman!*"[37] Mary Todd, on the other hand, could share Lincoln's passion for his political career.

The two may have tested the waters of mutual interest during the first three months of 1840—that was the longest stretch of time that year that they were both in Springfield—the year of their presumed courtship. Lincoln was tied to Springfield through March, busy with the state legislature, the Illinois Supreme Court, and the Sangamon Circuit Court. Meanwhile, following his own "Plan of Campaign of 1840," he was organizing Whigs around the state, writing letters to Party members. He also helped start up the campaign newspaper *The Old Soldier*, which was published from the *Sangamo Journal* office. Evening parties at the Edwardses', campaign events, and hot-tempered outbursts—"[Stephen] Douglas, having chosen to consider himself insulted by something in the 'Journal,' undertook to cane [editor Simeon] Francis in the street. Francis caught him by the hair and jammed him back against a market-cart, where the matter ended by Francis being pulled away," Lincoln wrote Stuart on March 1—gave occasion and subject for conversation with Miss Todd.[38]

But for the next half-year they barely saw each other. In April, Lincoln began making stump speeches for Harrison outside of Springfield, combining campaigning with his annual spring trip on the Illinois Eighth Judicial Circuit. These were the nine counties, encompassing thousands of square miles, in central and eastern Illinois, in which court sessions were held successively twice a year, in spring and fall. Lawyers who needed the extra money could follow the circuit judge from court to court and be on the road for ten weeks at a time, traveling by horseback or in buggies, staying together in farmhouses and inns. That spring, Lincoln was on the road handling cases and drumming up business for Stuart & Lincoln almost solidly until mid-June.

By the time he returned to Springfield, Mary had begun her own extensive trip, to her Missouri uncle David Todd's, and was out of town until September. But she was not out of Lincoln's mind. "Every week since I left Springfield," Mary wrote Mercy in July from her uncle's, "have had felicity of receiving various numbers of their interesting papers, Old Soldiers, Journals & even the [Democratic campaign paper] *Hickory Club*, has crossed my vision. This latter, rather astonished your friend, *there* I had deemed myself forgotten—When I mention *some letters*, I have received since leaving S— you will be somewhat surprised, as I *must confess* they were entirely *unlooked for*, this is *between ourselves*, my dearest, but of this more anon."[39]

Scholars have decoded Mary's coy hints to mean that she had two gentlemen correspondents: Lincoln (*Old Soldier* and *Sangamo Journal*) and Douglas (*Hickory Club*). Did she *feel* more for Lincoln? It is difficult to tell. Mary was, in her way, thrilled with her suitors, although she rather enjoyed construing these as merely flirtatious intrigues. Moreover, she was not so smitten as to be beyond the pleasures of having "so many beaux 'dancing attendance' " in Missouri. She liked playing potential suitors off one another, a form of power, and quite unlike the devoted Mercy, whom Mary even now tried to tempt with "a young Cousin, by my Mother's side . . . Were you to see him, I almost fancy & hope that *others* [i.e., Conkling] in your eye would be forgotten." So Mary amused herself through broad insinuations—a feature of her letters and, one presumes, her conversation—until her equally characteristic close, a flurry of polite phrases: "Be as *unreserved* as you find me, I forget myself writing to you, pass my imperfections lightly by, and excuse so miserable a production from your most attached friend."[40]

Mary's return in September, when she attended the meeting of the Tippecanoe Singing Club, where Conkling saw her, would have been the first opportunity she and Lincoln had to see each other since March. But if she were hoping to see him, she was disappointed, because Lincoln had left for a long speaking trip to the southern part of the state in mid-August and did not return until late September. Even then he was in Springfield for only a few days before leaving to join the fall county court circuit for six weeks, and he did not return until a few days after the presidential election of November 2. In October 1840, Conkling saw Mary at a wedding, where she seemed "not . . . as merry and joyous as usual . . . as if she looked around for former friends and asked, 'Where are they?' "[41] Mary would not have been the first or last unmarried woman to exhibit signs of loneliness and depression at another woman's wedding, and as the wedding party was unusually small, Mary may have been missing any number of friends; but among those "missing" she could have counted Lincoln.

During the fall, Lincoln continued to write to her, most likely with news about the progress of the campaign, and she presumably answered. Somewhere along the way, they reached some kind of romantic understanding, an expectation at least, to continue their relationship on his return. After his return, they fell into company again, sometimes meeting at parties given by Helen and Benjamin Edwards, who lived across from the Second Presbyterian Church, where a special session of the legislature was being held.

Neither affirmed or denied a relationship when their friends quizzed them. (The status of the relationship is still unclear, whether they were engaged or, through a misunderstanding, Mary assumed they were and Lincoln thought not. Mary's family would say they were engaged, but Lincoln's male friends, including his best friend Speed, never used the word when referring to this period.) Naturally, their secrecy encouraged teasing, which Lincoln probably endured silently, unlike Mary, who became indignant when "a group of girls" poked fun at Lincoln's height, saying she'll need to "take a ladder to get to Abraham's bosom." (In later years, Lincoln would turn their fourteen-inch height difference into a joke; they were, he'd say, "the long and the short of it.")[42]

But already Lincoln was experiencing a change of heart. For one thing, he was probably taken aback by Mary's appearance that fall—they had not seen each other since March—for like Mary Owens, she had grown fat, "grow[n] out of our recollection. . . . and bids fair to rival Mrs. Glenn if she does not exceed old Father Lambert," Conkling cruelly joked in September. Mary was self-conscious about her weight, although by December she could report to Mercy, "I still am the same ruddy *pineknot*, only not quite as great an exuberance of flesh, as it once was my lot to contend with, although quite a sufficiency."[43]

Mary's weight, however, was not the couple's biggest problem. By the end of November, another woman had caught Lincoln's eye: the beautiful, eighteen-year-old Matilda Edwards, a cousin of Ninian's, whose father, Cyrus Edwards, was an important Illinois Whig. To make matters worse, Miss Edwards, while on her visit to Springfield, was staying at her cousin's along with Mary.

Matilda arrived on the scene about the time Mary and Lincoln were probably beginning to rekindle a relationship that had been carried on only by mail since March. (None of this correspondence has survived.) For the first time, they were in one another's company in a way they had not been the previous winter, before the letter writing, and their relationship was obviously reaching a critical point. That Lincoln should back off now might have been a sign that he was scared to take the plunge, a logical extension of his history with women. Matilda was not interested in him or anyone, although apparently nearly everyone was interested in her (including Joshua Speed), with quite a number of them proposing (twenty-two by at least one count).[44] Certainly, it would have been convenient for a man who was frightened of commitment to fall in love with a gorgeous, young, and *unavailable* woman.

However, it is also true that, spending time with Mary in a way he had never done before, Lincoln may have seen signs of the temper that had scared others off. He certainly gave her cause for angry displays. Lincoln failed to show up "at a ceremonious occasion" when Mary was expecting him, a humiliation that could be kept from some of the guests, but not family—and her family was extensive. Indeed, given the small, incestuous interrelationships of their circle of family and friends and the very public way courtships were managed, it would have been hard to keep secret that she was being treated badly. But Lincoln's friends were certain that "seeing an other girl" and falling for her made him realize that "he did not love [Mary]"—and this does seem to be the case.[45]

All he could see was that he had made a mistake. Mary Todd was not what he remembered. Or expected. Or imagined. The happy sentiments that letter writing had warmed and nourished now deflated and collapsed. In some ways, Matilda's presence was the precipitating trigger, but fundamentally incidental.

Initially, Lincoln wanted to write a letter to break it off, but Speed (his confidant, despite their apparent rivalry) advised against it: "Words are forgotten—Misunderstood—passed by—not noticed in a private Conversation—but once put your words in writing and they Stand as a living & eternal Monument against you." You should go see her and speak to her, Speed said, "If you think you have the *will* & Manhood Enough." Afterward, Lincoln reported to Speed what happened when he told Mary "he did not love her." She seemed to blame herself. "She rose—and Said 'The deciever [*sic*] shall be decieved wo is me' " (probably thinking of Douglas and the widower Webb, both of whom she had been flirting with). Then Lincoln, feeling sorry for her, "drew her down on his Knee—kissed her—& parted." That "last thing," Speed declared, was "a bad lick," but "it cannot now be helped." Lincoln promised Speed he would stay away from Mary.[46]

Although Lincoln never mentioned Matilda when he spoke to Mary, Mary had seen his attraction to her. Matilda's effect on men was obvious. As Mary wrote to Mercy in mid-December, after Lincoln had broken off, she was "a most interesting young lady, her fascinations have drawn a concourse of beaux & company round us, occasionally, I *feel as Miss Whitney* [unidentified], we have too much of such useless commodities, you know it takes some time for habit to render us familiar with what we are not greatly accustomed to." Undoubtedly jealous of her rival, Mary graciously conceded, "A lovelier girl I never saw. *Mr. Speed's* ever changing heart I suspect is about offering *its young* affections at her shrine, with some others."[47]

After Lincoln's rejection of her, and certain that he was among Matilda's acolytes (in fact, his attraction was common knowledge in their circle), Mary followed up her emotional advantage by confronting Lincoln with his crush on Miss Edwards. Yes, she would "release . . . him," she said, but her heart was unaltered (unlike his fickle one, she implied); indeed, she would "hold the question open." However, she told him, he was "honor bound to marry" her. According to Douglas L. Wilson, this was a devastating attack. Here was the vulgar bumpkin being told by a gentlewoman that he was behaving dishonorably. Here was the man who had made himself wretched trying to elicit from Mary Owens an admission that *she* was not interested in *him*, to relieve himself of the guilt of breaking a silly promise to her sister to propose. Being told that Mary Todd was unchanged in her feelings effectively undid her release in his mind, and nothing could have affected him more than to have his honor thrown in his face. Mary, who did not want to lose Lincoln, knew that pride dictated that she let him go; however, she also knew how to get what she wanted. In the case of Mr. Lincoln, making him suffer for dishonoring and humiliating her was the best way to keep him tied to her. "I want in all cases to do right, and most particularly so, in all cases with women," he had written Mary Owens.[48]

Over the next few weeks, Lincoln showed signs of breaking down. His utter physical and emotional deterioration led friends to label this his "crazy spell." Even before his confrontations with Mary, he was exhausted, strained to the limit. He had gone without a break from the draining discomforts and pressures of months on the campaign trail and circuit to his legal duties in Springfield, without the help of Stuart, who was serving his term in Congress. In addition, upon his return, as the Whig leader he found himself at the center of an emergency session of the state legislature, called by the governor to deal with the crisis of state debt. In this vulnerable state, he had crossed the volatile Mary Todd. The distress and depression he felt after their encounters, which threatened his hard-won, yet shaky sense of social identity and triggered his deeper anxieties about women, undid him in a way that must have felt like a repeat performance of his crash after Ann Rutledge's death.

To read Mary's letter to Mercy during this time is to think that nothing so striking had happened, certainly nothing approaching being cast off by a suitor who then proceeds to have a mental collapse. The only real clue that she was feeling unsettled is the nonstop shifting and switching of topics and affect in her letter, a quality inherent to some degree in all her letters of any length. Beginning with her report on Matilda's charms with self-mocking humor and her satirical prediction that Speed would soon propose (Speed did, another blow to Lincoln, even though he was refused), she then laid out the social scene. As she presented it, it was not just Lincoln who was backing off; rather, he was part of a general retreat. With the high spirits and sexual charge of an overheated political campaign behind and the beautiful Miss Edwards present, there *was* a change in the whole merry band. Like Robin Hood's men (of whom a balladeer wrote, "Whan they were clothed in Lyncolne greene/ they keste away theyre greye"), "Speed's *'grey suit'* has gone the way of *all flesh*, an interesting suit of *Harrison blues* have replaced his *sober livery, Lincoln's, lincoln green* have gone to dust, Mr. Webb sports a *mourning p[in]* by way of reminding us *damsels* that we *'cannot come it,'* of the new recruits I need not mention, some few are gifted & all in our humble estimation interesting."[49]

If the "old" suitors had "gone to dust," at least the "new recruits" were interesting. The tug of the melancholic undertone against the glittering surface is a familiar friction in Mary's letters. So she continued, circling her loss, advising Mercy, who was with her family in Baltimore and missing Conkling, to tell her sister to stop singing her sad songs, because "I know *by sad experience that such dolorous ditties* only excite one's anxiety to see a beloved object." Mary was writing only days after her twenty-second birthday and not long before Christmas, prime season for feeling lonely. There *was* something to look forward to, at least: "a pleasant jaunt . . . to Jacksonville" to John and Sarah Hardin's, proposed for Christmas week by "Mr. Hardin & [Orville H.] Browning," in which she was to form a party with "Miss E[dwards], my humble self, Webb, Lincoln & two or three others." She may have hoped for some kind of reconciliation then. But for some unknown reason the "jaunt" turned out badly, discouraging the Hardins from arranging such outings again.[50]

By January, the contrast in the pair's behavior was striking. He missed legislative sessions; she did not miss a party. On the twentieth Lincoln wrote Stuart, "I have . . . been making a most discreditable exhibition of myself in the way of hyponchriaism and thereby got an impression that Dr. [Anson G.] Henry is necessary to my existence." Three days later Lincoln wrote again to Stuart: "I am now the most miserable man living. If what I feel were equally distributed to the whole human family, there would not be one cheerful face on earth." The happily engaged Conkling was among those canvassing the matter who could not suppress amusement at Lincoln's plight, caught in the knot of unrequited love twice over, being on one side in relation to one woman, and the other side in relation to the other: "Poor L! How the mighty are fallen! He was confined a week, but though he now appears again he is reduced and emaciated in appearance and seems scarcely to possess strength enough to speak above a whisper. . . . I doubt not he can declare 'That loving is a painful thrill, And not to love more painful still' but would not like to intimate that he has experienced 'That surely 'tis the worst of pain To love and not be loved again.' "[51]

On the other hand, Mary, by all reports, was having a most successful season. On the twenty-seventh a visitor from Kentucky wrote home to a relative, "Miss Todd is flourishing largely. She has a great many Beaus." A day earlier, Mary's cousin Sarah Hardin wrote her husband, John, that she "has come to the conclusion that it would not break her heart if Mary and Matilda was to marry them all."[52]

After the Lincolns were married, Mary would confide to Mary Stuart (John's wife) that "when they broke off she was very sad." With her childhood of losses and her hopes and ambitions thwarted, her suffering must have been acute. But this was not the Mary most people saw. Even a regretful letter to Mercy ended with a characteristic game of flirtation: "The interesting gentleman, whom Mrs Roberts gave you for a beau is now resident of this place, Mr. [Lyman] Trumbull, is Secretary of State, in lieu of *Judge Douglass* [Douglas was spelling his name with a double 's'], who has been rapidly promoted to office—Now that your fortune is made, I feel much disposed in your absence, to lay in my *claims*, as he is talented & agreeable & sometimes *countenances* me." Family and friends made sense of her behavior by deciding that it was a strategy to make Lincoln jealous, though they were not sure whether Douglas was really serious.[53]

Whether it was pride, revenge, defiance, a realistic view of things, impulsiveness, calculation, grief, or anxiety—or some combination—that drove her to undisguised flirtation is difficult to know. It was not because she had given Lincoln up. For meanwhile, she was confiding her unhappiness to Orville Browning, a friend of Lincoln. (It was Browning's wife who had been Lincoln's confidante after his break with Mary Owens.) She sat up with Browning "sometimes till midnight" in her brother-in-law's parlor talking "about this affair of hers with Mr. Lincoln." She could not hide her "bitterness" toward Matilda, whom even others viewed as a coquette. To Mercy she confessed in June that her own flirtations might have driven a jealous Lincoln away. Responding to something Mercy said about Mr. Webb, she wrote, "You appeared impressed with the prevalent idea that we were *dearer* to each other than friends, the idea was neither new nor strange, dear Merce, the knowing world have coupled our names together for a month past, merely through the folly & belief of *another* [Lincoln?], who strangely imagined we were attached to each other . . . I have deeply *regretted that his constant visits, attentions &&* should have given room for remarks." Still avoiding mentioning Lincoln by name, she continued: "Mr. Speed['s] . . . worthy friend deems me unworthy of notice, as I have not met *him* in the gay world for months, with the usual comfort of misery, imagine that others were as seldom gladdened by his presence as my humble self, yet I would that the case were different, that he would once more resume his Station in Society, that 'Richard should be himself again,' much, much happiness it would afford me."[54]

Mary would often be drawn to smart, ambitious, and melancholy outsiders, people with whom she identified on some level, she who had felt herself an outsider in her childhood home. Moreover, impulsive and childish herself and ever seeking replacements for her parents, she clung closest to people who conveyed some sort of ideal parental qualities: reliability, clear-mindedness, firmness, and steadiness. Lincoln, who was nine years older and possessed the air of a much older man, had these qualities in spades; he moved as if from a central core of being. In him, Mary might have sought the father she never quite had: the striving politician and lawyer whose ambitions were fulfilled and the tenderhearted and steady provider whose home life centered on her.

However, Mary's family's reactions to the courtship were mixed. "After the first crush of things," Elizabeth and Ninian were against the marriage; they told Mary that she and Lincoln were too different in "natures, mind—Education—raising" to marry happily. It was advice she not only rejected, but held against them. Despite their differences, Mary and Lincoln did understand each other's capacity for psychological suffering. She was right about his continued misery, and he was not fooled by her gay manner. Sixteen months after breaking off, Lincoln was still struggling against his guilt. "I should have been entirely happy," he told Speed, "but for the never-absent idea, that there is *one* still unhappy whom I have contributed to make so. That still kills my soul. I can not but reproach myself, for even wishing to be happy while she is otherwise."[55] Of all the men she knew, it was the melancholy Lincoln who would have empathized with Mary's underlying sadness.

So, apparently, things went on from January 1840 through October 1842. Lincoln avoided the Edwards house, although each was unavoidably aware of the other's movements. There are no surviving letters of Mary's from this time, so little is known about the details of how she felt. But her Springfield friends related that she was "either in the garret or the cellar," either ecstatically happy or deeply depressed. As for Lincoln, his extraordinary letters to

Speed reveal that he spent those twenty-two months struggling to climb out of the cellar by resolving the crisis of Mary Todd that he blamed himself for creating. It was not exactly a crisis "with" her, but "of" her—an internal conflict he fought within himself. In the end, a series of unrelated events, which to Lincoln felt like fate, brought them together. "My old Father used to have a saying that 'If you make a bad bargain, *hug* it the tighter,' " he wrote to Speed in the midst of it all.[56]

Foremost was that his best friend Speed, after returning to Louisville, fell unexpectedly in love at the end of the summer (during a visit from Lincoln), became engaged, and married the following February. The months leading up to the marriage found Lincoln monitoring long-distance Speed's anxieties and *"forebodings"* over what Lincoln called *"the rapid and near approach of that crisis on which all your thoughts and feelings concentrate."* He was using Speed's experience to come to terms with his own marriage crisis, and his heart and mind would never lie so exposed to us—or to anyone—again. When he opened the "promised" letter that Speed sent him after the wedding, it was "with intense anxiety and trepidation—so much, that although it turned out better than I expected, I have hardly yet, at the distance of ten hours, become calm." He was sad at what he felt was the loss of intimacy with Speed: "You will be so exclusively concerned for one another, that I shall be forgotten entirely."[57]

Once happily—and safely—married, Speed would urge Lincoln, who himself was feeling much better, to take steps to resolve the Mary Todd situation one way or the other. To this, Lincoln's response was telling. Before I do anything, he wrote in July, "I must regain my confidence in my own ability to keep my resolves when they are made. In that ability, you know, I once prided myself as the only, or at least the chief, gem of my character; that gem I lost—how, and when, you too well know. I have not yet regained it; and until I do, I can not trust myself in any matter of much importance."[58] Once he recovered his sense of self, he would act.

But before he was ready, another incident involving his honor occurred, with which Mary was tangentially connected. In September, Lincoln was challenged to a duel by the Democratic state auditor, James Shields, for a pseudonymous satirical letter he wrote and had published in the *Sangamo Journal* lampooning Shields personally as well as politically. Lincoln's letter was only one among several that were supposed to be from a place called The Lost Townships and written by a farmwoman named Rebecca. They were written independently by different authors, who apparently saw the fun of piling onto the vulnerable Shields, a genial but puffed-up man. For sport, Mary Todd became involved with this affair. In reaction to Shields's public demand of editor Simeon Francis to reveal the author of the letter so that he might defend his honor, her friend Julia Jayne, with Mary's help, wrote another Rebecca letter to the *Journal*, making fun of Shields's "threatenin to to [*sic*] take personal satisfaction of the writer"; a week later Mary's mock-epic poem appeared, announcing the marriage of Rebecca and her challenger.

Lincoln was against dueling, but could not have declined the challenge, not if he wished to be counted a gentleman under the accepted code of honor—or if he wished to regain his sense of himself as a man of resolve who follows through. Friends effected reconciliation, and afterward it was an incident Lincoln recalled only with embarrassment. However, as Douglas L. Wilson suggests, he may have drawn a link between this affair of honor and the one with Mary. And the fact that Mary was involved must have struck both of them, as well as their friends.[59]

The rest unfolded rapidly, and not altogether transparently. On September 27, five days after the duel was averted, Mary and Lincoln saw each other at the wedding of Martinette Hardin in Jacksonville, where they were most likely guests of John and Sarah Hardin, who had (it seems) recovered their matchmaking instincts after the disastrous jaunt of Christmas 1840. There, reconciliation occurred. Then, by arrangement of their friends Mr. and Mrs. Simeon Francis, Mary and Lincoln began meeting secretly at the Francis home. On October 5 Lincoln wrote Speed, "The immense suffering you endured from the first days of September [Speed's engagement] till the middle of February [when Speed married] you never tried to conceal from me, and I well understood. You have now been the husband of a lovely woman nearly eight months. That you are happier now than you were the day you married her I know well. . . . But I want to ask a closer question—'Are you now, in *feeling* as well as *judgement*, glad you are married as you are?' From any body but me, this would be an impudent question not to be tolerated; but I know you will pardon it in me. Please answer it quickly as I feel impatient to know."[60] Speed's positive answer sealed Lincoln's fate.

One month later, on the morning of November 4, without warning, Lincoln paid a call on his friend James Matheny to ask him to be a groomsman at his wedding that evening. Meanwhile, Mary headed over to Uncle John Todd's house to tell her secret to her cousin Lizzie Todd. When Ninian learned of the couple's plan to be married at the Episcopal Church, he insisted, as Mary's guardian, that the ceremony take place at his home. Elizabeth protested against the couple's haste, at least in part because she had no time to prepare a wedding meal. Helen Edwards remembered that when Elizabeth jokingly said that she would have to send out for gingerbread and beer, Mary retorted, "Well that is good enough for plebeians." She also recalled that Mary wore "neither veil nor flowers in her hair." Cousin Lizzie remembered Mary wearing a simple muslin dress, which she brought to "an old colored woman to launder" that very morning.[61]

A wedding pulled together with such haste and urgency was bound to be small, and this one was, with a few friends and Mary's family present. Lincoln might have been hoping that, like Speed, he would find himself happier after the marriage than before. William Butler said that when his little boy saw his boarder getting dressed that evening and asked where he was going, Lincoln replied, "To hell, I suppose." The groomsman Matheny described Lincoln as looking like a lamb being led to the slaughter. Yet the wedding ring, which Lincoln bought for Mary at a jeweler's on the public square, would be inscribed with these words: "A.L. to Mary, Nov. 4, 1842. Love is Eternal."[62]

Mary Owens, the Mary who refused to marry Lincoln, told a story that offers a key to understanding Lincoln's decision to return to Mary Todd after rejecting her. What moved him, it suggests, was empathy and pity: "In many ways he was sensitive to a fault. He told me of an incident; that he was crossing a prairie one day, and saw before him a hog mired down, to use his own language; he was rather fixed up and resolved that he would pass on without looking towards the shoat, after he had gone by, he said, the feeling was eresistable [*sic*] and he had to look back, and the poor thing seemed to say so wistfully—*There now! my last hope is gone;* that he deliberately got down and relieved it from its difficulty."[63]

Did Mary let herself register Lincoln's feelings toward her? We do not know. She may have been thinking only of her triumph that day: at the center of a party, marrying the man of her choice, and closing with her ambition. In the end, however, she had married a man whose sense of honor and feelings of pity were what drove his decision to be married to her, and she would suffer through a lonely marriage for it.

CHAPTER SIX

$\mathcal{B}$y the time Lizzy was returned to Virginia, by
early 1842, Armistead Burwell had died and her old
mistress was living with her daughter and son-in-
law, Anne and Hugh A. Garland, on a farm called
Mansfield overlooking the Appomatox River, just
southwest of Petersburg. This is where Lizzy and
her son were sent. After half a dozen years of separation, Lizzy was happy to be reunited with her
family and old friends. Working in the main house
were her mother, her Aunt Charlotte and Charlotte's three daughters, and Arabella from the old
Burwell farm, along with one or two men. Besides
Lizzy's George, there was another young boy, John,
who would be listed in an inventory of Garland's
property as Aggy's son. (If he was her brother, Lizzy
never mentioned him in her memoir.) As for her
white family, there were also the Burwells' unmarried daughters, Fanny and Betty (Elizabeth), the
youngest daughter to whom Lizzy was promised
when she married.[1]

The country was in a severe economic depression and Garland's income from various unsuccessful commercial enterprises was stretched thinly across the extended household. Although Garland housed and fed his female relatives, he could not long support so many impoverished dependents. Already there were five little Garlands and another on the way (all told, there would be eight children). And he needed his sixteen slaves, half of whom worked the farm.

His distress was canvassed in family letters. To help out, early in 1842, Fanny Burwell took a position as a live-in governess for a minister's family in Gloucester County. She was approaching thirty, with no expectations of marriage. Then Anna wrote from Hillsborough with the proposal that her mother-in-law come south and rent a house with Betty, who then could teach French in her school, while Mrs. Burwell could take in boarders. Mrs. Burwell, caught between living with her difficult daughter-in-law and a pile of unpaid store and doctor bills, reluctantly agreed. Robert "could not offer [Betty] a fixed salary," she explained to Fanny, "but he would give her: her board & what was made by the music scholars. . . . your brother says the music & French have always been worth $4 or $500," although he expected that the new school in Raleigh would drain students away from their school. Mrs. Burwell had thought of asking her other sons for money but was afraid she would still fall short. In the nationwide depression, teaching seemed one of the few paying options. "I believe teachers are all the persons making money now a days," wrote a Burwell cousin to Fanny; "how many of our county folk are brought down in their circumstances."[2]

Mary Burwell also worried about what to do with her slaves. Aggy and Lizzy were legally her property but were being handled as Garland slaves. However, Charlotte and her three daughters—twenty-five-year-old Amy, twenty-two-year-old Hannah, and fourteen-year-old Lucy—were hers to dispose of. She could not afford to keep them all but did not want to sell them and permanently break up the family. One acquaintance offered to hire Hannah, and that would bring in some income; she also thought that she might let them have Lucy, too, "for her victuals & clothes." But "I don't know what to do about Charlotte sometimes Anne [Garland] talks of keeping her by way of favour she seems not to be able to do much Amy will stay here. [A]nd I hardly know what she will do without her Mother. I want to do for the best with them."[3]

Finally, after a delay of several months due to a want of money for traveling expenses, Mrs. Burwell and Betty moved to Hillsborough. They took Lucy with them, having hired out Hannah for $50 a year and left Charlotte and Amy with the Garlands. In Hillsborough, Mrs. Burwell was pleased with Lucy. "She is the earliest riser I have ever seen," she marveled, "and just goes ahead cleaning any room. I help her make the beds and she does all the rest and keeps it in very good order has a very good notion of sewing and is learning to darn stockings." According to Lizzy, who was ten years older than her cousin, Lucy was also good at washing and ironing.[4]

Lizzy may have watched her cousin's departure with sympathy, for Lucy was the exact age that she had been when she was separated from her mother and sent to Hillsborough. However, Lizzy could have drawn comfort from knowing that with Mrs. Burwell to protect her, Lucy was less vulnerable than she herself had been.

Fortunately, Hillsborough was behind her now, and she was much happier in Virginia with the Garlands. In later years she would remember them fondly, especially the youngest daughters, Nannie and Maggie, whom she helped raise. Nannie was a toddler and Maggie an infant when Lizzy became their slave nurse, and Maggie grew up thinking of her as a second mother, an attachment of which Lizzy was quite proud. In all, Lizzy would be the Garlands' slave for about twenty-three years, sharing their fortunes and misfortunes, and she filled the role of trusted and valued domestic. The Garland girls relied on Lizzy for her counsel and comfort, as much as the Burwell girls had relied on Aggy. (When thirty-three-year-old Fanny Burwell wrote home from Gloucester in 1844 to announce her engagement, her mother wrote back, "Aggy says tell Miss Fanny I told her so.")[5] She even respected the scholarly Mr. Garland, whom she would have remembered from Hampden-Sydney College. Although none of this entirely eased the pain of slavery, if Lizzy ever experienced something like happiness as a slave, it was with the Garlands.

Mansfield, a farm of about 273 acres, was one of four plantations originally owned by a wealthy eighteenth-century English-born farmer and merchant named Robert Atkinson. Like other Dinwiddie plantations, Mansfield's stately mansion was set on a rise amid outbuildings, orchards, and fields. One can envision the relief of such expansive surroundings for Lizzy after the close, crowded quarters of Robert and Anna's house. (Indeed, after six months Mrs. Burwell would leave Hillsborough and return to Virginia "because there was no room for her," and Betty would complain about the "small" and "uncomfortable" rooms and the prospect of having to share "a room with six.")[6]

At Mansfield, Lizzy was also liberated from Alexander Kirkland. And the fact that her white-skinned child had neither a Burwell nor a Garland for his father prevented his existence from being the insult and irritant that hers had been to Mrs. Burwell when she was small.

A letter Lizzy wrote to Fanny Burwell in the spring of 1842, when Fanny was still a minister's governess, suggests her relative ease of mind. No letter Lizzy ever wrote from Hillsborough, where she was a minister's slave, conveys the same lightness of spirit. "My Dear Miss Fanny," she began, "In your letter to Miss Betty you said that you were expecting a letter from me, so I guess you will not be surprised when you receive *this*. I will begin with news as I know anything from home will interest you." Thereupon, she delivered a sprightly report of a neighbor's party and an overnight visit from relatives, and then an account of a Mr. Jones, whose saddled horse appeared one evening without its rider, followed that night by Mr. Jones, who told them that he had stopped to pick some flowers when his "horse broke loose and ran off." Lizzy also reported on family matters, and was not shy about giving her views:

> Nannie is standing by the window singing . . . she is as sweet as ever and just as pretty, she has not improved very much in her letters (Abc). I am very busy making shirts, I have had to stop two or three days to cook, as the women are dropping corn [planting], I have got to make Miss Bet's frock to wear to Miss Betty Scotts wedding. Miss Anne and [Miss] Charlotte dont pretend to lace the[ir cor]sets at the bottom, Miss Charlotte has'nt learnt to hold up her head yet, and I am afraid she never will. Mrs [*sic*] Randolph [a Garland cousin] looks like an old man 50 years old his beard is quarter of an inch long and I let Maj Hughs off at an inch. Fanny *and* Fanny [a Garland daughter and cousin] say you must answer their letters, you must not answer them in mine as I want a long letter. Mary [a Garland daughter] has been sick with the Ague and fever she is up to-day and much better. Every one of the servants send their love to you Mammy [Aggy] in particular, and also all of the white people little and big. I shall have to stop soon as paper is getting scarce and the times are too hard to send a double letter and to waste any more ink and spoil an *excellent* pen, as you will see by this writing. Mistress [Mary Burwell] is in Boydton she will return after commencement, when Mr. Garland will go up. Miss Bet has the prospect of two beaux Dr. Spencer and Mr. William . . . son who has been quite [att]entive lately. Yours truly Lizzy.[7]

However, this oasis of domestic calm was short-lived. Two years later, Garland was on the brink of bankruptcy, and he reluctantly gave up Mansfield and moved the family to his Petersburg house. Hugh A. Garland would fit the mold of white people whom Lizzy served: educated and insolvent. To be fair, in the widespread depression, he was one of many farmers and businessmen who failed; but Garland does seem to have been particularly bad at making money. He was a shy, mild, and scholarly man, who cherished literary ambitions more than anything else—certainly over law or business, by which he tried to earn his living. Before his death at age forty-nine in 1854, he would write biographies of his two Virginia heroes, John Randolph and Thomas Jefferson, as well as a five-act tragedy about the Indian massacre at colonial Jamestown in 1622.

He also wrote a study of African slavery, a grand historical and philo-sophical work, in which he argued that Africans had been brought to America to be redeemed from barbarism through slavery. But his proslavery views did not blind him absolutely to opposing positions. True to his Virginia heroes, he was a liberal thinker, and in his large library one could find antislavery books and pamphlets on the shelves alongside volumes on law, philosophy, politics, history, and literature. Lizzy respected her new master for his intellectual strivings—true to her slave father's parting advice, she had a lifelong respect for book learning—but she herself would prove to have a far better head for business than Garland ever did.[8]

In 1841, just before Lizzy's return, Garland retired to Mansfield from an early stint in politics in order to write. It was then that he invested in his various business ventures, and it was the failure of these that tumbled him into a debt from which he never recovered. By 1845, all of his "land, slaves, library, furniture, interests and other property," including "Household and kitchen furniture . . . not at his dwelling house [in Petersburg] containing the usual variety of articles of genteel housekeeping," were put up as collateral against his debts. (The slaves were "Albert, Adam, Jim, Arabella, Aggy and her child John; Lizzy and her child George.") He entered a new partnership, but nothing took. In late February and early March, a severe coastal storm remembered as "the Great Gust," which brought high winds and heavy downpours of rain, sleet, and snow from Norfolk up the East Coast, caused numerous deaths and half a million dollars in damage, making that year particularly hard. His wife, determined to help, opened a small boarding school in 1846. In the fall, she still had only two students, although she expected more after Christmas; however, even these two evaporated by January 1847, and her mother, who was visiting, found her "sometimes very much cast down." Only two months earlier, she had given birth to her seventh child.[9]

Mrs. Burwell found the move from Mansfield to Petersburg jarring, writing to Fanny, "Don't it seem strange that Mr. G is living in Petersburg." She herself did not like the busy manufacturing town, "where money carries the day" and the family was unable to keep up financially with their social circle. Indeed, Petersburg was a humiliating experience for the downwardly mobile family, and it was not long before they planned to move again. "I suppose Mr. Garland is fully determined to go some where & I don't blame him," Mrs. Burwell told Fanny in November 1846.[10]

"Some where" materialized as St. Louis, Missouri, a booming city, which was filling up with Easterners and German and Irish immigrants. It was soon arranged that Garland would head out before Christmas, taking with him the slaves Albert and Jim. The rest of the family—including Adam, Arabella, Aggy, Lizzy, and the boys—would follow a year later. "The servants here are perfectly delighted at the thought of moving West," Mrs. Burwell reported, "but when I think of it dread it very much."[11]

With her husband dead and her children dispersed, Mrs. Burwell had found herself nervously shuttling between her children's homes. The experiment of living with Anna and Robert now ended, Betty had moved to Vicksburg, Mississippi, to the home of her brother Armistead Jr., who, as a lawyer and planter, was far and away the most successful of the Burwell sons. Vaguely, Mrs. Burwell had thought of opening a school herself—after all, her daughters had done it—but in the end it was decided that when Anne and the family left for St. Louis, she would move to Vicksburg as well.[12]

For nine long months the women and children stayed behind in Petersburg after Garland left, with Anne leaning heavily on her slave women, especially Lizzy and Aggy, for help. She put them in charge of looking after the six older children as well as doing all of the family sewing. They also ran errands in town while Anne managed things at home. There were boarders again in the house, which made more work and only went so far toward paying the bills. "I am tired to death of debts," Anne confessed to her sister. Then there were the bouts of illness (measles and threats of cholera), leaving the women shorthanded and requiring some shifting of tasks. During the summer Amy, who took care of the baby, was sick for several weeks, so Lizzy stepped in. "This of course put me back with sewing work," Anne wrote her sister, "as Lizzie has to mind the baby so much."[13]

As would be the pattern for the next decade, the Garlands' misfortune would create opportunities for Lizzy. For her, living in Petersburg was no doubt an eye-opening experience. It was the biggest town she'd so far seen, over 15,000 people by 1850, and the most commercial, a center of tobacco factories, mills, and merchants. Vessels owned by Petersburg businessmen regularly carried tobacco and cotton to Europe from City Point, fifteen miles to the north, where rail and stage connections made travel relatively easy.

But there was something else: a sizable free black population. In fact, out of a population of which about half were black, nearly a third of the black people were free. Even more notable: most of these were unmarried, self-supporting women. Indeed, women headed more than half of the town's free black households and were the majority of the paid free black labor force. And many of these unmarried women were property owners (unlike their white counterparts, who, if they could, got married).

Lizzy would have noticed these free women as she walked from shop to shop alone, hunting up medicines, groceries, and other supplies for her mistress. She could see their occupational options were limited: most were washers, ironers, seamstresses, house servants, and cooks—traditional female tasks—or employed in the tobacco factories. However, there were women (some of them emancipated slaves) who were professionals and entrepreneurs: cuppers and leechers, midwives, nurses and even doctors, storekeepers, tavern keepers, and proprietors of cook shops. These women could not afford to be shrinking violets. One early businesswoman, taking advantage of economic hard times and a steamy hot August, billed her bathhouse as a chance for "HEALTH Purchased Cheap!" at reduced cost, only 25 cents a bath. (The advertisement continued: "She will make no comments on the necessity of Bathing in warm weather: —suffice it to say, that with Mr. Rambaut's FAMILY MEDICINES, and some Cold or Warm BATHS, the health of her friends will keep at a proper degree of the thermometer, without the aid of Calomel or any other mineral Medicines.")[14]

In these working- and middle-class black women Lizzy could see the possibilities beyond slavery for someone like her. With the taste of autonomy new in her mouth—never before had she had so much freedom of movement or of thought as here in Petersburg—she began hungering for more. She was almost thirty, with a small boy to think about.

Meanwhile, bad luck dogged Hugh Garland, beginning with the initial journey to St. Louis itself. Coach accidents were common and Garland apparently had one on the National Road, the major route west, near Wheeling, Virginia (today West Virginia), at the point where the Ohio River peels away from Pennsylvania. He was injured enough to require a short recuperation, during which time he had to hire out Albert and Jim to make ends meet. He passed the last leg of the journey by steamboat unscathed, making connections at Cincinnati and Louisville before docking in St. Louis. This, according to Charles Dickens, who had traveled the same route to St. Louis, was lucky: "Western steamboats usually blow up one or two a week in season." In fact, with the furnace fires and machinery exposed and in close proximity to the wooden deck, "one feels directly that the wonder is, not that there should be so many fatal accidents, but that any journey should be safely made."[15]

In St. Louis, Garland quickly established a small law practice, and in June wrote his father to say that he was very pleased with his new home and doing a lucrative business. But somehow, when his family appeared in the fall they "found him so poor that he was unable to pay the dues on a letter advertised as in the post-office for him."[16] (Stamps were available, but until 1855 one could mail a letter and expect the recipient to pay.)

His family could not have been more surprised and disappointed. The "lucrative business" had evaporated, and with it, it seemed, their prospects. Meanwhile, it occurred to Garland to hire out Aggy, who could be employed as a domestic and seamstress, positions much called for in the city, and add her wages to the family's income. When Lizzy heard about this plan, she objected. Because her mother had never worked for another family, she felt it would be cruel to force her to change now. She, on the other hand, was young and flexible, and she offered to go out as a seamstress instead.

It was a turning point in Lizzy's life. Indeed, one feels that behind her offer, much more than a wish to protect her mother, was a desire to see what she could do for herself, to test the limits of her enslavement. This is not to suggest that her motives were selfish. It was natural that she would want this, almost inevitable given her talents and character. She would have seen her mother's difference from her, generational and experiential. From the age of fourteen, when she was sent to North Carolina, Lizzy had in many ways been on her own, and she had acquired the level of literacy and the self-reliant habits of mind that were not only useful to earning a living but made it intolerable not to do so. Moreover, she had a genuine gift as a seamstress, one developed during her years of fitting dresses onto her white half-sisters. She still took orders, but she had been thinking independently for years. Being hired out would mean more independence and autonomy: walking to and from jobs alone and regulating her own time. Most important, it would be a chance to establish relationships outside of the slavery household. This would be the key to freedom.

For even then, she must have been anticipating a time when she might buy her own freedom, as her slave father wished to do and others she knew had done. In Petersburg she had seen how much money an ambitious black woman could make, and she knew that the money she kept, after handing over the portion her master would demand, could be put toward buying herself.

Perched on a bluff on the border between North and South, freedom and slavery, St. Louis was the kind of slave city that would have stirred reveries of freedom. On any given day, Lizzy could walk down to the Mississippi and look over into the free state of Illinois or even take the ferry across, as she sometimes did. St. Louis had a small and steadily shrinking percentage of slaves, almost equal to its population of free blacks, and there were so many slaves hired out that even Lizzy could mistake a slave for a free person, although she would not have claimed, like some travelers, to see no evidence of slavery at all, "none of the aspects of a slave city," as Anthony Trollope would write.[17]

St. Louis's free black communities were proud and active. A tiny but influential core of wealthy free "brown" families lived in various neighborhoods off fortunes running as high as half a million dollars. "Colored aristocrats," they thought of themselves, most the products of interracial families, or, as their insider chronicler Cyprian Clamorgan wrote, "many of them separated from the white race by a line of division so faint that it can be traced only by the keen eye of prejudice." Clamorgan, born in 1803, was himself the scion of a family that had made its money in barbershops and "Italian baths" and was typical of this population, whose income as barbers, saloon owners, boat stewards, boardinghouse keepers, seamstresses, nurses, and high-class prostitutes was increased by lucrative investments in business and real estate. (The Clamorgan brothers' "Depot of Elegant French and English Perfumeries, Toilet and Fancy Articles, Combs, Brushes, Razors, &c." stood not far from Garland's law office on Chestnut Street; their barbershop and bathhouse, with a bowling saloon in the basement, was eight blocks from the Garland Olive Street home.) Disinclined to radical activism, preferring to wield financial influence over candidates in political contests in which they could not vote, the "brown" families were nevertheless firmly antislavery, regarding the abolition of slavery as necessary for racial equality.

These "colored aristocrats" were also snobs, who once "threw out of society" one Mrs. Virginia Berry for committing the "*faux pas*" of accepting an invitation to a ball given by "the colored people of the second class." (Her indignant husband, London Berry, kicked up a fuss, but to no avail, and she was not invited to a first-class ball for some time afterward.) Lizzy could never be admitted into this society as an equal, but she could enter that "second class" of people with backgrounds closer to her own (middle-class former slaves, as she would be). Conscious of their standing in the eyes of whites, upwardly mobile free African Americans were keenly aware of caste and class. Indeed, Marylanders and Virginians considered themselves superior to Missouri and Kentucky blacks, a ranking Lizzy accepted.[18]

Despite the visible success of some free blacks, the practice of hiring out slaves coupled with the relatively large black population created a sense of racial danger among whites in this border town, lending urgency to the white population's desire to control its black neighbors. This was especially true in the twenty-five years before the Civil War, the years of the country's sprawling growth across the West and of a rapidly rising sectionalism, when traditional party loyalties succumbed to the sectional regional interests that would ultimately divide the country between North and South.

Frequent renewals of oppressive state ordinances respecting "slaves, free negroes and mulattoes" tell a story of the need to reassert white rule from time to time. In 1847, the year Lizzy arrived in St. Louis, the General Assembly of the State of Missouri passed an act outlawing schools "for the instruction of negroes and mulattoes in reading or writing." The act also prohibited "Negroes or mulattoes" from assembling for meetings for "religious worship, or preaching" unless attended by a "sheriff, constable, marshal, police officer or justice of the peace . . . in order to prevent all seditious speeches, and disorderly and unlawful conduct," to be punishable by fine or imprisonment. In addition, an 1843 law imposing daunting restrictions on free blacks entering the state was sharpened into a law forbidding free blacks from entering at all.[19]

Black locals knew where to find the law's resisters. For instance, the Reverend John Berry Meachum, a former Virginia slave who had bought his and his family's freedom with money earned working in Kentucky saltpeter caves and then (it was said) walked from eastern Kentucky to St. Louis, had been running a school in his church, the First African Baptist. He evaded the ordinance against black schools in Missouri by buying a steamboat and holding classes on the river, which was federal territory. (There is no evidence that Lizzy taught secret classes under the guise of running a sewing class, as some scholars have claimed.) The laws against congregating were aimed against all forms of assembly, including the enormously popular midnight voodoo ceremonies, which continued to be held secretly. At these, an old black woman, known as the queen, would chant multilingual incantations over a bubbling cauldron while men and women danced wildly until they sank from exhaustion.[20]

In addition, whatever a white traveler such as Trollope might have seen, no black traveler, and certainly no slave entering the city, would have missed the blatant presence of the city's active slave dealers, numbering over thirty before the war. And no slave would have ignored the stories of mistreatment and injustice; indeed, William Wells Brown, a Lexington-born mixed-race slave who was brought to St. Louis in the 1830s, wrote that St. Louis masters were "noted for . . . barbarity." (Brown's St. Louis experience was typical: he was hired out to a series of employers, including a slave trader named James Walker, whom he helped to cheat prospective buyers by blackening the hair of old slaves for the auction block; he also worked in the printing office of Elijah P. Lovejoy, the antislavery preacher-editor. Brown eventually escaped and became a prominent antislavery activist and writer.)[21]

One feels that whatever new hope of freedom Lizzy acquired on coming to St. Louis would have been tempered by her characteristic fatalism. For, like all other newcomers, she would have been apprised of local laws and local history. Well-known stories of racial violence, raw as open wounds, were circulated among the townspeople. One event of over a decade before, an incident that had drawn national attention, was still able to start an argument. In 1835, a white mob seized and lynched a free mulatto, Francis McIntosh, who was in jail for murdering the sheriff and injuring a guard. After Judge Luke E. Lawless directed a grand jury to decide against trying any of the accused citizens on the grounds that it was impossible to try a "multitude," another mob destroyed the printing press of Elijah Lovejoy's *St. Louis Observer* for its account of the lynching and grand jury decision. Lovejoy moved his newspaper to Alton, Illinois but in Novemeber 1837, was killed by a mob while defending his printing press. Those who sympathized with the lynchers "described McIntosh as a defiant killer" and praised "the heroic actions of the men who apprehended him and the collective action of the community in killing him." On the other side were those who agreed with Lovejoy that this was an example of "mob violence that threatened the foundation of law and civilized society."[22]

One of these was Abraham Lincoln. In 1838, he delivered an address to the Young Men's Lyceum in Springfield on the importance of the "perpetuation of our political institutions" (specifically, the system of laws) and conjured up the "horror-striking scene at St. Louis," in which McIntosh was dragged from prison, "chained to a tree, and actually burned to death." The twenty-nine-year-old Lincoln used Lawless's decision and the attack on Lovejoy to reinforce his point: "Whenever the vicious portion of the population shall be permitted to gather in bands of hundreds and thousands, and burn churches, ravage and rob provision stores, throw printing presses into rivers, shoot editors, and hang and burn obnoxious persons at pleasure, and with impunity; depend on it, this Government cannot last."[23]

For decades to come, long after Elizabeth Keckly had moved to Washington, St. Louisans would remain haunted by the McIntosh lynching, a vivid reminder of the racial dynamics in the border city. During Lizzy's time, however, the lynching was often recalled alongside memories of the night of April 17, 1841. That night, four black men (one slave and three free men) set fire to a counting house that stood on the levee after killing two white men who worked there and robbing the building. In the fire, the gable of the building fell, killing the fire company's engineer. The four men confessed, and were hanged before a crowd said to be in the tens of thousands.[24]

If the family's poverty provided Lizzy with opportunity, to Anne Garland it brought only the prospect of being trapped in a dingy fate. The family was now living in a house on Olive Street, between Eleventh and Twelfth, in a residential area up the hill from the river on the western edge of the city; already, their neighborhood was becoming more commercial and the fashionable residential district moving west of their block, leaving the Garlands behind. Faced with poverty where she had been promised better, Anne often felt like "giv[ing] up in despair." Nothing—not even the excitement occasioned by the performances of the Swedish Nightingale, Jenny Lind, and the Shakespearean actress Charlotte Cushman (who appeared in the winter of 1851)—could lift her spirits.

In fact, Lizzy's experiment in wage earning had begun as the ink was drying on the many legal deeds that were meant to stabilize her master's finances. At least this time Garland protected his home by putting the house in his wife's name. But with his home off-limits to creditors, Garland was busy leveraging his slaves and library against his debts. Soon after his family arrived he sold Albert, a carpenter, to his creditors for $1 to cover a $400 debt, with the understanding that he could redeem him within four months for the amount he owed; if he could not, his new owners could sell Albert at public auction. By March 1848, Garland's library was again in trust against a debt (this one of almost $300), although until he defaulted he would be permitted to use it. (Somehow, Garland did manage to keep his library, valued at over $600 at his death, the equivalent of over $11,000 today.)[25]

Lizzy worked in St. Louis for twelve years, during which time she devoted herself to cultivating the patronage of the city's white gentry. She had the advantage of the Garlands' social and professional connections, for despite their lack of cash, their family background entitled them to entrée into St. Louis society. They had joined the elegant Episcopal Christ Church, run by the young but already eminent Bishop Cicero Stephens Hawks. Their eldest daughters, Mary and Caroline, married into two of St. Louis's most prominent families, the Papins and the Farrars. And Mr. Garland's law practice, handling property disputes, soon put him in the way of the city's leading political and business families.

But it was Lizzy's gifts that propelled her forward. She quickly mastered the art of networking, and with ladies recommending her to one another, her reputation as a seamstress of unusual skill and taste spread. Her intelligence, soft voice, and natural dignity inspired confidence. She also became known for trustworthiness in money matters, and in this way established herself with the husbands, who could put cash in her hand to buy material and trimmings and know that she would return with a shrewd purchase and the proper change. Determined, prompt, reliable, and serious, she resembled no one so much as her former mistress, Anna Burwell, who had had to support herself and others steadily since she was eighteen.

A major transportation hub just eighteen miles south of where the Mississippi and Missouri Rivers converge, St. Louis in 1850 was a "commercial metropolis" of 78,000 people. Hundreds of steamboats, gently bumping against the wooden piers along the levee, disgorged goods and travelers from all over the world into the city's markets, shops, restaurants, and fancy hotels. In town, fashion-conscious ladies, many of French descent, had fortunes to spend from family businesses in trading and fur, making St. Louis an ideal place for Lizzy to hone her dressmaking skills. It was where she first made her name as a dressmaker, a name that later carried her to the White House, where the Midwesterner Mary Lincoln would hear good things about her from some St. Louis friends.

As the nearest big city to Springfield, just over a day's journey, it was to St. Louis that Mary Lincoln in the early 1850s looked to purchase "the fall styles." By then, her husband was a former Congressman and prosperous lawyer. Keeping up with the latest fashions from her outpost in Illinois took some doing. But as she was never shy about asking for what she wanted, Mary would enlist a St. Louis friend whose husband went back and forth between Springfield and St. Louis on business to buy her what she could not find at home: "white trimmings & white feather . . . of the prettiest quality"; "a drawn satin bonnet made of this brown, lined with white . . . if fine black lace, will be used this fall, perhaps *that* would be pretty with it, for the outside."[26]

The typical cycle of consumption, from desire to finished product, during which a lady determined what she wanted and had her dressmaker run it up, often began with a study of European fashion plates that had been reproduced in *Godey's Lady's* or with a friend's firsthand report from "the city." Mary might have looked to St. Louis, but ladies in St. Louis took their direction from the truly wordly New Orleans, where the sophisticated *bon ton* set a standard for display. One St. Louis businessman, Solomon Sublette, in New Orleans in the winter of 1851, sent back to his eager wife, Frances, minute descriptions of what the most vanguard ladies of that city were wearing. It could only have been by her special request, or else he was a very remarkable man indeed.

According to Sublette, the robes worn by the women to breakfast ("the most fashionable ladies attend at 10 o'clock") were both high-necked and low: "The high necks were ruffs ribons quilled or edgen coller the low necks generally worked capes, the sleeves are very large at the hand and tight above the elbow . . . of light materials. . . . the Street or walking dress are as verrious as the rainbow *Except in fineness* which is of the finest Silks are mostly used, ruffs . . . tucks & edges are plain are all in fashion, the bodies are pointed plain full Breast, the Backs are mostly plain, some fur have folds laid and made to fit tight." Further observation brought a report of dinner dress, when "Genteel neatness" prevailed (as opposed to "genteel Sloverness" at breakfast). Ladies turned out for a correspondingly late 3 o'clock dinner in dresses "of the finest material, Silk is the go, worked figured and of all collors and shades (excepted watered & poplin is not used) crapes and . . . of light collors, come cold are out of fashion low necks are mostly used with caps, sleeves large & Short at the wrist with large full undersleeves with wrist bands made to fit the wrist tight, ruffle or edgen."[27]

In the 1840s, when men could already outfit themselves in ready-to-wear clothing, women could buy only ready-made cloaks. Indeed, according to one historian, the "elaborate designs, tight fit, and rapidly changing vogues [in women's fashion] thwarted the ambitions of would-be manufacturers" until the twentieth century. The precisely fitted, complicated garments of the nineteenth-century woman's wardrobe also befuddled would-be home sewers. According with contemporary Victorian beliefs about female domesticity, women were thought to have natural skills in sewing, as in cooking and mothering. The wide availability of commercial sewing machines in the 1850s and the publication of dressmaking and millinery manuals—for instance, *The Ladies' Hand-Book of Millinery and Dressmaking* and *The Lady's Self-Instructor in Millinery, Mantua Making and all Branches of Plain Sewing*—made home sewing increasingly popular. A woman could study the sewing self-help columns in ladies' magazines, like the ubiquitous *Godey's Lady's Book*, which ran a regular feature of sewing tips and advice called "Hints to Dressmakers and Those Who Make Their Own Dresses." Later, inventions of pattern drafting systems and proportional patterns for cutting and fitting promised to make dressmaking a "scientific" enterprise that any woman could learn. Yet the democratic (and stereotyped) idea that all women could sew drew the disdain of the highly skilled dressmakers, who saw amateurs encroaching on their livelihood and amateurish incompetents plying their trade. Besides, even with a sewing machine, a basic dress, using twenty-five yards, requiring twenty-eight buttonholes, a lining, a pleated bodice, and the elaborate trimming that was in style (abundant ruffles, flounces, lace, and fringe were popular), could take two months to make, if one occasionally worked exclusively but sewed mostly at odd times.[28] Needless to say, women who could afford to, relied heavily on dressmakers and were loyal to them. A remarkable dressmaker, like the future Madame Keckly, could loom large in her clients' lives.

For a typical client like Mrs. Sublette to realize such styles as her husband described meant multiple time-consuming trips to her dressmaker, in this case, a Mrs. E. Smith, according to her receipts. But first came the shopping trips to T. & J. McGrade Importers, Jobbers, and Retailers of Fancy and Staple Dry Goods, located on Market near Main, where Mrs. Sublette rang up costly purchases of yards and yards of silk, satin, sateen, and velvet; of the less expensive linen, muslin, cambric, and cotton; and of yards of ribbons and edging for decoration. From there to Mrs. Smith, who sewed the raw material into the necessities of the 1850s woman's wardrobe: wrappers, mantles, capes, dresses, bodices, skirts, linings, and undersleeves, the outer garments covered with decorative embroidery and braiding. Mrs. Smith did a good deal of sewing for her money: she charged $1.25 for a walking dress, $3.50 for a mantle, $8.50 for two dimity capes, 60 cents for linings for two dresses and a skirt, $5.00 for an "infants suit," and $2.50 to put embroidery, braiding, and a band on a pair of sleeves. (For comparison, Mr. Sublette paid a bill of $15.00 for room and board for sixty days—25 cents a day—for his slave Pellina, who had sought refuge in the Locust Street slave pens operated by the aptly named slave dealer Bernard M. Lynch.)[29]

It is easy to see why well-dressed women considered themselves almost intimates with their dressmakers. The laborious dressmaking techniques of the day made close relationships between women and their dressmakers largely impossible to avoid. To begin with, cutting and fitting—the secret to a successful garment—was a hands-on, time-consuming affair. Lizzy, like most early nineteenth-century dressmakers, used what one costume historian has called the "pin-to-form" technique. First, to make a pattern for the lining, she draped and pinned inexpensive fabric or paper on her client's form (if she used fabric, that became the lining). Then she basted together the lining for her customer to try on as many times as needed until, after numerous fittings and adjustments, she was satisfied enough with the lining's fit to risk cutting the more expensive material for the outside garment. Such a method threw Lizzy and her clients together repeatedly and for long periods of time in the intimacy of the lady's boudoir; however, pinning to form was considered by perfectionists like Lizzy to be the only way to ensure a proper fit. (Interestingly, cutting on the figure was how Lizzy learned to make slaves' clothes, so as not to waste any material.)[30]

Sewing was the dressmaker's private labor: a dressmaker could take a good pattern, go away, and return with a finished outfit. For the bodices, meant to fit "like wall paper," Lizzy would use tiny, interlocking stitches. These could withstand the pull across the body and avoid gaping. Skirts, however, required longer and looser stitches, otherwise the seams could pucker, ruining the lines of the skirt as it fell to the floor.[31]

In the hierarchy of dressmaking, Lizzy soon rose to the top and could legitimately advertise herself as a mantua maker. Not all dressmakers could sew the complicated and popular mantua, a dress whose bodice was made to fit snugly through vertical pleats stitched in the back. Fitting the bodice took extra care, skill, and time. Then there was the voluminous skirt that draped over a dome-shaped hoop made of whalebone or metal and extended around the lower body. It could end in a circumference of eighteen feet, taking twenty-five yards of material all by itself. By the mid-1850s, hoop skirts denoted status, expense, vanity, and sophistication. Women from small villages sent to the cities and larger towns for hoops; slave women starched their skirts to imitate their billowing silhouette. The hoop skirts could fill stagecoaches, parlors, ballrooms, and the like rather quickly. In New York City, omnibuses charged a higher fare for women in hoops. During the Civil War, there were complaints about the dangers to the wounded and sick soldiers threatened by ladies sweeping through the hospitals in wide hoop skirts.[32]

In addition to the satisfaction of developing her craft, Lizzy would have taken enormous pleasure in working for wages for the first time. The long hours she put in were hours that she was, at least at first, happy to give. But pride and ambition could not long be subservient, and she soon grew resentful of her labors. She had not forgotten her first master's taunt that she would never be worth her salt, and she kept track of the exact amount of time, the "two years and five months," that she supported the seventeen people in the Garland household. All the while, she saw Mr. Garland, who, by virtue of his privileged birth, maintained his social standing while flailing against the usual undertow of debts. She could have earned a fortune, but it would not have been *her* fortune and she would still have been *his* slave. In a way, Lizzy almost savored the bitter irony of the situation. "While I was working so hard that others might live in comparative comfort in those circles of society to which their birth gave them entrance, the thought often occurred to me whether I was really worth my salt or not."[33]

The long hours and stress soon took their toll, however, and it was not long before Lizzy's health, in her words, "gave out." The close work and physical awkwardness of sewing, hours of stooping and squinting over material, often under dim lamps, doomed many seamstresses to headaches, dizziness, weak eyes, and exhaustion (this is why Lizzy later insisted that her sewing students sit with straight backs and not pin their work over their knees). Then, too, Lizzy still had her duties in the Garlands' house, with only Sunday afternoons off, as was the local custom. Meanwhile, about the city, disaster followed upon disaster. During the 1848–49 winter a smallpox outbreak hit; in May the steamboat *White Cloud* exploded on the riverfront, setting off a fire that destroyed twenty-three boats on one mile of waterfront and fully one-third of the city (the fire could be seen from forty miles away); that summer, a cholera epidemic killed nearly one-tenth of the population who had survived the previous year. The church bells tolled for funerals nonstop, until the mayor ordered that they not be rung for each death.

In 1850, Lizzy was thirty-two years old, striking to look at, independent-minded, and accomplished. "About this time," Mr. Keckly, "whom I met in Virginia, and learned to regard with more than friendship, came to St. Louis." An apparently free black man whom she likely met in Petersburg, Keckly asked Lizzy to marry him. Such an offer might have looked like a blessing, but at first she refused to even "consider his proposal; for I could not bear the thought of bringing children into slavery," as any child born to her would have been.[34]

Lizzy's feelings about marriage were common among slave women in similar positions, and yet, dooming children to perpetual enslavement and enriching the coffers of slaveholders were only the two most obvious reasons for rejecting marriage. Other difficulties presented themselves. Marrying a free man would place her in a vulnerable position. A free man could grow frustrated with his wife's virtual imprisonment and, over time, resent his bonds to her. Some husbands managed to buy their wife and children; others could only stay close by and hope that their masters never sold or moved them. Then there were those who, chafing against the enslavement that hampered their roles as husband and father, eventually abandoned their family to their fate. Reasonably, given the nonlegal status of slave marriages, some of these men married again.

Mr. Keckly's offer of marriage made Lizzy realize that she could never accept his proposal until she was free. There were three ways for a slave to accomplish this: run away, sue for freedom, or buy oneself. Of these three, only the last made sense for her. In St. Louis, there were secret societies, organized by free blacks, devoted to helping slaves run away (the Knights of Liberty was one). And there were white lawyers willing to represent slaves in lawsuits against their masters. (Edward Bates and Montgomery Blair, future members of Lincoln's administration, represented slaves; meanwhile, Mr. Garland was involved in defending a mistress against such a suit.) But Lizzy would have seen that running away not only was a bad risk, but also meant abandoning a good business, and she had no grounds for a freedom lawsuit. In contrast, purchasing herself was not only logical, it also fit her character. The objection raised by some abolitionists—that buying oneself meant support of the principle of holding humans as property—would not have troubled her. She was a pragmatist, not an idealist, and, as one who had to fight for it, she prized respectability. In fact, paying for herself would be a measure of self-reliance and success and, therefore, a source of pride. Truly, she would be "worth her salt."[35]

As for Mr. Garland's rights, she respected his legal authority to own her, in the way that, as a young woman in Hillsborough, she had accepted her master's "right" to whip her. This was not the same as believing in a master's *moral* authority. Even others of a more radical bent took this practical position. Eight years earlier, ex-slave Frederick Douglass had published in Garrison's *Liberator* a response to the charge that allowing friends to buy his freedom ratified slavery. Douglass had already published the first of three autobiographies and was emerging as a leading abolitionist figure, unmatched in intellect, eloquence, and charisma. He argued that being purchased was simply the most efficient and safe way to release him from his master's "power" and the "legal liabilities to slavery." He called the transaction government-sanctioned robbery, done out of necessity, "in order to secure that which is the birth-right of every man. And I will hold up those papers before the world in proof of the plundering character of the American government."[36]

Furthermore, had Lizzy wanted it, there was a close-to-home model: using his own money, the Reverend Meachum had bought twenty slaves and either freed them or allowed them to work off their purchase price. Lizzy decided she wanted to buy herself and her son. But the first time she approached Garland to propose this, he rejected her "bluntly" and "commanded [her] never to broach the subject again." Angered by his response, she refused to be put off. She brooded over the significance of her son's perpetual enslavement. She believed, like others around her, in biological theories claiming that race was determined by "blood," and she was angered by the logic that condemned her son to slavery, a boy in whose veins "the Anglo-Saxon blood as well as the African flowed."[37] By birthright, strictly adhered to, he was as "white" as he was "black"; in looks, more "white" than "black." (If she did not apply this logic to herself, it may have been because of her darker complexion. Such things mattered.) George could read and write—she would have made sure of that—and he was smart. He could grow up to be an accomplished man if given the chance.

She approached Garland again and "insisted on knowing whether he would permit me to purchase myself, and what price I must pay for myself." It was an audacious demand; Garland, seeing in a flash the consequences of letting Lizzy negotiate deals with her dressmaking clients, which had helped her to become a cool bargainer, responded by reaching into his pocket and drawing out a silver dollar. "I have told you often not to trouble me with such a question," he said, with irritation. "If you really wish to leave me, take this: it will pay the passage of yourself and boy on the ferry-boat, and when you are on the other side of the river you will be free. It is the cheapest way that I know of to accomplish what you desire."[38]

Lizzy knew this was a cynical offer, one that he never expected her to accept; she also knew that he was pleased when she refused. Like most people in St. Louis, Lizzy had crossed the river many times already, and, as Garland correctly assumed, had she wanted to run away, she could have gone already, without his paltry dollar. Instead, Lizzy insisted on being allowed to buy her freedom, as she said, "according to the laws of the country."[39] It was an important distinction, because in 1850, the federal law requiring the return of fugitives to their masters had been strengthened.

The year 1850 brought the culmination of three decades of legislative attempts to deal with rising sectionalism around the problem of slavery and westward expansion, and in that troubling history Missouri was key. In 1819, when Missouri had applied for statehood, a two-year battle ignited in Congress over the question of whether Missouri, part of the vast territory gained through the Louisiana Purchase of 1803, would be a slave or free state. To settle the matter, Congress devised a compromise, made possible by Maine's petition to join the Union: Missouri would be admitted as a slave state, and Maine would be a free state. In addition, slavery would be banned in the rest of the Louisiana Territory north of latitude 36°30´. This was the Missouri Compromise, meant to balance Northern and Southern political interests and ameliorate the widening divide between slaveholding and free states.

But by 1848 the defeat of Mexico and the appropriation of more than 50,000 square miles in the West—more territory in one fell swoop than ever before or since—triggered even more explosive debates in Congress over the spread of slavery. In 1846, at the beginning of the Mexican War, a freshman representative from Pennsylvania named David Wilmot had introduced an amendment to prohibit slavery from any territories won from the conflict with Mexico. In a bipartisan coalition (whose participants were motivated by various reasons), Northern Democrats and Whigs voted for Wilmot's proviso. Their united opposition against Southern Congressmen was a watershed moment. As one newspaper observed, "As if by magic, it brought to a head the great question which is about to divide the American people." Before the Senate could vote, Congress adjourned. Wilmot's Proviso was still being bitterly debated two years later when, for first time, the issue of slavery would dominate a presidential election.[40]

By 1850 rifts were deepening between Southerners and Northerners over the status of slavery in the lands to the west; there were even Southern threats of disunion over slavery. At this point, Congress made another heroic effort at compromise. Led by three elder statesmen senators, the nationalists Henry Clay and Daniel Webster and the sectionalist John C. Calhoun of South Carolina, who together warned that the Union would survive only if there was a balance of power in it between North and South, Congressmen began their efforts to cobble together a series of measures to forestall disaster.[41]

But it was a member of the new generation, the rising Democratic star Illinois Senator Stephen A. Douglas, Mary Todd's onetime suitor, who masterminded the legislative package and put together the votes needed to pass it. This was the Compromise of 1850 (and the crucial context for Lizzy's demand for legal freedom). Under its provisions, California was admitted into the Union a free state, the boundaries of Texas were fixed, the slave trade in Washington, D.C., was ended (keeping legal slavery intact), slavery in the new territories of New Mexico and Utah was left up to the people living there (no Wilmot Proviso, so despised by Southerners), and a stronger Fugitive Slave Law was enacted. This last required enforcement of the constitutional provision that runaway slaves who had successfully escaped to the free states be returned to their owners.[42]

A compromise had been reached, but it had been pushed through in the face of increasingly apocalyptic rhetoric on both sides, which had fueled an intensifying of emotions and expression that few would forget. The dying Calhoun prophesied that the admission of California as a free state would "destroy irretrievably the equilibrium between the two sections" and force the Southern states to secede, for under the circumstances they could not "remain in the Union consistently with their honor and safety." On the opposite side, New York Senator William H. Seward argued that slavery was dying. "You cannot roll back the tide of social progress. . . . there is a higher law than the Constitution," and that is God's law in whose eyes all humans are equal.[43]

Some optimistically thought the Compromise of 1850 would bring relief. If it did, though, it did not last. Southerners accepted the Compromise because they believed that opening the new territories to slavery and the enactment of the Fugitive Slave Law were crucial answers to the much-hated laws prohibiting slavery from all new territories. But they deplored what they considered the act's Northern infringements on slavery. Meanwhile, the Fugitive Slave Law was instantly reviled by Northerners, mobilizing African American communities and making outlaws of otherwise law-abiding citizens: "I will not obey it, by God," Ralph Waldo Emerson wrote in his journal at his home in Concord, Massachusetts, speaking for many New Englanders. From Rochester, New York, in his three-year-old antislavery weekly *The North Star*, Frederick Douglass attacked Daniel Webster for supporting the law. In Philadelphia, a resolution presented at the Brick Wesley African Methodist Episcopal Church called the law "so wicked, so atrocious, so utterly at variance with the principles of the Constitution; so subversive of the objects of all law, the protection of lives, liberty, and property of the governed." Signers of the resolution vowed to "resist to the death" any efforts to enforce the law. Prominent on the drafting committee was Robert Purvis, a wealthy black activist and a friend of William Lloyd Garrison. Throughout the North, these protesters made good on their words and early attempts at enforcement failed spectacularly.[44]

With such a law in place, a fugitive slave in free territory who possessed no legal proof of emancipation was fair game for the slave catchers. In effect, Garland's offer to allow Lizzy to cross the river and leave was worthless. If she could not buy her freedom "according to the laws of the country," she could not be free.

In proposing to pay him for herself and her son, Lizzy must have been calculating on Garland's need for money to smooth her way. However, as a proslavery author and lawyer, Garland was strongly committed to the perpetuation of slavery, and this may have made him reluctant to grant her request. He had no sympathy with laws prohibiting slavery "beyond a certain line"; he thought the Missouri Compromise "obnoxious," and said so publicly. Moreover, by 1850, the year Lizzy approached him, he was already engaged in a major case that concerned the very issue of the status of slavery in free territory, a case that may also have tinged his response to Lizzy. By January, Garland and his law partner, Lyman D. Norris, had been retained by Mrs. Irene Emerson, who since 1846 had been defending herself against the lawsuits for freedom that had been filed on behalf of two of her slaves, a married couple, Dred and Harriet Scott, and their two daughters. Considering the substance of the suit, Garland, known for his appeals court work and proslavery views, was a good choice to replace Mrs. Emerson's previous lawyer. He could also have been recommended by one of his most prominent clients, Pierre Choteau, the father-in-law of Mrs. Emerson's brother, John F. A. Sanford, who was most likely supervising his sister's legal affairs.[45]

The Scotts' claim was that they were free because they had lived on free soil with their St. Louis master, Dr. John Emerson, an assistant surgeon in the United States Army, during the seven years that Emerson was stationed in the north, starting in 1833, first at Fort Armstrong in Illinois, then at Fort Snelling in the Iowa Territory. When Dr. Emerson died in 1843, the Scotts became the property of his wife, and it was against her that they brought their suits for unlawful imprisonment and assault. The case (in which Scott had backing by his original owners, the Blow family) had already gone two rounds in the Circuit Court of St. Louis County: the first judgment, in June 1847, ruled against the Scotts; the second, in January 1850, overturned the initial judgment, with the jury deciding that according to Missouri law, the Scotts had been free since 1833.

Immediately upon taking over the case, Garland and Norris filed an appeal with the Missouri Supreme Court. They argued that the Scotts had been freed on the basis of civil law, but that during Dr. Emerson's residence in free territory, he lived under military jurisdiction, so civil law did not apply in this case. Also, Dr. Emerson's stay in free territory was not voluntary, so he could not be said to have taken his slaves into free territory voluntarily.

At that point, the court postponed its consideration of the case until the October 1850 session, one month after the Fugitive Slave Law was passed, when Northern resistance to the law was on the rise and Southern proslavery sentiment was hardening in response. In this climate, the Missouri Supreme Court judges decided unanimously to overturn precedents upholding the Northwest Ordinance's exclusion of slavery from the territories. However, the opinion of that session was never written, leaving Mrs. Emerson and her lawyers to bring their case before a newly elected slate of judges the following year. In March 1852, they finally received the decision they wanted: a divided court, reversing the lower court's decision, declared that the Scotts were still Mrs. Emerson's slaves.

It was a political decision, not surprising in a state bordered on three sides by free territory and therefore supremely sensitive to the territorial question. Even the presiding judge acknowledged that the court was ignoring eight Missouri precedents favoring Scott. "Times are not now as they were when the former decisions on this subject were made," wrote Judge William Scott. "Since then not only individuals but States have been possessed of a dark and fell spirit in relation to slavery. . . . Under such circumstances it does not behoove the State of Missouri" to do anything to reinforce antislavery positions.[46]

As the lawyer who had won the case by persuading the courts to take this position, Garland might have put himself psychologically and intellectually beyond the reach of Lizzy's arguments for freedom. Nor was he done with the Dred Scotts: under new counsel they brought a new suit for freedom to the federal circuit court in Missouri, and Garland was hired to lead the defense by Mrs. Emerson's brother, John Sanford, who was the named defendant in the new suit. (Mrs. Emerson had remarried and was living in Massachusetts.)

Yet Lizzy's desire to be free merely increased with each denial. Although he was proslavery, Garland was a thoughtful man, in private and public matters, and could see the justice in her request; she had served his family "faithfully" and, in working hard, "deserved [her] freedom."[47]

Then, too, more than ever, the Garlands needed the money. There had been no respite from the poverty of their first year in St. Louis, despite Garland's apparent legal success. Anne, who ran the household, was in despair over her empty pantry, a dire situation that reached its nadir in early spring 1853, when for some time she had "not a cent . . . even to send to market." To sister Fanny she poured out her heart: "Nearly seven years of almost hopeless poverty, finds me *writhing* under it with excruciating agony at times—my constant prayer is for resignation to bear even *poverty* with contentment—but it is hard to see those you love wanting even necessary clothing & be unable to supply their wants."[48]

Poverty was not the family's only cause of suffering. Three of the Garlands' eight children had died within months of one another: their two young married daughters, Carrie and Molly (who had two small children), and their youngest, two-and-a-half-year-old Louis, who succumbed to scarlet fever on the first day of March, "taken sick Thursday & died the next Tuesday morning about 9 o'clock," as his mother wrote. "It almost seems too much for human hearts to bear without braking . . . yet I know it would be a sin to grieve too much for them—To me the loss is incalculable but theirs is *infinite gain*."[49]

Aggy and Lizzy shared the family's rituals of death and mourning. Anne wrote, "[Louis] was a great pet in the house, and poor Mammy Aggy is almost heartbroken about him—She was more devoted to him than any mother could be & the little fellow was so fond of her." (What, one wonders, would Aggy say?) When Molly died painfully from an intestinal ailment, Lizzy was with the family at her side. In Molly's final moments, according to her mother, "she was very cold, we all rubbed her & did all we could to produce reaction but all in vain." A devout Catholic, Molly attempted to pray, "with stiffened tongue." Her last words were to Lizzy: "*Rub my hands*."[50]

The deaths took their toll on the parents. "Mr. G. is a changed man," Anne wrote her sister. The stricken parents turned to religion. Hugh began regularly attending services at Christ Church, seeking some relief from thinking about his dead children. Anne, too, found consolation in services, regretful "that I did not sooner seek the quiet Haven of the *Church*."[51]

Not much later, Garland agreed to Lizzy's proposal. Perhaps he felt grateful for her loyalty; perhaps his own guilt feelings played a part. In any event, one day he told her that she could buy herself and her son for $1,200. It was an enormous sum, yet it gave her hope for a future, "a silver lining to the dark cloud of my life," as she would describe it.[52]

The prospect of liberty dissolved her objections to marriage, and in a short time, she became James Keckly's wife. She would remember proudly how the wedding "took place in the parlor, in the presence of the family and a number of guests. Mr. Garland gave me away, and the pastor, Bishop Hawks, performed the ceremony, who had solemnized the bridals of Mr. G's own children." She felt as if she already had her foot on the threshold of freedom.[53]

According to Lizzy, the couple settled in their own home. However, the city directory shows no listing for Keckly until 1859, when only Lizzy is listed, identified as a "col'd dressmaker" living on Fifth Street between Green and Washington. But her happiness in her new situation did not last. She must have discovered almost immediately that her new husband was not, as he had represented himself to be, a free man. (He was most likely a fugitive from Virginia.) This, added to habits of drink that made him "a burden instead of a helpmate," sank the marriage. Other than mentioning that she lived with him for eight years (thus, they were married by 1852), Lizzy would say little more about her husband, at least in writing.[54] Beyond this, the story of his existence fades to near invisibility. As a slave, Lizzy had had no power to construct the narrative of her own sexual history. Her sexuality had not been her own, and for her there was no privacy, two points driven home by Alexander Kirkland. Once free, however, she would claim power over her body and her story, and when she wrote her memoir, she would say almost nothing about her most intimate life.

Following her marriage, Lizzy still worked long hours at the Garlands', where she was needed as much as ever. Aggy was "very often sick," Anne reported in January 1854, "but is now up again." The following month, a friend observed how careworn and ill Garland looked: "He is very shy . . . and so broken down with trouble of one kind or another that one has to be very civil to him to draw him out at all." During this time, Lizzy would recall, "I went to work in earnest to purchase my freedom, but . . . Mr. Garland's family claimed so much of my attention—in fact, I supported them—that I was not able to accumulate anything."[55]

Despite ill health, Garland would appear before the Missouri circuit court that spring to renew his arguments against the Scotts' federal suit. In 1854, the court had no permanent home, but sat in a small, rented room over a store on Main Street. Everyone in attendance at the trial in May was aware of the angry congressional struggle over the status of slavery in territories to Missouri's west. Moreover, a new battle was reaching its climax, this one over the Kansas-Nebraska bill, sponsored by Senator Stephen A. Douglas, that would effectively neutralize the slavery restriction of the Missouri Compromise by replacing it with the idea of popular sovereignty (letting the voters in the territories decide whether to have slavery). The Scott case came to trial on May 15, one week before the House of Representatives voted, and passed, the bill (the Senate had already passed it in March). Meanwhile, Garland once again won his client's case. Following the judge's explicit instructions that the law was on the defendant's side, the jury ruled that the Scotts were and had always been slaves. Then, as everyone involved had expected he would, the Scotts' lawyer responded to the predictable verdict by taking steps to bring the case to the Supreme Court. But by that time, Garland was too unwell to think of going with it.[56]

Hugh A. Garland may already have been dying in the spring, although he hung on until October, when he died in his bed, with his wife and slaves at his side. Of the servants, the most important were clearly Aggy, Lizzy, and Chapman, one of his father's slaves whom they had brought from Virginia. Garland's belief in the glory of God seemed to bring peace to his final hours and, according to his wife, inspired all who saw him. On the night they expected him to die, as Anne wrote her sister Mary, she herself, along with "Mammy Aggy" and Lizzy, took Communion with her husband. He survived the night, however, and the next morning he rallied and "had something to say to all." To Chap and Lizzy "he gave good advice & to the others who were weeping around his bed (for they loved him dearly) he said your Mistress Anne will take care of you—no conscious thought seemed to cloud his mind—a little while we shall all be reunited—perform your duties faithfully and trust in God, that is all that is required of you." Then as all remained watching, he asked the pastor, a widower, to kneel by his side so that he could advise him to marry again. "You cannot be happy without," he said, "but be *prudent*—be *prudent*." His final words were, "Anne: that will do." The next day, the twenty carriages hired by Mrs. Garland to carry the mourners followed his hearse from St. Paul's through the city streets to Bellfontaine Cemetery.[57]

The deathbed scene, in which a much-loved parent, spouse, or child died in the bosom of the family, was an important affirmation of the "hearth and home" values of Victorian middle-class households; in the case of Garland's death, it evidently brought comfort to his wife and drew the admiration of those who knew him. As for Lizzy, we cannot know how she felt or what advice (what "good advice") he gave her. We do know, however, that she had no illusions about her mistress's abilities to "take care" of her, nor had she any intention of letting Anne try. Her master's death was the signal for her to gain her freedom once and for all.

After the funeral, Anne sat down to her husband's debts. He had left no will, so there was a great deal of legal work to do. Her brother Armistead, in whose home Mrs. Burwell was living, came up from Vicksburg to help settle the estate. A successful lawyer and planter, Armistead Burwell Jr. would be a Unionist when the Civil War came, even writing President Lincoln a letter urging him to restore Mississippi to the Union, arguing that "there are thousands in Miss: who desire most ardently the restoration of the United States Government."[58] He arrived in St. Louis in the late spring or early summer of 1855 to attend to his sister's affairs.

But another's affairs would also concern him. Lizzy approached him with her proposal to buy herself and her son. (She did not buy Aggy, who would stay a slave and go to Vicksburg with her old mistress, Mrs. Burwell, and she was not interested in buying James, her deceiving and dissipated husband.) Armistead listened sympathetically. Seven years older than Lizzy, he had known her from the time she was born. He may also have known about her trials at the home of his brother Robert (to whom he was not close), as well as her valiant support of Anne's family. Perhaps he remembered who her father was, although the consequences of recollecting those linkages were not always beneficial to the black relative.

Lizzy would remember Armistead as a "kind-hearted man." He promised "to afford me every facility to raise the necessary amount to pay the price of my liberty," she later wrote. Anne had already agreed to honor her husband's word and, in June, had signed a paper pledging "to give Lizzie and her son George their freedom, on the payment of $1200." But first, there had to be a transfer of ownership to Anne Garland from her sister Betty Burwell, now Mrs. E. P. Putnam of Vicksburg, who on marrying had become Lizzy's legal mistress. Thus, a deed was produced giving the two slaves to Anne "in consideration of the love and affection we bear toward our sister . . . and for the further consideration of $5 in hand paid." Then, in a separate deed, Mrs. Putnam "relinquished her dower . . . and any other claim she might have in and to the property therein mentioned [Lizzy and George]"; moreover, she did so "freely, and without fear, compulsion, or undue influence of her said husband."[59]

At her present rate of earnings (estimated by one historian to be about $3 a day) Lizzy could never earn the $1,200 she needed for freedom. So, on the advice of "friends," she decided to go to New York, "state my case, and appeal to the benevolence of the people." She probably hoped to find aid from one of the vigilance committees that were created across the North to prevent kidnappings into slavery and to help runaways establish themselves in freedom. Word of these committees was smuggled into the South by means of the "black underground": pamphlets, newspapers, letters, and even agents who traveled about talking to slaves. In the North, at monthly meetings in their churches, committee members listened to runaways' testimony of imprisonment and escape, suffering and daring. The vigilance committees provided fugitives with food, shelter, clothing, and medicine, helped them find jobs, and gave them legal counsel. For fugitives who had their master's cooperation, they raised money for their purchase price. They were also crucial in protecting fugitives from the Fugitive Slave Law.

The most important vigilance committee was the all-black New York Vigilance Committee, founded in 1835 in New York City (although it no longer existed). Its founder and secretary was black abolitionist David Ruggles, who, in 1838, harbored the twenty-year-old Maryland runaway Frederick Douglass for almost two weeks, made arrangements for his marriage to Anna

Murray, a free black housekeeper he'd met in Baltimore, who sold one of her two feather beds to help pay for his escape, then sent the newlyweds to New Bedford, Massachusetts, with a $5 bill and a letter of introduction to an African American couple who ran a catering business. Other committees, most with racially mixed membership, were still operating in New York and upstate. Lizzy and her friends may have talked about her applying to the New York State Vigilance Committee, which had been founded in 1847 in New York City by Quakers and the next year reorganized under white philanthropist and dedicated abolitionist Gerrit Smith. From January 1851 to April 1853, it aided 686 fugitives and former slaves.

Nothing came of this plan, however. As Lizzy was preparing to leave, Mrs. Garland told her that she would not let her go unless she had the names of "six gentlemen" who would vouch for her return and make up her loss financially should she not return. Confident in her reputation for integrity, Lizzy set about collecting the necessary signatures. The first five men she approached, most likely husbands of her clients, signed readily; but when the sixth, a Mr. Farrow (possibly William Farrow, a boat builder), agreed to sign, he made it clear that he did not believe she'd ever come back: "You *mean* to come, that is, you *mean* so *now*, but you never will. When you reach New York the abolitionists will tell you what savages we are, and they will prevail on you to stay there; and we shall never see you again." Lizzy objected. "I not only *mean* to come back, but *will* come back, and pay every cent of the twelve hundred dollars for myself and child." She could not, however, make Mr. Farrow consent to believe her, and it made her "feel sick at heart, for I could not accept the signature of this man when he had no faith in my pledges. No; slavery, eternal slavery rather than be regarded with distrust by those whose respect I esteemed." With that, she turned away and walked home.[60]

She felt shamed by Mr. Farrow's persistence. "Humbled pride," she described it. Her mistress's distrust she evidently accepted: not only would Lizzy's disappearance cost Anne, but Lizzy's relations to her, despite their shared paternity, were governed by the laws and conventions that tied slave to mistress, and these Lizzy deferred to. However, her relationship with Mr. Farrow had been contractual and, therefore, proceeded according to laws and conventions that prevailed among free people everywhere. If she could not persuade her client to trust her word, she could not succeed in that "other" world. Social acceptance and recognition: these were the necessary conditions of self-esteem. More than anything, what Elizabeth Keckly wanted was a kind of middle-class *normalcy*: her marriage, her business, her dreams for her son were the unextraordinary stepping-stones out of the humiliating prison of slavery. In questioning her integrity, Mr. Farrow quashed so much. "I reached my own home, and weeping threw myself upon the bed."

After a while, she noticed "a carriage stopped in the front of the house; Mrs. Le Bourgois, one of my kind patrons, got out of it and entered the door." (The Le Bourgois family was related by marriage to three prominent St. Louis families: the Chouteaus, the Blows, and the Charlesses.) Having heard that Lizzy was going to New York "to beg" her freedom, she "had been thinking over the matter, and told Ma it would be a shame to allow you to go North to *beg* for what we should *give* you." Her plan was "to raise the twelve hundred dollars required among" Lizzy's St. Louis patrons. "I have two hundred dollars put away for a present; am indebted to you one hundred dollars; mother owes you fifty dollars, and will add another fifty to it; and as I do not want the present, I will make the money a present to you. Don't start for New York now until I see what I can do among your friends."[61]

Finally, this was the way it happened. Mrs. Le Bourgois, "God bless her dear good heart," rallied her friends during the hot summer months of 1855, and as the sums added up, Lizzy presented installments to Mrs. Garland's lawyer, Willis L. Williams, who deposited them on her behalf in the banking house of Darby & Barksdale. (John F. Darby, one of the bank's founders and a former mayor of St. Louis and Congressman, was a native of North Carolina, where coincidentally he had studied under William Bingham, father of Lizzy's Hillsborough persecutor.) Williams also arranged to give Lizzy one percent of her deposit per month for expenses, pledging that he "be responsible for [it], as well as for the whole amount, when it shall be needed by her."[62]

On November 13, 1855, Anne signed the deed of sale of her two slaves: "Know all men that I, Anne P. Garland, of the County and City of St. Louis, State of Missouri, for and in consideration of the sum of $1200, to me in hand paid this day in cash, hereby emancipate my negro woman Lizzie, and her son George; the said Lizzie is known in St. Louis as the wife of James, who is called James Keckelly [*sic*]; is of light complexion, about 37 years of age, by trade a dress-maker, and called by those who know her as *Garland's Lizzie*. The said boy, George, is the only child of Lizzie, is about 16 years of age, and is almost white, and called by those who known him as *Garland's George*." Two days later, Lizzy held the separate deed of emancipation in her hand. She would no longer be anybody's Lizzy but her own, and she had given her son the future that had been stolen from him at birth. Before she left for Washington in 1860, she would pay back the $1,200, refusing to see the donations as anything but loans. George helped, contributing a portion of his earnings, which Lizzy would subsequently estimate at $100 a year.[63]

Four years after Lizzy purchased her freedom, the following entry was added to the "List of free Negroes Licensed by the County of St. Louis County": *"Keckley, Lizzie, Age 39, Height 5' 2", Occupation Mantua Maker, Date of License May 1859."*[64]

Chapter Seven

$\mathcal{M}$ ary Todd stepped out of her sister's parlor as Mrs. Abraham Lincoln around the time that Elizabeth Hobbs returned to Virginia with her infant son to become the Garlands' slave. Mary may have begun her married life with a man who did not love her and with whom she had spent hardly any time alone, but at least she had chosen her future; up until the moment Mr. Garland finally agreed to sell Lizzy to herself, she had had few options open to her. And she would never forget that, before marrying James Keckly, she had had *no* choice in her intimate relations with men. A great gulf divided the life of a free white woman from her enslaved black sister, as the language of abolitionists of the day would put it.

The Lincolns' first home was a room at the Globe tavern, a plain, two-story, wooden inn near the State House where, for only $4 a week, the Widow

Beck provided the newlyweds with room and board. Aside from economy, there was not much to recommend it to a new couple, offering little privacy and less quiet. The Globe housed the offices of several stagecoach lines and whenever a coach arrived, the clerk would ring a large bell mounted on the roof. Parties for Springfield's seasonal influx of legislators and lawyers (once of vital interest to Miss Todd) congregated noisily downstairs. There was also the mealtime regimen to contend with, as boarders taking their meals communally were required to sit down together at regular times. This was probably fine with Lincoln, who was accustomed to boarding out and in any event liked the camaraderie of the communal board. Mary, predictably, was less tractable, often arriving late and once exploding in rage and leaving the room in tears when her husband "whimsically chided" her in front of the others. He had much to learn about teasing his wife.[1]

Even Lincoln was self-conscious about their situation. "Are you possessing houses and lands, and oxen and asses, and men-servants and maid-servants, and begetting sons and daughters?" he compared patriarchal notes with his friend Joshua Speed in May 1843. Yet if it was not the best beginning, it was not the worst. Surveying her domain from the edge of her bed, Mary might have consoled herself with the thought that as a newlywed her sister Frances had lived in the same room—although having no more than her sister could be worse than having less, as she could not declare herself to be badly treated. But there was certainly consolation in her husband's ambition. Since the winter he had been maneuvering for the Whig nomination for Stuart's now open seat in Congress, where he "very much" wanted to go.[2] At least their ambitions were well matched.

Glimpses into their intimate life suggest they were well matched sexually, as well, and that they found pleasure in and, later, comfort from their physical relationship. Indeed, by the time Lincoln wrote Speed, his lawyer friends who were with him on the court circuit had noticed how "desperately homesick" he was when he was away from Springfield for three weeks that spring. They were also teasing him about "coming events." (Before this, they had joked about their bachelor exploits with prostitutes, and among his male cronies, Lincoln was known for his near compulsion for dirty stories.)[3]

To be sure, Mary was already pregnant and anxiously awaiting her "time of trouble" (her phrase for childbirth), the anticipation of which could only have intensified her mood swings and by now regular headaches. Although the New Englander Dr. Oliver Wendell Holmes Sr. published a paper that very year on puerperal fever (the childbirth fever that had killed Mary's mother and Lincoln's sister), showing how it was spread by doctors going from childbirth to childbirth, it was years before this breakthrough in germ theory was widely accepted, and the risks of childbirth in 1843 were virtually unchanged from Mary's mother's time two decades earlier.[4]

However, all went well, and on August 1, 1843, the Lincolns' first son was born in their room at the Globe. By then, the couple knew they were not headed for Washington, at least this time. Seeing he could not win the nomination for Congress, Lincoln had withdrawn from the race in favor of his friend, the popular and oratorically gifted Edward Baker, who in turn lost to Mary's third cousin, John Hardin, who went on to win the congressional election; however, thinking ahead, Lincoln had persuaded the nominating convention to establish a principle of rotation for the seat (a rule followed in other states), so that after one year Baker would replace Hardin, and after that (he thought) his own turn would come. Time enough to establish themselves as the rising political couple, Mary might have thought.

They named the newborn Robert Todd after Mary's father, who in the fall made a rare visit to Springfield to see his tiny namesake. Having lost two sons named Robert, Mr. Todd (still a father of small children himself) was particularly touched by this gesture, which he expressed by putting $25 in gold in Mary's hand and telling Lincoln to handle a lawsuit to collect a debt of $50 for him and keep the money. His generosity would make it possible for the couple to look for a real home.[5]

As Mary's niece would sympathetically observe, the "primitive" surroundings offered at the Globe "could not fail to be anything but distasteful to Mary, reared as she had been," and now that she had a child, the contrast between her family's homes and this surely tried her nerves. With no slaves to call on, she might have thought of her sisters, but whether from a cooling of relations or preoccupation with their own young families, they did not rally to her side after Robert's birth. Instead, during the customary two weeks of postbirth confinement, she relied on the wife of one of her husband's friends who came in every day to wash and dress the baby and tidy the room while Mary rested, sewed, or read. The woman's six-year-old daughter, who liked babies, would take Robert outside, where she alternated between dragging him around the tavern yard and laying him in the grass to nap or play. Mary's slavery model for child care, in which the littlest slave girls (like Lizzy Hobbs) were set to watch infants barely five years younger than themselves, may explain—as Robert's child nurse would later wonder—how "Mrs. L. could have trusted a particularly small six year old with this charge."[6] Meanwhile, Lincoln was back on the circuit, away almost continuously from mid-September to late October.

Soon, however, the baby's wailing made even Mr. Lincoln unpopular at the Globe, and after three more months the couple rented a cottage not far away. Then, in January, for $1,200 in cash (the purchase price of Lizzy and her son) and a city lot they owned worth $300, they bought a one-and-a-half story, five-room cottage from the minister who had married them. Situated on an eighth-of-an-acre lot at Eighth and Jackson Streets, it had a woodshed, a privy, and a place for a carriage. It was no hilltop mansion, like Elizabeth and Ninian's home, but it was nicely located, only a few blocks from Lincoln's office in the Tinsley Building at Sixth and Adams on the square. Mary would have the help of the Edwardses' slave (listed this way in the census), a woman named Epsy Smith, who was in her twenties and from Kentucky and whom she knew and liked.[7]

In April, a month before they moved in and when Lincoln was off on the circuit, Mary withdrew $46.50 from the family's bank account and began furnishing their house, thereby inaugurating a pattern of shopping when her husband was away. Not all women took these matters into their own hands. Her newly married friend Julia Jayne Trumbull, for instance, did not; her husband, the lawyer Lyman Trumbull, bought their furniture while on the circuit and wrote his wife to say that he hoped she liked it. That Lincoln did not mind the arrangement in his house was, for its time and place, one of the striking features of their marriage. As he told a fellow lawyer, these were "the little things" he let his wife manage; "I myself manage all important matters." However, to Mary he evidently said, "You know what you want—go and get it."[8]

From the start, Mary's home was not her only project of improvement. Growing up in Lexington had left her deeply impressed by the value of display and things—of the "*outward show*," as she would call it—and here she was with a husband sorely in need of refurbishment. In this project Lincoln participated. In the space of two weeks the previous May, the month of his jaunty letter to Speed, Lincoln had reoutfitted himself: he paid his tailor $9 for a new serge suit (requiring alterations later); then he brought home a leghorn straw hat and then a satin necktie. Personal hygiene also received a boost, with the purchase of a 25-cent hog bristle toothbrush. The smooth fabrics and the finely plaited leghorn straw suggest Mary's gentrifying influence, smoothness being a mark of gentility as compared to coarser, rougher fabrics and weaves. Six months later he had a winter suit made of beaver cloth (a felted wool) with "more expensive trimmings." Yet despite his earnest and best efforts, Lincoln's dress consistently fell below his wife's standards, dragging him down a social notch or two in her eyes. "Why don't you dress up and try to look like somebody?" she would say, a particularly pointed barb at his origins.[9]

Mary was also determined to smooth Lincoln's coarse, country manners (his hair was beyond anyone's taming), and she launched her campaign immediately, for there was work to do and she obviously considered it a necessity for his political future, not to mention her own satisfaction. Like Mary Owens, she noted Lincoln's indifference to convention, but unlike the first Mary, this one assumed that, under her influence, he would change. She raised "merry war," as one of her sisters gently put it, against her husband's habit of eating butter with his knife, of opening the door instead of letting the servant do it, of sitting down to table in his shirtsleeves. His breaches of etiquette, especially in front of people Mary hoped to impress, not surprisingly grated on her aristocratic nerves, and the wars she raised, according to nonfamily, were anything but "merry." It was as if she "got the devil in her," according to their next-door neighbor, a shoemaker named James Gourley—who, even so, thought the Lincolns "got along tolerably well" otherwise and considered Mary a "good friend of mine."[10]

A typical dust-up from this time occurred one day when Lincoln was reading in his favorite position on the floor, lying against a pillow that was propped against an overturned chair, and some ladies came to call. Opening the door (of course, in his shirtsleeves), he told them in his homespun fashion that he would "trot the women out," a phrase that so annoyed Mary that she made things "exceedingly interesting" for her husband, while her guests no doubt fumbled about, until he slipped quietly out of the house, a coping strategy he used throughout their marriage. This was a story told by a daughter of Lincoln's half-sister, a girl named Harriet Hanks, who at the time was living with the Lincolns while attending school. Indeed, her presence "created a fight, a fuss" between the Lincolns over Mary's treating her "like a servant, a slave." Years afterward, Harriet declared that she "would rather Say *nothing* about [Mary], as I could Say but little in her *favor* I conclude it best to Say nothing."[11] Evidently, the temptation to speak was great.

With her high opinion of her background and low opinion of his, Mary might have assumed that teaching Lincoln the skills he needed to rise was her family's natural role. After all, she had seen him submit willingly to being mentored by two of her cousins: first, as the junior law partner to John Stuart, a smooth and polished politician (although known to be rather crude in private); and then for three years, starting in 1841, as junior partner to the older and brilliant (though slovenly) Stephen Logan, from whom Lincoln picked up much about technique and style in courtroom argument. Moreover, she had married a man who rejected core elements of the male frontier culture, a man who did not hunt, drink, curse, chew tobacco or smoke, or gamble. Now she would be his social mentor, a role she could relish and in which she was his indisputable superior. Certainly, she could tell herself, he needed her direction to make himself more presentable in the halls of power. She agreed with the character in Catherine Maria Sedgwick's popular novel *Home*, who said, "There is nothing that tends more to the separation into classes than difference in manners. It is a badge that all can see." Indeed, that President Lincoln put his hat on "country fashion," "with his hand on the back part of the rim," was striking enough to merit remark by the young Colonel Robert Gould Shaw in a letter to his mother at the start of the Civil War. Shaw was the blue-eyed, well-born Bostonian who would die commanding the 54th Massachusetts Colored Infantry.[12]

Mary's family saw her desire to train her husband as self-protective: criticism of him was criticism of her. However, her efforts to make him "more conventional" were so unrelenting that finally one of them said to her, "If I had a husband with a mind such as yours, I would not care what he did," a compliment to which she responded, "It is foolish; a very small thing to complain of."[13] But complain she did.

She was proud that he was no "dunce," like the fellow Campbell who married her cousin (even with all his money and property), and prouder still that she had been clever enough to see his worth; and she was steadfast in her conviction that he would someday bring her the "fame & power" she desired. One day, Mary was visiting with a circle of women, among them her sister Elizabeth and her old rival, Matilda Edwards, who by then had finally accepted a proposal and was Mrs. Newton D. Strong. The women were apparently talking about their husbands. Why, Matilda was asked, did she marry "such an old dried up husband—such a withered up old Buck?" (he was thirty-four when they married; she twenty-two). "He had lots of houses & gold," she replied. Eager for revenge against the woman for whom Lincoln had broken off their relationship, Mary said, "Is that true—I would rather marry a good man—a man of mind—with a hope and bright prospects ahead for position—fame & power than to marry all the houses—gold & bones in the world."[14]

Ironically, Lincoln's first bid for Congress had failed in part because of his marriage: he was tagged "the candidate of pride, wealth, and aristocratic distinction," as he disgustedly wrote a friend. Obviously, the people of Sangamon had forgotten that twelve years earlier he had been "a strange, friendless, uneducated, penniless boy, working on a flat boat—at ten dollars per month." Yet he was more distressed by the apparent mistrust of his old friends and neighbors because of his marriage "*in the Aristocracy*" than by the loss of the nomination. Taking aside one of his friends, the young James Matheny, who had been a groomsman at his wedding, he told him, "Jim—I am now and always shall be the same Abe Lincoln that I always was." So difficult and private was this communication—"Said . . . with great Emphasis"—that Lincoln brought Matheny to the woods to tell him. He wished to avoid as much as he could any trace of disloyalty to his wife.[15] However, his need for Matheny to see that he had not changed, appearances to the contrary, suggests the enormous gap at the time between his own and Mary's understanding.

In fact, the two *were* building separate worlds, albeit interdependent and side by side, energized by their mutual ambition, made tender by their shared melancholic natures and love of poetry, entwined in their child and their hope for more—but in the end fundamentally separate, based on opposing principles of being. She saw everything in personal terms; he aimed for the disinterested, impersonal. She was shrewd and impulsive; he was deliberate and a thinker. She wanted power and pleasure, which she regarded as ends in themselves, and spent her life fighting to attain both; he strove always to act on right principles as he saw them, but in the end he was a fatalist, whose "maxim and philosophy was—'What is to be will be and no cares of ours can arrest the decree.'"

Having no daughter to confide in, Mary would come to rely on female companions to dispel her loneliness, loneliness she felt even when her abstracted husband was at home. "What would I not give, for a few hours conversation, with you this evening," she wrote to a friend after seventeen years of marriage. "I hope you may never feel as lonely as I sometimes do, surrounded by much that renders life desirable."[16]

In 1844, with Mary's encouragement, Lincoln devoted himself to the presidential campaign of his political idol and her old neighbor, Henry Clay. Along with Logan, Baker, and Stuart, the top Whig stumpers in the region,

Lincoln was out nearly every evening that winter speaking before "crowded houses," whipping up support for a campaign that felt almost as thrilling and urgent as the one of 1840. (Clay's loss, his third presidential bid, led some of his more devoted followers to vow to go without shaving their beards or cutting their hair until Clay was President. Forty years later William H. Herndon saw "one man who had lived up to this insane resolution.")[17]

Mary, however, sat this one out. She nursed Robert, sewed, read novels (Walter Scott was a particular favorite), attended church, visited her family, neighbors, and friends, including Julia Trumbull, whose son was nine months younger than hers and whose husband rode the circuit as well; she did some work in the garden with sister Frances; and with the help of a "hired girl," she washed, cooked, and cleaned. She wondered what her father would think if he saw her slaving away in the kitchen. She also gave a party to which she did not invite her favorite Springfield cousin, Dr. Todd's daughter Lizzie, who had expressed the view that Robert "was a sweet child but not good looking."[18]

True to her training, she threw herself into making a genteel home; besides, it was something enjoyable and absorbing to do with Lincoln so often away. She slogged through dirt or mud to and from Robert Irwin's store to purchase numerous items, including yards of calico, a cheap cotton she could use for curtains, furniture covers, servants' and baby clothes, a looking glass, and materials for a corset—needles, fabric, whalebones, sewing accessories and for the trimming lace and gimp (silk, worsted, or cotton twist, with a thin wire running through it). Meanwhile, Lincoln was out on the circuit and the stump seven weeks out of the four months since April, returning home toward the end of July.

During the period from September to early November, when Lincoln was home only eleven nights, Mary's shopping excursions increased: more yards of fabric, a fireplace shovel and tongs, a small piece of cambric, a pair of black hose, some tape for holding hoops in place, a pair of children's shoes, kid slippers, and another comb came home from the store. She also began her winter sewing, and on one of Lincoln's rare days home in October, she sent him out for 12¼ yards of cloth, 6 yards of flannel, and a dozen pearl buttons for their winter underwear.[19] So went the first full year of marriage.

The following year saw little outward change to this arrangement, although, if her purchases are any indication, Mary was discovering how much "going out and getting what she wanted" suited her (at the time Lincoln's income was a comfortable $1,500 to $2,000 a year). During the 1845 spring circuit, she splurged on a new, deep-brimmed "Neapolitan Bonnet" ($7.50), the most expensive hat Irwin's sold, which she trimmed with ribbon herself and wore shaded by her new spring parasol; during the fall circuit she had her new seamstress (an apparently recently added expense) pick up some fabric and thread for her. The year after that brought other causes for dilation. In 1846, Lincoln ran for Congress, this time outmaneuvering John Hardin, who, rejecting Lincoln's proposal for rotation, had put himself forward again. Mary was thrilled when her husband won, the victory a confirmation of her marital choice, even though campaigning had contributed to his being away more than ever before, nearly five months. That was also the year their second son was born, arriving on a day in March that his father happened to be in Springfield.[20]

Throughout their marriage, like many couples in their circle, the Lincolns spent long periods apart. For nineteenth-century women like Mary—educated, ambitious, genteel women without an occupation to distract and refresh them or the freedom to travel alone—life was defined by domesticity. Lincoln's extensive absences at once liberated and provoked Mary. She did what she wanted, but she resented his being away—not just his absence, but his being wherever he *was*, his masculine prerogative to move about, to meet people, to see things. It would have been hard not to feel jealous of a husband (when bathing a screaming child, for instance) whom one watched ride off to his boon companions on the circuit, where "the court was like a big family consultation" and "there was a freedom and familiarity as of old friends meeting upon a public occasion," where "dinners, receptions, and suppers followed one another" and evenings were spent trading stories. As a consequence, shopping and visiting, blessed relief from being cooped up at home, were essential female activities. Church activities were another outlet for pent-up energy. But the Springfield sewing societies, which met evenings to raise money for the church and to which the women arrived bundled together in the back of a wagon that drove from house to house to pick up passengers, could not compare to her husband's experience. However "rattling" Lincoln's buggy and crowded the accommodations (bed sharing was common), there were new faces to see and interesting news to tell and hear. And there was no time to be lonely, unless one was lonely for home. In later years, when Mary was traveling, she never felt this particular loneliness. Nor, it seems, did Lincoln now.[21]

Then, too, Lincoln's long absences resurrected the twin specters of abandonment and loss that haunted Mary's childhood and now her dreams. It was her own need for security that had her children sharing her bed when Lincoln was away; even so, her neighbors would send their boys to sleep over so she would not feel alone. The fearless "tomboy" Mary Todd had become a somewhat fearful Mary Lincoln.

She also simply missed Lincoln, was "sad away from" him, she would write him. In Springfield there were many women in a position to sympathize, "widows" to the circuit or other businesses, with husbands who were too frequently away, leaving them with demanding children. Julia Trumbull, a new mother like Mary, broke down in tears when her husband left for the circuit. She wrote him that she was stricken with fears that "some evil was to befall one of us" and that she had "taken sick" within hours of his departure. Mary's neighbor a decade later, Mrs. William Black, also nursing a newborn, marked the days in her diary when her businessman husband "William came" and "William left." On one particular day "William left us," she wrote, "and I was cast into the very depths of despair—I felt as though I could not live longer separated from him." Mary gave many days and evenings to this community of left-behind women, who found solace in their mutual complaints about their absent husbands. One evening, following an afternoon visit from Mary, Julia sat down and wrote her husband that she had "little expectation of seeing him till my hair becomes grey, and this boy a man. [I sometimes] am afraid it is wrong in me to wish to see you before the courts are all over," Julia continued; "did I love you less, I should be less anxious to be ever with you." Mary, for her part, one day told her neighbor James Gourley, "If her husband had Staid at home as he ought to, she could love him better," a flirtatious suggestion of the physical relationship she missed.[22] By the time Mary was confiding in Lizzy Keckly, she had had nearly twenty years of creating her own everyday life apart from her husband.

Marriage also brought Mary the challenge of raising children. This was an era in which middle-class Americans were having smaller, child-centered families, a notable contrast to previous generations. Yet even among their friends, the Lincolns were held to be notoriously indulgent parents to their four sons, as if in compensation for their own bleak childhoods. "Had they s——t in Lincoln's hat and rubbed it on his boots, he would have laughed and thought it smart," declared Lincoln's new law partner, the intense William H. Herndon, who endured many office visits from the two youngest boys, Willie and Tad, who were born in the 1850s. "*These* little devils," Herndon called the pair. Mary was equally inclined to pet, praise, and warmly indulge: keeping her promise to Willie for a ninth birthday party, she gathered "some 50 or 60 boys and girls" for a "gala," although she concluded "they are nonsensical affairs." ("I feel it is necessary to keep one's word with a child," she wrote on another occasion.) Yet, impulsive and childlike herself, Mary also found being the mother of rambunctious boys to be a nerve-racking ordeal; in fact, as biographer Ida M. Tarbell observed, "she went to pieces at the slightest emergency in the family."[23]

The neighbors were used to hearing her panicked cries for help. When Robert was a toddler, Mary came running into the front yard "as usual, screaming, 'Bobbie will die! Bobbie will die!'" Apparently, she had caught him eating some lime out of the lime box, which was used for the privy out back. A neighbor "washed his mouth out and that's all there was to it."[24] If there were echoes in her head of her toddler brother's death, also a Bobby, only she could hear them.

Lincoln's characteristic response to Mary's alarms was to stay calm. Writing to Speed from his Springfield office in 1846, Lincoln was interrupted by an emergency at home. "Since I began this letter," he explained to Speed when he returned, "a messenger came to tell me, Bob was lost; but by the time I reached the house, his mother had found him, and had him whipped—and, by now, very likely he is run away."[25]

At this period in Mary's life, swamped by new responsibilities and already suffering from what would eventually become debilitating, periodic migraine headaches, Lincoln was in a way the worst kind of husband for her. He was undemonstrative when she needed constant shows of affection, cold when she craved heat. (More concretely, he could be hours late for dinner, absent-mindedly ignoring a summons home.) And she was intelligent enough to be provoked by the masculine mocking in his bemused calm in the face of her many anxieties.

It was widely known that Lincoln "paid no attention" when she was pitching a fit, that he met many a "tongue lashing" or upraised broom handle by leaving the house and staying away, day or night. Yet on occasion "he would rise and cut up the very devil for a while, make things more lively and 'get,'" in the words of Herndon (who would become Lincoln's most important, though controversial, early biographer). At other times, he would try to soothe her. In retreat, exhausted and strangely bereft, beset by severe headaches, Mary rode alternating tides of rage and guilt, a legacy of her childhood.[26] In choosing her husband and confidantes (including her oldest sister and later Elizabeth Keckly), she instinctively sought the steadier hand that could lead her back away from the edge of that terrifying, internal cliff toward which she was forever hurling herself.

Mary saw Washington, D.C., for the first time in December 1847, upon Lincoln's entry into Congress.

"Being elected to Congress, though I am very grateful to our friends, for having done it, has not pleased me as much as I expected," Lincoln wrote Speed in the fall of 1846. But Mary was enormously pleased. In a flurry of domesticity (perhaps anticipating a larger role as hostess), she had Lincoln buy her the bestselling *Miss Leslie's Directions for Cookery* and *Miss Leslie's House Book or Manual of Domestic Economy for Town and Country*. (In a later edition of the cookbook, the author, a Philadelphian named Eliza Leslie, declared she had received numerous testimonials from satisfied "countrywomen" who with her book at hand were "made practical housewives of young ladies," as well as thanks from their husbands, "who told me of great improvements in the family-table.")[27]

According to her neighbors, Mary Lincoln sewed every day in preparation for going to Washington—for, unlike most congressional wives, she fully intended to go. "Mrs. L, I am told, accompanies her husband to Washington city next winter," wrote Whig lawyer and fellow circuit rider David Davis to his wife. "She wishes to loom largely," he concluded.[28] He was right.

Like her husband, she sat for a local daguerreotypist who had recently opened his "Daguerreotype Miniature Gallery," the results of which sessions are the earliest known photographic images of each (there exists no portrait of the couple together, or family portrait, reportedly due to Mary's dislike of their appearance side by side, he so tall and she so short). The daguerreotype, "sun-printing" on silver-washed plates, had made it possible for nearly anyone to obtain an inexpensive personal image, and thousands of Americans flocked to daguerreotype studios, which had become common even in small towns in the West.

In his portrait, Lincoln sits angled so that the right side of his face is in shadow, his long legs crossed and his arms arranged stiffly, with the right elbow jutting out so as to require him to tilt back and almost twist in his chair to keep its position on the armrest. His dress clothes and neatly combed and plastered-down hair give him the look of a boy sitting for his school portrait; however, his expression is watchful, inward, self-possessed. Mary, in contrast, looks eager to shine. Sitting up and forward, she turns almost full-faced toward the photographer, her arms draped gracefully, her lovely plump hands on her lap, with her wedding ring glinting on her left ring finger. Her hair is parted to the side and smoothed over her ears, with ringlets falling neatly behind. She is clearly in love with her stylish, energetically trimmed outfit: a silk dress with gathered bodice coming to a long point, narrow sleeves with lace at the cuffs, and a full skirt, the whole of which she has decorated with ribbons, rosettes, and a waist ribbon. She also wears a lace shawl kept in place at the neckline by a large brooch, on which appears to be a miniature portrait of a dark-haired woman. Her gaze is direct, but narrow and tired, although her mouth is relaxed in a slight smile. She is not beautiful, but very pretty, just as friends and family described her to be.[29]

The Lincolns rented out their house and in October 1847 headed to Washington by way of Lexington, where they spent three weeks with Mary's family. The journey to the Todds' took nine days by stage, steamer, and finally, the three-car Lexington and Ohio railroad from Frankfort to Lexington. Traveling with four-year-old Bobby and eighteen-month-old Eddie presented a challenge, at least to other passengers. A nephew of Mary's stepmother happened to be on the Lexington train with the Lincolns without knowing who they were and, before the Lincolns reached the house, had already had time to complain to Betsey Todd about the "two lively youngsters on board who kept the whole train in turmoil, and their long-legged father, instead of spanking the brats, looked pleased as Punch and aided and abetted the older one in mischief." In truth, "I was never so glad to get off a train in my life."[30]

At home were two sisters and one baby brother whom Mary had never seen; in return the Todds were curious about the two sons and Brother Lincoln, as the family customarily addressed in-laws. Mary passed much of the three weeks catching up with her Parker and Todd relatives and old friends. Meanwhile, Lincoln spent hours reading newspapers and books in Mr. Todd's library, lingering over the popular genteel volume *Elegant Extracts, or Useful and Entertaining Passages from the Best English Authors and Translations.* He memorized William Cullen Bryant's poem "Thanatopsis," about accepting death amid life, and turned down the page for William Cowper's "Charity," marking its strong passages against the slave trade, its "merchants rich in cargoes of despair, / Who drive a loathsome traffic."[31]

En route to Washington, Lincoln was thinking about slavery. He had seen enough of the trade's horrors on his boat trips to New Orleans, St. Louis, and Louisville, where he found the sight of "ten or a dozen slaves, shackled together with irons . . . a continual torment to me; and I see something like it every time I touch the Ohio." But he had never lived down the street from a slave market and jail, as he did now during his visit to the Todd house. If he was brooding over his revulsion, he probably said nothing ("I bite my lip and keep quiet," he would describe his policy as an antislavery, pro-Union man), but Mary was thrilled to see her family's "old slaves" and "wished she had such a good old black nurse" for her own children.[32]

In Lexington on November 13 Henry Clay launched his fourth bid for the presidency with a speech against Democrat President Polk's declaration of war against Mexico, and the Lincolns went to hear him. Clay's charge—that the war was not an act of self-defense but of "unnecessary and of offensive aggression . . . actuated by a spirit of rapacity" and a desire to open new territory to slavery—was a position Lincoln held, and he took these arguments with him to Congress, aiming to position himself as one of the leaders of an antiwar, antislavery Whig Party.[33]

When they finally arrived in Washington, the couple's mutual excitement at finding themselves in a bigger city than either of them had ever seen made their experience, at least initially, a shared adventure. During the day, Mary could shop at the city's public markets, which sold everything from fruits and vegetables to Parisian millinery and English woolens, or at the fancy shops along a cobblestone stretch on Pennsylvania Avenue. When the government offices closed at three o'clock, Lincoln could meet her and they could join the locals in promenading along the "Avenue" before dinner at four.[34]

Of course, the city offered the usual varieties of entertainment: plays, concerts, lectures, and art exhibits. They heard the Marine Band, which played twice a week on the west terrace of the Capitol. At Carusi's Assembly Rooms, Mr. and Mrs. Lincoln saw the Ethiopian Serenaders, a black-face minstrelsy group, recently back from performing for the Royal Family in England, who were popular for their sentimental style of singing. (They were a contrast to the broad, raucous humor of Christy's Minstrels, regulars in New York City's working-class Mechanics' Hall and more like the minstrel shows Lincoln preferred and saw with his circuit friends.) There were also official receptions and parties. In March, the Lincolns attended Washington's National Birthday-Night Ball, postponed because of Congressman John Quincy Adams's death in February in the speaker's room in the House. There were the New Year's Reception and regular levees at the Executive Mansion, although because the humorless Polks banned dancing and gave their guests nothing to eat or drink, these were currently unpopular affairs.

On nice days, the family could walk across the Mall toward the Potomac to watch preparations for a monument to George Washington just under way or admire the construction of architect James Renfrew's red sandstone Norman castle. So different from the white stone and classical style of other public buildings, the castle was finally going up after a decade of congressional wrangling over the propriety of following the wishes of wealthy Englishman James Smithson, who had left his entire fortune "to the United States of America to found at Washington, under the name of the Smithsonian Institute, an Establishment for the increase and diffusion of knowledge among men."[35]

Lincoln, unlike Mary, had to work, which he did, with diligence, missing only 13 of the 456 roll calls during his two years in Congress. Just before Christmas, Mary was sitting in the gold-and-red galleries in the House when Lincoln made his first attempt to "distinguish" himself by answering President Polk's request for more funds for the Mexican War, with his "Spot" resolutions to Congress. Lincoln, wanting to show that the war was an act of U.S. aggression, challenged the President to reveal "all the facts which go to establish whether the particular spot of soil on which the blood of our *citizens* was so shed, was, or was not, *our own soil*." Three weeks later, Mary returned to hear her husband's forty-five-minute follow-up speech.[36]

But in their boardinghouse room, during the writing and rewriting of the speech—Lincoln said he "condensed all [he] could for fear of being cut off by the hour rule"—Mary was apparently in the way. Indeed, he thought she "hindered [him] . . . in attending to business," and after three months in the capital, she was back in Lexington with the two boys.[37]

One biographer, Jean H. Baker, contends that Mary was "a casualty of boardinghouse confinement," surely a part of the difficulty. After a short stay in Brown's Hotel, the family of four shared a room in the boardinghouse of Mrs. Ann G. Sprigg on Duff Green's Row, a row of houses just east of the Capitol, where the Library of Congress stands today, from which they could see the temporary wooden Capitol dome. These boardinghouses were called "messes" because of their newspaper ads offering "to accommodate a mess of members." Mrs. Sprigg's was a Whig stronghold. Stuart and Baker had stayed there during their terms, and seven other Whig Congressmen (including the ardent antislavery man, Ohio's Joshua R. Giddings)—and none of their wives—were now in residence. By the mid-1840s, the longer, busier congressional sessions prompted a growing number of Congressmen to bring their families to Washington for the winter social season, but they generally rented suites of rooms (Stephen Douglas, a first-term senator, and his new wife lived at Willard's); the single rooms in the messes were by and large a male preserve.[38]

Some wives found the mix of boarders unappealing: "We . . . went up to . . . board, to Mrs. Wise's, but there was a mess of clerks, and that sort of people there, and wretched living," Varina Howell Davis, wife of Senator Jefferson Davis (and Lizzy Keckly's future client), wrote her mother to explain why they had left the mess. With three other senators' families, they were renting a house next to the United States Hotel, where they ate in a private dining room. At Mrs. Sprigg's, common meals were served by three black waiters, one of whom was working to earn his purchase price for freedom.[39]

Lincoln shone in this world of male bonding, with "his simple and unostentatious manners, kind-heartedness, and amusing jokes, anecdotes, and witticisms." And it was not just at meals that the men enjoyed one another's company (despite the occasional woman's presence). For relaxation, they bowled at Casparis's bowling alley nearby, sometimes joining for matches against other messes, or gathered in the morning in the small post office in the Capitol, where they told each other stories. That Mary was excluded from this male-centered society was a given. At the same time, because she had no established social life to fall back on, few other opportunities for informal socializing presented themselves, for although Washington's permanent residents were used to welcoming back "old" outsiders by now, they had no reason to welcome the unknown wife of an unknown junior representative from the West, and she had no rooms in which to entertain.[40]

At Mrs. Sprigg's, meanwhile, Mary evidently had her share of run-ins: "All the house—or rather, all with whom you were on decided good terms—send their love to you. The rest say nothing," Lincoln wrote her after she left.[41]

Barely a handful of personal letters between Lincoln and Mary survived their son Robert's deliberate burning of his family's private papers when he was an old man. Of these, there are four by Lincoln from Washington and one by Mary in response, giving a brief glimpse into the inner workings of their marriage at the time.

After almost six years of marriage, topics once sure to start fights had become private jokes. Lincoln could tease Mary about her former rival, Matilda Edwards, now married to Congressman Strong and planning a visit to the capital. "Suppose you write her a letter," Lincoln proposed, "and enclose it in one of mine; and if she comes I will deliver it to her, and if she does not, I will send it to her." Mary returned volley with a mention of her old beau, Mr. Webb, and her intention to arrange to meet him "and carry on quite a flirtation, you know *we*, always had a *penchant* that way." Her weight, too, had become fodder for marital banter. "I am afraid you will get so well, and fat, and young, as to be wanting to marry again," Lincoln told her. "Get weighed, and write me how much you weigh."[42] (To which Mary did not respond at all. Perhaps she knew he was more than a little curious about her weight. After all, this *was* the man who had expressed revulsion at the idea of marrying a fat woman.)

There was between them the usual domestic chat, interesting to no one but themselves but revealing of Lincoln's willingness to adapt himself to Mary's concerns: "Very soon after you went away, I got what I think a very pretty set of shirt-bosom studs—modest little ones, jet, set in gold, only costing 50 cents a piece, or $1.50 for the whole." There was interesting gossip about "our two girls," two prostitutes whom they had spotted at Carusi's, who wore "black fur bonnets" and were "never . . . seen in close company with other ladies." A member of Congress went home with one, Lincoln reported, and "if I were to guess, I would say, he went away a somewhat altered man—most likely in his pockets, and in some other particulars."[43]

However, more conflicted feelings also emerge. When Mary was in Washington, Lincoln wanted her to return to Lexington, but now that she was gone, he missed her. "In this troublesome world, we are never quite satisfied," he wrote mid-April. "When you were here, I thought you hindered me some in attending to business; but now, having nothing but business—no variety—it has grown exceedingly tasteless to me. I hate to sit down and direct documents, and I hate to stay in this old room by myself." It seemed nothing was working out. The speech he had told her that he planned to make he never had a chance to, and since then he had lost interest in the subject. His efforts to fulfill her latest shopping request had also failed: "I went yesterday to hunt the little plaid stockings, as you wished; but found that McKnight has quit business, and Allen had not a single pair of the description you give, and only one plaid pair of any sort that I thought would fit 'Eddie's dear little feet.' "[44]

Lincoln was also anxious about Bobby and Eddie. Not unlike Mary's own heightened fears whenever he was away, Lincoln now had a "foolish dream about dear Bobby" that worried him so that he could not "get rid of the impression . . . till I got your letter written the same day." A comment that Mary had carelessly (or pointedly) made about the boys' forgetting who he was upset him: "Don't let the blessed fellows forget father." Chagrined, Mary took back her remark, hastening to assure him that she was only "jesting" about the children "forgetting you . . . E's eyes brighten at the mention of your name."[45]

Besides his solicitous remarks and tender misgivings, Lincoln also reproached Mary for some of her behavior, revealing another facet of their marriage. In Washington, among strangers whom he sought to impress, he must have been struck by the trail of impressions his wife had left behind. With her gone, he had time to ruminate on the impact of her behavior on his efforts to establish his own character on his own terms. "Suppose you do not prefix the 'Hon' to the address on your letters to me any more," he asked, referring to her habit of indicating his formal title for all to see. "I like the letters very much, but I would rather they not have that upon them. It is not necessary, as I suppose you have thought, to have them to come free." On another, more serious and personal matter, he gingerly suggested, "I wish you to enjoy yourself in every possible way, but is there no danger of wounding the feelings of your good father, by being so openly intimate with the Wickcliffe family [when your father is suing Mr. Wickcliffe over family property]?"[46] To these hints, there is no record of her response.

By June 1848 Mary wanted to rejoin him in Washington, but Lincoln had worries about her proposed return: "Will you be a *good girl* in all things, if I consent? Then come along, and that as *soon* as possible." Lincoln addressed Mary like a wayward child, but in this context, it was less clear-cut paternalism than a reflection of the pathological structure of their marriage. Thirty-year-old Mary *liked* being his "child-wife" (as Lizzy Keckly would recall), and he her "father-husband." (He also called her "Ma," thereby completing the family romance, in Freud's sense.)[47]

Yet, having received permission to come, she did not, and by July her lonely husband, no longer in a position to extract obedience, had to cede control to her: "Father expected to see you all sooner; but let it pass; stay as long as you please, and come when you please. Kiss and love the dear rascals, Affectionately."[48]

Mary *was* doing what she pleased. For, despite missing him—"How much, I wish instead of writing, *we* were together this evening, I feel very sad away from you"—she found her stay in Lexington comforting and gratifying. Lincoln was enclosing in his letters the money she asked for, and she could read at her leisure the copies of newspapers and speeches that he sent along (reminding her of the nicest period of their courtship). Happily, she had none of the headaches that had tortured her every spring since Lincoln had known her—and, perhaps, no wonder: she was nestled in the comforts of her father's home, with her "old slaves" again to wait on her and mind the children, and, at Lincoln's urging, she also hired a "girl" to "take charge of" the boys. Even her stepmother was "very obliging and accommodating" and sent her up "a glass of ice cream" for which she was grateful on a warm evening, although "if she thought any of us, were on her hands again, I believe she would be *worse* than ever." Indeed, Betsey's one outburst, "so striking" those days, was to "order the servant near, to throw out" a kitten that "our little Eddy" had rescued—"*your hobby*," she emphasized. This, over the child's loud "protest[s] and scream[s]." In the meantime, Lincoln was in the process of discovering the seeds of what was to be another sore point between them. He had been presented with unpaid bills from two Washington shops, but "I hesitated to pay them, because my recollection is that you told me when you went away, there was nothing left unpaid." Mary had denied these outstanding debts; why is unknown. In the local world of Springfield shopping, where everyone knew her or was related to her, such a thing could never happen. Washington, on the other hand, was too tempting, and her husband's position, she felt, gave her license.[49]

Toward the end of July, Mary and the two boys rejoined Lincoln, and in September the family left Washington. His term more than half over, Lincoln's experience in Congress was turning out to be a disappointment. Hardly anyone had paid attention to his "Spot" resolutions; at home, the thirty-nine-year-old Lincoln was generally criticized for his antiwar stance, especially as his former congressional rivals had both fought in the war with Mexico. Hardin had "acknowledged no fealty to any party but our country" and died at the Battle of Buena Vista, and Baker, with mixed feelings about the war, had also served heroically.[50]

Nor would Lincoln have more success in promoting his antislavery views when he returned to Washington without his family in December. In Congress, he avoided the bitter battling over the Wilmot Proviso, seeing it was doomed to fail, but voted for it when it came up. However, what he hoped to be his major antislavery contribution in the new session of Congress the following year—his carefully composed proposal for compensated emancipation in the District, whereby owners were compensated for lost property (a plan approved by his abolitionist messmate Giddings)—went nowhere. At the time, the Potomac port was one of the busiest intersections in the slave trade; "only seven blocks from the Capitol stood the warehouse of Franklin & Armfield, the country's largest slave traders," a place referred to by Lincoln as "a sort of Negro livery-stable."[51]

Lincoln seemed resigned to obscurity. Responding to a request for his "signature with a sentiment," Lincoln wrote, "I am not a very sentimental man; and the best sentiment I can think of is, that if you collect the signatures of all persons who are no less distinguished than I, you will have a very undistinguishing mass of names."[52] This was a sentiment Mary never shared, for she was unrelenting in her wish for distinction.

Lincoln returned to Springfield in early 1849 with no clear sense of his future. Then, in the spring, an opportunity presented itself. Lincoln, who had campaigned hard for newly inaugurated President Zachary Taylor, was beginning to be talked about for the powerful patronage position of commissioner of the General Land Office. Not only would he increase his salary to $3,000 a year, but with all public lands under his oversight, he would have a great deal of control over Western settlement. At first, Lincoln was reluctant to go after the position, being "so hedged about with other aspirants from his own State" (as Herndon put it), but soon he was heading back to Washington to make his case. In the meantime, Mary had sat down and copied out duplicates of a form letter, written by her husband but evincing her more characteristically urgent tones, soliciting support from prominent Illinois Whigs and signing them "A. Lincoln."[53]

However, the appointment went to a Chicago Whig (a competing branch of the state party), and Lincoln quickly rejected the bone thrown to him next, the office of secretary to the governor of the Oregon Territory. Later that summer, when he was tempted by the offer of the governorship itself, it was Mary who, according to Herndon, "put her foot squarely down on it with a firm and emphatic No. That always ended it with Lincoln."[54] Mary's negative would prove to be an accurate assessment of the greater political and economic promise of remaining in Springfield.

Mary had other reasons for not wishing to travel so far a distance over difficult terrain. In late July 1849, she received word that her father had died unexpectedly in a cholera outbreak in Lexington. This blow, followed scarcely a week later by the death of Julia Trumbull's boy Lyman, added weight to Mary's fears about their three-and-half-year-old Eddie, who had always been a frail child. Her fears were borne out when Eddie became ill the following December. For fifty-two days, the Lincolns watched over their son as his fevers and racking coughing fits—the signs of pulmonary tuberculosis, for which there was no known treatment—inexorably wore him down until he died on February 1, 1850. His death was horrible for his parents. Lincoln broke down in tears at the sight of the card on which was written the doctor's last prescription for the child. Mary was unable to stop weeping or take anything to eat. The next day, exhausted by watching and grief, they held his funeral at their home. Mary would not have gone to the graveyard, where women customarily did not go. Instead, not unlike Anne Garland, she turned to the comforts allotted to her by convention: she composed a mourning poem entitled "Little Eddie" for the *Springfield Journal* and joined the First Presbyterian Church, whose new minister, James Smith, had conducted Eddie's funeral and counseled patience and submission to God's ways. "Bright is the home to him now given/For of such is the Kingdom of Heaven," she wrote piously. Yet three years later (unlike the pious Anne), Mary wrote in private to a childhood friend, "I grieve to say that even at this distant day, I do not feel sufficiently submissive to our loss."[55]

Within a month after Eddie's death, Mary was expecting another child. William Wallace, named after Frances's husband who had helped take care of Eddie, was born December 21, 1850, distracting his parents out of their mourning. A gentle, intelligent child, Willie was considered the son most like Lincoln, and both parents adored him. A little over two years later, they had their fourth son, whom they named Thomas, after Lincoln's father, who had died the January following Willie's birth. "Tad," as his father called him, short for "tadpole" because of his enormous head, completed the family. The nearly three-year intervals between these two sets of sons was apparently determined by Mary's long nursing, in this instance, until Willie was eighteen months old, and he was temporarily sick as a consequence.[56]

Encouraged by the special status of childhood in Victorian culture, many parents were having smaller families, but health reasons also may have kept the Lincoln family small. Mary was ill after Willie was born, and after Tad's complicated birth, she experienced the onset of a cluster of ailments, which she grouped together "as a disease of a womanly nature," a veiled reference, typical of the age. It has never been clear to historians what she meant, but symptoms she described later in life and attributed to women's "troubles," following the uncertain diagnoses of the time, were most likely those of long-untreated diabetes.[57]

During these years, Lincoln was home much more than he had been before the family went to Congress. With his political career on hold and having turned down a lucrative offer to join a Chicago firm, he returned to being a Springfield lawyer and devoted his time to Lincoln & Herndon, building up a lucrative caseload with the railroad companies, which were in the middle of a building boom. Mary was delighted that he was bringing home larger fees, although disgusted that he split them equally with his junior partner. (Lincoln had precedent to do otherwise; as Logan's junior partner, he had taken home only 33 percent of the fees.)

By the mid-1850s, railroads were running regularly between Springfield and other Illinois towns. No longer limited to the 5 mph of horsepower, Lincoln could now come home circuit weekends. As an adult, Robert would remember his father as mostly being away when he was small, but Lincoln was a regular presence for young Willie and Tad. In a culture in which fathers were not expected to assist with any child care, Lincoln did a great deal, taking the boys for long walks, helping them dress in the mornings, and looking after them when Mary was busy or ill. He made a striking figure on Sundays, his head in a book, wheeling the two small boys up and down the street in a wagon when Mary went to church. "Henpecked" is what the neighbors called him, an opinion predictably fueled by the sight of Mary running up the street, loudly scolding her husband when one of the boys tumbled out of the wagon, unnoticed by their preoccupied father, who kept walking.[58]

Yet this period of settled domesticity was internally difficult, a time of transition for each. Mary had returned from Washington full of her superiority to her provincial neighbors. "The *advantages* of some winter's in Washington," as she put it, became her touchstone for sophistication and accomplishment.[59] The tragedies of the first year, however, undid this initial buoyancy of spirits. During Eddie's illness, Mary learned that her beloved Grandmother Parker had died in Lexington. Losing her maternal grandmother, father, and son in one year changed her. She had always been highstrung, demanding, and impulsive, but she had been able to temper the pull of her darker moods with a keen sense of the ridiculous and a pluck that enabled her to recover quickly. Now she became increasingly fearful, querulous, and self-indulgent; she seemed to act out every anxiety and act on every impulse, good or bad. Other young women lost parents and children, of course, but the disruptions of her childhood had left her with no ordinary sense of a stable world coming right again, or of her own power to shape events according to her desires. Particularly in later years, this deep-seated insecurity and sense of powerlessness, feelings that underlay what look like manic-depressive mood swings from today's perspective, drove her to efforts at control, especially over other people, whom she divided into two types: those who were for her and those who were against her. Eventually, what had once been her ready flirtatious charm could come across as selfish manipulation and a lack of candor.

Her husband, in the meantime, was undergoing his own internal evolution. Since coming home from Washington, Lincoln had begun a new round of studying (he was reading Euclid, for example), made newly self-conscious about his lack of formal education by his term in Congress. Although he was not intimidated by his colleagues, he could see the difference between their education and his own, and had spent his free time, to his colleagues' amusement, poring over books in the Library of Congress.

He was also, as others observed, abstracted and depressed. The deaths of his father and son likely triggered his own deep feelings about his childhood losses: the deaths of his brother, mother, and sister. Beyond that, his response to his father's death was complicated by their difficult relationship; Lincoln had refused to visit his dying father, even though his stepbrother had written him several times asking him to come. Lincoln's ability to shut down once he'd made a decision was one Mary recognized whenever "he compressed his lips tightly. . . . When these things showed themselves to me I fashioned myself and So all others had to do sooner or later." This determination showed itself in his explanation for ignoring his stepbrother's letters: "It is not because I have forgotten them—but because it appeared to me I could write nothing which could do any good."[60] This death, therefore, may have provoked a more pervasive withdrawal.

Also, his political father figure, Henry Clay, had died (of tuberculosis in the National Hotel in Washington). More than shared beliefs, it was personal loyalty to Clay and Webster, who had also just died, that had held the Whig Party together. By 1852, sectional interests were putting enormous strains on both Whigs and Democrats, but the Whigs were more deeply divided between North and South because of intensifying antislavery beliefs among Whigs in the North. For Lincoln, as for other Party men, the death of the Whig fathers had to be an emotional as well as ideological turning point.

Depressed and preoccupied, Lincoln had withdrawn from national politics, but watching from the sidelines proved to be a source of keen frustration for him; as for Mary, feeling marginalized in any way was intolerable. Lincoln's political and amatory rival Senator Stephen Douglas, the "architect" of the Compromise of 1850 (although Lincoln disparaged that view, charging he'd stolen it from Clay and Webster), was the Illinois politician whose name everyone knew—not Abraham Lincoln. Yet Mary never wavered from her original choice of Lincoln over Douglas. "He may not be as handsome a figure," she once said to Herndon, "but the people are perhaps not aware that his heart is as large as his arms are long."[61]

Then, in 1854, a recently widowed Senator Douglas, intent on building a railroad from St. Louis or Chicago through the Northwest to the Pacific coast, threw himself into brokering a bill to organize the territories west of Iowa and Missouri and extending north to the Canadian border, which had been named Nebraska, after the Indians. But what began as a railroad argument was soon overtaken by the explosive question of slavery. Douglas's original plan did not exclude slavery, but because much of the unsettled territory lay north of the 36°30′ line, slavery would have been prohibited under the Missouri Compromise of 1820. Pressured by powerful Southern senators who made it clear they would kill his bill should Nebraska be closed to slavery, Douglas first tried to skirt the 1820 prohibition by his democratic-sounding principle of "popular sovereignty"—that is, by removing the question from the federal government's authority and leaving it up to the settlers of the state. However, popular sovereignty did not satisfy Southerners, who wanted the act of 1820 repealed explicitly, a radical move that Congress had already twice refused to make when the Mexican territories were on the table. This time, however, the Southern political bloc prevailed. Douglas relented, included the repeal, divided the territory into two—Kansas west of Missouri and Nebraska west of Iowa and Minnesota—and in May (when Garland was arguing against Dred Scott) argued ferociously for its passage in Congress. Thus, for the first time, all the land of the Louisiana Purchase was opened to slavery. In swift reaction, outraged free-soilers "both in and out of Congress" vilified Douglas, who would later say he "could have traveled to Chicago by the light of his own burning effigies."[62]

Lincoln was one of those who was aghast at this total reversal of a long-held principle of containing slavery. "I was losing interest in politics, when the repeal of the Missouri Compromise aroused me again," he said. Two years earlier, eulogizing Clay, Lincoln had cited Jefferson (his only other political hero), who, alarmed by the enactment of the 1820 law, had predicted that it would prove dangerous to the Union. "A geographical line," Lincoln quoted Jefferson, "co-inciding with a marked principle, moral and political, once conceived, and held up to the angry passions of men, will never be obliterated; and every irritation will mark it deeper and deeper."[63] As Lincoln now argued, this erasure of the 36°30′ line did nothing to obliterate and much to deepen the divisions between slavery and nonslavery states. Already he saw what would become his gospel, quoting Jesus four years later: "A house divided against itself cannot stand."

Lincoln had been evolving his position on slavery for years, and so when the crisis came, he was ready. Indeed, about 1850, on the cusp of this decisive decade, Stuart and Lincoln, while riding home on the circuit, had a conversation about slavery's intensifying impact on all their politics. "Lincoln the time is Coming," Stuart said, "when you & I will have to be Democrats or Abolitionists." "When that time Comes," Lincoln responded, "My mind is fixed—I cant Compromise the Slavery question."[64]

By 1854, the time had come. In July, the abolitionist Cassius Clay, who knew Mary from childhood in Lexington, came to Springfield to denounce the Kansas-Nebraska Act. Refused the forum of the statehouse rotunda, he spoke in Mather's Grove, on the west side of town. He wanted to unite the opponents of Douglas, the "Free Soilers, Whigs, and Democrats." He demanded, "Slavery must be kept a sectional, and liberty, a national institution."[65] Lincoln, stretched out on the grass, whittled a piece of wood throughout the speech, while Mary listened from a wagon nearby.

Other abolitionists came to Illinois to speak. Frederick Douglass appeared in Chicago to address a crowd at Metropolitan Hall on the Kansas-Nebraska bill. Against charges that he was an "intruder" on Senator Douglas's home turf, he defended his "special" right as a black man to speak against the bill: "The people in whose cause I come here tonight are not among those whose right to regulate their own domestic concerns is so feelingly and eloquently contended for in certain quarters. They have no Stephen Arnold Douglas . . . to contend . . . for the Popular Sovereignty. They have no national purse—no offices, no reputation, with which to corrupt Congress, or to tempt men, mighty in eloquence and influence into their service. Oh, no! They have nothing to commend them but their unadorned humanity. They are human—that's all—only human."[66]

Alarmed at the prospect of Democratic election losses, Stephen Douglas had embarked on a campaign to defend himself in his home state. The black Douglass's supporters tried to arrange a debate between their champion and the white Douglas. Not surprisingly, that debate did not take place ("There can never have been much hope that Douglas would share a platform with any black man, let alone this one," his biographer, William S. McFeely, wrote.) However, another one did. On October 3, in Springfield for the opening of the Illinois State Fair, Douglas gave a rousing speech supporting the Kansas-Nebraska Act; while he finished his speech to mounting applause, Lincoln was pacing back and forth in the statehouse lobby. Then, as the crowd dispersed, Lincoln stepped forward and shouted that the next day either he or Lyman Trumbull would respond.[67]

Lincoln had followed Douglas's speeches closely in the papers, eager for a chance to rebut them, and it was he who answered Douglas on October 4. For three hours, dressed in shirtsleeves against the hot and sticky day, Lincoln strove to unify opposition to the Kansas-Nebraska Act by presenting it as a hypocritical betrayal of the nation's founding principles. In so doing, like Frederick Douglass, Lincoln asserted the humanity of black people: "All men are created equal; but now from that beginning we have run down to the other declaration, that for SOME men to enslave OTHERS is 'a sacred right of self-government.' These principles cannot stand together. . . . Let no one be deceived. The spirit of seventy-six and the spirit of Nebraska, are utter antagonisms; and the former is being rapidly displaced by the latter." To preserve the union, he argued, we must regulate slavery and limit its spread in the expectation that it will wither and die. This was what Lincoln believed the founding fathers intended. He did not think slavery could be abolished without destroying the Union, and so where slavery existed, he asserted that it must be left alone.[68]

This was the moderate antislavery position at the time—a free-soil, Unionist position—and abolitionists saw it as a pact with the devil. "Free soilism is lame, halt, and blind," wrote Frederick Douglass in 1855, "while it battles against the spread of slavery, and admits its right to exist anywhere."[69]

For the remainder of the decade, whether speaking as a candidate or stumping for others, Lincoln kept to the same arguments. Slavery was a "monstrous injustice" because it violated the principles of liberty and self-government, inseparable from the right to the fruits of one's own labor. Lincoln knew what it was to be forced to do physical labor for another, which is the position he had felt himself put in by his father. It was not surprising, as Douglass would note, that Lincoln sympathized with slaves, for he himself had come up from being poor and socially marginalized as a child. As Lincoln would put it in 1858, "It is the eternal struggle between . . . two principles—right and wrong—throughout the world. . . . It is the same spirit that says, 'You work and toil and earn bread, and I'll eat it.' No matter in what shape it comes, whether from the mouth of a king who seeks to bestride the people of his own nation and live by the fruit of their labor, or from one race of men as an apology for enslaving another race, it is the same tyrannical principle."[70]

According to Mary's Springfield relatives, in their Illinois days Lincoln read his speeches to Mary before he gave them. He would begin, "Mary, now listen to this," and she would offer comments. "Saying so-and-so would sound better."[71] Growing up hearing her father debate slavery, Mary was no stranger to the issues, making her an informed listener. Her views on slavery, however, differed from her husband's, being more in keeping with her upbringing.

Although she shared Lincoln's view on limiting the spread of slavery, Mary looked at slavery through two mutually reinforcing prisms: her childhood reliance on slaves, and her present difficulty with hired domestics, mostly immigrant Irish women. Her model was the dynamic between mistress and family slave, a model that did not work smoothly with free, white women. Not every "girl," Mary quickly discovered, could be trained to "become as submissive as possible"—her words and her ideal. She sometimes found herself without servants when in a rage she fired them or in a rage they quit. Regarding her current lot "outside the limits of a slave State," she could, as late as 1860, compare her situation to that of some St. Louis cousins who "live in a very handsome house, four stories, plenty of room & some Kentucky *darkies* to wait on them."[72]

Mary's disagreement with her husband about the serving classes put her in growing company in her adopted state. A steep recession in 1854–55 intensified resentment against the latest immigrants, who were seen as competitors for jobs, and made anti-immigration sentiment a pressing issue in the 1856 presidential campaign. (This was the first time a candidate ran from the brand-new Republican Party.) At the time, Mary accurately defended her husband against her family's suspicions that Lincoln's support for the Republican John C. Frémont, the romantic Western explorer, meant they could "include him with so many of those, who belong to *that party*, an *Abolitionist.*" As she wrote to her half-sister Emilie in Kentucky, "All he desires is, that slavery, shall not be extended, let it remain, where it is." Nor was she as radical as her moderate husband. "My weak woman's heart was too Southern in feeling, to sympathise with any but Fillmore [the ex-Whig, former President], I have always been an admirer of his, he made so good a President & is so just a man & feels the *necessity* of keeping foreigners, within bounds. If some of you Kentuckians, had to deal with the 'wild Irish,' as we housekeepers are sometimes called upon to do, the south would certainly elect Fillmore next time."[73] (Fillmore was the candidate of an anti-immigration party that had grown out of Protestant secret societies about 1854 and was called Know-Nothing by its opponents, after what its original members were supposed to say to outsiders who questioned them. It was called the American Party by its members.)

If the Lincolns ever argued these points between themselves, Lincoln may have said to Mary what he told Speed: "Our progress in degeneracy appears to me pretty rapid. As a nation we began by declaring that '*all men are created equal.*' We now practically [in practice] read it 'all men are created equal, *except Negroes.*' When the Know Nothings get control, it will read 'all men are created equal, except Negroes, *and foreigners, and catholics.*' "[74]

To one aspect of Lincoln's views—his support of colonization of freed slaves ("to Liberia,—to their own native land")—we have no evidence of Mary's response. However, her father and Henry Clay had advocated colonization, and she had generally agreed with them. She also agreed with Lincoln (as with her father and Clay) about the inferiority of black people, sharing his distaste of imagining black people as political and social equals. This was a point Lincoln also argued in his Kansas-Nebraska speech, when he said, "My own feelings will not admit of this [equality]; and if mine would, we well know that those of the great mass of white people would not."[75]

Elizabeth Keckly spent the decade before she first became acquainted with Mary Lincoln becoming free in various ways; that is, in addition to buying herself, she learned how to run her own business and handle paying clients and she established herself socially among free black people beyond the limits of her white family's world. In the meantime, Mary Lincoln undertook to learn how to be an employer of free women, some of them former slaves like Lizzy Keckly, but many of them neither black nor formerly enslaved. For Southern women, the confrontations with a "new" serving class almost inevitably mixed issues of class and race. In the mid-1850s, when two teenage Burwell cousins visited New York City for the first time, they were astounded not only by the tumult and noise, but also by the *white* servants: they were used to being served by people who were black.[76]

Mary was more comfortable with black serving women and girls than with the Irish immigrants who worked for her (and African Americans were probably more skilled at adjusting their attitudes to this former slave mistress's expectations). She liked her sister's Aunt Epsy Smith, the former Kentucky slave who had helped out when Robert was an infant; a young girl named Ruth Burns, who worked for the family when they returned from Congress; another girl, Ruth Stanton, who worked for neighbors but helped Mary with housework and cooking; and Mariah Vance, who came in to do laundry twice a week in the 1850s. But free black people were a small percentage of the Springfield population, and like other middle-class housewives, Mary had to turn to the rising population of immigrants. Difficulties were also more likely to erupt when the help lived in: a Portuguese woman who as a girl came in to wash for the Lincolns and later became their cook remembered Mary as very hard to please, but that she pleased her. (One wonders if there was a language barrier that also helped.) By the 1850s, the Lincolns could afford regular live-in help, and the 1850 and 1855 censuses each show a teenage girl living in, while in 1860, after the house had been enlarged, two domestic servants lived with them.[77]

One Irish domestic Mary Lincoln liked was the "Mary" of her 1859 letters. It was she who had "become as submissive as possible," who, in Mary's eyes, was a "faithful servant"—thereby, rhetorically "black." She washed, ironed, baked, and milked the cow, although Lincoln, over his wife's objections, insisted on doing the milking when it was extremely cold. However, another Irish woman, Margaret Ryan, thought Mary "cranky" and "half-crazy" and would have left much sooner had Lincoln not secretly promised to pay her 75 cents more than Mary was offering. Anxious to keep her, Lincoln asked her "not to fuss with Mrs." As Margaret later told Herndon, Mr. Lincoln would put his hand on her head "and tell her to Keep courage." Margaret stayed, but another young serving woman, with whom Lincoln hoped to make a similar arrangement, did not. She threatened to leave unless Mary paid her the going rate of $1.50 a week, 25 cents more than Mary was willing to pay. However, Mary overheard her husband speaking to the "girl" at the back door and, declaring that she would not be deceived, ordered her to leave. Then, turning to her husband, she told him that he should be ashamed of himself.[78]

When Lincoln went back into politics full swing in the fall of 1854, he had his eye on the United States Senate. Unfortunately, some supporters published an announcement of his candidacy for the state legislature in the Whig *Illinois State Journal* (the former *Sangamo Journal*) without his knowledge, at a time when he was out of town. Mary, understanding and backing her husband's intentions to seek a seat in the Senate, ran down to the newspaper office, where she found the editor, Simeon Francis, in whose parlor she and Lincoln had secretly met before their marriage, and demanded that Lincoln's name be withdrawn. Becoming a legislator "after a term in . . . [Congress], looked like a backward movement," according to biographer David Herbert Donald, one neither of them wanted. Moreover, if he were a state legislator, he could not legally be elected to Congress, and he knew that the state legislators were about to replace the incumbent Democrat, James Shields (Lincoln's opponent in the premarriage duel).[79]

Mary's habit of taking matters into her own hands on her husband's behalf has become part of her lore, prompting criticism far more than praise. Yet her assertiveness flowed naturally from her childhood, when she refused to give way before her stepmother or interrupted Henry Clay's dinner to show off her horse and declare her desire to go to the White House.

Mary was adamant, but when Lincoln returned to Springfield, under pressure from his friends he allowed his name to stand in the race for the legislature, persuaded, it seems, that it would strengthen the Whig ticket in the county and state. Mary was not happy; nor indeed was Lincoln, who was pulled in one direction by ambition and his wife, and in the other by loyalty to Party and friends. Lincoln was elected. But having spent the fall making stirring appearances at Whig conventions in Carrollton, Jacksonville, and Bloomington and even more powerful anti-Douglas, anti-Nebraska speeches in Springfield, Peoria, Urbana, and Chicago, he saw his opportunity and began soliciting support for a Senate campaign; finding it, he declined to accept the seat he had just won.

The special legislative vote to replace Shields was scheduled for the end of January, leaving Lincoln time to navigate through the complicated new political scene of shifting affiliations and parties: the "unpredictable array of Know-Nothings, Anti-Nebraska Democrats, Free-Soilers, temperance advocates, as well as Whigs and Democrats" sitting in the legislature, as one historian put it. In the weeks before the vote, he bought a stack of small notebooks, labeled all the legislators by party, and calculated his chances. He thought they were good, although "what mines, and pitfalls" his opponents "had under" him he did not know, and he was unsure how it all would go.[80]

In the meantime, Mary readied herself for what she was sure would be her husband's victory. As usual, she turned to contemplating what a Senator's wife should look like and spent the weeks before the election sewing, perhaps putting finishing touches on the dress she planned to wear, with her new gloves, to the postelection celebration party to be given by Elizabeth and Ninian in their honor. Then a freezing snowstorm, which shut down the railroads, pushed the election back one week and drew out the suspense. With time on his hands, Lincoln trudged down to John Williams's store and brought home a pair of overshoes, two shawls, and some hair combs for his wife.

When the day of the vote finally came, Mary was watching from the gallery beside Elizabeth and the sprightly Emilie, who was visiting from Lexington. The initial ballot went as Lincoln had expected: he led with forty-five votes against forty-one for Shields and five for Lyman Trumbull, Julia's husband, who was the candidate of antislavery Democrats. Fifty votes were needed for election, so another, then another ballot was cast. By the ninth ballot, Lincoln's support had dwindled and Trumbull's had risen. More important, both were trailing behind the Democrats, who, by prearrangement, had switched their votes to the popular Democratic Governor Joel Matteson. Seeing Matteson on the verge of winning, Lincoln gave his votes to his circuit friend Trumbull, who, as a result, won. "The agony is over at last," wrote

Lincoln, one day after the vote. He was regretful, but not depressed. "On the whole, perhaps it is as well for our general cause that Trumbull was elected." To another friend he confided, "It was rather hard . . . and a less good humored man than I, perhaps, would not have consented to it."[81]

Mary, however, was furious, and when Mary was thwarted, someone had to pay. Her nearest target was her friend and former bridesmaid, Julia Jayne Trumbull. Mary abruptly stopped speaking to her, meting to her the same fate as the childhood friend who declared that Jackson was handsomer than Clay and her father "rolled into one." Indeed, Mary refused even to acknowledge Julia when, two years later, they met outside of church. "I took some pains to meet Mary," Julia wrote Lyman at the time, "but she turned her head the other way and though I looked her full in the face she pretended not to see me." Thereafter, Mary deemed Julia beneath notice and, projecting her feelings on everyone else, assumed that all of Springfield agreed with her. "'Tis unfortunate, to be so unpopular," she wrote of Julia. Yet even her family continued socializing with Julia, and Lincoln accepted at least one invitation to tea at the Trumbull home that Mary turned down, claiming to be unwell. "I am sorry Mrs. Lincoln was too *unwell* to attend your party," Lyman wrote to Julia from Willard's in Washington.[82]

Mary's behavior embarrassed Lincoln, who tried to make up for her rudeness by being particularly gracious to its target. A week before Mary snubbed Julia at church, Lincoln and Stuart spotted her on a Springfield-bound train. "I met Mr. L's eye," Julia described the scene to Lyman, "& he started up & came down the aisle to shake hands. 'Why how do you do?' You know his lungs are strong—but he elevated his voice a little as he called out 'Stuart, here, do you know this lady?' " Then Lincoln switched to the seat beside her "& kept it," until they arrived at the station, where he "jumped up" to find her father, who was waiting for her at the depot.[83]

It was at about this time that Lincoln bought Mary a copy of a book called *The Elements of Character* by Mary G. Chandler. One of many of its kind, a popular Victorian genre, it was a guide to building "the wisely trained character," written in the common self-help blend of psychological and moral language. Evidently, Lincoln meant to give Mary something useful, for the book showed how to marshal a "determined will . . . [to overcome] the defects of the mind," one of the most prominent being a "hasty temper."[84]

*E*lizabeth Keckly in a photograph taken in the 1860s.
Credit: Ostendorf Collection.

*T*he Reverend Robert A. Burwell,
Lizzy's Hillsborough master.
Credit: Historic Hillsborough Commission.

*M*rs. Margaret Anna Burwell,
Lizzy's Hillsborough mistress.
Credit: Historic Hillsborough Commission.

*L*etter written by Lizzy Hobbs to Fanny Burwell
in 1842 after Lizzy moved back to Virginia.
Credit: Swem Library, The College of William and Mary.

*T*he earliest known
photographs of the young
Mr. and Mrs. Lincoln,
taken in Springfield
in 1846, the year Lincoln
was elected to Congress.
Credit: The Library of Congress.

*M*ary with her sons Willie
and Tad in Springfield, in a
photograph taken shortly after
Lincoln's election in 1860.
Credit: Courtesy of the Illinois State
Historical Library.

*R*obert Lincoln, the Lincolns' oldest son,
at the time of his marriage in 1868.
Credit: Courtesy of the Illinois State
Historical Library, Springfield.

*S*tephen A. Douglas, onetime suitor of the
young Mary Todd and Lincoln's Illinois
political rival, in a portrait by Mathew Brady.
Credit: The Library of Congress.

*H*ugh A. Garland, Lizzy's last master, in St. Louis in 1853, when he was the lead lawyer for the defense against Dred Scott's suit for freedom.
Credit: Missouri Historical Society, St. Louis.

*T*he Reverend Henry Highland Garnet, Lizzy's minister at the exclusive Fifteenth Street Presbyterian Church in Washington, circa 1881.
Credit: National Portrait Gallery, Smithsonian Institution.

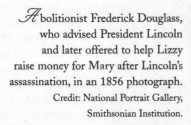

*A*bolitionist Frederick Douglass, who advised President Lincoln and later offered to help Lizzy raise money for Mary after Lincoln's assassination, in an 1856 photograph.
Credit: National Portrait Gallery, Smithsonian Institution.

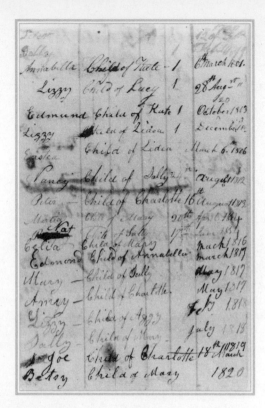

*P*age from the Burwell commonplace book listing slave births. The birth of Elizabeth Hobbs ("Lizzy") is recorded fourth from bottom in Mary Burwell's handwriting.
Credit: The Virginia Historical Society, Richmond.

Mrs. LINCOLN'S WARDROBE ON EXHIBITION IN NEW YORK.—Sketched by Stanley Fox.—[See Page 686.]

*M*ary Lincoln's wardrobe on display at W. H. Brady's in New York City was the subject of this *Harper's Weekly* illustration in 1867.
Credit: The Library of Congress.

List of Free Negroes, Licensed by the County Court of St. Louis County.

NAMES.	AGE.	HEIGHT. FT.	HEIGHT. IN.	OCCUPATION.	DATE OF LICENSE.
Johnson, Mary	48	5		Washer,	May 1843.
Jones, Paul	65	5	½	Waiter,	"
Jones, John	21	5	11	Steward,	June 1843.
Jones, Wm.	25	5	5	"	"
Johnson, Chas.	44	5	6	Cooper,	"
Jamison, Patrick	39	5	4½	Cook,	September, 1845.
Jones, Patsey	4		9	Washer,	Dec. 1846.
Jefferson, Letitia	43	4	11½	"	"
Jamison, Lewis	24	5	6½	Boat Hand,	"
Johnson, Geo. W.	31	5	10	Minister,	"
January, Mary	35	5	5	Washer,	"
Johnson, Harriet	21	4	11	"	"
Jackson, Ann M.	26	5	3½	"	"
Jones, Lewis	32	5	11	Drayman,	"
Johns, Henry	25	5	6	Steward,	"
Jackson, Eddy	36	5	3	Washer,	"
Jackson, Margaret	28	5	2½	"	"
Jesse,	33	5	4½	Drayman,	"
Jackson, Sally	27	5	2	Washer,	"
Jackson, Ann	27	5	3	Washer,	Dec. 1846.
Johnson, Horatio, Jas.		5	5½	Boat hand,	Feb'y. 1846.
John,	27	5	2	"	March 1847.
Jones, Julia	30	5	2½	Washer,	May, 1847.
Jenkins, Henry	49	5	6	Cook,	June 1847.
Jack, alias John Johnson	30	5	7	Drayman,	Feb'y. 1848.
Julia	20	5	7½	Housekeeper,	June 1848.
Johnson, Mary Ann	20	5	2	Washer,	Aug. 1849.
Johnson, Nicodemus	52	5	11	Servant,	June 1850.
Jones, Thos.	22	5	7½	Boat hand,	Aug. 1850.
Jackson, Chas.	37	5	10½	Steward,	"
Johnson, Isaac	27	5	10½	"	"
Isam, Jas.	25	5	8	Porter,	Dec. 1851.
Jamison, Leah	46	5	½	Washer,	June 1852.
Johnson, Isam	24	5	4½	Drayman,	Aug. 1852.
Jefferson, Alexander	40	5	5½	Steward,	Jan'y. 1853.
Johnson, Abram	21	5	5½	Barber,	March 1853.
Jackson, Fulton	42	5	6	White Washer,	Sept. 1853.
Jackson, Letty	32	5	1	Washer,	"
Jaynee, Parthenia	27	4	11	"	May 1854.
Jennings Benj.	22	5	8	Cabin Boy	Feby 1855
Jamison Stephen	27	5	7	Cook	Nine "
Jackson John	35	5	10	Laborer	"
Johnson Amanda	42	5	2	Washer	May "
Ferguson Rudolph	50	5	8	S.B. hand	Oct "
Johnson Betsy	50	5	4½	Servant	Jany 1856
Josephine	16	5	3	"	Mar "
Johnson Robert	36	5	10½	Cook	May "
Johnson Cynthia	23	5	11	Washer	June 1856
Johnson Jackson	30	5	7	Porter	Oct "
Johnson Jordan				Licensed as Cooper	May 47 "
Johnson Jennette				"	Nov 57 "
Jacobs Franklin	24	5	5	S.B. hand	Nov 1857
Keziah,	50	5	3	Chambermaid,	Sept. 1842.
Kennedy, Alexander	18	5	8	Boat hand,	May 1843.
Kerr, Sarah	24	5	5	Washer,	Feb'y. 1847.
Kayle, Letitia	33	5	3 1-2	"	May "
Kerr, Harriet	36	5	1	Chambermaid,	August 1853.
Kerr, William	44	5	4	Tinner,	"
Keane, Ann	21	5	2 1-2	Washer,	Dec. 1853.
Keith, Catherine		5	2	"	Dec. 1846.
Kennedy Mary F.	23	5	8	Vegetable Dealer	Feby 1858
Kibbut Geo W.	29	5	10½	Drayman	Nov "
Keckley Lizzie	39	5	2	Mantua Maker	May 1859

A page from the List of Free Negroes, licensed by the
county court of St. Louis County, with "Lizzie Keckley"
added to the bottom of the K's in 1859.

Credit: Missouri Historical Society, St. Louis.

$\mathcal{P}$resident Lincoln in a portrait taken by Mathew Brady, probably in 1863. Credit: The Library of Congress.

" $\mathcal{M}$rs. President" in a formal portrait taken by Mathew Brady in 1861. Credit: The Ostendorf Collection.

It was just the kind of book such a man as Lincoln might choose. He had, in a sense, studied his way out of a young manhood beset by periods of profound inner struggles against ungovernable moods. He still had to will himself out of depressions; indeed, his famous reliance on stories and anecdotes was a way to lift his moods. Then, too, his political doctrine of self-government fit naturally with ideas about self-government in character. His own experiences would lead him to such a book were he reaching a critical point in his feelings about his younger, seemingly unruly wife. However, the book's marked passages are, it is thought, all Lincoln's, and there is no indication that Mary, who understandably preferred novels anyway, ever read it.

In the late 1850s, Lincoln's increasing wealth and legal and political prominence gave Mary an expanding social circle that was no longer dependent on her older sister. She felt that she was coming into her own. She added an entire floor to the house, creating two parlors downstairs, where she could entertain on a grand scale. During the 1857 winter season, she invited five hundred people (she claimed) to a party, "yet owing to an *unlucky* rain . . . and the same evening" a wedding party in Jacksonville, "300 only favored us by their presence." Proudly could she report to Emilie, "You will think, we have enlarged *our borders*, since you were here."[85]

As her "borders" grew, so did her vanity, and her behavior became outsized as well. It was not just that she was imperiously cutting off whoever she believed crossed her. Reports of papers and books flying out the front door, of Lincoln's spending nights at the office or with friends, of his bandaged nose, of wild chases in the yard and street attest to increasingly violent tirades against her husband. Indeed, it was in the late 1850s that Mary was reportedly seen running after Lincoln in the street, waving a knife in her hand. When he realized that they "had been or would be discovered," Lincoln turned, grabbed Mary, and "hustled" her back toward the house. "There d—mn it," he said, "now Stay in the house and don't disgrace us in the Eyes of the world."[86] Little could have mattered more to the rising politician than his reputation, and the gentle hints in his letters from Congress years earlier would not suffice to modify his wife's behavior.

Half a dozen years later, right after Lincoln's assassination, at a time when Springfield might have sympathized, a visitor could not hear a kind word about Mary Lincoln. "I have not heard one person speak well of Mrs. Lincoln since I came here," wrote Sarah Sleeper in a letter home. Mary's vanity, arrogance, and temper appalled people. Even sympathetic Elizabeth knew she "made the world hate her," for though "Mary has had much to bear . . . she don't bear it well." In Springfield, where comparing Mary and Abraham Lincoln was a parlor game, his popularity made her *un*popularity more pronounced.[87] After snubbing so many, she had few friends to defend her.

But dislike of Mary must be seen in the context of her persistent violation of cultural expectations for women. *Godey's Lady's Book* was one of innumerable nineteenth-century journals and books to advise that a wife's proper sphere, "the seat of her dominion," was her home, not beyond. "Much to be deplored is any circumstance which draws a woman from this sacred sphere. I care not whether it be fashion or fanaticism, pleasure or politics." (Thus *Godey's* equated politics with fanaticism.) Mary was nobody's model of womanhood, despite her acknowledged domesticity—she was not quiet, she was not modest, and she was not meek. She could not take what *Godey's* praised as the "cheering view of female influence": the submerging of her triumphs in her husband's.[88] She wanted the perks, power, and adulation of triumphing herself—the "glitter Show & pomp & power," as Elizabeth put it.

But it would be equally a mistake to consider her an early feminist. Mary did not consciously seek autonomous power in nondomestic roles, and her trespasses into male domains were the work of impulse, not principle. Women's rights did not interest her and, like other Southern women, she probably associated feminism with abolitionism. (The women's rights movement began in the North, among women who were often also antislavery activists; the first woman's rights convention was held in 1848 at Seneca Falls, New York.) Moreover, unlike political activists, Mary's concerns were never universal. She was interested in her personal rights, and she narcissistically saw her husband's advancement as her own—"our advancement," she termed their going to the White House.[89]

CHAPTER EIGHT

*I*n October 1860, Elizabeth Keckly was examining lace at the Harper & Mitchell trimming shop in Washington, D.C. She had arrived in Washington the spring before with no money, but after a brief search, she found work as a seamstress for $2.50 a day. This was 50 cents more per day than a streetcar driver and 50 cents less per day than a government clerk, and it made it possible for her to find a place to stay. However, she could not afford the fee for the license required of all free blacks who wished to remain in the city. According to law, within thirty days of arrival, females over fourteen and males over sixteen needed to give evidence of "their title of freedom" and present letters to the mayor vouching for their "good and orderly conduct." Ever resourceful, Lizzy approached one of her new clients, Miss Ringold of Virginia, who knew Mayor James G. Berret. At Miss Ringold's request, the mayor granted Elizabeth Keckly a license free of charge.[1]

Lizzy always knew how to use her connections—it was one of her crucial survival skills. Now here she was, a free woman in Washington, with the shop owner Mr. Harper waiting on her himself. He was "polite and kind," she remembered; more important, he would give her $25 commission on her purchase. She had with her $100 and unequivocal directions from the husband of her latest client (another Miss Ringold connection) "to spare no expense" on trimmings for the dress his wife was to wear to a much-anticipated private dinner party for the nineteen-year-old Prince of Wales.[2]

Keckly's employers were as close to American royalty as one could be: the fifty-three-year-old Virginia cavalry officer Colonel Robert E. Lee was the son of a Revolutionary war hero and post-Revolution Virginia governor, and his wife, Mary Anne Randolph Custis Lee, was a great-granddaughter of Martha Custis Washington. Naturally, they were among those invited to dine privately with the Prince, while the hoi polloi would have to be satisfied with catching a glimpse at a White House public reception. The future King Edward VII, who was the first heir to the British throne to visit the former colonies, was staying three nights in the White House, going about town disguised as "Lord Renfrew."[3]

The Prince's masquerade fooled no one, not even the girls at Madame Smith's exclusive French school, a stop on his itinerary, who were warned not to address their guest (who joined them in a game of tenpins) as "Your Royal Highness." Nor was anyone fooled by the put-on gaiety of the dinner parties and ball in "Lord Renfrew's" honor. The atmosphere in Washington, a town of mostly Southerners, was one of unbearable tension. If the antislavery Republican, Abraham Lincoln, was elected President next month, the Southern states were going to secede. It would not be a question of "if," but of "how soon" and "how many."[4]

For 150 years, white Americans had looked on violence against black people as an acceptable price for slavery. But in the five years leading up to 1860, white citizens turned violently on each other. In the spring of 1856, antislavery Republicans and proslavery Democrats in Congress were introducing bills to admit Kansas as a state when guerrilla warfare broke out in Kansas between free-soil and proslavery settlers. "Bleeding Kansas" hardened sectional hatred between Northerners and Southerners as nothing had before. In May, the tireless abolitionist Senator Charles Sumner rose up in Congress to deliver a scathing speech on "The Crime Against Kansas," which he called a "rape of a virgin territory, compelling it to the hateful embrace of slavery," committed by "murderous robbers from Missouri, hirelings picked from the drunken spew and vomit of an uneasy civilization." Two days later he was writing letters at his desk in a nearly empty Senate chamber when the young Congressman Preston Brooks of South Carolina, enraged by what he considered the Northerner's libel on his state and his relatives, whom the Massachusetts senator had singled out for attack in his speech, approached with a heavy, gold-headed cane and began beating him over the head. The powerful Sumner, blinded by his own blood, his legs pinioned under the bolted-down desk, finally wrenched the desk from the floor as Brooks kept beating him, more than thirty blows in under a minute, until the cane shivered to splinters and Sumner collapsed.[5]

Brooks instantly became a hero in the South, honored with dinners and rewarded with gold-headed canes. "The truth is [Abolitionists] have been suffered to run too long without their collars. They must be lashed into submission," declared the *Richmond Enquirer*. In the North, however, the attack symbolized the rapacity of Southern slavery. "Are we too, slaves, slaves for life, a target for their blows, when we do not comport ourselves to please them?" asked the free-soil editor and poet William Cullen Bryant. It was not long before "Bleeding Sumner" and "Bleeding Kansas" inspired a fiery-eyed abolitionist named John Brown, who had joined the settlers in Kansas, to enlist four of his sons and three other men to seize five proslavery settlers from their cabins one night and "coolly split open their skulls with broadswords."[6]

In the meantime, the 1856 presidential campaign reached a new level of rhetorical violence. This election, in which the Republicans ran a candidate for the first time, was a foreshadowing of the 1860 race. The new Republican Party was identified with Northern interests, and the Democratic Party was the party of the South. (When the first issue of the *Springfield Republican* arrived at the Lincoln's home in the February following the election, Mary canceled the subscription to what she called "another useless little paper.") With this sectional alignment, the arguments about slavery, race, and, above all, *Union*, had reached a critical level of danger. Southern Democrats charged that Northern Republicans intended to trample their right to ownership of their slaves and elevate the black race to equality with whites. The more radical Southerners threatened to secede if Republican John C. Frémont was elected. Defensively, Northerners countered that Southern secession was the real threat to the Union; moreover, black equality, they said, was never their goal, even if limiting the spread of slavery was. In the end, the race-baiting rhetoric and threats of secession persuaded conservative ex-Whigs to preserve the Union by helping the lackluster Pennsylvania Democrat James Buchanan into the White House.[7]

Then Dred Scott, the St. Louis slave whose lawsuit for freedom had occupied the last years of Hugh Garland's life, became a national symbol. In the 1856–57 U.S. Supreme Court session, new lawyers on both sides stood before the nine justices, a majority of whom were Southerners and Democrats. These included the frail, eighty-year-old widower, Chief Justice Roger B. Taney of Maryland. Taney's passionate, broad opinion, which he read in a quavering voice in March 1857, was essentially a defense of his beloved South in its determination to push back Dred Scott's claims to less than nothing. Not only was Scott a slave, but in fact *no* black person could be a U.S. citizen with rights that anyone was bound to respect, which meant that Scott had no right to bring his lawsuit in the first place. Then Taney reached even further beyond the case to rule on the question of slavery in the territories. For as to the claim that living in free territory made Scott free, Congress had no right to prohibit slavery in a territory. In short, the Missouri Compromise was unconstitutional. (After losing their suit before the Supreme Court in March 1857, the Scotts were bought and freed by one of the Blows, their original owners, in May 1858, and were registered as "free Negroes" on the same St. Louis licensing list as Lizzy Keckly. Their listing reads: *Harriet Scott, age forty, five feet four inches, washer, and Dred Scott, age fifty, five feet four inches, steward.* Dred Scott died the following September.)[8]

In 1857, Lizzy Keckly was thirty-nine years old. Nearly thirty-eight of those years had been spent in slavery. She was living in St. Louis, using the tentative freedom she had bought herself to build a dressmaking business. Her expectations of her hard-earned liberty were the minimal human rights of being allowed to keep her own wages and to move at will. Nevertheless, in the current climate, she came to believe that her best future lay north. All that kept her in St. Louis was her goal to pay back her loans. Her mother had died suddenly in March in Vicksburg, where Mrs. Burwell had taken her when she moved into Armistead Jr.'s home. "I need not say what a loss she is, as counsellor & friend," wrote young Fanny Garland to her aunt.[9] Fanny, Anne's daughter, was the fourth generation of Burwells that Aggy had served.

With her mother's faraway death another severed tie, Lizzy began looking beyond St. Louis. James, her husband, was little more than a burden, one she would eventually slough off. As for her son, who was working and turning over to his mother more than $100 a year out of his wages, she had high hopes for him. She enrolled him in Wilberforce University in Ohio, a new, select black school, founded in 1856 and sponsored and run by white members of the Methodist Episcopal Church. Before being taken over by the African Methodist Episcopal Church in 1863, Wilberforce was especially popular with the mixed-race children of Southern planters.[10]

At the same time, in nearby Springfield, Mary Lincoln was in alternating states of elation and recovery from various exertions connected to her husband's growing fame and influence. There was a trip East with him, with sightseeing at Niagara Falls, New York, "& other points of interest"; there were regular strawberry picnics and "fetes" and dinner parties and teas at her newly enlarged home.[11] She relished her role as social and political host, one she had been raised to fill.

No one, least of all Mary, would have argued that her husband's *upbringing* had foretold his current station. Yet it was Lincoln's identification with the oppressed that magnetized his fervent, eloquent responses to the Dred Scott case and attracted national attention. His reaction to this watershed case helped raise him above the local horizon, setting him on course to becoming one of the brightest Republican stars.

With the Dred Scott ruling, Southerners were thrilled by what they saw to be the Court's vindication of their way of life; moreover, they gleefully declared, the decision "crushes the life out of that miserable . . . Black Republican organization." But, if anything, it galvanized the Republican Party. As Lincoln told Illinois Republicans in 1858, such a ruling set a dangerous precedent, for "then [by] the next Dred Scott decision" the Supreme Court could "decide that no State under the Constitution can exclude [slavery], just as they have already decided that . . . neither Congress nor the Territorial Legislature can do it." Soon, "we shall *lie down* pleasantly dreaming that the people of *Missouri* are on the verge of making their State *free*; and we shall *awake* to the *reality*, instead, that the *Supreme* Court has made *Illinois* a *slave* state." Extending slavery would destroy the Union: " 'A house divided against itself cannot stand.' I believe this government cannot endure, permanently half *slave* and half *free.*" Democrat politicians, who claimed not to care about whether slavery was extended as long as settlers could vote on it fairly, were endangering the Union. It mattered that Republicans were elected, for it was they who "consider slavery a moral, social, and political wrong," who "will oppose . . . the modern Democratic idea that slavery is as good as freedom, and ought to have room for expansion all over the continent."[12] They alone would save the house from destruction.

Lincoln's increasingly urgent tones found answer in the stirred-up feelings of the thousands of ordinary people who turned out (and stood or sat for hours in open fields) to hear him debate against the primary target of his anti-Democratic remarks, his long-standing rival Stephen A. Douglas. From late summer through fall, the men met one another in seven debates in seven prairie towns, part of their 1858 campaigns for the U.S. Senate and the culmination of their long-standing opposition. Mary stayed in Springfield for all but the last debate, which was held in nearby Alton and to which she took a train with her husband and fifteen-year-old Robert.

By then, nothing mattered in American politics as much as slavery; indeed, the "sole topic [of the debates] was slavery." And when they were over, and the debates had been printed in the newspapers, Douglas (in the words of historian James M. McPherson) "confirmed his standing as a leader of his party in the North and its strongest presidential candidate for the next presidential nomination," and the previously local Lincoln was suddenly a "Republican spokesman of national stature." Two years later, Lincoln stood before a large audience in New York's Cooper Institute delivering a memorable address; from there he went to New England, where he gave eleven more speeches.[13]

African Americans knew what was at stake for them in the contest between Republicans and Democrats. For those still enslaved, the Republican Party, although not abolitionist, was their one hope; for free blacks, there was no question that the Democrats were their greater enemy. Democrats had placed antiblack racism at the center of their campaign against the "Black Republicans" (as they called them) to keep nonslaveholding Southern whites in line. In the Illinois debates, Douglas had used the crudest form of race baiting to arouse his target audience: voting white men. He had seen "the negro" Frederick Douglass at Freeport, "reclin[ing]" with a white woman inside a carriage, while her daughter and husband rode outside. This man Douglass, the Little Giant told his listeners, was one of the "colored brethren" working for the "success of their brother Abe." At the time, Douglass was the most prominent black man in the United States, famous for two versions of his autobiography, his abolitionist newspaper, and his extensive speaking tours. Now, "if you, Black Republicans, think that the negro ought to be on a social equality with your wives and daughters, and ride in a carriage with your wife, whilst you drive the team, you have a perfect right to do so." In response, Lincoln strove to placate his white auditors with assurances that racial equality was not a Republican goal: "I will say then that I am not, nor ever have been in favor of bringing about in any way the social and political equality of the white and black races. . . . I do not understand that because I do not want a negro woman for a slave I must necessarily want her for a wife. My understanding is that I can just let her alone."[14]

Not surprisingly, it was easy for Frederick Douglass to loathe the Democrats, but he was ambivalent about a Republican Party that, as he put it, "was more opposed to slavery as a *political power* than to slavery itself" and that had no interest in racial equality. (Moreover, social equality was no abstract question for the forty-year-old Douglass. Husband to a black woman who had helped him escape slavery and had his four children, he was now intimately involved with a white German journalist named Ottilie Assing and would, at sixty-six, after his first wife died, marry a white woman.) Yet he admitted that the Party "carries with it the antislavery sentiment of the North, and that a victory gained by it . . . will be a victory gained . . . over . . . pro-slavery" forces. "He that is not against us," he wrote after the Dred Scott decision, "is on our part."[15]

The 1860 presidential election pitted the moderate Republican Abraham Lincoln against a Democratic Party so divided that it had yielded three presidential candidates on three opposition tickets: Illinois's Stephen Douglas, Kentucky's John Breckinridge, the current vice president, and wealthy Tennessee slaveholder John Bell. Southerners, doomed to splitting their votes, saw that if Lincoln took the North, he would be President. For Washington society, victory for the Republicans meant the end of Washington as they knew it. Even if the Union split up peacefully, Washington, wedged near the boundary between North and South, would never remain the capital and, without government business, would sink into insignificance. And if there was war, as more and more people believed there must be, the city would become a battlefield. In a famous campaign speech of 1858, the New York Republican William H. Seward had declared North and South to be on a collision course toward "an irrepressible conflict."[16] Many now, invoking Seward's phrase, believed the time had come.

Warnings of dire consequences should Lincoln win rose up throughout the South. From Georgia came the apocalyptic prophecy: "Let the consequences be what they may—whether the Potomac is crimsoned in human gore, and Pennsylvania Avenue is paved ten fathoms deep with mangled bodies . . . the South will never submit to such humiliation and degradation as the inauguration of Abraham Lincoln." From Mary Lincoln's Kentucky, a crucial border state, came a similarly dire, though toned-down message delivered by Senator John J. Crittenden, once heir to Clay's unionism: "[The South] has come to the conclusion that in case Lincoln should be elected . . . she could not submit to the consequences, and therefore, to avoid her fate, will secede from the Union."[17]

Southern unionism stood little chance. Abolitionism had found its martyr the year before in the stark figure of Kansas fighter John Brown, whose mad plan to seize the U.S. Arsenal at Harpers Ferry, Virginia, and to arm the slaves he expected to join him in a mass revolt had ended with his hanging and virtual canonization in the North. Henry David Thoreau called Brown "a crucified hero"; for Ralph Waldo Emerson, Brown had made the "gallows as glorious as the cross."[18] Outraged, the South saw Northern John Browns everywhere.

Lizzy's Washington employer, Colonel Lee, was one of two U.S. cavalry officers, the other being Lieutenant J. E. B. Stuart, who had been sent to Harpers Ferry to capture John Brown. It was another example of Lizzy's knack for being connected to the principal people and events of the day. With her St. Louis recommendations, she had found most of her work with the Southern women who formed the central web of Washington society. Commissions had trickled in over the hot, parched summer of 1860, but the dress she made in October for Colonel Lee's wife was such a success that her business grew steadily thereafter. Close friends Mrs. Mathilda Emory of Texas, Mrs. Margaretta Hetzel of Virginia, and Mrs. Varina Davis of Mississippi were devoted to her. More than clients, these ladies were her "patrons," as Lizzy always called them; they helped her to navigate the Washington bureaucracy, gave her credit with its shopkeepers, and, above all, introduced her to their friends.

It was Margaretta Hetzel who recommended Lizzy to Varina Davis, her neighbor on I Street, whose husband, Jefferson, was one of the South's largest slaveholders and a prominent senator. Sharp-tongued Varina had been a leading light in Washington society since Zachary Taylor's administration.[19]

As a slave, Lizzy had negotiated the mulatto house slave's double life, moving between the white world in the Big House and the black world in the slave quarters. Freedom allowed her to pry loose to some degree the one world from the other, to create a space between her black and white worlds. In other words, she had privacy, something she could only dream of when she was a slave. True, she could not elude the experience that W. E. B. Du Bois would call the black American's "double-consciousness, this sense of always looking at oneself through the eyes of others, of measuring one's soul by the tape of a world that looks on in amused contempt and pity."[20] But she could distance herself from the white world, and reflect back on it.

Lizzy's life in Washington was divided between a well-to-do white world and her black middle-class community. Although it seems she sewed exclusively for white women, she also established herself in the tight-knit, hardworking black community. For years she boarded with the family of Walker Lewis, who was a messenger then a steward in the government. Lewis had bought himself from slavery and now lived with his wife, Virginia, a seamstress, and their five children at 388 Twelfth Street, a brick row house just north of K Street, the unmarked boundary that separated the white core from the black neighborhoods. (The house is still there, now number 1017 Twelfth Street.) The poorest blacks lived in wooden houses in hidden alleyways behind the street houses, quite separated from the white population. At least one census taker looked at the Lewis family and listed them as "white," an ironic comment on designations of race and on the disappearing line between the races. (Virginia Lewis, the daughter of a slave father and a free black woman, apparently was fair-skinned.) The free black community Lizzy found in Washington was the largest, most established she had yet seen. According to the 1860 census, of the just over 60,000 inhabitants in Washington, nearly 20 percent were free blacks and only 4 percent were slaves. They were also the best educated: of the 11,000 free black inhabitants, over 42 percent were literate and some 1,100 black children were enrolled in private schools (no public schools for black children yet existed).[21]

In this city, where she had never been enslaved, Lizzy discovered new ways of expressing her freedom. No longer pressured by Burwell and Garland preferences, she joined the Union Bethel Church, part of the African Methodist

Episcopal Church, which was founded in Philadelphia in 1816 to give black people a place to worship away from whites and without being relegated to the galleries. (It was only after Lincoln's death that she became a member of the elitist Fifteenth Street Presbyterian Church.) Like all black institutions, black churches had to work around oppressive city laws, which controlled their operations. One such stricture was the 10 o'clock nightly curfew, which grounded the entire "colored population" of Washington, except for anyone driving a cart, wagon, or carriage. This code interfered with nighttime meetings at the church, so in 1838 Union Bethel members set about raising money to buy a lot on M Street for a meetinghouse in the western part of the city, where many of its members lived.

Historically, black churches have played a central role in the struggle for education and equality, its members organizing and funding causes to promote the advancement of the race. Union Bethel ran a school, and ladies of the church organized concerts and festivals to raise money for black institutions and relief organizations. Yet black churches also functioned as monitors of social respectability, which was a way to counter images of black inferiority. Union Bethel board members saw it as their solemn duty to chastise members who, for example, used "offensive language," wore rings on their fingers, or missed meetings. They preferred to punish their brothers and sisters with stern lectures, but in egregious cases resorted to suspension. Lizzy's measured behavior, her careful modes of address and dress can be seen as products of this same philosophy. Conspicuous displays of the three "C's"—character, culture, and cash—would not merely separate upper-class from lower-class blacks, but in the larger white society were crucial acts of racial self-assertion. Good conduct, good manners, and good dress told that other world that you were its equal, a message not lost on white observers. "The finest and most fashionably dressed women I find to be Negroes," wrote one surprised Illinois lady visiting the capital. "I rather think they imagine themselves the better class here."[22]

Attuned to racial ironies, Elizabeth Keckly must have felt all of the strangeness of awaiting the election results from her dual position straddling both worlds. She no doubt shared her community's eagerness for a Republican victory, but, in the presence of her white Southern patrons, she knew to express sympathy, if only by a discreet silence, with their nervous dread. It was not safe to wear one's pro-Republican heart on one's sleeve. In October, hecklers attacked a few brave black supporters who followed a parade of the Republican Association with cries of "Damn Niggers! They oughtn't to be allowed on the streets." Already, Lizzy had her eye on sewing for the next inhabitants of the White House—whoever they might be—and she would not have jeopardized her success by being open about her political views. She most certainly would have held her tongue after Lincoln won the election in November, for her most important patron, Varina Davis, announced that "she would not associate with Republicans" any longer. True, Lincoln had won with less than 40 percent of the national popular vote, but he had swept the free states—an ominous sign for the future of the Union. However, according to Varina's austere husband in a letter to a Boston editor in January, written one week after his state of Mississippi seceded, it was not "the Election" that "was . . . the Cause" of secession, "it was but the last feather which you know breaks the Camel's back."[23]

Back in Springfield in November Lincoln had awaited the election returns in the telegraph office. He stayed until about 2 o'clock in the morning, when the New York returns came over the wires and he knew his victory was certain. When in May he had received the telegram from the Republican convention in Chicago, telling him he had won the nomination, he excused himself from the celebrations by announcing, "There is a little woman at our house who is probably more interested in this dispatch than I am," and went home to tell Mary. This time Mary knew the results when she heard musicians coming to serenade the winner. Feeling the weight of the responsibility on him, Lincoln did not sleep that night; not many days later, stretched on a lounge in his office chamber, he saw his image reflected in the mirror with two faces, one much paler than the other. Unsettled, he told Mary what he saw, and she read his vision as a "sign" that he would be elected twice, but not live out his second term. Mary, who was no stranger to frightful visions of her own, would make it one of her self-appointed tasks in Washington to distract her husband with carriage rides and social occasions to relieve his characteristic gloom.[24]

The Jefferson Davises left Washington for the South at the end of January, after Mississippi's secession and Davis's emotional farewell to the Senate. "I am sure I feel no hostility to you, Senators from the North," he said. "I am sure there is not one of you, whatever sharp discussion there may have been between us, to whom I cannot now say, in the presence of my God, I wish you well."[25]

Until their departure, Lizzy sewed every afternoon in their home, coming at noon after a morning's work elsewhere, because the Davis family liked to sleep late. During the months she spent working for the Davises, the household was filled with intense conversation about the crisis. Southern "politicians and statesmen" met there at night, talking long into the morning hours. Lizzy, eager to pick up whatever news she could, heard about these meetings from the live-in servants. Often, the Davises and their friends talked over "the prospects of war" in her presence, as if she were not there.[26] That servants were invisible, nonentities, was a convenient illusion relied on in many households.

Lizzy was employed primarily making clothes for Mrs. Davis and the children; though she seems to have sewn mostly by hand, she may have used Varina's sewing machine. However, for Christmas, Varina wanted to surprise her husband with a hand-sewn silk dressing gown. Lizzy was working on it late Christmas Eve when the Senator, worn-out and nervous, came upon her suddenly. Leaning against the door, he said, "That you, Lizzie! Why are you so late? Still at work; I hope that Mrs. Davis is not too taxing." Lizzy said no, but that she had promised to finish this gown that night. "Well, well," he answered, "the case must be urgent." Peering at it with his bad eyes in the gaslight, he knew it was for him, but according to Lizzy he was too thoughtful to spoil his wife's surprise. It later struck her that he would have worn it during the "stormy years" of the war.[27]

Since the middle of December, Jefferson Davis had been exhausting himself to the point of sickness trying to forge an eleventh-hour compromise between Northern and Southern interests in Congress. But there was little hope. Just a few days before Christmas, the state of South Carolina, with its plantation, slave-dependent economy and entrenched proslavery ideology, had seceded, the first state to leave the Union. Then, on January 9, South Carolina artillery fired on an unarmed merchant vessel, *Star of the West*, which was carrying reinforcements to the federal garrison at Fort Sumter, four miles off the coast of Charleston. Kentuckian Major Robert Anderson, in charge of Sumter, did not fire back and the war did not begin. But by the end of January, Florida, Mississippi, Alabama, Georgia, and Louisiana had seceded, with Texas following shorly after. Thus, the Lower South had left the Union. (Mary had two half-sisters living in Alabama and four half-brothers in New Orleans.)

In February, Jefferson Davis, former United States Senator, was elected

President of the Confederate States of America. It was an honor he did not want, but which he accepted out of a sense of duty and purpose. Of his February 18 inauguration in Montgomery, Alabama, he confided to Varina, "Upon my weary heart was showered smiles, plaudits, and flowers but, beyond them, I saw troubles and thorns innumerable."[28]

Of all the worried households in the United States that winter, no two could have been witness to more anxious discussions about their own and the nation's future than the Lincoln and Davis homes. That the link between them would be a recently freed African American is ironic, yet appropriate. White Americans, who were willing to sacrifice their all for the war, liked to see themselves as fighting a white man's war, but in fact, African Americans were at the heart of their struggle.

As the Union unraveled, Washington appeared to many to be sliding toward lawlessness. Pickpockets and burglars seemed to prowl the streets, while every night "incendiary fires" were lit in every neighborhood and fire bells rang out in alarm. Rumors of mob violence and treason circulated wildly, and guards were posted on street corners and at government buildings. Nervous citizens slept with loaded revolvers by their beds.[29]

In the meantime, Southern Congressmen and other "seceders" throughout the government resigned their posts and began packing up to move back home. Many of them, like Varina Davis, had been longtime residents and had deep-rooted ties, and they did not want to leave. One day, Lizzy heard Mrs. Davis tell a friend, "I would rather remain in Washington and be kicked about, than go South and be Mrs. President." It was an unguarded moment; as early as mid-November, when her future was not so clear, she wrote to her husband, "That one thing we do know, and that is that we quit here the 4th of March"—inauguration day.[30]

Although Varina Davis had accepted the inevitability of returning South, she was certain that the North would go down to defeat quickly and that she would soon return to Washington in triumph. It was under this impression that one day in January she invited Lizzy to go with them. "I will take good care of you," she told the startled Lizzy. "Besides, when the war breaks out, the colored people will suffer in the North," because they will be blamed for being "the cause of the war." The South had made the belief in slavery as a "natural and normal condition" for an inferior race the cornerstone of the Confederacy, and Northern insistence that this was a war for Union, and not against slavery, would not hold forever. When it was over in a few months, Varina told Lizzy, with the assurance that had provoked a friend to nickname her "Queen Varina," "I may come back to Washington . . . and live in the White House." Mr. Davis was going to be elected the South's President, she went on, and "we will raise an army and march on Washington, and then I shall live in the White House."[31]

Lizzy took Mrs. Davis's offer seriously and thought about it for some time. She regarded the "proposition" to be a kind one, and at first she was tempted to accept. It is telling of her sense of service that one argument in favor of going was that she had "served" Varina Davis "faithfully" and that Mrs. Davis had rewarded her by paying her respect. Indeed, Mrs. Davis had "learned to place the greatest confidence in me," Lizzy remembered with immense satisfaction. It was not as if Lizzy had sought to live in free territory, for even when she left St. Louis to move north, she had gone only as far as Baltimore before moving to slaveholding Washington. Then, supposing that Mrs. Davis was correct about the Southern victory, her path to the White House ran with the South and the Davises. But if Lizzy talked over her problem with anyone in her church or boardinghouse, there is little question but that they would have advised her to stay in Washington. After the war, she would say that she had believed the North would be victorious in a sectional war, just as it had been victorious in the recent election, and that this had influenced her decision. However, one would think that being a black woman would have been reason enough "to cast my lot among the people of the North."[32]

While Elizabeth Keckly was considering Mrs. Davis's offer, Mary Lincoln was enjoying her first shopping trip to New York City, where she had come to buy a wardrobe befitting the wife of the President-elect. She had left Springfield escorted by a brother-in-law the day after the firing on the *Star of the West*, leaving her husband in Springfield in the midst of choosing his Cabinet. Since November, Lincoln's office and home had been thronged with visitors who came to discuss his administration and to take his measure. They had also looked over his wife. Excited reporters wrote flatteringly of her elegance and graciousness, but king makers and office seekers who came intent on influencing her husband emerged with a less benign view of the woman who refused to shrink resignedly into the background. As one critic privately remarked, Mrs. Lincoln ought to "be sent to the cooper's and well secured against bursting by iron hoops." Old friends saw her New York trip as typical of Mary's need to outshine everyone else without paying much attention to circumstances. Wrote her old and upright friend Mercy Conkling to her son (a childhood friend of Robert Lincoln) at Yale: "Mrs. Lincoln has gone East to get an outfit for the *White House*, which her friends here think quite unnecessary in the present state of political affairs."[33]

However, nothing happened to deflate Mary's ambitions on this New York trip, her first excursion as a public figure with her own entourage. Robert, now a student at Harvard, whom his mother missed almost desperately and was "*wild* to see," met her in New York, where the two could read about their movements in the New York papers, the lighter *Frank Leslie's Illustrated* or the more serious-minded *Herald* or *Tribune*. "Aren't you beginning to get a little tired of the constant uproar?" Robert had teased his mother in December after reading about her in the Boston papers, knowing that "uproar" was her water and air. Mary's New York visit was being reported as a shopping tour—"whether to purchase rails or calicoes is not mentioned," quipped *Frank Leslie's*—and shop she did. In the meantime, reporters were already busy detailing what she was wearing, with the following, approving description typical: "Her dress was a brown or oak-colored silk, with grayish flowers and leaves. It was made full, with flounces fitted well, hung gracefully about her person, and trailed just a trifle. Her bonnet was of black silk, trimmed with cherry ribbon, which, with a dark mixed shawl, neatly-fitted kid gloves, and rich lavend[e]r-colored parasol, completed her costume."[34] No wonder that Mrs. Lincoln's first priority on reaching Washington, D.C., was to locate the best dressmaker in town.

The to-do made over Mary Lincoln by solicitous merchants, who were quite happy to extend credit to the future Mrs. President, was an undeniably thrilling experience, and Mary did not hang back from picking out whatever she wanted. But even better was the fawning welcome of the city's leading citizens: powerful, wealthy, and sophisticated New Yorkers. Soon she was stretching her political muscles. By mid-January she was writing to David Davis, Lincoln's campaign manager, a "*Confidential*" letter to object to one of the candidates for the Cabinet, the news of whose consideration for appointment she had gathered while eavesdropping on the banter of several gentlemen seated near her at breakfast in her New York hotel. "Evidently strong Republicans," she wrote Davis, they were "laughing at the idea of [Norman] Judd, being in any way, connected with the Cabinet in *these times*, when honesty in high places is so important." The gentlemen "did not know, who was near," she noted with self-importance. Because of this, she wanted Davis to persuade her husband against the appointment.[35] That she tapped an intermediary, rather than write Lincoln directly, suggests the distance that had already grown up between them; under the combined pressures of national and personal crises, it was a distance that would increase in the White House.

After her New York stay, perks followed Mary all the way back to Springfield. In Chicago, Wheeler & Wilson's Sewing Machine donated for display the elegant machine, made of rosewood inlaid with mother-of-pearl and enamel, that it planned to present to Mrs. Lincoln. "It is worthy of the possession of a duchess," wrote an admiring reporter, and in fact Wheeler & Wilson's gave the same machine to both an English and a Russian duchess.[36]

On February 11, 1861, the Lincolns left Springfield to make their way to Washington. The roundabout twelve-day railroad trip, intended to show Lincoln to his supporters, began with Robert's temporary misplacement of the "grip-sack" containing his father's inaugural address, which had been written by Lincoln alone in Springfield. It ended with the President-elect slipping unseen through Maryland and sneaking into Washington at 6 A.M., after a Pinkerton detective and a War Department agent warned of an assassination plot in secession-friendly Baltimore. The trip gave Mary a glimpse of the highs and lows of her future position. At times feted and cheered alongside her husband, along with Robert, Willie, and Tad (Robert was greeted as "the Prince of Rails"), she was literally locked in her room in Harrisburg, Pennsylvania, by the President-elect's men, who could think of no other way to silence her "unmanageable" demands that "if Lincoln's route [through Baltimore] was changed she must accompany him." They feared she would compromise the secrecy on which Lincoln's safety depended.[37]

Ten hours after her husband quietly arrived in Washington on Saturday, February 23, the train carrying Mary and the rest of the Lincoln party pulled into the depot at New Jersey Avenue and C Street. Emerging into the late-afternoon light, she saw towering before her the massive white marble Capitol, its colonnade still domeless beneath black scaffolding, with the arms of cranes sticking out, making the top look like a mutilated spider. To the right wooden sheds and huts stood in an open muddy field, beyond which were small brick houses and church spires. The black hackney coach drivers crowded outside the station calling out for potential passengers, but waiting for her with a carriage were New York's slight, silver-haired Senator William Seward, Lincoln's choice for Secretary of State, and Illinois Congressman Elihu Washburne, an old friend. She would have welcomed the sight of the cautious and loyal Washburne, but not so the affable but ambitious Seward. Her husband's most formidable Republican rival at the Chicago convention, Seward intended to be the "power behind the throne," and Mary, sensing this, neither trusted nor liked him. Lizzy Keckly would later remember Mary telling President Lincoln that Seward "had no principles" and was a "hypocrite" who would "twine you around his finger as if you were a skein of thread."[38]

From the station, the carriage drove up tree-lined Pennsylvania Avenue, passed the sprawling stalls of the Centre Market (where the National Archives stand) and the uneven buildings that housed the Avenue's shops, hotels, bars, and "bawdy houses," which took up whole blocks on the south side of the street. Ahead lay an unimpressive brick building, the State Department, behind which loomed the vast stone Treasury Building; beyond these was the Executive Mansion, where in a few days Mary would be touring the house and chatting with President Buchanan's niece, the blonde, thirty-year-old Miss Harriet Lane, who had acted as the official hostess for her bachelor uncle. But now, turning right off the Avenue, the gentlemen carried Mary Lincoln to Willard's Hotel at E and Fourteenth Street, where the family was to stay until the inauguration. (The bill for nine days, which included several private dinners and receptions, came to $773.75.)

Before the war, Willard's, the city's preeminent hotel, was a favorite residence for well-off Northern legislators. In the weeks leading up to March 4, the rambling, six-story building was packed on all decks with would-be courtiers, supplicants for position in the new government. Up and down the halls "doors were opening and shutting for men with papers bulging out of their pockets, who hurried as if for their life in and out and the building almost shook with the tread of candidature," wrote the London *Times* correspondent William Howard Russell. "It probably contains at this moment more scheming, plotting, planning heads, more aching and joyful hearts, than any building of the same size ever held in the world."[39] Now Mary Lincoln and, soon, Lizzy Keckly would add their mite of human striving to the clamoring mass.

Barely a week before Mary's arrival, Lizzy Keckly had been busy sewing in her rooms on Twelfth Street when she heard a bustle in the hallway and, looking up, saw one of her patrons, Mrs. McLean. Another close friend of Varina Davis, Margaret McLean was one of four daughters of cavalry officer Colonel Edwin V. Sumner, who had volunteered to travel to Washington with the Lincolns; her husband was Colonel Eugene McLean of Maryland. Like many of Lizzy's "ladies," past and future, Mrs. McLean was a demanding employer who had an "emphatic way" of speaking; barely greeting her dressmaker in whose sewing room she now stood, she plunged into the reasons that brought her to Twelfth Street. She had been invited to "dine at Willard's on next Sunday," the day after the Lincolns' scheduled arrival, and she had "positively . . . not a dress fit to wear on the occasion. I have just bought material, and you must commence work on it right away."[40]

It was a feature of Lizzy Keckly's manner of handling her more imperious patrons to demur in her own gently emphatic way to their self-absorbed requests. She answered that she had "more work now promised" than she could do. "It is impossible for me to make a dress for you to wear" in time. "Pshaw! Nothing is impossible. I must have the dress made by Sunday," Mrs. McClean said. Lizzy could see that her patron was growing impatient, and she began to apologize, though without backing down, when Mrs. McClean interrupted her. "Now don't say that again," she said. "I tell you that you must make the dress." Then Mrs. McClean said, "I have often heard you say that you would like to work for the ladies of the White House. Well, I have it in my power to obtain this privilege. I know Mrs. Lincoln well, and you shall make a dress for her provided you finish mine in time to wear at dinner on Sunday."

"The inducement was the best that could have been offered," Lizzy later wrote. She would do what she needed to—sit up all night, hire helpers, put off her other patrons—to hold up her end of the bargain. She might never again have such a chance. "After much worry and trouble," she finished the dress, and Mrs. McLean wore it to Willard's on Sunday.

It was either that night or the following, when the Lincolns greeted callers for two hours in the muggy hotel parlors, that Mary Lincoln or a waiter spilled coffee on the lavender gown she was planning to wear to a party after the next week's inauguration, and now she needed a new one. Seizing her opportunity, Mrs. McLean told Mrs. Lincoln about Lizzy Keckly. Lizzy Keckly? Mary repeated the name. She had heard of Lizzy Keckly from friends in St. Louis, and they all said good things. Could Mrs. McLean recommend her? "With confidence," she said, and promised to send Lizzy to her.[41]

A week passed before Mrs. McLean summoned Lizzy Keckly. It was a mild, springlike Sunday, the day before the inauguration, and Lizzy, considering Sunday her day off and seeing no urgency as Mrs. McLean had given no reason, "was determined to wait until Monday morning," as she put it. It was good to assert one's will after years of slavery.

Early the next morning, a raw, overcast day, the streets of Washington were alive in anticipation of the afternoon's events. Out-of-towners who, in the words of biographer Ida M. Tarbell, "had come to see the inauguration of the first Republican President, and who had been unable to find other bed than the floor, were walking the streets; the morning trains were bringing new crowds." By 10 o'clock, Pennsylvania Avenue "was black with humanity," recalled one eyewitness. "Added to the stir . . . were sounds unusual in Washington—the clatter of cavalry, the tramp of soldiers." Under orders from Winfield Scott, General-in-Chief of the U.S. Army, companies of soldiers were moving into position in intervals along the Avenue, blocking off the cross streets, and sharpshooters were making their way to the rooftops. That afternoon, a ring of volunteer guards would encircle the crowd amassed before the east portico of the Capitol. General Scott was determined to protect the new President.[42]

Lizzy Keckly was determined on her own mission: when nearly everyone else, it seemed, was preoccupied with what would happen later that day at the Capitol, she was making her way the few blocks to Mrs. McLean's house opposite Willard's. The self-reliance she always said she learned from slavery and for which she claimed to be grateful was perhaps little more than the powerful instinct to let nothing interfere with her survival. If she was the only person in the world at that moment thinking of Elizabeth Keckly's future, it was enough: as a slave, she had felt isolated, futureless, unbidden by hope. Of course, she noticed the anxious faces all around her and shared the common "deep interest" in the inauguration and in the threats of assassination and rumors of war swirling about. But for the time being the commotion presented only a "difficulty" in her path to Mrs. McLean's door.

At the McLean house, an aide to the Colonel told her that she was wanted at Willard's. She crossed the street and, managing her way past the crowded entrance, found Mrs. McLean inside. Immediately, the lady scolded Lizzy for not coming the day before. "Why did you not come yesterday, as I requested? Mrs. Lincoln wanted to see you, and I fear that now you are too late." Calmly, Lizzy answered that as she had not said why she wanted her yesterday, she "judged that this morning would do as well." Still upset, Mrs. McLean gave Lizzy the Lincolns' suite number, saying, "She may find use for you yet."[43]

Lizzy's entrance into parlor No. 6 brought her face-to-face with the woman who was to claim her attention for the next six years and would remain a fixture in her memory for the rest of her life. Moreover, without Mary Lincoln, Elizabeth Keckly would not be known today. For Mary Lincoln, it also was an important meeting, although it would be silly to claim an equal importance to Lizzy's circumstances and historical memory. Mary would quickly come to rely on the extraordinary qualities of the woman who stood before her. "She is a very remarkable woman herself," she told cousin Lizzie Grimsley, who met Lizzy Keckly at the White House frequently during her long stay there that first year.[44]

Their meeting that day was brief and uneventful; Mary was getting ready for the inauguration and, without introducing herself, simply told Lizzy to come to the White House the next morning at 8. It was "where I shall then be," Mary said, with emphasis. As was her custom, Lizzy bowed herself out of the room. Then she went home, where she spent the rest of the day.

For her, inauguration day "passed slowly"; all she could think about was her interview tomorrow with Mary Lincoln. Only blocks away, thirty thousand people were crammed into the fenced-in Capitol Grounds. (They were mostly white people, because for the past thirty years, black people had been forbidden to enter the grounds of the Capitol.) Above, the sky had cleared. Shortly after noon, the President's carriage, surrounded by cavalry, rolled solemnly along cobblestoned Pennsylvania Avenue toward the Capitol, following the route taken by every President to his destiny since Thomas Jefferson. Unseen by Elizabeth Keckly, the inauguration ceremonies went forward; she did not see her future mistress seated, with her family, on the platform on the Capitol steps; she did not see the tall, black-clad Lincoln step forward, hat in hand, then stand perplexed, not knowing what to do with his hat; nor the much shorter gentleman (Stephen A. Douglas) reach out, take the hat, and hold it for the rest of the ceremony. Unseen by her, Lincoln adjusted his glasses and, unheard by her, read out his inaugural address.[45]

Only days before the inauguration, Frederick Douglass expressed the "cautious optimism" felt by many African Americans who wanted only to know what the new President's policy toward the seceded states was to be. "Of one satisfaction, one ray of hope," Douglass could assure himself and his readers: that after March 4, "it will at least be a great relief to know [his policy], to rejoice in and defend it, if right, and to make war upon it if wrong." That Lincoln should hold firm to his campaign promise to preserve the Union, that he should resist the corrupting "atmosphere of Washington" and not compromise with the seceding South, was Douglass's most earnest hope. "Will Mr. Lincoln boldly grapple with the monster of Disunion, and bring down his proud looks?"[46]

Douglass's verdict on the inaugural address was that Lincoln would not. He was pleased to hear Lincoln condemn slavery and to vow to preserve the Union with "all the powers at my disposal." But Lincoln's promise to the South "not to interfere with the institution of slavery where it exists" confirmed Douglass's worst fears. He "found no hopeful impression" in Lincoln's delicately balanced address.[47]

For the moment, however, unaware of all that was transpiring beyond the walls of her rooms on Twelfth Street, Lizzy's hopes were pinned on her own industriousness, intelligence, skill, and ambition. That day, secluded in her apartments, she thought mostly of her interview the following morning. Self-reliantly, she was keeping watch over her own personal fate. "My long cherished hope was about to be realized, and I could not rest."[48]

CHAPTER NINE

On the morning after the inauguration, a dispatch from Major Robert Anderson at Fort Sumter, informing President Lincoln that the garrison's supplies were nearly depleted, lay on the new President's desk. The time Lincoln had sought to buy with his inaugural speech was already running out. Either he reinforce the garrison, at risk of starting a war, or evacuate the fort, essentially surrendering it to the Confederates and reneging on his inaugural promise to hold all government property. It was staggering news, and Lincoln had it sent to the aging, gouty General-in-Chief Scott and waited for advice on how to proceed.

A little before 8 o'clock on the same morning, Lizzy Keckly crossed Lafayette Square, walked up the semicircular drive around the bronze statue of Thomas Jefferson, and ascended the portico leading to the main entrance of the President's Mansion. At the door stood a short, elderly doorkeeper (she would later learn this was Edward McManus), who admitted her into the vestibule, which opened out into a wide hall. Once inside, she was shown to a waiting room, possibly by the White House butler, a light-skinned, former slave named Peter Brown. Brown, a Virginian, had worked under Buchanan, and his cash wages went to buy the freedom of his small son, who was now eleven years old and shining shoes in the grounds around the Treasury Building. The Browns lived three blocks from Lizzy on Twelfth Street, and given the insularity of the middle-class black community, it is likely that they knew one another.[1]

In the waiting room, Lizzy saw "no less than three mantua-makers [dress-makers] waiting for an interview. . . . Hope fell at once." Obviously, Margaret McLean was not the only woman who had recommended her favorite dress-maker to the new President's wife. "With so many rivals . . . I regarded my chances as extremely small," she would later recall.[2]

That morning, the new President, still reeling from Anderson's dire mes-sage, sent his private secretary, John G. Nicolay, from his office to the Senate with his Cabinet nominations for approval. Down the hall, the new Mrs. President, with her cousin Lizzie Grimsley, was busy interviewing dressmak-ers, choosing a critical member of *her* Cabinet.

In Washington at the time, association with a particular dressmaker could bring triumph or despair, praise or disdain. Throughout the 1850s, Mrs. Rich had been the favorite dressmaker of distingué Washington, according to the wife of the Alabama Senator, Mrs. Virginia Clay. Mrs. Clay was so fierce a Southern partisan that at the costume ball thrown by the wife of the very rich California Senator William M. Gwin in their mansion in April 1858, a week after the House refused by eight votes to admit Kansas as a slave state, *she* re-fused to shake the hand of the abolitionist Senator Seward. Reminiscing over forty years later about the decade before the Republicans wrecked her Wash-ington, Mrs. Clay described the "incomparable miracles" performed by Mrs. Rich, who would "transform provincial newcomers, often already over-stocked with ill-made costumes and absurdly trimmed bonnets into women of fashion!" Indeed, she wrote, still defending the honor of the South, "Mrs. Rich was the only Reconstructionist, I think I may safely say, on whom Southern ladies looked with unqualified approval.[3]

Mary Lincoln, who had made high fashion her special province since girl-hood, may have been less likely than most women of "far-off States" to com-mit the kind of "sartorial *faux pas*" Mrs. Clay amused herself by skewering. Quite the opposite: Mary's fashion goals were so complicated and sophisti-cated that it would be no common mantua maker who could help her realize her dreams. France's Empress Eugenie epitomized *"les modes Parisiennes"* (as

Godey's put it), featuring luxurious fabrics and wide hoop skirts elaborately trimmed, and it was *les modes* that Mary wanted.

Lizzy Keckly was the last to be called. She ascended the central staircase, which was fairly vibrating with office seekers wishing to see the President in his second-floor office. At the top of the stairs, she was ushered through the crowd to the oval family sitting room, where inside she recognized Mary Lincoln, standing by a window. She was having a "lively conversation" with another lady Keckly did not know, while looking over the unfamiliar view, a stretch of lawn that ran down from the White House and ended in a high iron fence; beyond, the pungent marsh led down to the Potomac.

"You have come at last," Mary stepped forward, addressing her warmly and respectfully. The interview took only a few minutes; when Mary heard that Lizzy had worked for Varina Davis, she made up her mind instantly. What remained was to negotiate cost, and Mary, true to form, meant to bargain for the lowest prices Mrs. Keckly would give. Do you have time to "do my work?" she asked. "I trust that your terms are reasonable. I cannot afford to be extravagant. We are just from the West, and we are poor. If you do not charge too much, I shall be able to give you all my work."

"My terms are reasonable," Lizzy asserted, so there will not be "any difficulty about charges." Well, Mary drove on bluntly, "if you will work cheap, you shall have plenty to do. I can't afford to pay big prices, so I frankly tell you so in the beginning."

Prior to this, Mary's experiences with dressmakers had not always been successful. A few years earlier, a story accusing her of having cheated her seamstress had made the rounds in Springfield parlors. In her own defense, Mary proclaimed, "I would as soon have her [the seamstress] to say this, as anything else, her name and *tongue* is well established. My seamstresses bear such different testimony to my *honesty* & justice." Just before coming to Washington, she had offended another Springfield dressmaker with a "slighting remark" about her work, which she made to a common acquaintance during an afternoon call. Word soon reached the dressmaker, Miss Snell, who threatened to drop Mary's work, and in the end, Mary Lincoln found herself paying an enormous bill.[4]

But the entrepreneurial Lizzy presented her with satisfactory terms. When Lizzy left the White House, she was carrying the first of the many dresses she would sew for Mrs. Lincoln: the "bright rose-colored moiré-antique" dress that Mary wished to wear to the first levee of the Lincoln presidency. (Moiré, the wavy or watered pattern on fabrics, was produced by passing the material through engraved cylinders; the crushed and uncrushed parts reflected light. It was a popular way of treating silk.) When she returned the next day to fit the dress—climbing up the central staircase, passing some of the same office seekers from the day before—she found Mary Lincoln in a white cashmere wrapper with quilting down the front, a morning dress recommended by *Godey's* as "elegant." It was the start of a pattern they would follow for the next four years (interspersed with Mary's visits to Lizzy's rooms for fittings), whenever Mary, who made numerous trips, was in Washington.[5]

Tellingly, in only a matter of days, another future ritual of their relationship emerged, when Lizzy found herself drawn into the family circle. The alterations Mary wanted took work, and Lizzy was not finished until the day of the levee. By the time she brought the finished dress to the White House, Mary was in a rage, "protesting that she could not go down" because she had nothing to wear. Lizzy felt "humiliated," as she would recall years later in an interview, but the patient Elizabeth Edwards and sensible Elizabeth Grimsley helped persuade her to let Lizzy get her ready. Soon, Lincoln came in and stretched on the couch, where he began laughing with Willie and Tad, pulling on his gloves, and "quoting poetry." "You seem to be in a poetical mood tonight," Mary said. "Yes, mother, these are poetical times," Lincoln answered lightly. (His light mood was misleading to Lizzy, but familiar to Mary as her husband's way of finding relief from deepening difficulties.) "I declare, you look charming in that dress. Mrs. Keckly has met with success." Mary was also pleased with the way she looked, and ready to head down. But first, there was a search for her lace handkerchief, which Tad, a frequent instigator of mischief, had hidden somewhere. Once found, "all became serene," and on the arm of her husband, a smiling Mrs. Lincoln "led the train below."[6]

From that day forward, Elizabeth Keckly was Mary's "regular modiste"; through July alone she made her new patron fifteen or sixteen dresses, an enormous amount of work. She also dressed Mary for levees and receptions. In the meantime, Mary employed other, less skilled seamstresses to do her "plain sewing," mending clothes, linens, or darning socks. In New York in February she had "procured" an Irish seamstress, Mrs. Mary Ann Cuthbert, to replace a "girl" she had brought from Springfield; Mrs. Cuthbert also did double duty as "dressing maid." Later, she was promoted to head housekeeper, and two African American Washington women, Mrs. Rosetta Wells and Mrs. Hannah F. Brooks, took over Mrs. Lincoln's plain sewing. Hannah Brooks had an inside track: her husband's cousin was William Slade, the President's messenger, who under President Andrew Johnson would become the White

House steward and supervise the other black servants ("Bossed all the help," said the talkative Rosetta Wells).[7]

For a newcomer like Lizzy Keckly, entrée to the White House meant more than just admission to the *white* Executive Mansion. The White House "colored" servants, virtually all descended from slaves, considered themselves the cream of black society, on a par with the city's leading black restaurateurs, caterers, barbers, and government messengers, who derived their status from their education and business success and by how far from slavery they were. Mostly members of the elitist Fifteenth Street Presbyterian Church, the "palest" of black churches, they were notoriously hostile to darker-skinned, lower-class blacks who tried to join their ranks. Many were less interested in politics than in culture, less invested, for example, in abolitionism than in education for free black children.[8]

Light-skinned, successful, always beautifully turned out, and remembered as "courteous to the Nth degree," Lizzy was exactly their type; even her descent from the Virginia Burwells was a favorable mark in her pedigree. Then, too, her landlord Walker Lewis, like the messenger William Slade, was an elder in the Fifteenth Street Church, another recommendation. Besides, it would have been difficult to snub Lizzy Keckly, who didn't take "tea for the fever" from anybody, in the words of Rosetta Wells, who was also of the opinion that Lizzy Keckly was "the only person in Washington who could get along with Mrs. Lincoln, when she became mad with anybody for talking about her and criticizing her husband."[9]

Not even Lincoln could override a snub by the house servants. Lincoln had brought a servant from Springfield to Washington, his personal valet, William Johnson. However, Johnson was dark-skinned, and the lighter-skinned servants in the White House treated him with active disdain. A mere two days of living in the White House were enough for William (as Lincoln called him). As Lincoln put it in one of the letters of recommendation he wrote for him, "The difference of color between him and the other servants is the cause of separation." Lincoln's letter to Secretary of the Treasury Salmon P. Chase had effect, and Johnson was employed by the Treasury Department, a major employer during the war. To finance the war, Chase resorted to printing "greenbacks" (the first legal tender banknotes), a massive task requiring more than 1,600 new clerks and one that forced Chase to hire even women, who worked mostly as cutters (they literally *cut* the money).[10]

In the meantime, the country was hurtling toward the war that Major Anderson's dispatch portended and Chase would have to finance. On April 4, against General Scott's recommendation, Lincoln gave orders to send provisions to Fort Sumter, sending a subsequent message to Governor Pickens in Charleston that told of his intention to do so peacefully. On April 12, before the relief arrived, Confederate soldiers opened fire on the fort. Thirty-three hours of bombardment later, Major Anderson surrendered. On the fifteenth, the President issued a proclamation calling for 75,000 militiamen for national service for ninety days, longer than most Northerners figured it would take to put down the Southern rebellion.

Lincoln's call for volunteers ignited the flames of "war[s] within the larger war" between unionists and secessionists across the eight states of the upper South. Almost immediately, Virginia, Arkansas, North Carolina, and Tennessee left the Union. At the same time, the western counties of Virginia seceded from the state, to later enter the Union as West Virginia. And though Delaware, Maryland, Kentucky, and Missouri did not secede, the last two especially sent many men from their large secessionist minorities into battle against Union forces.

Mary's family found itself caught in the self-division of the South. Her brother George fought in the Confederate Army; so did three half-brothers and three of her half-sisters' husbands. Indeed, her earliest heartbreak in the war was when Ben Hardin Helm, the West Point graduate and Kentucky-born husband of Emilie (whom the Lincolns affectionately called "Little Sister"), refused Lincoln's offer of the commission as paymaster in the United States Army during the couple's April visit to the White House. Mary had hoped to have Emilie keep her company; instead, it turned out to be a farewell visit. Helm consulted Colonel Robert E. Lee, who not only turned down Lincoln's offer of command of the Union Army, but resigned from the army altogether and became commander in chief of Virginia's forces, all within the space of five days. Soon after, the Helms left Washington and Ben accepted an appointment as general in the Confederate Army.[11]

Mary's loyalties were already the subject of negative innuendo during the secession crisis, before her husband's inauguration. On March 2, the popular Northern *Harper's Weekly* described "Mrs. Lincoln's sisters" as "the toast of Southerners." Throughout the war, Northern suspicions that the Kentucky-born First Lady was a rebel sympathizer and even a spy never quite faded, and she was never free of the taint of association. When Emilie visited the White House after the death of her husband, many Northerners were outraged. And in the spring of 1864, Northern papers picked up a story that Mrs. Lincoln's sister was smuggling supplies to the rebels across Union lines, using a pass from the President to get through at Fortress Monroe in Virginia. Lincoln, who ignored most attacks as they were too numerous to answer, had secretary John Nicolay investigate. A few days later, a disavowal of the story appeared in Horace Greeley's *Tribune*, in which the charge had first appeared under the headline "Aid and Comfort for the Enemy."[12]

Southerners were no more kind, since Mary was in fact staunchly loyal to her husband and the Union, and they considered her a renegade from her Southern roots, a traitor. Yet her loyalties were personal, the devotions, she reasoned, of a true wife. "Why should I sympathize with the rebels?" she told Lizzy. "Are they not against me? They would hang my husband to-morrow if it was in their power."[13]

She was also ridiculed as a plebeian Westerner, dismissed on the spot as too provincial, too vulgar, too ignorant, too parvenu. The contrast with the popular Harriet Lane, the previous mistress of the White House, was harped on. Miss Lane was "always courteous, always in place, silent whenever it was possible to be silent . . . she made no enemies," one Washington lady recalled; she had "exquisite taste in dress. She never wore many ornaments, many flowers, nor the billows of ruffles then in fashion." Indeed, Mary's refusal to hide from shame was irritating, and some Washington old-timers, who considered the Lincolns pretenders in the White House, thought that "he is better than she, for he seems by his manner to apologize for being there."[14]

So widespread were the "amusing [Mary Lincoln] anecdotes" told by "Secessionist ladies" that the London *Times* correspondent confessed he was "agreeably disappointed" when he met her at the first state dinner for members of the Cabinet on March 28 and found that the worst he could say about her was that she punctuated every sentence with the word "sir" (a Kentucky habit), fanned herself energetically, and was perhaps too obviously "desirous of making herself agreeable." "Consciousness that her position requires her to be something more than plain Mrs. Lincoln, wife of the Illinois lawyer," he thought, "stiffened" her manners. Lizzy Keckly heard the gossip, too, not surprising for someone who was spending her time fitting dresses onto Washington's female aristocracy; she had been equally surprised when she first met Mrs. Lincoln to find her every bit a lady, graceful, "confident and self-possessed."[15] Lizzy, more successful at finding acceptance among Washington's black elites than Mary was with the parallel white establishment, and accustomed from early on to discriminating between classes and behaviors of white people, easily felt herself in a position to judge Mrs. Lincoln's manner.

Thus, in a sense, Mary existed in a geographical and political no-woman's-land. During her first months in Washington, the Southern-born ladies who had dominated society, and whom she may have dreamed of impressing, snubbed her invitations and boycotted official receptions. Even the first levee, which was so jammed that people who wanted to get out left through the windows, was deemed by society a total failure, packed with strangers and the unwashed masses. John B. Blake, Buchanan's Commissioner of Public Buildings, whose job it had been to supervise the White House purchases, wrote a smug report of the lowly affair to Harriet Lane: "The only ladies present, who visited you socially, were Mrs. Palmer, Mrs. Franklin, Mrs. Magruder, Miss Woodbury, the Lorings, Miss Johnson, and the younger Miss Pleasanton. The great mass of the crowd consisted entirely of strangers, and the remainder mostly of citizens, who had not been in the habit of being present on such occasions." Blake would have appreciated the exchange at the President's first Cabinet dinner between Mrs. Lincoln and twenty-year-old Kate Chase, the auburn-haired daughter of the Secretary of the Treasury, who planned to see her father succeed Lincoln as President. In response to Mary's greeting, "I shall be glad to see you anytime, Miss Chase," she replied, "Mrs. Lincoln, I shall be glad to have *you* call on *me* at anytime." During the years the Lincolns were in Washington, Kate Chase, more than twenty years younger than Mary, would be the First Lady's social rival.[16]

Mary did give people things to talk about, however. At one of the Marine Band concerts on the White House lawn, she spotted the mother of the two boys who had already become her sons' best Washington playmates, Mrs. Horatio Taft, whose husband was chief of the Patent Office. Staring at Mrs. Taft's bonnet, which was trimmed with purple ribbon and tied under her chin, she approached and took her aside. The fashionable French milliner they shared, Willian on Pennsylvania Avenue, had "trimmed her bonnet with this same ribbon but is unable to get enough for the strings," and Mrs. Lincoln wanted the ribbon off Mrs. Taft's bonnet. When Mrs. Taft told the story to Willian, he promised that if she gave Mrs. Lincoln the purple ribbon—for he wished to oblige his important new customer—he would give Mrs. Taft even nicer ribbon to replace it.[17]

Mary's personal style also provoked critical comment, particularly her stylish low-cut, off-the-shoulder gowns, heavily ornamented, and her flower-bedecked headdresses ("Mrs. Lincoln had *her bosom* on display and a flower-pot on her head," one disgusted senator wrote home to his wife). Above all, she aimed to look au courant, which was the equivalent of looking youthful: women past forty were expected to have outgrown the need to follow fashion trends. As a result, Mary's look—her hair combed smoothly over her ears, her off-the-shoulder necklines, purple and white silks, use of every possible trimming, and flowered headdresses—was considered inappropriately girlish ("like some over-grown Ophelia," one journalist remarked). Her style of dress contrasted sharply with the modest necklines, simple headdresses, and staid browns, blacks, and blues worn by sister Elizabeth and cousin Lizzie. But fashion spotters recognized what she was about. Reporting on the first levee, savvy Washington correspondents called Mary's bright rose gown "magenta," the newly discovered, madly popular, brilliant color named for an Italian town and rival to delicate "mauve," a slightly earlier mid-nineteenth-century creation. Only her niece, dressed in crimson, approached her aunt in up-to-date vividness.[18]

Nevertheless, plunging ahead as was her wont, Mary was in high spirits through the end of March, when she wrote to her Springfield friend Harriet Shearer on the afternoon before the Cabinet dinner: "This is certainly a very charming spot & I have formed many delightful acquaintances. Every evening our *blue room* is filled with the elite of the land. . . . I am beginning to feel so perfectly at home, and enjoy everything here so much." Better yet was the report from sister Elizabeth, who had returned home and written to say that "she cannot settle down at home, since she has been here. We *may perhaps*, at the close of *four* years, be glad to relinquish our claims." And yet the genuine, and understandable, delight Mary took in her novel circumstances—"Very different from home. We only have to give our orders for the dinner, and *dress* in proper season"—could not dispel an intensifying dread.[19] It had many sources: her fear for her husband's physical safety; her feeling exiled from his political life; the public criticism, which raised the specter of her own failings; her loneliness. Indeed, more and more, she felt diminished and neglected.

Mary had always lived at the center of a world she knew. She had never lived in a town not run by her family or in a place where her name did not open doors. She had never had to prove herself among strangers. When her husband was away on the circuit or the campaign trail, she had a ready-made community of women who understood her and were more forgiving toward her than she was toward them. When he was home, she had a captive audience.

Now she was in a town where she was not only *not* welcomed, but was actually repulsed. And it was as if the all-male circuit in which Lincoln thrived were living inside her house; in fact, Lincoln's young secretaries, Nicolay and the even younger John Hay, did share a room down the hall from the family's rooms. It was a male culture in which she had no place: her notes to Cabinet members and officials about appointments were thought meddlesome and alienating; her battles for control over White House functions—Nicolay was in charge of these—regarded as overreaching and self-aggrandizing. Cousin Lizzie remembered Lincoln's reaction to those who hoped to flatter their way through the "ladies of the family" into positions in the government: he'd say that the "[women] hav[c] no influence in this administration." But Mary ignored this fact, and when she was not trying to go around her husband, she was known to badger him about appointments. Hay nicknamed her the "Hell-cat." (Lincoln was "Tycoon," after the all-powerful Japanese emperor.)[20]

Unfortunately, as Lincoln's workload increased and he grew closer to the men around him, Mary, feeling shut out, abandoned, and agitated, in her childlike way turned impulsively to anyone who paid attention to her, for good or ill.

At first, she was surrounded by her family; indeed, had it not been for the Todd relatives, twelve of whom came to Washington that first March, and other familiar Springfield faces who had flocked east for the inauguration ("Half the town seems to have gone to Washington," noted Mercy), Mary would have felt more keenly how isolated she was from the start. As it was, she grew anxious when her family began peeling away after the inaugural festivities ended. Faithful Lizzie Grimsley, who kept Mary company after everyone else went home, also tried to leave in March, but Mary would not let her. "Whenever I mention my return home," Lizzie wrote to cousin John Stuart on the twentieth, "Mary instantly objects, and I have no excuse to hurry home as all are well." Two months later, sounding desperate, she was not above suggesting a ruse: "I have overstayed my time so long because Mary has urged and urged and seemed to feel hurt at the idea of my leaving her, and now I am no nearer getting away than I was six weeks ago. You all write you are getting along so well without me, that Mary thinks me very selfish if I speak of going home. The only way will be for Father or Mother to write me word to *come home*." (Years later, when Lizzie Grimsley wrote a reminiscence of this visit, she chose as its title "Six Months in the White House.")[21]

In July, anticipating Cousin Lizzie's departure at the end of the summer, Mary urged her friend Hannah Shearer, who was expecting a child, to visit, hoping to woo her with the promise of an August holiday in the North. In the self-absorbed, imperial, and finally sadly pleading tones that were familiar to family and friends, she wrote:

I am now sitting down, to explain to you, why you *must* keep your word, & what a *quiet*, comfortable time, you will have, by so doing. . . . Remember I claim you for two months. Do not disappoint me. You shall be kept perfectly quiet. Mrs. Grimsley you will love very much. She is very anxious, to have you join us. It will give you strength, for a year to come. We go to the sea shore, to be perfectly quiet. We are invited, to bring any friend with us, we desire, and there is no one I am so anxious to see, as your dear self. If you are not well, my word for it, you can always keep yourself, as quiet as you wish.

I feel that I must have you with me. . . . I want you to write, directly you receive this. If you love me, give me a favorable answer. I have set my heart on having you with me.[22]

Indeed, Mary's isolation was so obvious that in a letter begun on the same day, kindhearted Unionist and Kentucky-born Elizabeth Blair Lee wrote her husband, "The women kind are giving Mrs. Lincoln the cold shoulder in the City & consequently we Republicans ought to Rally." But Washington-savvy Elizabeth Lee was an uncommonly generous diplomat. Her father was the elder statesman Francis Preston Blair, an adviser to Andrew Jackson and now counselor of Lincoln; one brother was the outspoken Congressman Frank Blair who held Missouri in the Union; another, the earnest, conservative Montgomery Blair, who had argued Dred Scott's Supreme Court case and was now Lincoln's Postmaster General. Yet despite her family's unquestionable Union pedigree, she had managed to remain friends with Varina Davis. And she did so in spite of Mrs. Davis's pronouncement that she was no longer associating with Republicans. When Varina asked her friend if she "was going south to fight her—I told her no. I would kiss & hug her too tight to let her break any *bonds* between us." Elizabeth Blair Lee would be one of the few Washington women Mary wished to see after Lincoln died.[23]

Elizabeth Lee's efforts on Mary's behalf could not undo the damage Mary did herself by behaving—at least to outside eyes—as if there were not a war on. But there was. On April 19, a Baltimore mob attacked the 6th Massachusetts Regiment, which was headed toward Washington. Frightened soldiers fired back, and by the time the riot ended, four soldiers and twelve citizens were dead and scores of others were injured. To keep more Northern regiments from passing through the city, Baltimore leaders ordered the destruction of railroad bridges into the city from Pennsylvania. When secessionists tore down the telegraph lines as well, Washington was cut off from the North. Gripped by a state of emergency, citizen volunteers, under orders from General Scott, sandbagged and barricaded public buildings. To protect the White House, the Frontier Guards of Kansas slept in the East Room. "We are in a Beleagured City with enemies on every side and . . . at our doors," Horatio Taft wrote desperately in his diary on Monday the twenty-second. "The ratling of musquetry and the booming of cannon may startle us any moment."[24]

"No troops from the North," Taft wrote on the twenty-fourth, as Washingtonians kept vigil, awaiting the arrival of more Union volunteers. "No mails since Friday, and in fact no *news* at all from the North." That same day, Lincoln told officers and wounded men of the 6th Massachusetts at the White House, "I begin to believe that there is no North."[25]

Therefore, when the New York 7th Regiment came through the following day, the city breathed a collective sigh of relief and poured into the streets, on foot and in carriages, to watch the troops drilling on the Capitol grounds. Mary rode out in the President's carriage with her husband, Secretary of State Seward, and Seward's son and daughter-in-law. More regiments from the North soon followed, making the capital look, and sound, like an armed camp, with "Drums beating and Bugles sounding all the time," and the sharp report of musket practice and the "deep booming of a heavy Cannon from Fort Washington, or from the Navy Yard or perhaps from some vessel on the River." Quartered in the White House, the Capitol, the Treasury, and the Patent Office, in the Georgetown seminary, and in tents at various points in the city, including the White House South lawn, the soldiers—untrained volunteers in uniform, really—filled the barrooms, hotel lounges, streets, squares, and every other public space. To supply the troops with bread, the government opened a bakery in the basement of the Capitol. Many had never been near the South, and on one particularly hot day, several fainted in the streets. Many had never seen so many black people before; some had never seen any. In the scramble for money, food, and services, pickpockets and gamblers found easy victims, and black men found it necessary (as historian Constance Green wrote) "to take special precautions to avoid arrest for white men's thieving."[26] Many a fugitive or former slave must have found the nightly mounted patrols frightening.

It was toward the end of May that the Lincolns had to attend a funeral in the East Room for the first officer killed in the war, the boyish and charming Colonel Elmer Ellsworth, who had read law briefly in Lincoln's law office and had come on the train to Washington with the family, catching measles from Willie and Tad en route. After leading his New York Fire Zoaves (1,100 New York City firemen) on the successful mission to seize the heights from Arlington to Alexandria, Virginia, he was shot after removing a "Secession" flag from atop a hotel in Alexandria. For weeks, Lincoln had stared at that rebel flag through a telescope aimed out of one of the south windows of the White House. Only days before his death, Ellsworth had wandered into photographer Mathew Brady's Washington studio and posed with his walking stick, wearing a flowing cape and military cap tilted at a jaunty angle; the carte-de-visite of the young dead Union officer became one of the first souvenirs of the war and Jackson's hotel in Alexandria a stop for sightseers.[27] The eeriness of this unexpected death—that of all the men who could have died, it was this young man whom they had brought with them—must have struck the omen-reading Lincolns.

Two weeks later another man close to the Lincolns died in the service of his country. The "Little Giant" Stephen Douglas, with whom Mary had danced at the Inaugural Ball, in failing health probably from cirrhosis of the liver, had taken up the mantle of patriotic retainer and gone west to urge his countrymen to rally behind their President against the Union "traitors." The strenuous trip probably killed him. His dying words were for his sons: "Tell them to obey the laws and support the Constitution of the United States."[28]

In the third week of July, confident of polishing off the rebels before their three-month term of service was up, Union troops singing "John Brown's Body," a song that a Massachusetts regiment had recently made popular, crossed the Potomac behind General Irvin McDowell and marched into Virginia to attack the Confederates who were stationed along the slow-flowing Bull Run near Manassas, not thirty miles from Washington. This was to be the first turning-point battle of the war. Reporters and civilians drove out from the capital to watch, but "they could see little but smoke from their vantage point two miles from the fighting." In Washington, the steady rumble of guns could be heard since dawn. Willard's was crowded with people urgently seeking news. Word of victory—that General McDowell was advancing "Forward to Richmond"—briefly raised hopes.[29]

It was devastating, therefore, when the awful details of the Union rout reached the city, arriving with the still-retreating and stunned Union soldiers.

From the start, confusion and miscalculation (including mistaking Southern troops for their own men and therefore not firing on them for several fatal minutes) had hurt what had been the Union's chances for victory. Toward the end, fresh troops sent in to reinforce the Confederates dealt the final blow. As the Confederates swept forward against the exhausted Union men, who had been marching and fighting without reinforcement for fourteen hours, an eerie, piercing scream filled the air, a scream that would soon be known as the rebel yell. Startled and demoralized, the Union soldiers fell back, panicked, and then fled.[30]

In the White House, grim determination followed the initial shock of the defeat. The following day, Lincoln signed a bill calling up 500,000 men for three-year stints; the day after that, he signed a second bill for the enlistment of 500,000 more. By the end of the week, the youthful, self-confident General George B. McClellan had replaced the defeated McDowell as commander of the Army of the Potomac.

In the meantime, Lizzy continued to earn a living working on Mary's dresses. She would have been happy to make the one-third-mile walk between the White House and her home as much as needed; indeed, she even thought it proper that she should. But Mary, who did not like sitting still, preferred going to Lizzy's rooms on Twelfth Street for her fittings. Particular and, in Lizzy's word, "whimsical" in her tastes, Mary was regularly suggesting this or that "alteration in style," and the two women began settling naturally into a collaboration.[31]

Letters Mary wrote to her New York milliner, Ruth Harris, give a taste of the kinds of conversations she and Lizzy must have had. Her precise instructions for one hat ran: "I want you to make up a purple silk velvet headdress of the exact shade of the flowers in this dress, similar to the crimson velvet one, you made me, with real silk velvet strings, behind—trimmed exquisitely with heartease before & behind, of the same shade—I want it very beautiful, exercise your taste, to the utmost. . . . be very moderate with this purple headdress—you must not ask me over $5.00 for it—I want it the exact shade of this purple & real— a little green & gilt would not hurt it." When she was satisfied, she ordered more of the same: "I liked the undersleeves & collars—Please have me *two more*, white & blk collars mixed, with cuffs to match." When not satisfied, she asked for something else, and then added more: "I wished a much finer blk straw bonnet for mourning—without the gloss. Could you not get such a one? I want you to send me a bow of blk crape, for the top of the blk straw bonnet, *exactly* like the one, on top of the blk crape bonnet."[32]

Another dressmaker might have balked, but Lizzy was sympathetic, clever, and patient, and she and Mary got along. Her slavery experience had taught her how to adjust herself to a mistress's temperamental demands; she was not afraid of the sudden tantrums the labile Mary threw when she did not get her way, and she grew used to her complaints and, eventually, her tears. Mary Lincoln "had her ways, but nobody minded her" was the attitude of the "colored" White House servants, "for she never hurt a flea, and her bark was worse than her bite."[33] The nervous, talkative Mary, whose earliest confidences were shared with her favorite "mammy," must have relaxed considerably in the presence of this knowing black woman, especially after her trouble with the Irish domestics back in Springfield.

But perhaps more significant for their evolving, deepening relationship were their complementary backgrounds. Born the same year into similar cultures—Kentucky Bluegrass and Virginia Piedmont slavery households had been cut from essentially the same cultural cloth—Mary Todd Lincoln and Elizabeth Hobbs Keckly shared cultural assumptions. They understood one another's expectations without the need for labored translations, and it was this instant recognition that no doubt clicked at their initial connection. To be sure, their straightforward, interlocking roles—Mary as consumer, Lizzy as producer of stylish dresses—enabled them to become working partners. But it was the shared cultural background that formed the common ground on which they would eventually build something more: a friendship.

It was in early May, with the Union troops exercising and parading gaily to the delight of all who saw them and before the frightening defeat at Bull Run, that Mary took her first shopping trip to Philadelphia, New York, and Boston to refurbish the White House. The railroads were still closed, so at Lincoln's suggestion she left by steamer, taking with her Lizzie Grimsley and William S. Wood, a New Yorker and onetime hotel manager whom Thurlow Weed, the shrewd Albany publisher and Republican organizer, had recommended to handle the arrangements for their trip from Springfield. The good-looking, attentive Wood was also Mary's choice for the vacant position of Commissioner of Public Buildings.

Mary had been thinking of this project since before the inauguration. While at Willard's, she had ascertained that there was a $20,000 congressional allowance to each new administration to refurbish the White House. Having launched Lizzy Keckly on the course to refurbish her wardrobe, she turned to the much larger task of overhauling the President's residence. No one denied it needed major work. Years of neglect had left its thirty-one rooms in a shoddy state, with broken furniture, balding rugs, and ripped wallpaper. An "ill-kept and dirty rickety concern," wrote Nicolay; the "shabby-genteel" White House was no setting for a powerful leader.[34]

Unfortunately for Mary, her Washington shopping took on the shape and meaning of an obsession, a way to cope with the panic, anxiety, and dread inspired by the isolation of her new position and the war. In Springfield, there had been a built-in limit to this pattern of shopping-as-symptom: Lincoln's salary. Now, however, she felt unrestrained. This was the first of three or four shopping trips she fit in that year; she would make at least eight more, eventually spending thousands upon thousands of dollars for furnishings, clothes, and jewelry during her years in the White House.[35]

If Mary had a psychological need to accumulate things to try to replace lost human love objects, her acquisitiveness was also cultural. Her childhood town and all her neighbors were simply steeped in commercialism; it was one of the reasons Mary loved New York, a giddily commercial city. (A reason to dislike New York would have been the fact that the city was never a strong supporter of Lincoln, who lost the election there by 30,000 votes.) Its marble emporiums lining lower Broadway and catering to the wealthy enchanted Mary, and she became a recognized customer at the fashionable Lord & Taylor and at A. T. Stewart's opulent "Marble Palace" on Broadway at Chambers Street. It was here that the innovative Stewart offered his customers set prices, a "free entrance" (which meant they could browse at will without being attended by a clerk), staged fashion shows, and a "Ladies' Parlor" on the second floor, with full-length Parisian mirrors. The shrewd businessman also staffed his store with young, gentlemanly clerks, called "Stewart's nice young men," deliberately hired to gossip and flirt with the female shoppers. In 1862, Mr. Stewart would open his even larger "Iron Palace" further up Broadway, between Ninth and Tenth, near Mathew Brady's photography studio.[36]

These shopping trips gave Mary freedom of movement, the power of choosing, and exposure to society. They satisfied the restlessness she tended to feel when depressed or anxious; they gratified her vanity and her need to be the center of attention. Holding court at the lavish Metropolitan Hotel at Prince and Broadway, attending theater and dinner parties at night, she spent her days absorbed in selecting whatever she wanted. In part, her shopping—manic, intensive, all-consuming—demonstrated what Julia Taft, whose mother gave up her bonnet strings to Mary, remarked on as an "an outstanding characteristic" of the First Lady: "that she wanted what she wanted when she wanted it and no substitute!" The teenage Julia, who spent many hours in the White House while her brothers played with Willie and Tad, nevertheless found Mary Lincoln a warm and sympathetic listener to her adolescent woes.[37]

On the occasion of her first shopping trip in mid-May, Mary returned after two weeks, in time, it turned out, to attend Ellsworth's funeral. Then, after Douglas's death in early June, she returned briefly to Philadelphia, immersing herself in happier thoughts. She was considering ordering custom-made wallpaper from Paris and, evidently liking what she saw, had William Wood authorize the order by mid-June. She took another end-of-summer trip to the shore in New Jersey with Tad, Harriet Shearer, and Lizzie Grimsley; they were joined by Robert (on summer leave from Harvard) and Secretary John Hay, who, at about the same age, were often companions. The trip was taken partly to escape the unhealthy, bug-infested August heat, which made Tad ill (although after Bull Run Mary had refused General Scott's insistence that she and the boys go north for safety). In November, she made a visit to Boston, where she could also see Robert, and at last the bulk of her shopping for the year was done. By that time, she had bought a fancy carriage; a 190-piece porcelain dinner set "decorated with royal purple and double gilt" and the United States seal for the White House, and a duplicate Limoges set for herself, with her initials M.L.; glassware; another dinner service; the custom-made wallpaper from Paris; custom-made carpetings; mantel ornaments, chandeliers, silverware, draperies, and books. In addition, she bought "rare exotics" for the conservatory, from which came the numerous bouquets that she loved to dispense as gifts; ordered the White House cleaned and painted; and "modernized" it, adding furnaces, gaslight, and running water pumped up from the Potomac. While their rooms were being redone, she and Lincoln stayed in the guest room.[38]

What happened to the congressional appropriation of $20,000 is easy to see. Mary's bill from the New York importers H.V. Haughwout and Co. for china, silverware, and chandeliers amounted to nearly $6,000; for the custom carpeting and wallpaper from William H. Carryl of Philadelphia, a bill came in for $7,500—in other words, well over half her allowance.[39]

Yet, even before the bills came in, her shopping exposed her to public censure. She was vociferously denounced in the Northern newspapers that were habitually critical of Lincoln and, therefore, lost nothing by lashing out at the First Lady. To these critics, her self-indulgent extravagances looked unpatriotic beside the sudden urgent need to fund a war. Wrote one: "She has evidently no comprehension that Jeff. Davis will make good his threat to occupy the White House in July for she is expending thousands and thousands of dollars for articles of luxurious taste." According to another, she was not the model of Republican womanhood the country craved in a time of self-sacrifice. "Shall the inanities of a Ball Room and Theatre be now the order of your life," asked "A Strong-Minded Woman" of Washington, "when there is scarcely a family in our midst but immediately or remotely is suffering the cruel pangs of mortal bereavement?"[40]

On the other hand, praise in papers sympathetic to her husband's administration frequently backfired. Although hailing First Ladies as "queens" was a journalistic commonplace—Harriet Lane had been the "Democratic queen"—reportorial swooning over the "Republican queen's" new bonnets bearing names like "The Princess" infuriated serious-minded Northerners. Abolitionist writer Lydia Maria Child was not alone in thinking, "So *this* is what the people are taxed for! to deck out this vulgar doll with foreign frippery!"[41]

Sometime after Lizzy Keckly became Mary's confidante, Mary would justify her spending to her: "I must dress in costly materials. The people scrutinize every article that I wear with critical curiosity. The very fact of having grown up in the West, subjects me to more searching observation."[42] Whatever Lizzy thought, she kept it to herself. Certainly, she was a beneficiary of Mary's extravagance and even, ironically, of the attention it drew.

But Mary's behavior laid her open to another, more potentially damaging charge. Toward the end of June, Lincoln received an anonymous letter warning him against keeping Wood as Public Buildings Commissioner. Opponents "will attempt to stab you in the most vital part by circulating scandal about your most estimable lady and Mr. W.," it read. According to one Republican congressman who knew them both, Lincoln "spoke sharply" to Mary and they argued about Wood, but in September, Wood had to resign anyway, after a congressional delegation uncovered his financial interest in a company to which he had given a government contract. In the scramble for power, Wood had meanwhile charged another of Mary's new favorites with disloyalty: John Watt, the White House gardener, who was brokering deals for her. Mary, eager to disavow her former connection to Wood and defend Watt (who knew about her debts, and more), made certain to denounce Wood as well. Writing to Secretary of the Interior Caleb B. Smith, she charged that Wood, "either deranged or drinking," is "now proved to be a very bad man . . . who does not know, what *truth* means . . . a most unprincipled man."[43]

Ironically, no matter what was said about Mary Lincoln at the time, Lizzy Keckly's own reputation as dressmaker to the President's wife soared, and she was able to open workrooms across from her apartments on Twelfth Street and hire assistants. During the secession winter, her business had declined as the best of her Southern clientele pulled out, but she was now the desired dressmaker of loyal Union women who sought her services, especially during Mary's well-advertised absences from Washington. During August of that year, which began with a string of oppressively hot days, she fit in kindhearted Mrs. Mary Jane Welles, whose husband was Gideon Welles, Lincoln's snowy-bearded Secretary of the Navy, and the handsome Mrs. Ella Stanton, wife of Edwin M. Stanton, Lincoln's gruff second Secretary of War. She sewed mourning clothes for Douglas's young widow, the exquisitely dressed Adele Cutts Douglas, whose aunt happened to be the glamorous widow Mrs. Rose O'Neal Greenhow. Mrs. Greenhow, who managed to juggle her roles as Washington hostess, friend of Northern politicians, and Confederate spy, had sent warning to the Southern troops at Manassas (Bull Run) of the Northern advance; before the summer was out, she was arrested for "holding correspondence with the Confederates."[44]

In mid-August, with troops moving in and out of the city and Thaddeus Lowe's observation balloons, meant to spy on the Confederates, sailing dreamily overhead, Lizzy received the news that her son, George, was dead. Unable to enlist in the Union Army as a black man ("The government consents only that Negroes shall smell powder in the character of cooks and body-servants in the army," Frederick Douglass wrote a friend in disgust later that month), twenty-one-year-old George W. D. Kirkland had left Wilberforce to join the First Missouri Volunteers as a white man, being white enough to pass. He was killed in his first battle, on August 10, in the bloody confrontation at Wilson's Creek, far away in the rolling hill country of southwest Missouri. Nearly 2,600 men were killed or wounded or went missing that day. It was the second significant battle of the war in which, not three weeks after Bull Run, the Confederates dealt the Union another crushing defeat.[45]

Mary was in New York when she heard the news about George and sent Lizzy "a kind womanly letter" which the grieving mother found comforting. After returning to Washington, Mary wrote Lizzie Grimsley the sad news: "I know you will be sorry to hear, that our colored Mantuamaker, Elizabeth, lost her only son & child in the battle of Lex Mo—She is heart broken. She is a very remarkable woman herself." Given her self-control and pride, Lizzy may have told Mary little about her past until her son died, so that hearing her story for the first time prompted Mary to make note of how "remarkable" Lizzy was. (She may also have told Mary that her husband, James Keckly, had died, news she would have heard since leaving St. Louis.) By then, too, Lizzy may have begun performing the intimate, domestic tasks for the Lincoln family that made her a comfort to them all, tasks that she had been trained to do for her white family in Virginia: comb and brush the President's hair; look after the two little boys, Willie and Tad, who were often sick; and minister to Mary when she was struck down by one of her headaches. Mary's letter to her cousin revealed a growing intimacy ("Mrs. Keckly" had become "Elizabeth," or "Lizabeth," as Mary pronounced it) and a flow of feeling between them, filtered through respect on Mary's side and gratitude on Lizzy's.[46]

In other respects, Mary was losing her footing. By the fall, her enthusiastic White House renovation, coupled with her dread of Lincoln's discovering how much she'd overrun her budget, had gotten her into serious trouble. John Watt, a native of Scotland and the White House gardener since the early 1850s, bought provisions for the Mansion, ran the payroll for outside staff, and had his hand in the general, nonstop maneuverings for jobs. Under his tutelage, Mary learned how to pad bills and use the gardener's account to hide other expenses. She was accused of doing both when it came time to pay for the banquet she ordered for Napoleon III in early August. (Mary had to fight to be allowed to order the dinner, which, according to White House custom, was supposed to be given by the Secretary of State; as a compromise, Secretary Seward gave Napoleon a formal dinner, too.) Interior Secretary Caleb B. Smith refused to pay the $900 bill she submitted after he consulted with Secretary Seward, who claimed to have entertained the same number of guests, ordering from the same restaurant, for $600 less. When Mary could not prevail upon Smith, Watt agreed to make out false bills for flowers, manure, and a horse and cart for twenty-seven days of hauling in August and submit them for a kickback instead. Unfortunately, one of the gatekeepers complained to Smith about "sundry petit, but flagrant frauds on the public treasury," the products of "deliberate collusion." (By then, Mary and Watt were known as a team: when a job seeker sought Mary's influence with Smith, he went to Watt, who told him, "Mrs. L always *succeeds*, and is enlisted in my behalf.") Mary, evidently worried about what Lincoln would say if he knew about the debts and false bills, persuaded Watt to ask Smith to speak to the President. "Mr. Watts [*sic*] . . . says," she wrote to Smith, as if it were all Watt's idea, "he will ever be deeply grateful to you, if you would *to day*, attend to some business, which he says he has spoken to you about." What Watt told Smith is that Mrs. Lincoln "had no idea that any thing was done which was not authorized by law," and Benjamin Brown French, the new Commissioner of Public Buildings, covered the bills.[47]

But a larger problem was brewing. In early fall, ignoring French's warnings that there was no more money to pay for what she had already bought, Mary continued spending and sending in bills. Inevitably Lincoln had to know, and the two of them had an argument on December 13, her forty-third birthday; by the next morning, she was begging Commissioner French to speak to the President, who had "declar[ed] he would not approve the bills overrunning the $20,000 appropriation," which by then ran over the amount by $6,700. According to French, "Mrs. L. wanted me to see him & endeavor to persuade him to give his approval to the bills, but not to let him know that I had seen her!"[48]

Despite a "severe headache," one of his usual ones, which he had going in to his meeting with Mrs. Lincoln, French set off down the hall to Lincoln's office. A somewhat melancholy insomniac since his wife died in May and a fellow sufferer from dizzying headaches, French was inclined to sympathy for Mary and did her bidding as best he could. However, he found the President "inexorable." French described Lincoln's reaction in his diary: "He said it would stink in the land to have it said that an appropriation of $20,000 for furnishing the house had been overrun by the President when the poor, freezing soldiers could not have blankets, & he swore that he would never approve the bills for *flub dubs for that damned old house*. It was, he said, furnished better than any house *they* lived in, & rather than put his name to such a bill he would pay it out of his own pocket!"

"Not very pleasant," French summarized the meeting, "but a portion of it very amusing."[49]

Yet it was not only her collection of *things*, but also her collection of *people* that nearly sank Mary Lincoln that year. "Our 'blue room,' in the evenings, is quite alive with the 'beau monde,'" she wrote Hannah Shearer in October, virtually repeating her delighted, postinaugural pronouncement of the success of her gatherings in the sumptuous oval parlor. In Mary's mind, this room, done up splendidly in blue, silver, and gold, contained her salon, her own circle of men (rarely a wife). Evenings spent with her favorites grouped around her in conversation no doubt transported her to the days of her Springfield coterie, when she was a young and popular coquette and there were no war, no unpaid bills, no disapproving news articles, and no horrible Washington women to contend with.

One of the most devoted of her callers that year was Henry "Chevalier" Wikoff, a charming American who had spent his young adulthood roving the capitals and courts of Europe, where he had evidently honed his immense gift for enchanting conversation. More delightfully, he had a reputation for intrigue and danger, having been an English spy and served fifteen months in a Genoese prison on a seduction charge for kidnapping his paramour, a young heiress. As a writer for the influential James Gordon Bennet's New York *Herald*, he had spent the Buchanan years in Washington at the White House and now was back on assignment, sending flattering insider stories back to Bennet to print, for which Mary was grateful. She wrote the publisher a thank-you note on her own behalf: "Need I repeat to you my thanks, in my own individual case, when I meet, in the columns of your paper, a kind reply, to some uncalled for attack, upon one so *little desirous* of newspaper notoriety, as my inoffensive self."[50]

Now nearing sixty, Chevalier Wikoff had many stories to tell, some probably not included in his three memoirs. To Mary, who was dying to see Europe, this well-traveled, well-read speaker of several languages must have seemed a cosmopolitan miracle. He had also earned his keep by introducing into Mary's "blue room" another member of the beau monde, the diverting Dan Sickles, who shot and killed his wife's unarmed lover, who was pacing in front of his house in Lafayette Square trying to signal her with a white handkerchief. The Quaker lawyer Edwin M. Stanton (Lincoln's future Cabinet member) had won then Congressman Sickles a much-celebrated acquittal on a plea of temporary insanity.[51]

Wikoff's luster dulled, however, when *Herald* readers had the pleasure of skimming excerpts from the President's annual message before Lincoln delivered it to the Congress on December 3. Accusing eyes turned accurately to the Chevalier, well-known to be telegraphing news to Bennet. Then Greeley's *Tribune*, the *Herald*'s rival, accused Mrs. Lincoln of giving (or selling) "her Chevalier" her husband's message, and Wikoff was called before a House Judiciary Committee. Refusing to name his collaborator, he was jailed overnight in the Old Capitol Prison, then emerged the next day ready to identify "the gardener Watt" as the person who supplied him with Lincoln's speech. At this point, the committee decided to drop the investigation; in the dénouement, Lincoln banished Wikoff from the White House. He was a sore point between the Lincolns for some time. Watt took the blame and lost his job; however, he privately insisted that it *was* Mary who had slipped Wikoff the message one day in the library.[52]

Of course, Mary was not barred from the White House, but this episode further tarnished her reputation, and it was said that she was "one of the *leaky vessels*" of the Executive Mansion. It was also said that her husband had to personally go to Capitol Hill to urge "Republicans on the Committee to spare him disgrace." Thereafter, Lincoln warned Mary against idle talk, as she would later admit: "My husband always enjoined upon me to be quiet."[53] But by then, Lincoln was no longer confiding in her.

The President had more pressing problems, however. His new General in Chief, the ardent thirty-four-year-old General McClellan, had been amassing an army of unheard number since his elevation in November but steadfastly refused to do anything with it but drill. He had, it is true, urged action in October in his capacity as commander of the Army of the Potomac. But that battle, on the steep, wooded bank along the Potomac forty miles up from Washington, called Ball's Bluff, had been another Union defeat, as well as a personal tragedy for the Lincolns. Colonel Edward Baker, their old Springfield friend and second son's namesake, was delegated with the mission and died along with more than half of his 1,700 men. Subsequently, in December, the newly convened Congress voted to establish a Joint Committee on the Conduct of the War to investigate the military "disasters" at Bull Run and Ball's Bluff. The Committee was chaired by the righteous Ohio Republican Senator Benjamin Wade and dominated by radical abolitionist Republicans.

(Moderates, led by Lincoln, were antislavery, but feared the consequences for race relations of wholesale emancipation; conservatives wished for slavery's ultimate end but preferred the means of voluntary emancipation and colonization.) Its self-defined charge, to root out corruption and incompetence in the army, most obviously in its Democratic generals, including McClellan, became a lightning rod for partisan political feelings.[54]

Despite the dismal mood, the holiday season of 1861 demanded celebration. One evening in late November, Mary invited " 'Hermann' the 'Prestidigitateur,' " who was performing at the National Theater, to come to the White House after his show and perform his card and magic tricks for her guests. In December began the formal levees and the First Lady's afternoon receptions, occasions on which Mary could shine. Indeed, not a week after Lincoln's "flub-dubs" outburst, Commissioner French, whose job it was to stand by Mary's elbow introducing callers to her, revisited her character in his diary: "I like Mrs. L. better and better, the more I see of her and think she is an admirable woman. She bears herself, in every particular, like a lady, and, say what they may about her, I will defend her." Friendly news reports, transmittable all the way to Sacramento, California, along the recently completed transcontinental telegraph line, could block out the blather of critics. Admiring descriptions of the White House redecorations appeared in the *Herald*. Even the weather cooperated, being particularly mild. In January, Mary posed for her portrait in Brady's Washington studio, showing off two of Elizabeth Keckly's silk gowns.[55]

Eleven-year-old Willie and eight-year-old Tad and their two new friends of similar age, Bud and Holly Taft, brought their own brand of merriment to their parents during this trying season. Free to come and go as they pleased, the four boys ran back and forth between the Tafts' house on L Street and the White House where, as Mr. Taft observed, proudly, "Mr. & Mrs. Lincoln take particular notice of our boys. They have *dined with the President* on two or three occasions. They have the 'run' of the 'White House.' " It was Mary who extended the invitations, including an invitation to sleep over, although it was Lincoln who most enjoyed—and got relief from—looking in on the boys' games. After the New Year, the boys staged a show in the White House attic, for which Tad blacked up his face and Willie wore one of his mother's gowns, with musical entertainment on a banjo played by one of the household staff. Admission was 5 cents, but the boys admitted the President for free. Another day found the boys on the flat copper roof of the White House, where they had constructed their own "Ship of State," from whose deck they peered through a spy glass to report "all strange sails on the River and objects on the Virginia shore." Allowing that Lincoln was the Commodore and the Cabinet the officers, they claimed to be the ones who actually sailed the Ship, the most important part. The boys also skated on the frozen streets, rode the White House pony, and played with Tad's goats. In mid-January, when Robert came home from Cambridge for vacation, the family circle was complete.[56]

On the day of the boys' show, Lizzy was fitting a dress for Mary. The hectic winter social season was on Mary's mind when she asked her what she thought of a new idea for entertaining in the White House. Instead of the formal state dinners, which she had found to be "very costly," what did Lizzy think of her giving "three large receptions"? "I think that you are right, Mrs. Lincoln," Lizzy answered, wisely agreeing when Mary had clearly made up her mind.

Before Lizzy was through for the day, a depressed Lincoln joined the pair. Lizzy often found herself seated with the Lincolns, listening in on their conversations. On this occasion, Lincoln had just come from visiting the bedridden McClellan, who was laid up with typhoid fever. No sooner had he sat down than Mary "at once stated the case to him." Lincoln paused, then said he did not think large receptions would work, and when pressed to explain, said "mildly" that it was "breaking in on the regular custom." The custom was complicated: evening receptions alternately hosted by the President and the Secretary of State were given from the last week in January through March; in addition, the White House hosted weekly dinners, each for the different members of the government, and special receptions for the military and navy officers, diplomatic corps, and Supreme Court justices. (Secretary Nicolay carefully wrote out the rules of etiquette, Cabinet rankings, seating charts, and proper forms of address for the diplomats for his personal files.)[57]

Mary, who took the view that whatever the President wanted to do, he could do (poor Lincoln may have wished this were more true, considering his current frustrations with his haughty and recalcitrant army commander), argued that receptions were more economical, more democratic, "more in keeping with the spirit of the institutions of our country, as you would say if called upon to make a stump speech." We could invite "strangers in the city, foreigners and others" to the receptions, but not to our dinners. Mary was adamant. "So the day was carried," Lizzy recalled. "The question was decided, and arrangements were made for the first reception," an immense, formal party.[58]

At the beginning of February 1862 Nicolay wrote to his fiancée of Mary's innovation: " 'La Reine' has determined to abrogate dinners and institute parties in their stead. How it will work remains to be seen." The first party, slated for February 5, was not to be as democratic or as inexpensive as Mary had found it necessary to propose to Lincoln. Instead, it was to be a ball in the enormous East Room by invitation only. Over seven hundred invitations were sent out to the leading men in government and their wives and to a select group of acquaintances and nongovernment eminences from Washington and New York. "Half the city is jubilant at being invited while the other half is furious at being left out in the cold," was Nicolay's comment. With the servants dressed in new mulberry-colored uniforms, the champagne and wine from a New York merchant, and a banquet from the expensive caterer Maillard's, also in New York, the ball was predicted by at least one invitee to be "the most magnificent affair ever witnessed in America." By 9 o'clock on the appointed evening, the guests were filling the East Room, where the Lincolns stood at the center greeting. At midnight, the dining room doors were opened to a feast of oysters, turkey, foie gras, aspic, beef, quail, partridge, duck, and varieties of cakes, ices, and fruits. Baskets of spun sugar in elegant shapes were arranged at the center of one table, at the head of which was a sugar helmet, symbolizing war. On a side table stood a cake in the shape of Fort Pickens.[59]

Lizzy made Mary's dress for this special party. It was a low-cut, off-the-shoulder, white satin gown, trimmed with black lace flounces looped up with black and white bows, with a long train. On her head Mary wore a headdress of black and white flowers and on her bosom a bouquet of crape myrtle, a half-mourning style in honor of the recently widowed Queen Victoria. Eyeing her before the ball, Lincoln had remarked, "Whew! our cat has a long tail to-night. . . . Mother, it is my opinion, if some of that tail was nearer the head, it would be in better style." For once, Lizzy felt she had to disagree with Lincoln. It was her opinion that Mary "had a beautiful neck and arm, and low dresses were becoming to her."[60]

The party was meant to be Mary's triumph in the midst of a depressing, muddy season, the grand finale to a year of renovations with a party suited to a new, opulent Mansion and her own personal redemption after a season of criticism. Early descriptions were flush with awe, but in the end few could ignore the disjunction between the pomp and vanity of "Mrs. Lincoln's ball" and the "mourning, distracted, and impoverished" state of the country. Of those who had returned their invitations refusing to come, nearly one hundred had added indignant notes, like the one sent back by Senator Benjamin Wade, who was in the middle of investigating Lincoln's inept generals: "Are the President and Mrs. Lincoln aware that there is a civil war? If they are not, Mr. and Mrs. Wade are, and for that reason decline to participate in dancing and feasting."[61]

Willie Lincoln had gotten a fever a few days before the party, which grew worse as the day of the ball approached. At first, the Lincolns considered canceling, but then, after consulting with the doctor, who thought Willie was "in no immediate danger," they simply announced that because of illness, the Marine Band would play but there would be no dancing. On the night of the party, even though Willie's fever grew worse and his breathing labored, the doctor stood by his earlier diagnosis. His parents, reluctant to leave him, finally had to go downstairs. They asked Lizzy, an experienced nurse who already knew the boys well, to look after him. But Mary came several times during the evening to see how he was, and throughout the night, guests noticed how sad the President looked.

Gentle, intelligent, and thoughtful Willie was the child thought to be most like Lincoln and the favorite of both his parents; he did not recover from what turned out to be typhoid fever. At about 5 o'clock at the end of the bright, mild day of February 20, just days after word of the Union's immense victory at Fort Donelson, Tennessee, reached Washington, reviving Northern hopes, Willie Lincoln died. He had been suffering for two weeks. Nicolay was lying on the couch in his office when the President came in and stood before him: " 'Well, Nicolay—my boy is gone—he is actually gone'! and bursting into tears, turned and went into his office." Later, Nicolay found Lincoln lying down with Tad, trying to comfort and quiet him. Tad, also sick, was now terrified.[62]

Tad's mother was in no condition to soothe him. The blow of Willie's death, though expected in the final days, overwhelmed her, and she could think of nothing but her own grief and despair. On the night Willie died, she asked Illinois friend Senator Orville Browning, who had been in to see her, if he would send for his wife to come sit with her. Someone also thought to send for Lizzy Keckly, who came immediately. She had worn herself out with watching over a boy whom she had come to admire and care for and, sadly, she had not been in the room when "God called the beautiful spirit home." Now, she readily helped wash and lay out his slight body in the Green Room. At one point, Lincoln entered the room and, lifting the covers, gazed at his son's face. "I know that he is much better off in heaven, but then we loved him so. It is hard, hard to have him die!" He "buried his face in his hands" and sobbed, in front of an "awe-stricken" Lizzy.[63]

Lincoln's grief and tears stirred Lizzy; she would never forget the "solemn moments" when she watched him weeping over his son's body. In contrast, Mary's "convulsions" at the sight of Willie's "pale face" seemed to leave Lizzy dry-eyed. It was not that she had forgotten Mary's comforting kindness at her own son's death, or could not sympathize with her misery, but in the presence of Mary's "paroxysms" of grief, Lizzy seemed to become steadier, more self-contained. Later, she would often hold back at the points at which Mary let go; indeed, it was likely part of her appeal to Mary that she did so, since Lizzy's restraint evidently had a calming effect on Mary. To the former slave, emotional forbearance possessed an almost dignifying purpose and meaning, making Mary's undisguised lack of self-control, a luxury denied to women in Lizzy's position, something to look down upon. It would have been in keeping with her Presbyterian background, and also her personal doctrine of self-reliance, which had helped her make do against the pain of too much powerlessness and loss, for her to feel this way. Mary told Lizzy that had Providence spared Willie, he would have been "the hope and stay of her old age. But Providence had not spared him," Lizzy said in her straightforward manner.[64] She, too, had had such hopes for her only son, and Providence had not spared him either. It was part of Lizzy's self-protective faith to see the death of a son as one in a number of life's sorrows.

Haunted by feelings of shame and guilt, Mary came to see Willie's death as God's judgment upon her vanity, symbolized in the convergence of her party and his fatal illness. "Willie being too precious for earth," she would write a friend in May, his "severe illness" two years ago, when he had scarlet fever, was "but a warning to us, that one so pure, was not to remain long here and at the same time, he was *lent* us a little longer—to try us & wean us from a world, whose chains were fastening around us & when the blow came, it found us so unprepared to meet it." Yet, at the same time, she was ordering from her New York milliner mourning bonnets trimmed with "the *very finest*, & blackest & lightest" veils, and crapes, and lace, and "black & white crape flowers," and bows.[65] Lizzy Keckly would have her new orders, too.

Chapter Ten

*T*he year 1862 marked a turning point in the relationship between Mary Lincoln and Elizabeth Keckly. It resulted largely from Mary's personal tragedy, but it also came about in connection with the dramatic change in the intensity and scope of the war, when the battles became bloodier and the momentum toward emancipation as a necessity, if not an outright aim, increased. In the extended mourning she observed after Willie died, Mary's complicated feelings of guilt and vulnerability caused her to become more attached to the reliably steady Lizzy, just as, during the crises of her childhood, she had turned to the always present Mammy Sally. At the same time, the rising tide of emancipation and her own celebrity as a commuter between the races and their separate worlds gave Lizzy Keckly room to become more than Mary's dressmaker or "mammy" surrogate.

Willie's death occurred at the dawn of the next stage of the Civil War, when the war grew to a scale of unimaginably destructive proportions. The change came in early April with the slaughter at the Battle of Shiloh, in which in two days alone 20,000 men were killed or wounded, "nearly double the 12,000 casualties at Manassas, Wilson's Creek, Fort Donelson, and Pea Ridge *combined*." After the costly Union victory at Shiloh, battles that seemed like massacres became commonplace. Shiloh also dislodged all fantasies of a swift end to the war or the hope for some kind of Union-preserving compromise. General Ulysses S. Grant, Lincoln's "fighting" general who had been leading Union troops to victory in the Kentucky-Tennessee theater, had answered Confederate General Simon Bolivar Buckner's proposal to discuss the terms of his surrender at Fort Donelson with the firm declaration "No terms except an unconditional and immediate surrender can be accepted." After Shiloh, it became clear that only "unconditional and immediate surrender" of the enemy was going to end this war.[1]

At the same time, pressure mounted on Lincoln to confront slavery (as opposed to unionism) as being at the root of the war. The slaves simply would not go away. Since the summer of 1861, abolitionists had been arguing the strategic necessity of emancipating the rebels' slaves, who were the Confederate Army's labor force. "The very stomach of this rebellion is the negro," said Douglass. "Arrest that hoe in the hands of the negro, and you smite the rebellion in the very seat of its life."[2] At Fortress Monroe, the Union stronghold in the midst of Confederate territory on Virginia's eastern coast near Hampton, General Benjamin Butler declared that three escaped slaves he had put to work at the fort were "contraband of war" from a state no longer in the Union, thus preventing their master from claiming them under the Fugitive Slave Law. In July, the government ratified Butler's policy, and from then on the runaways who could be seen trudging wearily out of Virginia across the Long Bridge became known as contrabands. This created other questions about their legal status, but they were not considered emancipated.

In midsummer of 1861, the idea of actually freeing slaves by government edict was a Rubicon not yet crossed. But by the end of August, it was. On August 30, after the Union defeat at Wilson's Creek, John C. Frémont, onetime Republican presidential candidate and now Lincoln's new commander of the Western Department, issued a proclamation emancipating the slaves of Confederates in the state of Missouri. Lincoln, unaware of Frémont's intentions, was furious when he found out. Writing privately to Frémont, he requested that he rescind the order, explaining that it threatened to "alarm our Southern Union friends, and turn them against us—perhaps ruin our fair prospect for Kentucky." Frémont refused, and Lincoln publicly revoked his proclamation. But the countermand stirred up frustration and anger in the North. To antislavery activists, it fulfilled their worst fears that Lincoln was a reactionary. Abolitionist editor William Lloyd Garrison charged that it would "prolong the war and subvert the government." Even Orville Browning, a conservative Republican, criticized his old friend's move against Frémont's proclamation.[3]

Lincoln delivered his Annual Address to Congress in December with the slavery controversy heavy on his mind. In his message, he expressed his hope to avoid having the war "degenerate into a violent and remorseless revolutionary struggle." He recommended a plan for emancipation by which states that voluntarily freed their slaves would be compensated and the freed blacks be colonized "at some place, or places, in a climate congenial to them." The "integrity of the Union" must be the "primary object of the contest on our part" and all other questions "not of vital military importance" be left "to the more deliberate action of the legislature." But already, abolitionists and radicals in Lincoln's own party were calling the war "a revolutionary struggle between two social systems" that could not coexist.[4] And no one doubted but that the heart of the Southern system was slavery.

There came urgent calls for immediate emancipation. In a speech in mid-January 1862 radical leader George W. Julian of Indiana told Congress, "The mere suppression of the rebellion will be an empty mockery of our sufferings and sacrifices, if slavery be spared to canker the heart of the nation anew, and repeat its diabolical deeds." On the same day in Philadelphia, speaking before the largely black audience of a self-improvement society, Frederick Douglass similarly urged that the moment for eradicating slavery was now: "Now lay the axe at the root of the tree, and give it up—root, top, body and branches—to the consuming fire. . . . To let this occasion pass unimproved . . . would be a sin against unborn generations."[5] In March, Lincoln and members of his Congress were in the audience at the Smithsonian Institution when the Boston abolitionist orator Wendell Phillips made three triumphant appearances that would have been unthinkable in that slavery town only a year earlier.

At the same time, activists had been mobilizing citizens throughout the North, from which petitions calling for confiscation of slaves and emancipation began pouring into Congress. For years Southern congressmen had blocked measures that interfered with slavery. Now, in 1862, with the Southern politicians gone, long-awaited antislavery bills issued forth from Capitol Hill: prohibition of slavery in the territories; a treaty with Britain for more effective suppression of the international slave trade; diplomatic recognition of Haiti and Liberia (likely sites for colonization); and abolition of slavery in the District of Columbia. Turning to the problem of the contrabands, Congress also adopted an article of war forbidding army and navy officers to return fugitive slaves to their masters.

In was in the third week of April 1862 that President Lincoln signed a congressional act abolishing slavery in the District of Columbia. "I trust I am not dreaming," Frederick Douglass wrote to Senator Charles Sumner, "but the events taking place seem like a dream." Mary Lincoln's gentle defender, Elizabeth Blair Lee, wrote to her husband describing the bill's effects on the family slaves:

> Vincent [a slave] has announced his wish to go *in the world* to better his condition. Father at first was puzzled what to do—but I begged him to let him go & to take Alick in the house & I am quite certain at the end of six weeks to make him a better house servant than Vincent & not doing great things either—The rest of the servants are going to remain on their old terms—Henry says he is content where he is—& is not used to knocking about among common folks. Been used to quality all his days & wants to spend the rest of them with them. . . . I expected all of them would put out for the City & was rather surprised when Nannie Olivia & Henry told their purpose Nanny says she knows when she is well off but is evidently delighted that her children are free.[6]

Similar scenes were being enacted in households all over the District. The act included a provision for colonizing freedmen outside of the United States and offered compensation to their masters for the loss of property, up to $300 a slave. But in the eyes of most of Washington's white citizens, who had fought the bill with petitions, letters, and editorials, it was an inadequate sum, hardly compensation for the social transformation that they worried was taking place. Utterly law-abiding and practical, Lincoln had made compensation a central feature of his plans for emancipation—that, and colonization, which flowed not only from his belief in racial inequality, but also from his Jeffersonian opinion that slavery had caused too much hostility between the races to enable them to live peacefully together after emancipation. "Emancipation compensation & colonization—satisfies all shades of Republicans," Elizabeth Blair wrote, the view Lincoln hoped for.[7]

In the wake of this remarkable act, Lizzy Keckly became a minor celebrity. Two days later, Washington correspondent Mary Clemmer Ames wrote a celebratory article profiling several successful "late Slaves" that appeared in the New York *Evening Post*, featuring the most celebrated figure, Mrs. Lincoln's dressmaker "Lizzie."

> Lizzie is a stately, stylish woman. Her cheek is tawny, but her features are perfectly regular; her eyes dark and winning; hair straight, black, shining. A smile half-sorrowful and wholly sweet makes you love her face as soon as you look on it. It is a face strong with intellect, and heart, with enough of beauty left to tell you that it was more beautiful still before wrong and grief shadowed it.
>
> Lizzie's father was a gentleman of "the chivalry," and in her mother's veins ran some of the best blood of the Old Dominion.
>
> I cannot tell the wrongs of her childhood and early youth; if I were to try my hand would stiffen with horror, my heart, in its strong indignities, would stifle the words I might utter. . . .
>
> It is Lizzie who fashions those splendid costumes of Mrs. Lincoln, whose artistic elegance have been so highly praised during the past winter. It was she who "dressed" Mrs. Lincoln for "the party," and for every grand occasion. Stately carriages stand before her door, whose haughty owners sit before Lizzie docile as lambs while she tells them what to wear. Lizzie is an artist, and has such a genius for making women look pretty, that not one thinks of disputing her decrees. Thus she forgets her sorrow, interesting herself to serve each one who comes, as if to dress her was the chief business of her existence.

In many ways, the portrait typified abolitionist writing. For Lizzy's character, Ames reached into the popular genres of the day and pulled out the "tragic mulatto," the passive, sentimental heroine of much fiction, poetry, and drama, whom white readers could feel comfortable imagining as free. She was the exemplary victim of slavery: beautiful, intelligent, aristocratic, and long-suffering, who could have been a model of "true womanhood," virtuous and domestic, no different from the ideal white woman had not the taint of race doomed her. (Ames merely hinted at her sexual degradation, which by itself excluded Lizzy from white women's domestic culture.) In describing the post-slavery "Lizzie," Ames invoked another stereotype: the "Lizzie" who made fashion decrees, a version of the society dressmaker similar to Virginia Clay's Mrs. Rich. But here racial difference gave the stereotype a twist: the symbolism of the former slave issuing absolute decrees to obedient white women could not be missed. The result was a "Lizzie" embodying contradictory messages, an accurate reflection of the social confusion at the time. On the one hand, she was meant to assuage white fears of the degenerate, dangerous, ex-slaves in their midst. She was the perfect citizen, the model of a "late Slave": a true success story, up from slavery to the White House. On the other hand, this freedwoman threatened the old social order.[8]

For her own part, Lizzy may have wished to be an inspiration for the beneficiaries of the new act, like the Blairs' plucky Vincent.

During this period, Mary Lincoln was likely unaware of what was happening outside the White House. For weeks after Willie died, she stayed in her room trying to shut out the world that had caused her so much pain. All reminders of Willie sent her into convulsive fits of grief, and so she cut out of her life whatever she could that had been associated with him when he was alive. (She saved items associated with his funeral: the flowers from his open coffin and a published eulogy written by one of her blue room courtiers.) Unable to bear the sight of the Taft boys, particularly Bud, who had called daily at the White House during Willie's illness and held his hand on the day he died, she had written Mrs. Taft a note before the funeral: "Please keep the boys home the day of the funeral; it makes me feel worse to see them." She stayed away from the funeral herself and did not know that Lincoln sent for Bud so that he could see Willie before he was put in the casket. The Tafts were never invited to visit again. Mary also had all Willie's toys and games given away, and she afterward refused to enter the second-floor guest room where he had died. He was laid out in the Green Room, which she also avoided, except for a séance she organized three years later to communicate with Willie. She did go out at least once in the second week of April, when she went to her church, the New York Presbyterian, with her husband, but she looked to a Springfield friend to be "so hid behind her immense black veil, and very deep black flounce, that one could scarcely tell she was there." Even in May, pleading her mourning, she refused Navy Secretary Gideon Welles's request to begin the customary summer concerts on the White House lawn: "It is hard that in this time of our sorrow, we should be thus harassed." All this time, others took care of little Tad, who was sick with the fever that killed his brother and was obviously suffering from his loss, although he never mentioned Willie.[9]

One of those caretakers was sister Elizabeth Edwards, who was back in Washington before the end of February. She had been reluctant to come, partly because she felt needed at home to help with her grandchildren and partly because of a falling-out she had had with Mary. In the fall, Mary had found a "private letter" Elizabeth had accidentally left behind when she left Washington, in which Elizabeth's daughter, Julia Edwards Baker, had written unflattering things about her aunt. Elizabeth wrote trying to smooth things over, but Mary returned her letters to her "with insulting remarks." However, the ties between the sisters were strong, and even in her anger, Mary believed that Elizabeth was "the only one of my sisters who has appeared to be pleased with our advancement."[10] Elizabeth would never disavow her old role as caretaker for her troubled younger sister.

Elizabeth wrote Julia about Mary's condition three weeks after Willie's death: "Your Aunt Mary still confines herself to her room, feeling very sad and at times, gives way to violent grief. She is so constituted, and the surrounding circumstances will present, a long indulgence of such gloom." Unable to control her feelings enough to handle visitors, Mary relied on her sister as her intermediary. When Elizabeth Blair Lee came to the White House on March 1 "to enquire for the sick child & the Mother," Mary sent her sister down with her thanks and a "kind message," and the two women, according to Mrs. Lee, "had a very friendly chat."[11]

Elizabeth, who had endured the loss of a child of her own and felt a great deal for her sister's suffering, may have been one of the reasons Mary interpreted Willie's death as a punishment for her high style of living. "Your Aunt Mary's manner is very distressed, and subdued," she wrote Julia. "It is a seeming crush to her *unexampled frivolity,* such language, sounds harsh, but the *excessive indulgence,* that has been revealed to me, fully justifies it." She hoped that Mary would give up some of her "*pleasures,*" but did not expect she would. "Such is her nature, that I can not realize, that she will forego *them* all."[12]

Mary wanted her sister to stay through May, but Elizabeth, feeling homesick and oppressed by the pressure of having to socialize mostly with strangers, was anxious to leave. She spent April privately trying to persuade their other sister, Frances Wallace, to allow her daughter to replace her as Mary's companion. But Mary had also quarreled with Frances, who was less inclined to let bygones be bygones. "I wrote to your Aunt Frances," Elizabeth told Julia, "urging that Mary [Wallace, Frances's daughter] should come on. She might as well forget the past, and allow Mary to see *something of the world*—Her Aunt Mary is so nervous, and dependent upon the companionship of someone, that she need feel no apprehension, of not being considerately treated."[13]

Mary Lincoln was not the only one who wanted Elizabeth to stay. Lincoln, too, found Elizabeth's presence soothing. She took him into the conservatory "to Calm his mind—to Cheer him"; it turned out he'd never visited the place, one of Mary's favorite. Another time, she accepted Lincoln's invitation to drive with him to the Navy Yard and Arsenal, her first time out of the White House since she had arrived more than a week earlier. More important, Lincoln believed that her staying was necessary to his wife's mental health. Elizabeth would remember Lincoln's reaction when she told him she was leaving: "Mr. Lincoln Shed tears. . . . Said to me—Mrs. Edwards—'do Stay with me—you have Such a power & control Such an influence over Mary—Come do Stay and Console me.'"[14]

Mary Lincoln met the terrible crises of her adult life like the child she essentially was: by breaking down under the overwhelming release of her feelings and relying on others to step in, take care of her, and handle her affairs. Her panicked reactions to the ongoing discoveries of her overspending (particularly in the first and final years of Lincoln's administration) conformed to the pattern: Benjamin French was not the only man who would find himself listening to one of Mary's tearful requests to help her out of trouble with her husband or her debts. In the emotional crisis triggered by Willie's dying, Lincoln was too burdened by his own, and the country's, troubles to take care of Mary himself. Besides, he had retreated into his own misery, leaving her emotionally exiled in hers. After Elizabeth went home, Mrs. Rebecca Pomeroy, one of the army hospital nurses who served under Dorothea Dix, the reformer of insane asylums who had been named Superintendent of Female Nurses, was hired to take care of Mary. But Mary needed the attentions of someone who could feel more like family and would not leave. It was apparently after her sister returned home and because her niece did not come, that Mary began to regard Elizabeth Keckly as a possible companion. By fall she had invited Lizzy (as she then called her) to join her on an extended excursion to New York City and Boston.[15]

When Mary emerged from the fog of the months after Willie's death, she found about her an altered world. At Lincoln's urging, the foot-dragging General McClellan began moving a vast army toward the Peninsula in eastern Virginia, nearer to Richmond, leaving behind troops to guard Washington against Confederate invasion. The city itself had also changed. The capital that a year before had seemed a large and colorful parade ground was slowly becoming one vast hospital, filled with the stench and moans of sick, wounded, and dying soldiers, at its peak up to 50,000 men. The freshly injured soldiers, their "wounds full of worms—some swelled and inflamed," wrote Walt Whitman, one of the hospital nurses, were brought into the city by steamer, then loaded into ambulances and driven to the fifteen to nineteen army hospitals housed in schools, hotels, churches, government offices, and other improvised spaces around the city. One could also see soldiers limping into the hospitals themselves, some with their head bound up, others with their arms in slings. Even the dead contributed to the impression of unceasing commotion, as carts burdened with corpses "nightly lumbered through the streets leading to the cemeteries, to Oak Hill, or Glenwood, or Mt. Olivet, or, after June 1864, to the newly dedicated Arlington National Cemetery across the Potomac, on part of what had been General Robert E. Lee's plantation." Mary, subdued and in deep mourning for her son and for one of her half-brothers who had been among the dead on the battleground at Shiloh, was at last in sync with the national mood.[16]

In addition to a different kind of war, Mary also discovered an altered racial landscape when she began to go about again that spring of 1862. The April emancipation of Washington's slaves, followed by the repeal several weeks later of the black codes that had interfered with the social life of the free black community, sparked nothing short of a social revolution. District residents, possessing no power in Congress, did what they could to stem the tide of change. The city's board of aldermen had unsuccessfully sought to dissuade Congress against "*unqualified* abolition of slavery in this district at the present critical Juncture in our national affairs" before providing "Just and proper safe-guards against converting this city, located as it is between two Slaveholding States, into an asylum for free negroes, a population undesirable in every American community, and which it has been deemed necessary to exclude altogether from some even of the non-Slaveholding States."[17] But for Washington's African-American community and the nation's population of anxious black onlookers, enslaved and free, abolition in the district came not a moment too soon.

In some ways, white fears of an inundation of refugees from slavery were accurate. In April 1862, about 400 contrabands were counted in Washington; by October, that number had risen to 4,200; by the following spring, the population of contrabands reached 6,000. All in all, by 1865, the year the war ended, some 40,000 newly freed men, women, and children had come to Washington.[18]

The first groups of contrabands were absorbed into the city. Early in 1862, contrabands lived along Duff Green's Row on East Capitol Street, where the Folger Shakespeare Library stands today. But as their numbers grew, they moved into empty soldiers' barracks; into huts along the Canal, clustered around military hospitals, or near the forts on the edge of the city; or into shacks in the alleys hidden behind the houses. They built their poor shelters out of bits and scraps of "tents and blankets, ends of plank, barrel staves, logs, and mud," according to one eyewitness.[19] The more fortunate newcomers found rooms in homes or boarding houses owned by other African Americans.

By the summer of 1862, Congress enacted a law freeing the slaves of disloyal citizens who came under Union control and authorizing the President to employ "persons of African descent" to help suppress the rebellion. As a consequence, the federal government set up a system for registering contrabands, giving out rations and clothing and paying "able-bodied men" and some women (from 40 cents to $1.00 a day) to do menial work for the Union effort in and about the government corrals, army camps, and military hospitals. Because of the wartime labor shortage, there was much work to do. The men sawed wood, carried water, made fires, cooked, built ditches and drains, repaired roads, wharves, and stockades, and policed hospital grounds. Women were employed in hospitals as laundresses and cooks. Contraband workers were also given tasks that no soldier wanted to do: clean cesspools, remove slops from hospital wards, scrub privies, bury dead horses and mules, and cart refuse-filled soil beyond the city limits.

But the system of government support broke down at many points. Wages and rations were often withheld from the vulnerable black workers, leaving many—particularly women, children, the old or infirm—with little or no food or means of support. Union soldiers physically abused some of the contrabands. Overcrowded conditions in the contraband camps made them breeding grounds for dysentery, typhoid, and smallpox. Red wooden crosses stood at the head of roughly dug graves not far from the camps.[20]

It was not only white Washingtonians who feared being engulfed by black refugees. Many in Washington's middle-class black community, struggling to maintain their own precarious social foothold, did what they could to distinguish themselves from the mass of lower-class black people clamoring below. Reflecting the extremes of this desire, some government clerks in 1863 formed the Lotus Club, a secret society to which only leading, light-skinned African American families could belong, and which white people and contrabands knew nothing about. However, many more in the black middle class responded by reaching out to help the newcomers, if only because they understood that most white people painted all members of their race with the same broad brush of ridicule and contempt and it was self-preservation to raise up all African Americans. Indeed, already by July 1862, a congressional committee reported that with the elimination of the legal barriers of slavery "the prejudice of caste becomes stronger and public opinion more intolerant to the negro."[21]

Lizzy Keckly was one of those who helped that summer by founding a relief society to aid the contrabands. To be sure, she now had little in common with the masses of former slaves who flocked into Washington. She was literate, independent, and of mixed-race heritage; she had spent her years in slavery living with her white family and the last decade earning a living by making silk gowns for the "elite of the land." Many of the contrabands arrived in the rags they were wearing to plow their master's fields, where they had toiled far apart from the household slaves, when they dropped their tools and headed north. Most were dark-skinned, illiterate laborers who had never worked for wages and so had no experience with Yankee notions of "prompt and steady endeavor, the employer's right to discharge unwanted workers, and the laborer's right to change employers." White officers expressed surprise and admiration at the amount of work some of these black laborers produced under difficult conditions and sometimes without compensation. However, most Northerners looked with suspicion on people they regarded as foreign beings—of a different tribe, if not species. Contrabands looking for work gathered at the Contraband Depot at the foot of Twelfth Street, but potential employers in the white community liked to say that the contraband idea of freedom was "Nothing to do, and plenty to eat." Even Washington's established blacks took this view. As Lizzy put it, "Dependence had become a part of their second nature, and independence" brought responsibilities and cares they were not used to. "They came to the Capital looking for liberty, and many of them not knowing it when they found it. . . . the bright joyous dreams of freedom to the slave faded—were sadly altered, in the presence of that stern, practical mother, reality. . . . Poor dusky children of slavery, men and women of my own race—the transition from slavery to freedom was too sudden for you!"[22]

The tone of condescension in her response was typical of her caste, but Lizzy's sympathy was real. Less far from slavery than some of her Washington friends, she could remember how her own "dreams of freedom" had faded when, for instance, she found herself paying off the debts of her alcoholic husband. When she spoke of their "exaggerated ideas of liberty" and "extravagant hopes," she may have spoken from experience. She could also recall the shock of coming north, where people might mean well but were not by nature "warm and impulsive. For one kind word spoken, two harsh ones were uttered." Leaving home was painful, she knew, and the South, whatever else it was, had been home: "The emancipated slaves, in coming North, left old associations behind them, and the love for the past was so strong that they could not find much beauty in the new life so suddenly opened to them." The camps were so wretched that some of the men and women she met there told her that they wanted to "go back to slavery in the South, and be with their old masters."[23]

Lizzy's deepening relationship with Mary held out to her the prospect of wielding real influence in a culture that saw the mulatto as a mediator between the races. After Willie died, Lizzy was one of the few people Mary admitted to her presence during her self-imposed confinement; she helped soothe the poor, distraught woman and, as the weeks went by, fitted her for her mourning wardrobe. Lizzy was also one of the women who helped take care of Tad during this time. When Mary took Tad with her on her late-fall trip to the North, Lizzy Keckly was their logical traveling companion, as familiar in her caretaking capacities to Tad as she was to his mother. Lincoln must have assumed Lizzy's presence, too. As Mary would write to her husband in November from New York City: "A day or two since, I had one of my severe attacks, if it had not been for Lizzie Keckley, I do not know what I should have *done*."[24] Lizzy had become part of her routine and her retinue.

During the family crisis of the spring, Lizzy had also become an intimate observer of the family, another position of power she would use. Indeed, her "behind the scenes" testimony has helped historians understand the toll Willie's death took on Mary, mentally and physically. Lizzy believed that Willie's death actually changed Mary; most of all, she was struck by Mary's need to get rid of whatever Willie loved, by her intense, almost "supernatural . . . dread" of coming into contact with Willie's belongings, a reaction so different from her own love of mementoes. For Lizzy, being in possession of the belongings of a lost loved one was like being in possession of one's past and identity, contained in the material memories of one's most heartfelt attachments that not even slaveholders could repossess. For Mary, rage at the loss, at the narcissistic injury that the other's death dealt to *her*, overrode all other feelings, and ridding herself of the other's possessions, while devoting herself to amassing an elaborate mourning wardrobe, was her way of eradicating the injury and shoring up her damaged self.

Lizzy would also remember Lincoln's reaction to one of Mary's fits of grief, often cited by historians. Leading her to a window and gesturing across the Potomac toward the Hospital for the Insane, he told her "gently" that if she could not control her grief, it would drive her mad, and "we may have to send you there."[25]

Lincoln apparently confided to several people during this time that he believed his wife was "partly insane," language he would have used to describe her inability to control her emotions. That she was "dependent upon the companionship of someone," in Elizabeth Edwards's words, was evident. It had not been that different in Springfield, after all; back in Illinois, he had had to urge indignant or frightened servants to remain with his wife. Now it was Madame Keckly, as he always called her, whose presence he could appreciate.[26]

For Lizzy, having a white family depend on her was nothing new, but having social visibility in the white world was. Seven years after buying her freedom, she broke that particular bond of slavery. For slavery as a social institution rendered innumerable human beings invisible: most slaves came into the world and went through it and out of it with no documented—that is, no social—identity, essentially with no public record of their existence other than their master's tax and property lists. For Lizzy, Mary Clemmer Ames's article of April 1862 signaled her crossing a threshold into visibility few women of her background managed in their lifetime. As usual, Lizzy was to seize the opportunities that her recently gained access to the White House and new celebrity gave her.[27]

During the first part of the summer, Lizzy probably did not see much of the Lincolns, because Mary spent part of her time at the Soldiers' Home, the 240-acre farm on an overlook about two miles north of the city that the Lincolns used as a summer home; then she spent much of July in New York City and Boston, where she visited Robert. Mary's visit to the North was less gay than the trips of the previous year: she replaced the White House's shabby sets of Sir Walter Scott's *Waverly* and Shakespeare, and she visited the Brooklyn Naval Yard and the New England Soldiers' Relief Association, one of the many local aid societies that had formed in the North, many instigated by women who had been schooled in such contemporary reform movements as temperance, women's rights, antislavery, and education.

Most of all, as Mary privately told a Washington acquaintance, she managed to find in the North her own relief from months of severe depression: "In the loss of our idolized boy, we naturally have suffered such intense grief, that a removal from the scene of our misery was found very necessary." Yet, she confessed, the anguishing thought that *"he is not with us"* would overcome her no matter where she was: "How often, I feel rebellious, and almost believe that our Heavenly Father, has forsaken us, in removing, so lovely a child from us! Yet I know, a great sin, is committed when we feel thus." There was also reason to find relief from the despair of the war and fears of invasion. In early September, after the Second Battle of Bull Run, with the dark news spreading that Union General John Pope's newly formed Army of Virginia was falling back toward Washington, a Springfield friend discovered Mary pacing back and forth alone in the East Room, "wringing her hands and weeping."[28]

Militarily, it had been a grim summer for the North. By the end of June, Union forces had been outmaneuvered in the Shenandoah Valley and General McClellan's drive to Richmond had failed. The Napoleonic McClellan openly blamed Lincoln for his inability to take Richmond, as usual accusing the President of not giving him enough troops to overcome the enemy. "It is the nature of the case, and neither you or the government is to blame," Lincoln telegraphed to his angry general. ("He is a humbug," Lizzy heard Mary tell Lincoln; "he talks so much and does so little.") In early July, news of the Union retreat from Richmond spread through the disheartened North; so too did word of the appalling numbers of dead, wounded, or missing. In the last week of fighting in June, during what became known as the Seven Days' battles, they ran to 36,000 casualties for both sides.[29]

From then on, there was little doubt that the war would have to be waged until the North had destroyed the South. A comprehensive income tax law was passed and new recruits were mobilized. As part of his military strategy, Lincoln also resumed his push for emancipation beyond Washington, a subject he had been turning over in his mind for some time. On July 12 he pleaded with congressmen of the border states to accept a plan for gradual emancipation in their states, with provisions for compensation and colonization, warning that if they did not act soon, slavery in their states "will be extinguished by mere friction and abrasion—by the mere incidents of the war." They rejected his appeal two days later. However, two days after that, Congress issued a virtual emancipation act, freeing the contrabands who had already escaped and were under Union jurisdiction. Even before hearing the congressmen's answer, Lincoln had concluded that it was a "military necessity" to free the slaves. "We must free the slaves or ourselves be subdued," he told Cabinet members Seward and Welles on Sunday, July 13, as the three men rode in his carriage to the funeral of Secretary of War Stanton's baby. Then, on July 22, Lincoln privately revealed to his Cabinet his intention to issue a proclamation emancipating slaves in the rebel states, but following Seward's advice, he agreed to wait to announce it publicly until after a Union victory. Releasing the proclamation in the midst of defeats would look like desperation, Seward told Lincoln, who was instantly convinced.[30]

Unaware of Lincoln's temporarily tabled emancipation proclamation, abolitionists saw little to encourage them. Toward the end of August, in response to Horace Greeley's *Tribune*'s "prayer of twenty million people" for emancipation, Lincoln said that the policy he was pursuing was to save the Union, that regardless of his personal feelings about slavery, saving the Union was his "paramount object." He was trying to stave off a polarizing debate over slavery in the North. "If I could save the Union without freeing *any* slave I would do it, and if I could save it by freeing *all* slaves I would do it; and if I could save it by freeing some and leaving others alone I would also do that," Lincoln wrote the New York editor.[31]

More troubling for African Americans, a week earlier Lincoln had explained to a delegation of five black citizens he had invited to the White

House why he supported colonization and why they should accept his plan of colonization in Central America. He had listened to them attentively in the widely publicized meeting, the first time a President had met formally with black Americans. But his response bore the marks of the kind of cold and disassociated logic that sometimes drove him: "You and we are different races. . . . Whether it is right or wrong I need not discuss, but this physical difference is a great disadvantage to us both, as I think your race suffer greatly, many of them by living among us, while ours suffer from your presence." The presence of blacks had caused the war, he told them. "But for your race among us there could not be a war, although many men engaged on either side do not care for you one way or the other. Nevertheless, I repeat, without the institution of Slavery, and the colored race as a basis, the war could not have an existence." Regardless of his personal feelings, social inequality of the races was "a fact with which we have to deal. I cannot alter it if I would." Colonization would be a "sacrifice . . . of your present comfort" but one to be made "for the sake of your race."[32]

It has been argued that Lincoln's comments to his visitors reflected his need to find a practical solution to the vexing problem of race and, in the present crisis, to manage the racist violence that had erupted in Northern cities following the government's recent steps toward emancipation. Indeed, there were some freed men and women quite ready to leave a country in which they had been enslaved. But most Northern blacks reacted with hostility to Lincoln's words. In September, an outraged Douglass published an attack against Lincoln, in which he called him "a genuine representative of American prejudice and Negro hatred." Lincoln's beliefs were incoherent, Douglass said; blaming the war on the presence of black people was like a horse thief claiming the "existence of the horse" is the reason for his theft, not the "cruel and brutal cupidity of those who wish to possess horses, money, and Negroes by means of theft, robbery, and rebellion." As one who had backed the Republican President with hope and patience, Douglass felt betrayed by what he saw as Lincoln's blunt desire to "merely . . . get rid of" black people, rather than "improve the condition of the oppressed." Postmaster Montgomery Blair, acting on Lincoln's behalf, tried to enlist Douglass's help in the colonization scheme, an overture Douglass quickly rejected. He objected not only to colonization's premise of racial inequality, but also to its refusal to grant blacks American nationality. "I am an American citizen," Douglass had told a Boston audience during the winter. "In birth, in sentiment, in ideas, in hopes, in aspirations, and responsibilities."[33]

At the same time that the visibly weary Lincoln was struggling toward a policy on slavery and race that would not drive away potential allies, Elizabeth Keckly had begun making her own plans to "improve the condition of the oppressed." One evening in early August, Lizzy had been out walking in Washington with a friend when they heard music coming from a nearby street. Following the sound, they came upon a lit-up house and yard where a party was taking place. In response to their question, a guard at the gate told them that it was a festival for the benefit of the hospitals. "This suggested an idea to me," Lizzy wrote. "If the white people can give festivals to raise funds for the relief of suffering soldiers, why should not the well-to-do colored people go to work to do something for the benefit of the suffering blacks?"[34]

The next Sunday at Lizzy's church, the Union Bethel, she presented her idea for "a society of colored people" to give aid to the freedmen. Many liked her suggestion, and two weeks later the Contraband Relief Association had forty women members, with Lizzy as president. This was not the only relief association operating out of Union Bethel, although the other major organization, the Union Bethel Relief Association, was the provenance of the men in the church; in fact, Lizzy's idea followed a well-established tradition of black self-support. Paying $1 a night, these associations could have a hall in the church for their meetings, where they planned the benefit concerts and festivals they held during the year and coordinated the visits volunteers made to the contraband camps. Another aspect of fundraising involved sending their most prominent members to make direct appeals to potential friends and donors in the North, many of whom were white.[35]

Soon there would be many more freed people to aid. In mid-September, the North claimed the victory Lincoln had been waiting for since July, when, taking Seward's advice, he had put away in a drawer the draft for his Emancipation Proclamation. On September 17, near Antietam Creek in southwest Maryland, north of Harpers Ferry, the Army of the Potomac had repulsed General Lee's advance. Five days later, Lincoln called his Cabinet together to announce his intention of making his Proclamation public. Antietam was not the great victory he had wished for; McClellan had failed to pursue and "destroy the rebel army, if possible," as Lincoln had pressed him to do. But it was time. On the next January 1, Lincoln announced publicly, all the slaves in all those states still in rebellion "shall be then, thenceforward, and forever free."[36]

Reaction among antislavery people was muted, wary. It was not the sweeping, universal proclamation that most antislavery leaders hoped for. For one thing, it left untouched slaves in the border states in the Union; for another, it held the door open to rebel states to reenter the Union and accept a plan for gradual emancipation, with compensation and colonization. Still, it was a commitment, and it would help clear the way for black enlistment in the Union Army. And *it was time*; indeed, feeling himself that this was so, Lincoln would not have minded Frederick Douglass's notion that it was not the work of "individual design," but "the hands of the clock" that moved the nation toward emancipation.[37]

For free black Americans in the North, the months leading up to "the day of Jubilee," of Emancipation in the South, were filled with anxiety and expectation. When it happens, Douglass told an audience in November, "it will make justice, and liberty, and humanity possible in this country."[38]

Sharing in the anticipation, Lizzy had been using her influence and connections among black activists to promote her relief association. In November, the same month as Douglass's speech, Lizzy joined Mary and Tad at the Metropolitan Hotel in New York. The Lincolns had been in New York since late October and were soon planning to head to Boston, but when Mary fell sick with one of her unspecified "severe attacks" (likely her migraines and, perhaps, symptoms related to untreated diabetes), she wanted Lizzy as her companion.

For her part, although Lizzy went along to help Mary, she also saw the trip as an opportunity to further her own plans. Proudly, she would report how, "armed with credentials," she boarded the train for New York, her first trip to the North. Mary shopped for suits for Tad and furs for use in the carriage, went sightseeing, and visited with her New York friends. Lizzy "circulated among the colored people," raising money for her relief association. The nearly month-long trip highlighted the kind of balancing act of identities a woman like Elizabeth Keckly had to sustain. She would never live in a unified world, in which she would not have to be one way among white people and another among blacks. To be sure, she was the paid black servant of Mrs. Lincoln, but something in her presence and her character compelled Mary Lincoln to hold her "in a category all her own," in the words of Justin G. Turner and Linda Levitt Turner, the editors of Mary Lincoln's letters. Of course, Lizzy was not a competitor for Mary, as a white woman with her beauty, intelligence, ambition, and gifts certainly would have been; ironically, this was one reason Mary treated her so well. (Insecure, competitive, and ever subject to mood swings, Mary had made few friends in Washington among white women who were her peers.) And Lizzy kept many of her private feelings about Mary to herself. Lizzy lived, as she had as a slave, moving between black and white, skillfully negotiating the ambiguous, intense relationship she had with Mary Lincoln.

Being able to do so enabled her success. Her connections both in Washington's middle-class black community and in the White House opened the way for Lizzy into New York's and Boston's well-established activist communities as she sought to raise money to purchase supplies, mostly clothing, bedding, and shoes, for distribution in Washington's contraband camps. In New York, she met the educated black nationalist Reverend Henry Highland Garnet, the future minister of the Fifteenth Street Presbyterian in Washington, who presided over a meeting for the association at his Shiloh Presbyterian Church on Prince Street. Frederick Douglass, lecturing in England, would raise money for them from several English antislavery societies and also donate $200. At the elegant Metropolitan Hotel, where she was staying with the Lincolns, she persuaded the head steward to raise a collection from the black waiters in the hotel dining room. In Boston, while Mary and Tad visited Robert, Lizzy met the fiery Wendell Phillips and prominent black abolitionists, including Garnet's close associate, the Reverend J. Sella Martin and his wife. Martin had been born into slavery in North Carolina in 1832 and sold eight times as a child; he escaped in 1856. She also met Douglass's friend Reverend Leonard A. Grimes, who presided over a mass meeting at the Twelfth Street Baptist Church, where his wife also organized a branch of the contraband society.[39]

Lizzy's activism had Mary's support. By the fall, despite her periodic bad days, Mary had come back to life. She was prodding Lincoln to replace McClellan (which Lincoln finally did in mid-November), and encouraging *Herald* editor Bennet to urge Lincoln to replace "two or three men" in his Cabinet, by which she meant mainly the rivals Seward and Chase, each of whom she regarded as more ambitious for himself than for her husband (Lincoln did not replace them). "I have a great terror of *strong* minded Ladies," yet at a time like this, "we should not withhold" any view we might have, she told Bennet. With Lincoln, however, she was so vocal in her criticism of the Cabinet that he one day remarked, "If I listened to you, I should soon be without a Cabinet." As Lizzy recorded the conversation, Mary answered her husband's defense of Seward and Chase by advising him that "it is a safe rule to distrust a disappointed, ambitious politician."[40]

In some ways, Mary had emerged from the darkest hours of her mourning with a consciousness awakened to the troubles around her. While in New

York that fall, she exhibited a rare interest in a case that did not directly affect her. She wrote the governor of New York a plea to grant clemency to Mary Real, whose six-day trial and conviction for murdering her husband when she discovered he had a mistress had mesmerized readers of the *New York Times* in mid-October. Speaking perhaps from personal understanding, Mary argued, "She must have acted under the influence of a mind, distrait," without premeditation.[41]

It was also about this time that Mary turned some of her considerable energy to Washington's army hospitals. Under the auspices of the United States Sanitary Commission, organized in 1861, thousands of volunteers in the North, many of them women, were holding bazaars and "Sanitary Fairs" to raise money for the military hospitals. They sent bandages, socks, mittens, shirts, brandy, porter, books, puzzles, pencils, sweetmeats, pickled mangoes, tomatoes, even rocking chairs—whatever they could—to the wounded men. Several thousand paid and volunteer nurses came to the army camps and hospitals to give aid and comfort to the soldiers. Many of these were women who first came to take care of a wounded husband, son, or brother and then stayed on; other volunteers were single women out of their twenties, past the age of marriage, who wanted "something to do" to help the war effort, like Louisa May Alcott, who enlisted in 1862 after turning thirty.[42]

Mary had food sent to the hospitals from the White House kitchen, and she also arranged for gifts and supplies for the soldiers to be collected and delivered. She made visits to the wards, sometimes alone or with others, and at least once with Tad, distributing flowers from the White House conservatory, which the men kept or sent home to sweethearts, wives, or mothers. She served meals and sat by bedsides, writing letters home for stricken soldiers. Somehow this nervous, genteel woman managed to endure what were surely horrific scenes of rows of men, ill and wounded, groaning or silent in their beds, some delirious from fever, still others wandering the wards seemingly half-mad.[43]

Finally, in New York, while Lizzy was tending to Mary during her illness, Mary was paying attention in return to her companion's outside efforts to raise money and listening to her stories about the misery she was witnessing in the contraband camps. One imagines that Lizzy added to these accounts of others' sufferings some stories about her own sorrows as a slave. In response, Mary took up her pen to enlist her husband's interest on Lizzy's behalf. When Lizzy wanted to borrow money, possibly for expenses for her fundraising work, Mary asked her husband to send a check. And when Lizzy seemed to be having little luck in getting her collection off the ground, Mary wrote another letter, again asking for a contribution. Mary did not expect her husband to be as naturally sympathetic as she. She had been raised with the values of paternalism toward black slaves; she also had memories of her Mammy Sally helping runaways pass through Lexington, possibly influencing her inclination to help now. Mary suspected her husband might feel differently; his feelings were more with the wounded soldiers, with whom he identified and for whose sufferings he felt responsible, than with the ex-slaves. (He had always leaned toward the policy of leaving freed black people alone to make their own way, as he had done.) She also worried that he might hesitate to donate funds to a black-run charity. As usual, however, although Mary believed in racial differences, her politics followed her personal feelings, and her personal fondness for Lizzy led her across the color line to share in Lizzy's social cause. "I wrote you on yesterday, yet omitted a very important item," she began this second letter to Lincoln:

> Elizabeth Keckley, who is with me and is working for the Contraband Association of Wash is authorized by the *White* part of the concern by a written document—to collect any thing for them—*here* that, she can—She has been very unsuccessful—She says the immense number of Contrabands in W—are suffering intensely, many without bed covering & having to use any bits of carpeting to cover themselves—Many dying of want—Out of the $1000 fund deposited with you by Gen [Michael] Corcoran, I have given her the privilege of investing $200 her[e] in bed covering. She is the most deeply grateful being, I ever saw, & this sum, I am sure, you will not object to being used in this way—The cause of humanity requires it. . . . The soldiers are well supplied with comfort. Please send check for $200 out of the fund—she will bring you on the bill.[44]

Antislavery journalist Jane Grey Swisshelm, who met the Lincolns at the White House in the winter of 1863, believed that by that time Mary Lincoln had become "more radically opposed to slavery" than her husband, whom she regarded as a compromiser. If so, Mary had come a distance from the days in Springfield when she wished herself back in a slave state, and it seems likely that Lizzy had helped lead her to her new position. In listening to Lizzy, sympathizing with her loss, taking up her cause, Mary had opened up her heart and mind to a perspective many white people, including her husband, did not have. Yet another element may have contributed to her antislavery feelings. Mary never occupied a middle ground, and following Willie's death—when her mind was steeped in ideas of sin and punishment and penitence and she was racked with guilt that Willie had died because she had ignored God's warning to turn away from the material things of this world— she could have found an echo and strange comfort in the popular antislavery thinking that this bloodiest of wars was God's punishment for the nation's sin of holding slaves. The month Willie died, there appeared on the first page of the *Atlantic Monthly* Julia Ward Howe's new lyrics to the Union anthem "John Brown's Body." "The Battle Hymn of the Republic" roused the Union with the vision of God's righteous anger: "Mine eyes have seen the glory of the coming of the Lord/He is trampling out the vintage where the grapes of wrath are stored;/He hath loosed the fateful lightning of His terrible swift sword,/His truth is marching on." It was a millennial vision echoed in speeches by the nation's leading abolitionists. The war was "the lesson of the hour," preached Frederick Douglass, "written down in the characters of blood and fire. We are taught as with the emphasis of an earthquake, that nations, not less than individuals are subjects of the moral government of the universe, and that . . . persistent transgressions of the laws of this Divine government will certainly bring national sorrow, shame, suffering and death."[45]

CHAPTER ELEVEN

$\mathscr{A}$s the New Year of 1863 approached, Democratic voices were raised across the North against the coming day of Emancipation. After Lincoln announced his preliminary Proclamation in September, Northern antiwar Democrats (known as copperheads) had responded that they were not going to fight a black man's war, and they went to the polls in the off-year elections to elect Democratic governors and congressmen to emphasize their point. Democratic newspapers were making dire predictions that the promised Emancipation Proclamation was a national catastrophe in the making. Southerners were not alone in their nightmare vision of "primitive" black men (and women) roaming the countryside and cities overcoming "civilized" whites. Opponents of emancipation did accurately foresee that the edict that would strike the shackles from the slaves would also shake loose the barriers between free blacks and the rights of citizenship, and thereby the privileges of whites. They saw how Lincoln's war measures—the suspension of habeas corpus, the suppression of the press—had restricted *their* freedoms, and they were primed for preserving distinctions of race.

During the months leading up to January 1, few Northerners were sanguine about the future. Democrats feared that Lincoln would go through with the Proclamation despite the apparent rebuff of his Party in the elections. Abolitionists and radical Republicans feared he would not. War weariness, and few Union successes, dimmed everyone's hopes.

African Americans both feared and hoped. On December 31, the evening before the fateful day, black people all across the North flowed into their churches for freedom-watch meetings, to wait for the telegraphed messages announcing Lincoln's signing of the Emancipation Proclamation. Lizzy was most likely among the joyful who came from all over the city to her church, Union Bethel. The church was full by sundown, and while waiting for services to begin at 10 o'clock, the people sang, prayed, and talked about their "earthly experiences" in voices suffused with longing and anticipation. At 10, the pastor stepped up, opened his Bible, and began prayers; then, closing his book, he preached a sermon about "God, old Satan, Lincoln and the coming day of eternal freedom." He likely gave not only a speech that celebrated the coming freedom, but one about what freedom meant for African Americans. As another preacher in another church exhorted his white brethren: "Give unto us the same guarantee of life, liberty and protection in the pursuit of happiness that you so cheerfully award others, and make the very same demands of us to support the government you make of others." Give us the vote and give us arms to fight, he also said. "Your destiny as white men and ours as black men are one and the same; we are all marching on to the same goal."[1] Seen from atop a mountain of struggle, the prospect of black citizenship was thrilling.

Then, just before midnight, the Union Bethel minister told everyone "that he wanted no one to pray standing up with bowed head; nobody sitting down, with bended necks praying; and no brother kneeling on one knee, because his pants were too tight for him, but to get down on *both knees* to thank Almighty God for his freedom and President Lincoln too." Everyone knelt, and throughout the church there was silence, broken now and then by someone calling out for God to guide them when freedom came, just as He had guided them through bondage. People prayed to God to guide Lincoln, too. Many

Washington African Americans had a personal feeling for this strange white man, whom they could have seen walking about or riding through the streets.[2]

The next day, the Lincolns held the customary White House New Year's Day reception. It began at 11 o'clock, when the dignitaries arrived in groups one after another: the diplomatic corps, resplendent in their formal dress; the Supreme Court judges; and the fully turned out army and naval officers. At noon, the Mansion gates were thrown open for the two-hour public reception, a reception unofficially off-limits to blacks. At that point, Mary retreated upstairs, leaving with a nod to Commissioner French, who stood beside her making introductions. Not long afterward, Lincoln also withdrew upstairs. He went to his office, where Secretary Seward and his son, the Assistant Secretary of State, were waiting with the final copy of the Proclamation. Remarking that his arm was stiff and numb from shaking so many hands and that this was one time when people would look to see that he did not tremble when signing, Lincoln gripped his pen and signed his name to the document.

"This proclamation changed everything," declared Frederick Douglass, jubilant at last. He had spent the emotionally exhausting hours at the huge freedom-watch meeting at Tremont Temple in Boston, where a crowd of people, among them the abolitionists Lizzy met when she was in Boston, waited until late in the day for the telegraph to flash the news. A line of messengers had been set up between the telegraph office and the Tremont Temple to pass along the joyful word. At last a man ran into the crowd. "It is coming! It is on the wires!" he cried. It was like a bolt of lightning, like the dawn of a new day.[3]

For Lizzy, the consequences may have been less momentous, but they were real. With every widening of the path toward equality, she was ready to take another step forward. In the fall, with her fundraising, she had come into her own in her relationship with the First Lady. She had brought to the friendship her own desires and interests, had even brought Mary Lincoln further into her world. After Emancipation, she seemed able to make even more demands on the friendship. In March, she had likely told Mary that she needed to earn more money because Mary recommended her for a job in the cutting room at the Treasury Department, an unusual position for a black woman in those days. "Although colored," Mary wrote the Assistant Secretary of the Treasury, addressing the natural bureaucratic aversion to hiring a black woman, Elizabeth Keckly "is very industrious, & just had an interview with Gov Chase, who says he will see you. . . . She is very unobtrusive, & will perform her duties, faithfully."[4] However, Mary added, she would not be ready to work until the middle of April, after the winter social season ended, when Mary would need Lizzy's help less frequently. (However, there is no official record that Elizabeth Keckly worked at the Treasury Department.)

In May, Lizzy laid claim to a new right of citizenship. That month, about the time that the War Department created the Bureau of Colored Troops signaling the government's commitment to enlist as many black regiments as possible, Lizzy went to the United States Pension Agency to apply for the pension to which a recent law entitled her as a widow whose only son had been killed in action. However, to do so she had to bend the racial laws, because in the eyes of the government her dead son was white. One year after George's death, the black soldier had become an irresistible reality—and in some ways the most revolutionary feature—of the war. Although, as abolitionists had repeatedly pointed out, black soldiers had fought in all of the nation's previous wars, when George enlisted in 1861 blacks were officially excluded from Union forces; he had had to pass as a white man to join a regiment. (Being half white still relegated him to being black, according to the bipolar racial logic of his country, and therefore ineligible for enlistment.) Indeed, at that time in the war, Lincoln had regarded arming black men, like emancipation, a sure way to push wavering border states into the Confederacy, and had held back from authorizing black enlistment. His Secretary of War's recommendation in his annual report of 1861, that the government should arm slaves against their rebelling masters, drew Lincoln's wrath. But the fighting dragged on, swallowing up thousands upon thousands of white Union men and vomiting up their mutilated bodies, and the war became a war to destroy the South, and so Lincoln's feelings about black enlistment changed. In March 1863, when Mary recommended Lizzy for a Treasury job, Lincoln wrote Andrew Johnson, military governor of Tennessee, "The colored population is the great *available* and yet *unavailed* of, force for restoring the Union. The bare sight of fifty thousand armed, and drilled black soldiers on the banks of the Mississippi, would end the rebellion at once." By June, black regiments were parading up Pennsylvania Avenue. "I never saw a *new* Regt *march* better," wrote one white resident in his diary. Later that summer, after the courageous showing at Fort Wagner, South Carolina, of the 54th Massachusetts Infantry—the North's "showcase black regiment," led into battle by young Colonel Robert Gould Shaw, of a prominent Boston abolitionist family—Lincoln wrote a public letter declaring, "The use of colored troops, constitute the heaviest blow yet dealt to the rebellion." In the final two years of the war, nearly 180,000 black soldiers would join the Union.[5]

But George's participation had been as a white man, and it was as a white man's mother that Lizzy had to apply. To qualify for a pension, Lizzy had to make her son black again because she herself could not pass for white. This would not jeopardize her claim, because the government was ready to acknowledge the existence of black claimants. Yet she faced another difficulty: George's illegitmacy. And so, having confronted the ironies of her country's racial laws, Lizzy had also to confront the ironies of marital laws. She testified how she, a black slave, and Alexander Kirkland, a free white man, had married; how he then had died, leaving her with their eighteen-month-old son; and how, after that, she had bought her freedom and married Mr. Keckly, a black man.[6] It was about as unlikely a story as could be told, but everyone who witnessed the statement signed on to it. One only wonders who of those involved invented it.

There were several possibilities. Among those who helped Lizzy get her pension was the generous, pugnacious Illinois Congressman Owen Lovejoy. Lovejoy was a firm abolitionist; after his brother Elijah died in 1837 defending his antislavery newspaper against a mob, he vowed never to forsake the cause and was an early advocate of black enlistment. Nevertheless, he had stood by Lincoln's more moderate emancipation plans. When he died in 1864, Mary called him a "loved & esteemed" friend, although it was one of Lizzy's St. Louis patrons who took her to him. He gladly helped her prepare her claim, and after he returned to Illinois another brother, Joseph, a Democrat, agreed to take over. Meanwhile, making use of her network in the African American community, Lizzy sought out the greatly revered Bishop Daniel A. Payne, head of the A.M.E. Church, who endorsed the truth of her pension statement. She received $8 a month, eventually raised to $12, for the remainder of her life.

For Lizzy Keckly, January 1, 1863, delivered symbolic affirmation of who she had become after her years as an American slave had ended. But for Mary, January 1, 1863, stood for what she had lost. It was a gloomy day, a sad reminder of "how much we have passed through since we last stood here," she told Benjamin French that morning. She may have been brooding about what

Mrs. Cranston Laury, the spiritualist medium, had told her only the day before, when she drove out to see her at her home in Georgetown. "Wonderful revelations about her little son Willie," as she confided to Orville Browning, her old Springfield confidant, who recorded their conversation in his diary, "and also about things on earth. Among other things she revealed that the Cabinet were all enemies of the President, working for themselves, and that they would have to be dismissed."[7]

Indeed, in the past year, Mary had made several visits to spiritualists, hoping primarily to speak to her dead son but also inquiring about "things on earth." She also invited spiritualists to hold séances in the White House. In her search, Mary had the encouragement of Lizzy Keckly, who may have tried to contact her own deceased son or mother or to find out if her slave father was living or dead. One White House journalist thought that Lizzy "induced" Mary to listen to a spiritualist medium, Lord Colchester, who styled himself the illegitimate son of an English duke. In a darkened room at the Soldiers' Home, Lord Colchester transmitted messages from Willie.[8] Yet Mary would have needed no "inducement" from Lizzy. For both of these women, with their distinct histories of suffering, it was a way to escape an intolerable world; spiritualists could connect one to a powerful force in the world beyond. They were hardly alone in seeking solace through spiritualist mediums, who, like mesmerists and clairvoyants, spoke to the suffering unconscious.

Spiritualism had emerged in the late 1840s, after eleven-year-old Kate Fox discovered that she could communicate with the spirits whose nocturnal raps and bumps had kept the Fox family awake in their tiny house in upstate New York. When word spread, people began making pilgrimages to the Fox home to see if Kate or her sister, Maggie, could pick up spirit messages for them. One of the earliest messages Kate received was from the spirit of the dead five-year-old daughter of abolitionist Amy Post; after that, the intellectual and respected Posts became firm supporters of the new movement.

Spiritualism's therapeutic qualities attracted many bereaved parents. The unhappy Mary Cheney Greeley had her husband, Horace, bring Kate Fox from Rochester to their farm on the East River in New York City, so that she could hold a séance for them to communicate with their dead son. Harriet Beecher Stowe turned to spiritualism to contact her young son after he drowned. She said she saw his spirit in a circle with others; her husband also had spirit visions. In Washington, Gideon and Mary Jane Welles, who buried six small children, consulted clairvoyants after their children died.

From the start, spiritualism was the domain of women. It came to its female practitioners as a calling, offering them a source of real power for intervention in an age when the pulpit and podium were off-limits to the gentler sex. One of Mary's spiritualist mediums, the talented Mrs. Nettie Colburn Maynard, who held séances in the White House, claimed that a message transmitted through her had moved the President to emancipate the slaves.[9]

It also gave a voice to black women, a profoundly more disenfranchised group than white women. Throughout the South, the conjure or voodoo woman was a familiar and dreaded figure. In Washington during the war, an old slave woman named Oola, who was said to be a native African, was widely feared for her ability to conjure spells. Tall, gray-black, with piercing eyes, she told fortunes to whites and blacks alike. In early 1861 Oola had seen a prophecy of war in a comet that passed over Washington, in which she saw the North holding a sword pointed at the heart of the South. When Mary heard about this, she laughed it off; Lincoln was thought to be more impressed.[10]

Although skeptics doubted and religious conservatives disparaged it, to its followers spiritualism conveyed an aura of sublimity, a communion with invisible truths on a higher, more intense experiential plane. Harriet Beecher Stowe believed that spiritualism was "a reaction from the intense materialism of the age." Spiritualism made Mary the powerful bearer of messages from a superior world. She had been ashamed to reveal her shopping sprees to her husband, but she could tell him about her spirit communications, because he was at least half a believer too.[11]

Confirming what her devotees already felt, a spiritualist medium's predictions also empowered woman's intuition. Indeed, two weeks after receiving the spiritualist's message about the treachery of the Cabinet, Mary startled a few afternoon guests who had come over after church, Elizabeth Blair Lee reported, by saying "very loudly to be heard every where in the room . . . that there was not a member of the Cabinet who did not stab her husband & the Country daily except my Brother [Montgomery]—she did not know anything about Politics—but her instincts told her that much."[12]

On July 2, Mary was riding back alone to Washington from the Soldiers' Home when the horses took off wildly, breaking up the carriage, and she jumped out to save herself. Somebody had unscrewed the bolts holding down the driver's seat, and when the seat came loose, the frightened horses jumped and ran. In landing, Mary fell over, and the back of her head hit a sharp rock. Although the gash bled profusely and she appeared stunned and confused to the men who ran from the nearby army hospital to help her, Mary appeared only slightly injured.[13]

On July 4, a most glorious day that year, Mary was back on her feet after the accident, helping to set up celebrations on the White House lawn. The Marine Band's summer concerts had been resumed, although it had taken Secretary Welles privately informing Lincoln that "there was grumbling and discontent, and there will be more this year if the public are denied the privilege for private reasons" of attending the popular events.[14] On July 7 Lincoln was flush with the long-awaited news coming from Mississippi of General Grant's successful occupation of Vicksburg. It was only three days after the Gettysburg victory was confirmed. Lincoln felt it was a turning point in the war, and with the Potomac swollen from rain, was certain that, this time, the Confederate forces retreating from Pennsylvania would not be allowed to get away, that General George Gordon Meade, his third replacement of McClellan to head the Army of the Potomac, would capture Lee's army and end the war. Then Mary's wound became infected, requiring the doctor to reopen it, and she became dangerously ill.

On July 11, Lincoln sent a telegram to Robert, who was in New York City, telling him to come to Washington, but three days later Robert had neither arrived nor sent word of when he would be there. "Why do I hear no more of you?" a worried Lincoln again wired his son.[15] In New York City, a protest against the government's new conscription act (the country's first draft), begun by poor Irish workers who did not want to fight a war to free black people who would then come and take their jobs, had escalated into an uncontrolled riot. Federal regiments were just now being rushed to New York to quell the mob. After four days of rioting black homes and businesses had been destroyed, the Colored Orphan Asylum burnt to the ground, federal draft offices and the homes of Republicans and abolitionists sacked, and over one hundred people killed.

It turned out that Robert was already approaching Washington. When he arrived that afternoon, he found his father sitting in his office, his head on his desk before him, an image of despair. After being beaten at Gettysburg, General Lee's army had escaped back south across the Potomac.[16] And there was Mary, lying sick, far sicker than he had told Robert.

There was some speculation that the carriage vandal had hoped to injure the President. Threats against Lincoln's life were part of the daily routine, brushed off by the President but unnerving to his wife. With her head throbbing from the accident intended for her husband, Mary may have experienced the dubious satisfaction of having her instincts about the death threats against him confirmed. Yet despite his joking, the President had shown signs of his anxiety in many sleepless nights and, when he slept, foreboding dreams. "Think you had better put 'Tad's' pistol away. I had an ugly dream about him," Lincoln had wired Mary in Philadelphia in June. That spring, when he had been haunting the War Department telegraph office for news of the fighting from Chancellorsville, Virginia, Lizzy had heard Mary beg her husband not to walk the short distance from the White House alone. "Don't worry about me, mother, as if I were a little child," he told her, pulling on his gray shawl and overshoes, "for no one is going to molest me."[17]

Mary gradually improved. By the end of July, she had recovered enough to take a late-summer trip to New Hampshire's White Mountains with Tad and Robert, between the "inevitable stops" in New York for shopping. This time, she would stay away from Washington for two months. It was a summer trip that she had originally planned in April, and she had thought Lincoln might join the family in New Hampshire. But he could not leave Washington, even though the rest of the summer was a "relatively tranquil" time, and he spent the weeks mostly at the Soldiers' Home. He rarely left Washington during those years, except to inspect troops across the Potomac and to consult with one of his generals, or to give speeches in nearby Pennsylvania or Maryland—or, when the end of the war finally came in 1865, to enter a fallen Richmond.[18]

While Mary was away, Frederick Douglass made his first visit to Washington. Since escaping from slavery in 1838, Douglass had not set foot south of the Mason-Dixon line, but now, with the government's official attitude toward African Americans in flux and slavery in Washington abolished, he was eager to come. He met with Secretary of War Stanton and, more important, the President himself. Kansas Senator Samuel S. Pomeroy escorted Douglass to the White House and up the stairs to meet Lincoln, who, hearing Douglass's name, rose from his low armchair to shake his hand. Douglass had come to protest unequal treatment of black soldiers, who were paid less than white soldiers, were ineligible for promotion, and were not protected as prisoners of war but enslaved, abused, or killed when they fell into Confederate hands.

One particularly gruesome incident would occur at Fort Pillow, Tennessee, in April 1864, when Confederates murdered several dozen black soldiers after they had surrendered. Until things changed, he would no longer work to recruit black troops, he said. Lincoln listened "with patience and silence" but defended his belief that change must come slowly. Inequality in the army was a "necesary concession" to "popular prejudice" against having black soldiers at all, but he believed that "ultimately" blacks would be paid equally. He also told Douglass that he thought simple retaliation for the death of black soldiers at the hands of Confederates would not work, because Northern whites would not accept killing Southern whites to avenge black deaths. As for promotions, he would endorse whatever his Secretary of War recommended.

Douglass had not received the answers he wanted, but he left "so well satisfied with the man and with the educating tendency of the conflict" that he began recruiting black soldiers again. Even more important to this former slave was the way Lincoln treated him: "I was never more quickly or more completely put at ease in the presence of a great man than in that of Abraham Lincoln." In a room filled with white men—busy secretaries and other callers—Lincoln's attention was on what the black man had to say. "I tell you I felt big there!" Douglass told an audience in Philadelphia. Meanwhile, his three sons enlisted as soldiers.[19]

What Douglass called "the educating tendency" of the war on Lincoln's racial understanding would be reinforced by Lincoln's encounters with dignified black men like Frederick Douglass; yet Lizzy's presence in his family circle also likely contributed to his evolving comprehension of black life in America. By the time Douglass met with Lincoln, Lizzy had developed her own quiet relationship with the President. While combing his hair or sewing in the sitting room when he happened to enter, they sometimes fell into conversation, and like Douglass, she desired and treasured this powerful white man's recognition. Sometime after he instituted the draft, Lincoln called her to the window to look at Tad's pet goats. He knew she shared his love of animals and wanted her to admire the way the goats could jump. While looking at them, his face clouded; they reminded him of bounty jumpers, men who enlisted for the bounties offered, then deserted, then "repeat[ed] the play," as he put it. In the next moment, the goats looked up at the window, and Lincoln brightened again: "See, Madam Elizabeth, my pets recognize me." Then, according to Lizzy, as they were standing together, Mary called out to "stop staring at those silly goats" and come dress her for the evening. "Mrs. Lincoln was not fond of pets," Lizzy remarked, "and she could not understand how

Mr. Lincoln could take so much delight in his goats." But Lizzy could understand, she implied, thereby revealing a submerged rivalry with his wife.[20]

Yet, despite her contact with Lincoln, Elizabeth Keckly, unlike Frederick Douglass (or, indeed, Mary Lincoln), was not to be a presidential consultant; it was not part of even Lincoln's large generosity to admit black women to that circle (and, in fact, white women, including Mary, had been virtually shut out). But she must have taken pride in her Contraband Association, which after emancipation was called the Freedmen and Soldier's Relief Association. It became one of the philanthropic organizations whose activities helped persuade the War Department to appoint a Freedmen's Inquiry Commission, whose recommendations led to the creation of the Freedmen's Bureau in the last days of the war to monitor the transition from slavery to freedom. It was a long way from being the lonely victim of Alexander Kirkland's lust to being the black woman in the White House who helped others make it across the great gulf between slavery and freedom.

It must have pleased her, too, that the Lincolns sometimes stopped at the contraband camp on Seventh Street (where Howard University now stands) on their way out to the Soldiers' Home to hear the freed men, women, and children sing hymns. The singers would dress in their best clothes, sometimes scavenged from battlefields but more often picked up at relief offices, and line up to perform the "sorrow songs," like "Nobody Knows the Trouble I've Seen," "Swing Low, Sweet Chariot," and "Steal Away," always ending with "John Brown's Body." Visitors to Washington made special expeditions to the contraband camps. In November 1862, waiting for the Emancipation to come, Harriet Beecher Stowe had attended a special Thanksgiving dinner at one of the camps, at which the contrabands sang "Go Down, Moses," "the negro Marseillaise," as a friend of Stowe's called it. On December 2 of that year, Stowe had gone to the White House at the invitation of Mary, whom she had met a few weeks earlier in Brooklyn; as Stowe's biographer remarks, "One would give a good deal to know the details of this meeting between Harriet Beecher Stowe and Abraham Lincoln, but the accounts leave almost everything unsaid." Supposedly, Lincoln greeted the five-feet-high Stowe with "So you're the little woman who wrote the book that started this great war!"[21]

By the summer of 1863, after months of visiting for her association, Lizzy was a familiar figure in the contraband camps. She was one of the hundreds of white and free black volunteers, among them Sojourner Truth and Harriet Jacobs, who had begun their lives as slaves. The volunteers brought material aid and spiritual comfort to the people living in the contraband camps, taught reading and sewing and other practical skills, and sometimes just gave advice on what it meant to be free: what it meant to work for wages, to move from place to place, to make your own plans. It did not mean, as Lizzy advised an old woman, that the Lincolns, like your old master and mistress, would give you two dresses every year. Sojourner Truth "told them they must learn to love the white people . . . that they must learn to be independent—learn industry and economy—and above all strive to show the people that they could be *something*."[22]

By September, Mary was in New York and planning to return to Washington at the end of the month. Before she left, she received a letter from her husband with the news that Ben Helm, Emilie's husband, was one of six Confederate generals killed at the Battle of Chickamauga in Georgia. Soon after she returned to Washington she heard that her youngest half-brother, "everybody's favorite, ebullient red-headed" Aleck, only an infant when she had left Lexington for Springfield, had died the day before Ben, at a skirmish near Baton Rouge, Louisiana. Lizzy had already heard the news when Mary told her, but had not wanted to bring it up, fearing it would cause her pain. She was relieved when Mary played down the event. He was Mary's third, and last, half-brother to die in the war; the second-oldest boy, David, had died of wounds he received at Vicksburg during the summer.

However, Aleck's death was more of a blow than Mary would admit, perhaps even to herself. Given the persistent accusations that she was a rebel sympathizer, she may have felt she had to reject mourning for her dead relatives who had fought on the Confederate side. And in a way, as Confederate traitors, they were already dead to her. Mourning was already becoming the key feature of her identity, as it surely became after Lincoln was killed. Like many people, she found the anniversaries of her losses painful, something she felt "only those, who have passed through such bereavements" could understand. (She felt that Lizzy was one of the sympathizing ones.) Over a year after Willie's death she was still dressed in black for her son, inviting comment. Lincoln, also grieving, continued wearing black crape on his hat. With the deaths of "Little Sister's" husband and her brothers, especially baby brother Aleck, only four years older than her Bobby, it was as if she were losing all her "sons," starting with little Eddie thirteen years earlier.[23]

Understandably, sickness now terrified her. While in New York, she had wired Lincoln, apparently concerned about returning with Tad, who was frail and high-strung and often ill, if Washington was "unhealthy." "So far as I see or know, it was never healthier, and I really wish to see you," he wired back; they had been away nearly two months. After they returned to Washington, Tad did fall sick; his skipping breakfast one morning in November was enough to depress his father, who was leaving by train at noon for Gettysburg, where he was to make a speech at the dedication of the new cemetery. His mother became hysterical. That night, however, she wired Lincoln that Tad was better. Lincoln, attended by the devoted William Johnson, returned two days later with a fever, the beginning of varioloid, a mild form of smallpox, and was rather cheerful about being quarantined in the White House for three weeks.[24]

Family and friends were convinced that Mary's July accident had lasting effects on her behavior and thinking. Two years later, after Lincoln's assassination, Robert would tell his Aunt Emilie, "I think mother has never quite recovered from the effects of her fall."[25]

It may be that Mary began having the visions of her dead sons and brother only after July, for the only record of them comes afterward, in December, when "Little Sister" Emilie Helm was in the White House. The visit of the Confederate general's wife was a fact Lincoln did not want advertised, and although she was welcome, it was a difficult, emotional visit in many ways. Returning from her husband's funeral in Georgia, Emilie passed through the Union lines at Fortress Monroe and continued on to Washington. It was a sad reunion between the two stricken sisters, who spent hours alone talking and crying, carefully avoiding all reference to the war that made them political enemies.

While Emilie was in Washington, she was the confidante of both Lincoln and Mary; each of them was anxious to know how she thought the other one seemed. Lincoln told her that he believed Mary's "nerves have gone to pieces. . . . What do you think?" Mary asked her sister for her opinion on how Lincoln looked: "Do you think he is well?" To Mary, Emilie responded by saying only that Lincoln seemed thinner. Her response to Lincoln was more direct: "She seems very nervous and excitable and once or twice when I have come into the room suddenly the frightened look in her eyes has appalled me."

Emilie would soon have more reason to be appalled. One night, Mary came into her bedroom. She was "smiling though her eyes were full of tears," Emilie remembered. Mary then told her that each night, Willie came to her room "and stands at the foot of my bed with the same sweet, adorable smile he has always had; he does not always come alone; little Eddie is sometimes with him and twice he had come with our brother Ale[ck], he tells me he loves his Uncle Alec[k] and is with him most of the time." She wanted Emilie to know what a comfort this was to her, seeing that Willie was not "in immensity, alone. . . . [I still grieve that] he has no future in this world that I might watch with a proud mother's heart—[but] he lives, Emilie!"

"It *is* unnatural and abnormal, it frightens me," Emilie recorded her conversation with Lincoln in her diary. "It does not seem like Sister Mary to be so nervous and wrought up," she told him. "She is on a terrible strain and her smiles seem forced. . . . I believe if anything should happen to you or Robert or Tad it would kill her." Lincoln wanted Emilie to come back the next summer to keep Mary company; he had made a similar request of Elizabeth after Willie died. But it became obvious that it would be impossible for Emilie to live with them after she had an angry exchange one evening in the blue room with General Daniel Sickles, who had lost a leg at Gettysburg, and Senator Ira Harris, whose Union officer stepson had survived some of the war's worst battles. The careworn Harris, perhaps overheated by drink, had been taunting the young widow with the Union victories in the West, where her husband had been killed. "And, Madam," Harris finally turned to her, "if I had twenty sons they should all be fighting rebels." "And if I had twenty sons, [Senator] Harris," Emilie answered, "they should all be opposing yours." Afterward, Sickles clumped upstairs to find Lincoln, who had been feeling ill and was lying down. He wanted to know how he could have "that rebel in your house." Lincoln must have paused before responding to the proud survivor of the already mythic battle of Gettysburg. "Excuse me, General Sickles, my wife and I are in the habit of choosing our own guests."[26]

During the blue room confrontation, Senator Harris had also turned on Mary to ask why Robert wasn't in the army. Her face went white as she struggled to find an answer. Robert's joining the army was a fraught subject in the Lincoln household. Robert, who knew he was being criticized for not joining, wished to quit school and enlist, like other Harvard students, but Mary was adamantly against it. She worried constantly that Robert's resentment and public pressure would push Lincoln to overrule her; whenever it came up, he would argue gently with her but so far had always backed down. She had confided her fears to Emilie during her visit and to Lizzy, who more than once heard Lincoln tell his wife that "many a poor mother has given up all her sons, and our son is no more dear to us than the sons of other people are to their mothers."[27]

As the bereaved mother of an only son who left school and enlisted as soon as he could, and was then killed, Lizzy surely had her own thoughts about Robert's situation. She admired his sense of duty, even when it took the form of youthful severity, as when he disapproved of his mother's throwing a White House party for the impresario P. T. Barnum's newlyweds Mr. and Mrs. Tom Thumb (thirty-two and thirty inches high, respectively); it follows that privately she felt he was right to want to join.[28] Beyond that, it would have been hard for her not to feel that Mary was being selfish, even if she understood the reasons; if so, it was another thought that she kept discreetly to herself.

Emilie left by mid-December, leaving Mary better than when she had arrived. For despite Mary's mental and physical deterioration, she was more up to the social challenges of the 1863–64 winter season than she had been the previous year. In December, the twenty-foot-tall bronze statue of Freedom had been hoisted to her place atop the cupola on the Capitol dome and the scaffolding removed, revealing the inspiring figure, and Mary announced that after the New Year she would put off her mourning. At the New Year's reception, she wore a purple velvet dress decorated with white satin fluting and Valenciennes lace and a long train. Her headdress had an enormous white plume. The First Lady's return from official mourning was not the only change of note. For the first time ever in American history, four black men, described by one newspaper as "four colored men of genteel exterior, and with the manners of gentlemen," were formally presented in the receiving line to the President and his wife.[29]

Part of the renewed display was prompted by the fact that 1864 was a presidential election year, and Mary was determined to do all that elegant entertaining, gracious notes, and gifts of bouquets could do to assure Lincoln's renomination and reelection—which was by no means assured. Despite mounting Union victories, Lincoln's popularity rose and fell battle by battle; also at issue in his reelection was the question of reconstruction of the South, which Lincoln had begun addressing publicly in December. For Republicans who would have to rally behind him for Lincoln to win, reconstruction was a vexed issue. On December 8, responding to low Southern morale and division among Southern leaders, the President had issued a proclamation offering pardon and amnesty to rebels who took "an oath of allegiance to the United States and to all of its laws and proclamations concerning slavery"; Emilie took the oath before going home. Plans went forward for the reconstruction of Tennessee, Louisiana, and Arkansas, where large portions of the states were already under Union military control. By the end of 1863, even conservative Republicans who had been leery of emancipation had united behind it as a war goal, allowing them to turn Democratic opposition to emancipation into opposition to Northern victory. Lincoln never veered from insisting that slavery would be abolished in a reconstructed South, but that left many questions about the status of the newly free people: What role would black people play in reconstruction? Would black men everywhere vote? What provisions would be made to raise the "laboring, landless, and homeless class" of free blacks above the practical condition of slavery?[30] The Republicans were deeply divided over these and other related questions.

But opposition Republicans needed an alternative candidate. The obvious one was Secretary Salmon P. Chase, the father of the beautiful Kate, Mary's rival, who had spent the last three years using Treasury Department patronage to build a political machine that would limit Lincoln to one term—"on principle," Chase supporters said—and take the next term for himself.[31]

Mary was not going to let this happen. No one believed that she declined to attend Kate Chase's wedding to Rhode Island millionaire Senator William Sprague in November because she was ill, as she claimed. But she was not merely jealous either. She once told Lizzy that she did not want to promote the daughter "through political favor" to the father, nor would she wish to promote the father by socially recognizing the daughter. (Five years later, Lizzy would write that Mrs. Sprague "was a lovely woman, and was worthy of all the admiration she received." By that time, the social rivalry between Mary Lincoln and Kate Sprague no longer mattered, but Madam Keckly, still Washington's leading mantua maker, had a business to maintain.)[32]

So set was Mary against the Chase-Sprague machine that she told Nicolay, who was in charge of state dinners, to exclude Secretary Chase and the Spragues from the Cabinet dinner at the end of January. When Lincoln went over her head, ordering his secretary to include them, "there soon arose such a rampage," Nicolay wrote Hay, "as the House hasn't seen for a year, and again I am taboo," meaning "her S[atanic] Majesty" had banished him from the planning and the dinner itself. From what followed, one gets a sense of the power dynamics in the Mansion, of how little power Mary actually had in this Mansion of men. Nicolay, armed to defeat "the enemy," instructed his assistant, William O. Stoddard (who sympathized with her more than did Nicolay or Hay), to be no help to her, and he was not. Finally, on the afternoon of the dinner, a contrite Mary sent the doorkeeper Edward with an apology to Nicolay and an earnest request for his "presence and assistance." The "affair had worried her so that she hadn't slept for a night or two."[33] When an embarrassed Chase withdrew from the race before the spring, it was because of her husband's political maneuverings, not hers. But until the election had safely passed, Mary could not rest.

Once Chase was down, Lincoln's nomination came fairly smoothly, despite some rumblings of dissent, most significantly from radical supporters of the still-disgruntled John C. Frémont. But Frémont's candidacy went nowhere fast. At the June Republican convention in Baltimore, conventioneers under the less partisan-sounding name National Union renominated Lincoln with a "down-the-line Republican platform"; it included pursuing the war until the "unconditional surrender" of Confederates and the passage of a constitutional amendment to abolish slavery. Although the Thirteenth Amendment, already before Congress, would be stalled in the House the following week, people knew that if Lincoln won, ratification would be only a matter of time.

Against Lincoln, the Northern Democrats put forward his deposed commander of the Army of the Potomac, the youthful and popular General George B. McClellan, who had openly oppugned Lincoln's war policies, including emancipation. Lincoln, who wanted to win to finish the job he had started, considered McClellan a dangerous opponent, and at the end of August was glumly anticipating his defeat at the polls three months hence. The war had not helped. A spring of unimaginably brutal battles in Virginia under Ulysses S. Grant, Lincoln's new general in chief, and General William T. Sherman's apparently fruitless maneuvering around Atlanta, Georgia, had been followed by a summer of waiting for Grant and Sherman to deliver victories. "Whatever happens, there will be no turning back," Grant told Lincoln. By then, Grant had become the Union's hero, although dissenters (including Mary, who called him a "butcher") were appalled at his willingness to sacrifice as many lives as necessary for victory. But at a White House levee, wearing his worn-out traveling uniform, he had been forced to stand on a sofa so that the crowd could greet him. True to his word, the taciturn Grant had pursued Lee through the heart of Virginia for seven bloody weeks beginning in May—from the Wilderness, a tangle of scrub oaks and pines, southwest of Manassas, through

Spotsylvania, North Anna, Cold Harbor, and ending in a siege at Petersburg. During that time, thousands of Union wounded had flooded the Washington hospitals, and many of the local citizens had come to the hospitals to see what they could do to help. After one visit, one man went to the Sanitary (as the Sanitary Commission was called) to pick up two boxes, each containing five hundred cheap palm leaf fans, to give to the "poor fellows on their beds" to keep the flies away. Mary also had made her rounds, visiting at least once with Mary Jane Welles, her one friend among the Cabinet wives.[34]

Grant's Virginia campaigns had brought the war terrifyingly close to Washington. On July 11, Confederates led by Jubal A. Early marched unimpeded to within five miles of Washington, which had been left virtually unguarded except for militia, stragglers from army units, and the government clerks and convalescent soldiers who were given rifles by Lincoln's frantic chief of staff, Henry W. Halleck. Desperate appeals for help from the War Department finally persuaded Grant to send help. On July 12, Lincoln watched the skirmishing from a parapet at Fort Stevens. Ignoring warnings, Lincoln, "a conspicuous figure" in his stovepipe hat, kept standing up to get a view. After a man standing near him was shot in the leg, an exasperated young Captain Oliver Wendell Holmes Jr. snapped, "Get down, you damn fool, before you get shot!" Lincoln got down.[35]

Lizzy was one of those close to the Lincolns who would notice the President reading the Bible frequently that year. One day, after a depressing morning at the War Department telegraph office, he was absorbed in the Bible in the upstairs sitting room. Pretending to look for something that had fallen in the sofa, Lizzy came up silently behind him to see which section he was reading. It was Job, and she "almost imagined" hearing God "speaking to him out the whirlwind: 'Gird up thy loins now like a man: I will demand of thee, and declare thou unto me.'" She found the sight of this powerful "ruler of a mighty nation" seeking "comfort and courage" in the Bible inspiring. It made him seem "a simple Christian," not that different from a former slave who read and took "comfort and courage" from the same book. She believed that she herself sometimes managed to soothe Lincoln by combing his hair while he sat in a chair in front of her.[36]

In the meantime, Mary had returned to her spending sprees with a vengeance, racking up unpaid bills exceeding by thousands of dollars her husband's salary of $25,000 a year. This year's bursts of shopping were a manic dance with danger. As she told Lizzy, if her husband "is re-elected, I can keep him in ignorance of my affairs; but if he is defeated, then the bills will be sent in, and he will know all." She was, according to Lizzy, "almost crazy with anxiety and fear."[37]

Anxiety and fear drove her straight into the shops. The sight of the President's carriage stopped outside of a Pennsylvania Avenue dry goods store was a familiar one in 1864. A footman wearing gold braid and a cockade in his hat would hold open the carriage door so that Mrs. Lincoln, seated within, could lean out to examine the goods held up to her by an obliging clerk. While in New York in late April, Mary had been seen (according to the *New York Herald*) "from the early hours . . . until late in the evening . . . ransack[ing] the treasures of the Broadway dry goods stores" for shawls (paisley, lace, lama, and camel's hair); two cape and boa sets, one sable and one chinchilla; handkerchiefs; a parasol cover; flounces and fringes; fans, bonnets, coats, boots, and shoes; and scores of other personal items, for which she (her husband) was expected to pay. With the shawls ranging in price from $50 to $2,000 and a lace handkerchief costing $80 alone, Mary's personal expenses in 1864 surpassed her first-year expenditures on the White House.

Already, Mary's favorite Broadway merchant, A. T. Stewart, was one of the creditors who had threatened to sue the First Lady for unpaid bills. Stewart evidently backed down and remained a favorite. Undeterred by her outstanding debt, Mary continued relaying requests for such luxuries as "a black India Camel's Hair shawl," with a special plea for Stewart to accept "a delay of the Settlement of my account with you until the 1st of June—when I promise, that without fail, *then*, the whole account will be settled. I deeply regret, that I am so unusually situated & trust hereafter, to settle as I purchase." Meanwhile, she continued fixing up the White House, making $15,000 to $18,000 worth of purchases in this, the last year of Lincoln's life, mostly after his reelection, without telling Commissioner French, who was supposed to authorize her official spending.[38]

It was this free-floating yet keenly felt and frequently acted-out agitation—and no doubt the need for new dresses—that led Mary as intently as ever in Lizzy Keckly's direction. After Emilie had gone, Mary felt particularly lonely in a way her many social engagements could not assuage. She felt that she barely saw her husband anymore, although she blamed *her* busy schedule of entertaining as much as his working: "I consider myself fortunate," she wrote Mercy, "if at eleven o'clock, I once more find myself, in my pleasant room & very especially, if my tired & weary Husband, is *there*, resting in the lounge to receive me—to chat over occurrences of the day."[39]

In a way, Lizzy was part of Mary's shadow White House: the "downstairs" world of Mansion staff who more or less did her bidding. (This is in contrast to her blue room White House, with its salon-like atmosphere and its decidedly "upstairs" clientele, where the agenda was society and politics.) Mansion watchmen, laborers, doormen, and messengers (white people, generally) sought and received her patronage for low-level government jobs in the Navy, War, or Treasury Department. Mary Ann Cuthbert, the housekeeper, Edward McManus, the head doorkeeper, and Thomas Stackpole, the watchman promoted to steward, ran private errands and delivered confidential messages and received favors in return. Mary and Lincoln wrote separate letters recommending Stackpole for a permit "to go into the Oyster trade"; on the side, in addition, Mary helped him in a secret enterprise selling trading permits to a local friend: trading Northern goods for Southern cotton between the lines was a lucrative business given wartime shortages and inflation. In the end, the staff knew more about Mary's messy affairs than practically anyone else.

With a staff to command, Mary readily reverted to her Lexington days, when the family slaves stood at the ready; more deeply, perhaps, she was also identifying herself with the second-class family to which her stepmother and father had relegated her and her siblings. Out of all who became close to Mary, only Lizzy was not white, and she became the closest.[40]

Gradually, Mary enlisted Lizzy in her various schemes, a shift from their earlier bonding around the loss of their sons, experiences of slavery, and passion for elegant dress design. Mary's shopping debts and her political schemes became a central part of their conversation. Anxiously, she sought Lizzy's opinions—or at least, her reassurances. "What do you think about the election, Lizabeth?" Mary asked her dressmaker, who was busy with her work, pinning or sewing. From many Northern quarters was coming the view that Lincoln was too ineffectual, too indecisive, too unsystematic to bring the war to a satisfactory close. "I think that Mr. Lincoln will remain in the White House four years longer," Lizzy said, looking up from the material in her hands. She elaborated, saying that Lincoln "represents a principle . . . that loyal people of the loyal States" would vote to support. Mary had been listening to the politicians, who were not so sure, but Lizzy gave her the "people's" view and hope: that the President's honesty and faithfulness to the North during the nation's great trial would be enough to persuade voters "to confide in him" until the war was over.[41]

By the end of the summer, Lizzy had become adept at these political conversations. One day, when Mary came to her rooms for a fitting, Mary reopened the topic of her husband's reelection: "Lizz[y], where do you think I will be this time next summer?" "Why, in the White House, of course." "I cannot believe so," Mary answered. Like Lincoln, she was despondent about their prospects. "No matter," Lizzy dismissed her worries. "Mr. Lincoln will be re-elected. I am so confident of it, that I am tempted to ask a favor of you." "A favor! Well, if we remain in the White House, I shall be able to do you many favors," Mary answered truthfully. "What is the special favor?" Lizzy asked for "the right-hand glove that the President wears at the first public reception after his second inaugural." It would be a memento of "the man who has done so much for my race." "You have some strange ideas, Lizabeth," said Mary; were it up to her, she would throw the "filthy" used-up glove into the fire.[42] Mary liked her gloves new and, as Lizzy had already observed, did not like keepsakes.

At about this time, Mary also began entrusting Lizzy with the important business of seeing that she got what she wanted from New York. Mary could not be in Washington giving parties and at the same time in New York procuring shawls, and Lizzy was posted to New York when Mary had Washington campaigns to wage. In the fall, after Mary returned from her shopping to the capital in time for the election, Lizzy stayed in New York, remaining all of November. There she carried on Mary's business, getting estimates on yards of material for her, placing or "countermanding" orders, paying or deferring paying bills, and in general acting as a liaison between Mrs. Lincoln and the shopkeepers, according to telegrams that went back and forth between them.[43]

"I never in my life saw a more peculiarly constituted woman," Lizzy remarked. Not even the complex Anna Burwell came close to Mary Lincoln for contradictions. On the one hand, Lizzy believed that Mary was "well-versed" in human nature: "Her intuition about the sincerity" of certain people "was more accurate than that of her husband." Mrs. Lincoln was "shrewd and farseeing, and had no patience with the frank, confiding nature of the President." On the other hand, Lizzy, who was scrupulous about paying debts, must have wondered what compelled Mary to become so financially entangled.[44] (Only a sheltered white woman who'd never had to work a day in her life would have been so reckless with money; only a white woman who'd never been sexually exploited and enslaved would have allowed herself to become so dependent on men.)

Nor could she understand what she called Mary's "jealous freaks"—her irrational jealousy when any other woman paid "marked attention to the President." It was an issue that came up before every reception, according to Lizzy, and Lincoln eventually took to consulting his wife as to which lady he could talk to before they went downstairs.

" 'Shall it be Mrs. D?' ... 'No' ... 'What do you say to Miss C.?' ... 'No' ... 'Well, I must talk with some one,' " and so on, went the ritual, which Lincoln would perform "with a mock expression of gravity." Indeed, by 1864, Mary had grown tired of watching him make the traditional reception promenade with one or another of the political or military wives or daughters, and she confided to Lizzy, whose taste and sense of propriety she respected, that she wanted the President to lead her or nobody. Why should she allow some White House custom to make another woman "first with him" and her "second"? Besides, "If they recognize his position, they should also recognize mine."[45]

By the fall before the election, Mary, when she was not shopping, was focusing nearly all of her efforts on helping her husband in New York City, where the long-standing feud between conservative Republicans, the faction of Seward and publisher Thurlow Weed, and radical Greeley Republicans endangered the chances for Lincoln's reelection by driving a wedge into his Party support. Between her New York trips, during which she was entertained or escorted by ambitious Party men, and her blue room coterie, with its circle of New Yorkers who traded morsels of information with their hostess and one another, she had the heady sensation of having an inside track into the murky arena of New York Republican politics.

Using the prized patronage appointments in the New York Custom House was a time-honored way to secure political support, and Mary lobbied for her intimate, Abram Wakeman, the New York Postmaster and Weed man, to replace a former favorite, Rufus F. Andrews, as Custom House surveyor. Andrews had diligently sent gifts of English mutton "just received from the other side of the world" to the White House, but he was a Chase man and despised by Weed. After Nicolay returned from a mission in late August to negotiate appointments that would appease the New York boss, Lincoln named the smooth Wakeman the new surveyor and gave the title of collector, "with some reluctance," to the merchant Simeon Draper, whom Mary also was cultivating.[46]

The careful and correct Lizzy witnessed Mary's maneuverings with concern. As before, there were rumors that Mary had sexual relationships with Sickles and Wakeman (between Mary and Wakeman the President was frequently referred to as "the P," a familiar reference that was unusual for Mary to use, putting her husband on the level of her coterie), and she was regularly criticized for associating with "a certain class of men." Mary explained to her friend why she put herself in the way of malicious gossip: "I have an object in view, Lizabeth. . . . These men have influence, and we require influence to re-elect Mr. Lincoln. I will be clever to them until after the election, and then, if we remain in the White House, I will drop every one of them, and let them know very plainly that I only made tools of them." She didn't mind "double-dealing" with men who were already "an unprincipled set." "Does the President know what your purpose is?" Lizzy asked. "God! no; he would never sanction such a proceeding, so I keep him in the dark. . . . He is too honest to take the proper care of his interests, so I feel it to be my duty to electioneer for him." "Poor Mr. L," Mary wrote Wakeman at about this time, "who is almost a monomaniac on the subject of honesty."[47]

Although Lizzy might have questioned Mary's flirtations with conservatives who were somewhat less than respected, she could only have approved of Mary's favorite radical, the highly respected, formidable Massachusetts Senator Charles Sumner, who had been beaten on the Senate floor for his antislavery convictions and was a hero in the black community. Sumner disagreed with Lincoln's "soft" reconstruction policies toward the white South— "The only loyal Unionists of the South are black," he argued—and he had always believed that Lincoln moved too slowly against slavery. It was important that he not oppose Lincoln's reelection, and cynical observers concluded that the attention he received from both Lincolns was "to help [get] L. right with the N. Engl. antislavery people," as a friend of Sumner's wrote him. Whatever Mary's initial intention when she began inviting the aloof Sumner to the opera or on carriage rides, she was soon eager for the arrogant, intellectual Sumner's approval. The handsome, serious-minded fifty-three-year-old bachelor made Mary wish to temper some of her bad habits, to appear better than she was. After chiding him for not attending a reception, she hastily wrote a note of apology with a peace offering of a bouquet "for the inadvertent manner, in which I addressed you on yesterday. . . . I am aware, that you, do not usually frequent large crowds, or attend receptions." She herself found them "somewhat an *annoyance*, but a necessity, which of course, in this house cannot be dispensed with." One week later, hoping to ingratiate herself with the pro–equal rights Sumner, she dropped him a note to "introduce to your distinguished notice, these two colored persons, who come to us very highly recommended, from some of our most loyal families of Phila— . . . Mr. Hamilton . . . and Mrs. Johnson. Both appear to be very genteel & intelligent persons." They wished to meet him, she added, "you, whom all the oppressed colored race, have so much cause, to honor." After a time, Mary relaxed with her haughty and imposing guest and, as an intelligent woman, found discussing ideas a refreshing, inspiriting change from the usual gossip: "I learned to converse with him, with more freedom and *confidence* than any of my other friends." For the virginal Sumner, who did not marry until after his mother's death in his mid-fifties, and then to a widow half his age who left him the next year, charging impotence, Mary's attentions were pleasurable. He enjoyed their exchanges of notes in French, of French and English books, and of tidbits about European notables, with whom he was in regular correspondence. He even let her read the famous Europeans' letters.[48]

If Sumner's influence had an indirect effect on Mary's thoughts about Lizzy, it was clearly in accord with her initial reactions to her dressmaker. To be sure, using an introduction to a "genteel & intelligent" black person as a way to make a social impression is not the same thing as seeing a black person as a person. But to the extent that in Mary's mind a black Mr. Hamilton and a black Mrs. Johnson had become name-dropping material, being friends with a "genteel & intelligent" black woman like Madam Keckly did not require an impossible leap of imagination.

In the meantime, Lizzy had her own sphere of influence. In the fall of 1864, a white woman named Lucy Colman, an antislavery activist and spiritualist from Rochester, New York, approached her with a request. Could she secure a meeting between President Lincoln and her friend, Sojourner Truth? A former slave, nearly six feet tall, with a low, powerful voice, Truth was an itinerant preacher and an advocate for abolition and women's rights.[49]

There is no description of how Lizzy arranged the meeting, which took place on October 29, 1864. (When black leaders later wished to maneuver Lincoln's successor, President Andrew Johnson, who showed no interest in the welfare of blacks, into appointing Frederick Douglass to head the Freedmen's Bureau, they enlisted William Slade, newly promoted to steward, who wrote Douglass a letter on White House stationery encouraging him to take the post and then showed Douglass's written response to Johnson.) Nor is there a clear-cut description of what took place when Truth and Lincoln met. In Colman's version, Lincoln was less than gracious, growing irritated when Truth began praising him as the antislavery President, preferring to speak with Colman; he called Truth " 'Aunty' . . . as he would his washerwoman." As another friend described it, "A born Kentuckian, [Lincoln] could call her 'anty' in the old familiar way." In Truth's account, published in her narrative, Lincoln treated her with marked respect: they shook hands and he listened to her attentively; he signed her autograph book and showed her a copy of a Bible presented to him on July 4 by "the loyal colored people of Baltimore."[50] Who knows how to reconcile the differing accounts? Truth was not offended when Lincoln called her Auntie, so it may be that she had a different reaction to Lincoln altogether from the white Colman. However, Lincoln may have been less than obliging toward his striking, self-invited guest. Unlike previous black visitors, notably Frederick Douglass, Sojourner Truth was neither mixed-race, genteel, nor male.

Since Emancipation, African Americans had had access to the President as never before. Indeed, before Lincoln, no black person had ever been invited to consult with an American President. By 1864, Lincoln had come to see Frederick Douglass as his adviser on black affairs, inviting him back to the White House in August to talk over how to respond to the criticism he was getting from all sides about his proposals for Southern reconstruction. Nevertheless, except for two meetings with Douglass, a meeting with the black delegation to discuss colonization in 1862, and one famous interview with free colored gentlemen from New Orleans about black suffrage in 1864, Lincoln did not seek the counsel of his black supporters on how to deal with the problems of the freedmen. Still, by 1865, one could have seen that Lincoln had been "educated" (by Douglass's lights). He had moved from his moderate, gradualist views on emancipation to a more radical position supporting universal emancipation with limited suffrage. He had also obviously abandoned his previous belief in colonization as the only way to deal with postslavery race relations. Had he survived into his second term, when reconstruction would replace war as the key national concern, he may have learned to turn toward black leaders more.[51]

Not everyone who approached Lizzy for an introduction to the White House had good intentions. One woman offered Lizzy money to help her get a job as a chambermaid in the White House; after refusing to oblige, Lizzy discovered that the woman was an actress who hoped "to enter the White House as a servant, learn its secrets, and then publish a scandal to the world." Lizzy was proud of her White House position and saw it as a point of honor not to "betray the confidence" of her "employer."[52]

At the beginning of September, Lincoln's prospects for a second term suddenly improved. On September 2, Atlanta fell to General Sherman, and the tide of Northern victory swept Lincoln along to reelection. With victory, Mary Lincoln was saved from being a middle-aged woman beleaguered by debts and transformed as if magically into a returning queen, able to grant and press for favors. It also gave her justification for gratifying every impulse. Between November and March the feverish Mary had her milliner in New York make her a new black velvet bonnet "for *grand occasions*"; ordered a black velvet headdress from Tiffany & Co.; abruptly fired doorkeeper Edward Mc-Manus and accused him of spreading "vile falsehoods" about her; ordered a new 508-piece set of china to match the new official set she bought for the White House, replacing her 1861 china purchases; and bought herself three hundred pairs of kid gloves. Then, in March, in the midst of the postinaugural parties, she rolled back and forth between the White House and Galt & Bro. Jewelers on Fifteenth Street, where she spent $2,888.50 on pearl, amethyst, and diamond jewelry: pins, earrings, bracelets, and a ring.[53]

Elizabeth Keckly was also delighted. She received her one glove, yet, as four years earlier, she was not in the crowd that gathered outside the Capitol to watch the inauguration. Still, so much had changed from four years before. For the first time ever, black people were permitted onto the Capitol grounds to attend the inauguration. They may have heard Douglass's echo in Lincoln's inaugural address, in the apocalyptic vision of a righteous war: "Yet, if God will that it continue, until all the wealth piled by the bond-man's two hundred and fifty years of unrequited toil shall be sunk, and until every drop of blood drawn with the lash, shall be paid by another drawn with the sword, as said three thousand years ago, so still it must be said 'the judgments of the Lord, are true and generous altogether.' " Then, pulling back from this vision of God's vengeful justice, Lincoln offered human forgiveness: "With malice toward none; with charity for all."[54]

By March 1865, African Americans had many reasons to rejoice. On January 31, the House approved the Thirteenth Amendment abolishing slavery to the cheers and weeping of black people, who for the first time were allowed into the congressional galleries. The next day, Senator Charles Summer presented Boston lawyer John Rock for admission to practice before the Supreme Court, the first black man to be sworn in to do so. Eight years earlier, in the Dred Scott case, the Supreme Court had "denied U.S. citizenship to his race." After Lincoln's second inauguration, Lizzy Keckly, the Slades, and the Lewises would be among friends at the "colored" inaugural reception who would hear Douglass tell about his adventure earlier that day, when he broke the racial barrier at the inaugural levee at the White House and went in and shook Lincoln's hand. Douglass's pride and pleasure in the occasion—most of all, in Lincoln's warm greeting and open expression of admiration—was a mirror of Lizzy's feelings of pride about being in the White House.[55]

In the meantime, the nation was turning a hopeful face toward the resolution of the war. Witnesses to the second inaugural on March 4, 1865, said that when Lincoln came forward to take the oath, the clouds that had been overhead all morning parted and a ray of sunshine streamed forth. To the war-weary people, it was a sign of hope for the future. Southern cities were tumbling one by one. Sherman had "cut a swath [from Atlanta] through to the sea," and in Virginia, Grant's army was closing in on Lee.

Two nights later, before the Inaugural Ball at the Patent House, Lizzy helped Mary into the white silk dress she had sewn for the occasion and began fixing Mary's hair. It was the first time they had seen each other since the inauguration and, as Lizzy did her hair, Mary was telling her how her husband looked "so broken-hearted, so completely worn out," that she feared he would not survive the next four years. Then the President came in, and, beaming pleasure, Lizzy went up to him, shook his hand, and wished him congratulations. "Thank you," he answered, in a weary voice. After thinking a moment he said, "Well, Madam Elizabeth, I don't know whether I should feel thankful or not. The position brings with it many trials. We do not know what we are destined to pass through. But God will be with us all," he concluded. "I put my trust in God."[56]

Less than one month later, on Monday, April 3, Richmond fell into Union hands. When she heard the news, Elizabeth Keckly gave the girls who sewed in her workrooms a day off. All over the city, people were spilling out into the streets, eager to merge themselves with the throngs of other tearful and elated people who could not stay indoors. The otherwise strict Madam Keckly was amused to see "usually clear-headed" friends getting joyfully drunk.[57]

Lincoln, who had been in Virginia since the last week in March, was in

Petersburg on the morning of April 3 meeting with the victorious General Grant. Hearing the news of Richmond's fall, he decided to go there the next day. Back in Washington, Mary was busy making her own arrangements to go to City Point, on the James River near Petersburg and Richmond, where she expected to join her husband and proceed with him in triumph into the fallen Confederate capital. "Will you dine with us, in Jeff Davs', deserted banqueting hall?" Mary giddily asked Abram Wakeman before she left. Lizzy, hearing of Mrs. Lincoln's plans for the trip, asked to be included. Petersburg was her old home; and nothing could make her happier than to return to Virginia as a free woman.[58]

It was, in fact, a return trip for Mary as well; she and Tad had accompanied her husband to General Grant's headquarters at City Point the previous week. However, that trip had been a disaster for her. She had ferociously attacked Lincoln in public for allowing two officer's wives to ride alongside him on the field where they were reviewing troops while she was relegated to a slow-moving carriage in the rear with Mrs. Julia Grant. She had also lashed out at one of the officer's wives in front of a field of witnesses and loudly berated Mrs. Grant. As the day wore on, her rage escalated, and by the evening she was demanding, in front of others, that her husband dismiss the officer whose wife had so offended her. Possibly mortified by her behavior, Mary spent the rest of the trip on board the *River Queen*, too ill to venture forth. She returned to Washington, leaving Tad with his father, arriving home on April 2.[59]

Instantly, she was ready to try again, and on April 6, her party arrived by steamer at Fortress Monroe. Included were Senator Charles Sumner and his guest, a marquis who was the grandson of Lafayette; James Harlan, Secretary of the Interior, and his wife and daughter, who was being courted by Robert (now a captain on Grant's staff); and Elizabeth Keckly. Despite her hints for him to wait for her, Lincoln had entered the burned-out Richmond two days earlier where the first people to recognize him were some black workmen who fell on their knees shouting praises and tried to kiss the feet of the embarrassed President. Forty hours after Jefferson Davis abandoned it, he sat in the study of the President of the Confederate States. Upset that he had gone ahead, Mary sent her husband urgent telegrams, requesting that he wait for her in Richmond and, if he could not, would he "return [to Washington] on some other vessel, we are most uncomfortable on this & would like your boat." After some complicated arrangements, the party of Mrs. Lincoln was aboard the President's boat, the *River Queen*, "steaming up the James River."[60]

Elizabeth Keckly would remember the day as balmy, the air pure, the river flowing majestically. A flood of nostalgia washed over her. "A birthplace is always dear, no matter under what circumstances you were born," Lizzy wrote, "since it revives in memory the golden hours of childhood."[61] In the Virginia statehouse, where the Confederate congress had met, Lizzy picked up a sheaf of papers from the piles that were scattered about and found herself holding "the resolution prohibiting all free colored people from entering" Virginia. She sat in the chairs of Jefferson Davis and Vice President Alexander H. Stephens. Afterward, they toured the Davis mansion.

Not all went smoothly, however. That night Mary made a scene when a young officer innocently teased that upon entering Richmond the other day, Lincoln was "quite a hero when surrounded by pretty young ladies." "I do not think that the Captain who incurred Mrs. Lincoln's displeasure will ever forget that memorable evening in the cabin of the *River Queen*, at City Point," Lizzy remarked dryly.[62]

The party then traveled by special train to Petersburg, where Lizzy had been a slave twenty years before. There they met a ragged black boy, who used the word "tote" (meaning "to carry"), a word popular in the South that Lincoln had never heard; this led to a discussion with Sumner about its African origins. The trip to Petersburg was painful for Lizzy; whatever memories came to mind, they were not those of a golden childhood that, in any event, had never been. "I was not sorry to turn my back again upon the city," she wrote.[63]

The Saturday evening that they were to return from City Point to Washington, Lincoln came on board the *River Queen* exhausted from reviewing troops. "Mother," he said to Mary, "I have shaken so many hands to-day that my arms ache tonight. I almost wish that I could go to bed now." In the deepening twilight, the boat, which was lit up all over, looked to Lizzy "like an enchanted floating palace." A military band on board was playing music, and at Lincoln's request, played "Marseilles" and "Dixie." Officers were coming on board to say good-bye. Responding to calls for a speech, Lincoln rose slowly to his feet and apologized that he was too tired to speak that night but would make a speech in Washington on Tuesday, "at which time you will learn all I have to say." At 11 o'clock "the lights were taken down, the River Queen rounded out into the water and we were on our way back to Washington." On the ride back, the President read Shakespeare aloud for several hours. Whatever Mary Lincoln was feeling, Elizabeth Keckly had rarely felt so content and peaceful in her life.[64]

On Tuesday morning, as Mary was preparing to drive away from her apartments on Twelfth Street, Lizzy asked her if she and a friend could come to the White House to hear Lincoln's speech. Lizzy had never heard Lincoln make a public speech before. As long as she came early to dress her, Mary said, she could come with her friend. At 7 o'clock, Lizzy entered the White House and climbed the stairs. How many times she had done this over the past four years she could not tell. However, this time was different: she was coming at her own request, with a friend, and she was coming as an insider, permitted to witness the public event from inside the Mansion. To be sure, Mary had secured her services for the evening, but before going to Mrs. Lincoln's room, she snuck a private glimpse of history and peeked into the President's office, where he was seated at his desk, muttering over his notes.

That evening, as soon as the President stepped out into a second-story window, a roar went up from the crowd that was assembled in the dark before the White House, illuminated by tiers upon tiers of tiny candles affixed to strips of wood that workmen had nailed to every window. Most of the crowd had walked up Pennsylvania Avenue from the Capitol, where an enormous gaslit transparency had been hung with the words "This is the Lord's doing. It is marvelous in our eyes." Mary was watching the crowd and her husband from another second-story window. Looking on from yet another window on the second floor were Elizabeth Keckly and her unidentified friend. With Tad holding a lamp beside him, Lincoln began reading his speech, which was about his plans for reconstruction.[65]

To Lizzy's eyes, father and son "made a striking tableau," the "one lost in a chain of eloquent ideas," the other looking up proudly. Below, "thousands of free citizens" stood, black and white. Then, as Lizzy watched the light fall on the President, "making him stand out boldly in the darkness," a terrible thought darted into her mind. How easy it would be to kill the President "as he stands there," she whispered to her friend. "He could be shot from the crowd, and no one be able to tell who fired the shot." Mary would agree when Lizzy chose to tell her the same thing the next day. It was obviously the continuation of a subject they'd discussed often; Mary had a "presentiment that he will meet with a sudden and violent end. I pray to God to protect my beloved husband from the hands of the assassin." She knew that Lincoln was also haunted by fears of his own death. Before each major battle, he had had a recurring dream: of a ship moving toward a dark shore. It seemed to Mary a journey toward death.[66]

She could not know how close to journey's end Lincoln was. In the crowd watching Lincoln speak the evening before was an actor, John Wilkes Booth. "That means nigger citizenship," he muttered when he heard Lincoln's recommendations for suffrage for African Americans who were educated or had fought in the Union. "That is the last speech he will ever make." He urged Lewis Paine, one of his two companions, to shoot Lincoln on the spot, but Paine refused. Turning in disgust to David Herold, the other man, Booth made a vow. "By God, I'll put him through."[67]

Chapter Twelve

*A*t 11 o'clock on the night of April 14, 1865, Elizabeth Keckly was awakened by a neighbor, Mrs. Brown: "The entire Cabinet has been assassinated! Mr. Lincoln has been shot, but not mortally wounded!"

"When I heard the words I felt as if the blood had been frozen in my veins, and that my lungs must collapse for want of air." She dressed quickly, and hurried into Twelfth Street. There were people milling around, not knowing what to do. No one could tell her what was happening. She ran back into her boardinghouse and woke the Lewises. All she knew was that she had to go to the White House. Walker and Virginia Lewis tried to quiet her, but she was desperate to go. She knew Mrs. Lincoln would be wild with grief, and she wanted to go to her. "I felt that the house would not hold me." Finally, the Lewises agreed to go with her, and she waited while her two friends dressed; then they went out together to begin their walk to the White House.

On their way, the three passed Secretary Seward's house in Lafayette Square. It was surrounded by soldiers, with bayonets drawn. Hurrying on, they saw that armed sentries were also posted outside the White House. The guards would not let the three well-dressed black people pass, nor would they tell them more than that the President had been shot. Turning back into the streets, Lizzy saw an elderly man whose face seemed "so full of kindness and sorrow" that she felt she could ask him about the President. Gently touching him on the arm, she implored him to tell her if Mr. Lincoln was dead or not. His response was "Not dead, but dying, then indeed God help us!"[1]

The next morning at 11 o'clock, a messenger sent from the White House arrived at 388 Twelfth Street to bring Lizzy to Mrs. Lincoln. As they drove toward the Mansion in the cold, cheerless rain, Lizzy could see that the gas streetlamps, normally extinguished in the morning, were still burning. In front of several of the houses, which she recognized as the Cabinet members' residences, a single sentry paced back and forth. Already, flags "hung in silent folds at half-mast," and some of the shops and houses were draped in black crape. (At directions from Commissioner French, the Capitol and government buildings would soon be covered in mourning.) The streets seemed unnaturally hushed, as if people were afraid to speak above a whisper. On the White House lawn, she saw "several hundred" African Americans, mostly women and children, "weeping and wailing their loss."[2]

That morning, Commissioner French had ordered the White House closed, so Lizzy needed permission to get in. Hastily untying her bonnet, she ran upstairs to look for Mrs. Lincoln, who was not in her own bedroom. When Mary had been brought back to the White House that morning, she refused to enter any of the family bedrooms. She finally did agree to use a tiny, spare bedroom that she had made up for Lincoln to use during the summer, when they slept mostly at the Soldiers' Home. Lizzy, fearful of what she would find, entered the darkened room where Mary was lying moaning in bed. The only other person there was Mrs. Mary Jane Welles, who with Elizabeth Dixon, wife of Connecticut Senator James Dixon, had helped Mary away from the Petersons' house, a private home across the street from Ford's Theatre, where they had carried the wounded President the night before. It was there that Lincoln had died at 7:22 in the morning.

When her husband had been shot, Mary was hanging on to his arm. She saw a flash and heard the report of the pistol but, like most of the audience, thought it was part of the play. She looked at her husband, who was sitting with his head dropped forward, as he sometimes did when he was deep in thought. Then something brushed by her; there was a commotion, shouting, and blood.

Mary became aware of the familiar figure standing beside her bed. "Why did you not come to me last night, Elizabeth—I sent for you?" she whispered. She was exhausted from grief. "I did try to come to you, but I could not find you," Lizzy answered. Apparently, Mary had sent three messengers from the Petersen house the night before, but for some reason none of them was able to find her correct address.

With Lizzy in attendance, Mrs. Welles, who had been ill when she came out in the rain at dawn, felt herself able to leave. Mary became quieter, and Lizzy asked if she might go see Mr. Lincoln's body, which was laid out in the guest room. It was the same room where Willie had lain in his coffin three years before, where Lizzy had watched the President weeping over his beautiful young son. Now she was the one black woman among the white men who gathered in the guest room, some of them crying audibly. Walking up to the body, she lifted the white cloth from the President's face. "No common mortal had died. The Moses of my people had died in the moment of his triumph." For Lizzy, as for countless other black Americans, Lincoln's death transformed their Moses into a martyr and a saint. He was "the man I had worshipped as an idol—looked at as a demi-god."[3]

When Lizzy returned to Mary's room, she saw Robert. At the age of twenty-two he had gone from being a protected son to the head of a household. He was leaning over his mother's bed, while at the foot crouched Tad, "with a world of agony upon his young face. I shall never forget the scene," Lizzy later wrote. Mary was shrieking, while her terrified twelve-year-old was begging his mother to stop. Lizzy approached the bed and, taking over from Robert, tried to soothe her as best she could. Eventually, Tad's cries must have penetrated his mother's consciousness, because Mary struggled to control herself; but she soon broke down, overtaken by another wave of convulsive sobbing.[4]

Mary would remain in the White House for nearly six weeks, too heartbroken and overwhelmed to leave, while the new President, Andrew Johnson, stayed in a house at Fifteenth and H, where a guard marched up and down in front, and worked from a tiny room in the Treasury Department. Bedridden for weeks, Mary refused to receive any officials except Senator Sumner and Secretary Stanton, for whom she made a point to rouse herself. (President Johnson never wrote or tried to call; he might have stayed away knowing she had not forgiven him for his performance at the inauguration, to which he had shown up drunk.) As she had after Willie died, she now secluded herself from the outside world, only this time her anguish was beyond imagining and she permitted only a few close friends into her presence. Later, when Mary remembered who was with her at the time, she remembered Lizzy. "Our good friend, Lizzie Keckley, can give you, every particular, with regard to myself, in the deep affliction, I have been called, to pass through," Mary would tell a friend the next year. "Every other night, Lizzie K., for six weeks, watched faithfully by my side."[5]

Mary's grief was painful to behold, and her emotional needs so draining on her companions, that no one except Lizzy seemed able to stay with her for long. Mary Jane Welles and Elizabeth Blair Lee took turns, although one day Mary declined to see Mrs. Welles, and on another complained that she could not bear to see Mrs. Lee's smile. Elizabeth Lee had volunteered to "watch & wait upon her," but found Mary hard to take. "I shall return again this evening," she wrote her husband a week after Lincoln died, "& shall continue to go as long as I can stand it—or be of any use." On the day of Lincoln's funeral, which was held in the East Room, Mary remained upstairs, attended by Elizabeth Keckly and Elizabeth Lee, who left only after Robert and Tad returned to their mother after the service.[6]

Although Mary had periods of calm, during which she talked about her husband's final hours, she was frequently hysterical and even delirious. Commissioner French thought that "the sudden and awful death . . . somewhat unhinged her mind, for, at times she has exhibited symptoms of madness." Elizabeth Lee told her husband: "She addresses him in her sleep & in her delirium from raging fever in terms & tones of the tenderest affection." After the death of two sons and now her husband, it was not possible for Mary to resign herself into the hands of God. In these harrowing first days after Lincoln's assassination, the brokenhearted widow referred "constantly" to Lincoln's "religious faith—but never to her own," according to Mrs. Lee. Instead, Mary went to spiritualism for what little comfort she was able, or willing, to take. Her private physician, Dr. Anson Henry, an old Springfield friend who stayed in the White House when he visited Washington and was in City Point when he heard the dreadful news of Lincoln's murder, encouraged Mary in the belief that "our departed friends hover over and around us, and are fully cognizant of all that transpires, while we are not sensible of their presence." However potentially consoling a belief, she seemed to her friends to almost refuse to be comforted.[7]

None of Mary's relatives came to Washington this time around. Emilie had broken with her several months ago, after Lincoln turned down her request for a permit to sell cotton across Union lines. Elizabeth had taken her husband's side when Lincoln removed Ninian from his position with the Commissary Department, in charge of distributing food to the army; besides, Mary had already cut off her oldest sister after reading the insulting remarks Elizabeth's daughter had written about her in a letter. Whatever her sisters' feelings, they probably knew that she might very well refuse to see them. Lizzy believed that Mary's seclusion of herself during this time left her nearly friendless, and although she would hasten to add that she did not wish to "harshly judge her sorrow," it is clear that she thought Mary's behavior had a self-indulgent edge.[8]

Lizzy slept in Mary's room, along with Tad, who could not sleep alone. (After Willie died, his lonely brother often fell asleep on the floor of Lincoln's office when he was working late; afterward Lincoln would carry Tad in to sleep in his bed with him.) However, sleeping in Mary's room was not always a comfort to the twelve-year-old boy. His mother's sobbing would wake him. "Don't cry, Mamma, or I will cry, too," he would plead, an appeal that usually worked, as Mary could not bear to hear Tad cry.[9]

Lizzy felt sorry for this poor, vulnerable boy who, in losing his father, had lost his closest companion, for Lincoln had let Tad tag along almost everywhere. The President's assassination, according to Lizzy, forced Tad to grow up (until then, he had never even dressed himself). Only a few days after the assassination, he told his nurse while she was dressing him (who subsequently told Lizzy): "I am not a President's son now. I won't have many presents any more. I will try and be a good boy, and will hope to go some day to Pa and brother Willie, in heaven." ("Three of us on earth, & *three* in Heaven," he liked to say.) Soon after that conversation, he made his own decision to do without a nurse.[10]

As one whose own childhood had forced her to grow up fast, Lizzy could not look at Tad without measuring the distance between his life and that of a black child's. She knew his parents had let him neglect his studies, but she was shocked to discover how ignorant he was. Indeed, when she realized a few weeks later that Tad could hardly read she remarked that had he been a black boy, and not a President's son, he would have been "held up as an example of the inferiority of the race."[11]

By mid-May, Mary had for weeks been promising President Johnson that she would leave. Her husband's body had been carried by special train to Illinois, the route lined with millions of weeping men, women, and children, and buried in Oak Ridge cemetery in Springfield. Jefferson Davis had been captured in Georgia and imprisoned in Fortress Monroe, Virginia. Mary had rallied herself enough to win a battle with a group of prominent Illinois citizens who wished to bury her husband in a vault at the center of Springfield. But she dreaded vacating the White House. Even after she physically was able to leave, it was hard for Mary to give up who her husband's position had empowered her to be. "God, Elizabeth, what a change!" she said to Lizzy one day. "Did ever woman have to suffer so much and experience so great a change? I had an ambition to be Mrs. President; that ambition has been gratified, and now I must step down from the pedestal." Then guilt and self-pity set in. "My poor husband! Had he never been President, he might be living today. Alas! All is over with me!"[12]

Indeed, there were difficulties to be addressed before she could go. Foremost was deciding where she would go *to*. Springfield was out of the question. The house on Eighth and Jackson had too many memories of a happy life with her husband, and were she to try to live there now that she was "deprived of *his* presence and the darling boy, we lost in Washington, it would not require a day, for me to lose my entire reason." This was a frequent topic of conversation with Lizzy, because Mary knew that her husband's friends and even Robert thought that she should go back to Springfield, where she already owned a house. "My God, Elizabeth, I can never go back to Springfield! no, never, until I go in my shroud to be laid by my dear husband's side, and may Heaven speed that day. I should like to live for my sons, but life is so full of misery that I would rather die." This last sentiment found its way into many of her letters.[13]

Where she could afford to live depended on her finances—another difficulty. Lincoln had died without a will, so Mary had to wait for his estate to be settled, and that was up to its executor, Judge David Davis. An Illinois friend and campaign manager whom Lincoln had named to the Supreme

Court, Davis was unaware of the extent of Mary's indebtedness and thought she had enough to live on. Yet only months before, Mary told Lizzy that she owed $27,000, mostly to Stewart's in New York. True, after her husband's re-election, some of that had been paid, but she had continued to shop with abandon, and she now owed various merchants and bankers at least that amount, possibly more. She had just sent Dr. Anson Henry to New York to settle some of her bills, but that was only the tip of the iceberg. To be sure, no one was calling in their debts right now, but eventually they would, and Mary would need to find a way to pay up.[14]

She solved the more immediate problem, deciding where to go, by choosing Chicago. It was there, she claimed, that Lincoln planned to retire after serving out his second term. As the city in which Lincoln had received his first nomination as Republican candidate for President, it was associated with days of triumph, not despair. Also, she may have felt that Chicago was closer to home, and to Lincoln's grave.

"Packing," according to Lizzy, "afforded quite a relief." Into fifty or sixty crates and scores of trunks (by Lizzy's count, although other estimates were higher) went everything she'd brought from Springfield and every personal item she had bought in Washington, from bonnets and dresses to jewelry and fans. She also put in nearly five years' worth of gifts she had accumulated as First Lady on the presumption that they were hers, not the nation's, including tablecloths, yards of imported lace, silk, and embroidered fabrics, silver-ware, paintings, photographs, statuary, and books. More than once, Robert became impatient with his mother: "I wish to heaven the car would take fire in which you place these boxes . . . and burn all your old plunder up." Mary was philosophical: "Robert is so impetuous. He never thinks about the future. Well, I hope that he will get over his boyish notions in time." The malicious believed that into her trunks and crates she stowed away furnishings, china, and silverware belonging to the White House, a charge both she and Lizzy would answer in the same way—whether accurately or conspiratorially: that Mary, with Mr. French's permission, took only a small dressing stand that Lincoln had admired.[15]

What she did not pack she gave away. Lincoln mementoes went to the doorkeepers, guards, messengers, and valets, whom Mary had always made it her special business to notice. To William Slade, Lincoln's messenger, Mary gave one of Lincoln's many canes and his heavy gray shawl; Slade's wife received the dress Mary was wearing on the night of the assassination, a black silk with white stripes. (Over the years, Mrs. Slade would cut strips from it to give to family and friends as souvenirs.) To a White House guard whom she especially liked went the suit Lincoln was wearing when he was shot. In distributing these items, which she did in May, Mary was consciously contributing to the apotheosis of Lincoln. She sent another cane to Senator Sumner, with a note explaining that her "offer" of "this simple relic" was in recognition for his "unwavering kindness to my idolized Husband, and the great regard, *he* entertained for you." She also sent canes to black abolitionists, to Frederick Douglass and the Reverend Henry Highland Garnet, now minister of the exclusive Fifteenth Street Presbyterian Church, indicative of the change in her from the days when a superior black person was a superior servant. Another special offering, the last hat Lincoln wore, went to Reverend Dr. Gurley, who officiated at both her son's and her husband's funerals and was present when the President died. To Lizzy, now emerging as one of her closest friends, she gave the comb and brush she had used for the President's hair, a pair of overshoes, and the earrings, bonnet, and cloak she was wearing on the last night of her husband's life.[16] In selecting this first group of recipients, Mary chose from her heart. (Tad's precious goats she directed to be delivered to the nurturing Elizabeth Blair Lee, but they never arrived.) She also wrote a few letters of recommendation for men her husband had intended to help.

Finally, on Monday, May 22, Mary Lincoln, encased in black mourning, climbed heavily into the carriage that stood waiting outside the White House to take her to the depot for her trip to Chicago. With her was a sad entourage, consisting of Tad, Robert, Dr. Anson Henry, Elizabeth Keckly, and two White House guards, Thomas Cross and William Crook. Commissioner French was one of the few who bade Mary good-bye. He "felt really very sad," he recorded in his diary, "although she has given a world of trouble. . . . She is a most singular woman, and it is well for the nation that she is no longer in the White House. It is not proper that I should write down, even here, all I know! May God have her in his keeping, and make her a better woman."[17]

To Lizzy, Mary's departure was "so unlike the day when the body of the President was borne from the hall in grand and solemn state," when thousands lined the funeral procession. "Now, the wife of the President was leaving the White House, and there was scarcely a friend to tell her good-bye. . . . The silence was almost painful."[18]

Mary took herself away just in time to miss the Union celebration. The following day, 20,000 blue-clad veterans of the Army of the Potomac and Sherman's Army of Georgia were marching triumphantly down Pennsylvania Avenue toward a flag-draped reviewing stand on the White House lawn occupied by President Johnson and Generals Grant and Sherman. ("But Abraham Lincoln was not there," wrote one diarist. "All felt this.") French watched the Grand Review from the north portico of the Capitol, and then climbed to the top of the dome for a spectacular view of the tens of thousands of citizens and soldiers in the streets. He felt, he reflected later, grateful, joyful, and relieved. It was the start of a new era.[19]

Mary's new life began with a splitting headache, followed by a fifty-four-hour train journey to Chicago in the private green car that had often carried her between Washington and New York City. When she was not weeping, she "was in a daze; it seemed almost a stupor," recalled William Crook. "She hardly spoke. No one could get near enough to her grief to comfort her."[20]

Lizzy must have watched with mixed feelings, for she had not wished to go. In fact, when Mary had first asked her to go to Chicago with her, she "strongly objected." For one thing, she was worn out. "I had listened to [Mrs. Lincoln] sobbing for eight weeks, therefore I was never surprised to find her in tears," she would write testily after two weeks in Chicago. Also, for two months she had neglected her business, into which she had invested all her money, time, and ambition and which she never liked to leave for long. While in Washington, she had reminded Mary of that fact, and also that she had "the spring trousseau to make for Mrs. [Stephen] Douglas," which she promised to do in less than a week. "Never mind," Mary had insisted. "Mrs. Douglas can get some one else to make her trousseau." Then Mary remembered the businesswoman standing before her. "You may find it in your interest to go. I am very poor now, but if Congress makes an appropriation for my benefit"—she hoped for $100,000, representing the salary for the remainder of Lincoln's term—she promised Lizzy would be "well rewarded." The day she had hired Lizzy, the first morning after the inauguration, Mary had said she was poor and could pay only cheap rates; now she felt she could not afford to be cheap.

Lizzy demurred. "It is not the reward, but—"

"Now don't say another word about it, if you do not wish to distress me. I have determined that you shall go to Chicago with me, and you *must* go."

Mrs. Douglas was gracious about losing Lizzy's services and wished her to do all she could to help Mrs. Lincoln. Therefore, "finding that no excuse was accepted, I made preparations to go to Chicago with Mrs. L." Lizzy's only explanation for why she relented was ambiguous, although suggestive of an emotional bond. "I had been with her so long, that she had acquired great power over me." Trained to serve faithfully, she may have also felt as she had before the war, when Varina Davis asked her to return south with her family and she had considered going. Whatever the case, she could not bring herself to deny Mary's request, although she tried pulling away. No doubt, she also hoped to benefit from Mary's repeated promise to provide for her should Congress "provide for me." Mary's feelings were more straightforward: she needed Lizzy. On their first night on the train to Chicago, while Lizzy was bathing her temples, Mary looked gratefully at the familiar face. "Lizabeth," she said, "you are my best and kindest friend, and I love you as my best friend."[21]

For Mary, the world had always been divided into friends and enemies; after the assassination, this way of looking at the world intensified. Lizzy had done for her what no other friend had—indeed, what she had wanted no one else to do: she had endured the violence of Mary's private agony, talked to her about the hovering spirits of her husband and sons, had put her own life aside for weeks to nurse her. Lizzy had tended to her physically, as a mother would, bathing her temples, encouraging her to eat, helping her dress. What mattered most to Mary was that Lizzy had not abandoned her, something terribly important to someone whose list of people who *had* abandoned her was long. It reached back to her mother dying when she was six and forward to a husband who had left her alone at forty-six.

Lizzy would outstay Mary's other companions, remaining in Chicago for two weeks into June, until Mary could no longer afford her services. (Lizzy would receive a check from the Commissioner of Buildings for $360: $35 a week for a total of six weeks in Washington as "first Class Nurse & attendant on Mrs. Lincoln"; $100 for "traveling & incidental expenses" for accompanying her to Chicago; and $50 for "mourning apparel.") She stayed in Chicago long enough to see the Lincolns move from the expensive Tremont Hotel in the city, to three rooms in a hotel in the cheaper resort community of Hyde Park, seven miles south of the center of town. Meanwhile, Mary's boxes and crates were stored in a public warehouse in the city.[22]

Mary and Robert were miserable in their temporary home, which they found depressing and dreary. To Lizzy, though, the wind off the lake and the sparkling water, with here and there a sailboat gliding silently by, were "delightful." However, she too felt an overwhelming sadness, and the restful scene made her yearn for the peace of death: "I had seen so much trouble in my life, that I was willing to fold my arms and sink into a passive slumber—slumber anywhere, so the great longing of the soul was gratified—rest."[23] Lincoln's death touched the lifelong sadness she carried in her.

In June, Lizzy returned to reopen her shop in Washington, "with Mary Lincoln's best wishes for success in business," she proudly noted. Upon her return, she called at the White House to transact some unfinished business for Mary. "I had no desire to enter the house," she recalled, "for everything about it bitterly reminded me of the past." Ever loyal to Mary, she told friends she had no desire to work for Mr. Johnson's family.

Before Lizzy left, Mary had made her promise that if Congress gave her the appropriation she wanted, she would come back to Illinois, and the two would make a pilgrimage together to Lincoln's tomb. Mary had been reluctant to let her go. But the appropriation was not made, and Lizzy stayed in the East. They exchanged letters for the next two years, then they had their final, remarkable encounter. In the meantime, Lizzy continued sewing for Mrs. Lincoln, who disliked anyone else to do her work. Indeed, Mary did not even want any articles sent from Lizzy's workshop "*without* she [herself has] made them."[24]

Yet above all, like Hamlet to Horatio, the exiled Mary had charged the faithful Lizzy to carry her woeful tale to Washington. And Lizzy spread the word—to Mrs. Douglas, Mrs. Lee, Mrs. Welles, and any other potentially sympathizing lady she knew or sewed for—that Mrs. Lincoln was "practicing the closest economy," living in a second-rate hotel, and going without her best friend's help, because she was so poor.[25]

Back in Washington, Lizzy rearranged her own life. In late June, she changed her mind about staying away from the Johnson family and began sewing for the President's married daughters, who stood in socially for their all-but-invisible mother. However, the relationship ended abruptly when Lizzy refused to cut and fit a dress in the White House, with the explanation that she only did that part of the work in her shop. (In contrast, Mary had enjoyed coming to Lizzy's workrooms.) She could afford to be particular. Her business had prospered, and she was able to open another shop in the Market. Then, in November, in a significant step up the social ladder, she relinquished her membership at Union Bethel and was admitted to the Fifteenth Street Presbyterian, "after a satisfactory examination" and submission of a letter of recommendation.[26]

Instead of a pilgrimage with Mary to Springfield, Lizzy made an important personal pilgrimage in 1866 to Virginia, where, at their invitation, she had a reunion with the surviving members of the Garland family, including her mistress Anne. After the war, these reunions between former slaves and masters became possible, and a number of freedmen returned south. Their motives were complex. Some, like Frederick Douglass, who returned to Maryland to see his dying ex-master Thomas Auld, sought reconciliation and mutual forgiveness. Auld acknowledged that had he been in Douglass's place, he would have run away, and Douglass explained that it was not his master he ran away from, but slavery. Others, like Josiah Henson, Harriet Beecher Stowe's model for Uncle Tom, wanted to make a triumphal appearance in front of his impoverished, defeated ex-mistress. When she asked him what he had brought her from the North, he replied, "Nothing! I came to see if you had anything to give me!" But in each case, these reunions were personal reconstructions, not unlike the national political reconstruction: an effort to fashion a unified identity by reaching back into and coming to terms with one's slavery past, trying to incorporate the trauma of slavery, with its legacy of visible and invisible scars, into one's present life of freedom.[27]

Lizzy had often thought about her Virginia family since coming to Washington. "I recalled the past, and wondered what had become of those who claimed my first duty and my first love." Northern friends thought her naïve to "have a kind thought for those who inflicted a terrible wrong upon you by keeping you in bondage." But even to a slave, the past is dear, she answered. "To surrender it is to surrender the greatest part of my existence—early impressions, friends, and the graves of my father, mother, and my son. These people are associated with everything that memory holds dear, and so long as memory proves faithful, it is but natural that I should wish to see them once more."[28]

Much had changed for Washington's African Americans in the past few years. Four million slaves had been emancipated, and now every man, woman, and child was free. The black codes were gone, and a black person could sit wherever he or she pleased in the streetcars. More and more people were opening businesses, buying homes, and sending their children to "colored" public schools. Howard University was chartered in 1867, where, in addition to the normal school class, advanced students could study theology, medicine, and law. Men could vote in the local elections.[29] But bigotry and discrimination could not be eliminated by the stroke of a pen, and many sorrows would never be forgotten. Nevertheless, for Lizzy and her generation, who had seen so much trouble and come so far, hope was in the air. Visiting the Garlands as a free woman would be another marker of how much had changed.

Anne Garland had moved from St. Louis to western Virginia to live with her third daughter, Nannie, and her husband, Confederate General Gilbert S. Meem. To see them, Lizzy traveled by train across the battle-scarred Virginia countryside to Harpers Ferry, and then on to Winchester; there she took the stage to the little town of New Market in the Shenandoah Valley, which put her near Rude's Hill, the Meem family home. Rude's Hill was where General Stonewall Jackson had had his headquarters; now, as Lizzy said to herself, a former slave and intimate of the Lincolns was an honored guest. She remained in Virginia for five weeks and "was shown every attention," she would recall with satisfaction. Her connection to the Lincolns made her something of a local celebrity.[30]

For Lizzy, the reunion with her white family was a mix of triumph and reconciliation. "Do you always feel kindly toward me?" Anne Garland asked, during one of their many walks together after Lizzy told her how she used to tell Northerners that she could never forget her Southern family. Lizzy answered, "To tell you candidly, Miss Ann, I have but one unkind thought, and that is, that you did not give me the advantages of a good education. What I have learned has been the study of after years." She had spent her life trying to honor her slave father's parting wish that she "learn her book." Anne confessed that Lizzy was right and that she always "regretted" that she was not educated "as a girl." "But you have not suffered much on this score, since you get along in the world better than we who enjoyed every educational advantage in childhood." Like Josiah Henson, Lizzy took satisfaction and pleasure in recording these words of triumph over her former mistress.

After she returned to Washington, letters went back and forth between Lizzy and the Garlands, and there was at least one more visit. Maggie Garland, another of Anne's daughters, whom Lizzy had helped raise, stayed with Lizzy during a visit to Washington, and—to Lizzy's delight—"expressed surprise to find me so comfortably fixed." The unmarried Maggie was teaching to support herself and not much liking it. "None of 'Miss Ann's children were cut out for 'schoolmarms,' were they?" she wrote Lizzy. "I am sure I was only made to ride in my carriage, and play on the piano." Having surpassed the child of her former owners, Lizzy's triumph over her Southern past was as complete as it could be. Yet she took pride in their connections, even Confederate ones: She liked to tell about the visit she received from the wife of the Confederate General James Longstreet, who was Anne Garland's sister-in-law. And she was proud of the Garlands' professions of love for her. She especially wanted Northerners to know that Maggie Garland signed her letters to her " 'Your child, Mag,' an expression of love warmly appreciated by me." After these emotional reunions, Lizzy felt vindicated before her Northern friends, who "doubted that the mistress had any affection for her former slave." It was crucial for Lizzy's self-esteem that this white family valued her, not as an investment but as a human being. She had devoted a large part of her life to them, and they had given her whatever happiness she had known as a slave.[31]

It was this kind of ambivalent yet powerful and important attachment—one that only Southerners could understand—that Lizzy Keckly carried into her relationship with the Kentucky-born Mary Lincoln.

In the meantime, the two years following the assassination were harder on Mary Lincoln than on her friend; indeed, the troubles Mary faced would lead her back to Lizzy. "I am so miserable," Mary wrote a friend from Chicago in July 1865, a month after Lizzy left. "I still remain closeted in my rooms, take an occasional walk, in the park & as usual see no one—What have I, in my misery, to do, with the outside world?" While Tad attended school for the first time, and Robert went to work in a law firm in the city, Mary read and wrote letters, and went over the details of her husband's shooting with the few visitors she did admit. Yet, shut up as she was on "the *far* off shores of Lake Michigan," the outside world preoccupied her immensely.[32]

She was "growing very weary of *boarding*" and wanted to buy the kind of home "suitable to our Station," which she could not do on the $1,500 annual income from her husband's unsettled estate. "A clerk's salary," she called it. She felt cheated by the death of her husband, who had lost his life serving his country, and she wanted nothing less than what she thought she was owed: a congressional appropriation of his salary for four years and a widow's pension. And there were other possible sources of support: for instance, the subscriptions that were being taken up for her in cities in the East—one surprisingly started by the unpredictable Horace Greeley of the *New York Tribune* to raise money for "the late President's grieving widow and fatherless sons." Then there were her wealthy friends in New York and the veterans of her blue room salon, potential benefactors who she felt would come to her aid.[33]

Her options for raising money were limited. She could never have earned enough money by working herself, even if it had occurred to her to try. Despite her upbringing in a political household, as a girl she had been raised no differently from Maggie Garland, "made to ride in my carriage, and play on the piano." She had no desire to live off male relatives, and it evidently never crossed her mind to try to remarry, both tried and true ways for widows to find support. So, with characteristic resourcefulness and verve, she became determined to extricate herself as best she could.

Never one to wait for what she wanted to come to her, she began distributing Lincoln canes, a Henry Clay snuffbox, and even a piece of Lincoln's hair to prospective donors, although, as she told a friend with admirable practicality, she had only a small supply: "Only a bunch, as large as one of our finger's, was saved me—You shall have, as much as I can possibly spare you." To her rich New York friends she wrote what Robert angrily called "Mother's begging letters." Certain select donors could purchase "the handsome home in Chicago the President intended to buy [so that] instead of going North we might this summer come here [to Chicago] at our pleasure." One blue room friend was charged with trying to "settle the fur business," presumably bills for furs.[34]

But to launch a thorough attack, she needed an agent to represent her full time, someone whom she could trust and order about. By summer's end, she had hired Alexander Williamson, her sons' White House tutor, who owed his present clerkship in the Treasury Department to her recommendation. (It was characteristic and mirrored her actions of years past that she should reach down into her White House staff.) She wanted the politically inexperienced tutor to lobby Congress, visit and cajole potential donors, return unused purchases and renegotiate her debts—all without mentioning that he was taking orders from her. "It must not appear, that *I* am aware, of any thing, going on," went one admonition. And another: "*You* can aid me *now* & help yourself a little, at same time. Keep sacredly secret about it, but *work—from this hour*. . . . Take *no one* into *your* confidence."[35]

Williamson, a "gentle Scotsman," was wholly unsuited to this impossible task. Besides, he was working against two "obstacles": there was no precedent for paying the salary for an uncompleted term, and by June the newspapers had accurately reported that Lincoln's estate was a sizable $75,000. (In fact, unknown to Mary, it was nearer to $85,000, an amount owing much to her skill bargaining down prices, asking for items for free, and above all, getting others to pay her bills.) Mary, however, was undeterred, because she knew that she was to get only a third, with Robert and Tad each getting an equal portion. For three years she sent the hapless Williamson letter after letter, urging him on to this or that mission, like a commander in chief improvising strategy, with explicit instructions (and increasing impatience) about whom he should see and what he should say—and not say. Above all, he was to not say a word about her debts. "When you speak to Sen's & mem[bers] mention *no* indebtedness *in any* quarter," she wrote in the fall of 1865. Later, she would tell him that he could say "I have settled the estate, & am left, really impoverished—Say, Chicago residents tell you this. . . . work upon their feelings & have them sign—their names."[36] (This was in fact a year before the estate was settled.)

Indeed, had Mary tried to pay off her debts from Lincoln's estate she would have been impoverished. (By the time it was settled in 1867, the estate was worth just over $110,000, minus the $13,000 that had been used to support the family during the settlement period.) She had always been afraid of poverty and now, with creditors hovering and no husband to earn a living, she became almost crazed with fear. She had every reason to feel frantic. From Washington, Philadelphia, and New York the bills began pouring in for the diamonds, sables, and shawls that had been so necessary to her in the White House, but were like so many albatrosses to her now. When she was Mrs. President, her creditors had hesitated to press her. Now they threatened her with lawsuits and the humiliation of seeing her debts "published" in the newspapers, with itemized lists. Not even Mary knew what she owed, but it was thousands of dollars more than her annual income of $1,500 from the unprobated estate. She *did* know that before she could purchase a home, she had to pay off her debts.

In the White House, Mary had once told Lizzy that her wardrobe would be her fortune. Now was her time to make good that claim. She first tried returning her purchases, and in January 1866 she had her agent Williamson try to get the Washington jewelers Galt & Brothers to take back over nearly twenty items, including a set of eighteen "nut picks & spoons." Nothing was ever used, she claimed. Indeed, "as they have never been out, of their cases—I am sure—he [Mr. Galt] will let me return them for the price he asked," which she tallied at $2,152. The next day brought another idea. Would her friend, Sally Orne, the wife of a Philadelphia carpet maker, take several dress patterns that she has "on hand . . . to be placed in a store for disposal . . . [?] The price of living here is fabulous," she concluded by way of explanation.[37]

This was not Mary's first request to Mrs. Orne, one of the very few people she had let in to see her after her husband's assassination. Three months after leaving the White House, Mary asked if Mrs. Orne knew anyone who might be interested in buying "a *very* elegant lace dress . . . lace flounce for the bottom of the skirt" and "a double lace shawl, very fine . . . [that I wore], on the night of the Inauguration—for two hours . . . [and] next morning, most carefully, the gathers were drawn from the skirt—and it was folded *tenderly* away—the flounce, was not used. I wore the article, reluctantly," she added, "as it was too elaborate for my style & expensive, for my means." They cost "in New York . . . $3,500—of course—if I can get $2,500 it would be a great consideration to me." But Mrs. Orne could not help her sell this shawl and dress, nor "the most magnificent white moiré antique, that Mr. Stewart says, he ever imported . . . & never made up."[38]

As if waging financial campaigns were not enough, Mary was also engaged in an escalating struggle for control over Lincoln's memory. It had begun with the fight with Illinois dignitaries over the placement of her husband's grave and monument, battles that she had won. But the battle with countless biographers—present and future—she was destined to lose.

Her most visible antagonist turned out to be William H. Herndon, her husband's Springfield law partner. Within a month of the assassination, when Mary was beginning to emerge from the shock of her husband's murder, Herndon had already had the idea to collect other people's memories of Abraham Lincoln in order to write and publish something of his own on Lincoln's "inner life." Yet while Mary Lincoln was penning letters about her "idolized Husband," the "immortal Savior & Martyr for Freedom"—partly to stir up sympathy to help her fundraising, and partly because she really needed to see her merely mortal husband in this spiritualized way—Herndon was seeking out the kind of information that would not idealize the man. On June 8, he wrote Josiah Holland, a fellow prospective Lincoln biographer, of his own desire to search for "*the facts & truths* of Lincoln's life—not fictions—not fables—not floating rumors, but *facts—solid facts & well attested truths*."[39]

As wife and widow, Mary Lincoln could not escape her fate as a subordinate figure in the evolving narrative of her husband's life, which itself was wrapped up in an evolving national narrative of Civil War and Reconstruction. But it was one thing to study the politician's life, another to make his wife and children "public property," in Robert's phrase. On this, Robert agreed with his mother. "One of the unpleasant consequences of political success," he would write Herndon, "is that however little it may have to do with that success, [the politician's] whole private life is exposed to the public gaze—that is part of the price he pays. But I see no reason why his wife and children should be included—especially while they are alive—I think no sensible man would live in a glass house and I think he ought not be compelled to do so against his will."[40]

By the end of 1865, the loss of privacy was a recurring motif in Mary's letters. Finding herself already publicly exposed in print, her living situation—a hotel—came to symbolize her further lack of privacy from prying eyes. By that time, Congress had decided to give her only one year of Lincoln's salary with no hope of receiving the remaining three years or any other form of assistance. She received $25,000, minus tax and salary for the six weeks of the second term he had served. Embittered by the decision, she again wrote to Sally Orne: "We, as an afflicted family, *well knew*, we had lost our *all*—the *nation*, has sealed the decree, by their vote, that there, is to be, no privacy, for us, in the future, our grief & we, ourselves—can have, no retirement."[41]

Nor did the next year bring relief. The estate remained unsettled, her debts unpaid. Worse, she had incurred more debts. Depressed by the prospect of having to stay in a hotel, sharing rooms with thirteen-year-old Tad (Robert had moved to his own hotel apartment), in June she impulsively bought a new house on West Washington Street on the expectation of financial support from Simon Cameron, Lincoln's corrupt first Secretary of War, who was circulating a letter among his wealthy friends to raise "twenty-thousand dollars, soon" for "these orphans and this widowed Lady [who] have claims upon every patriotic man in the land." But these donations never materialized, and she wound up turning over to the builder more than three-quarters of the presidential salary payment she had from Congress. Furnishings and maintenance came out of borrowed money.[42]

In the midst of this crisis, things came to a head with Herndon, who had successfully collected letters, interviews, and statements, and by January 1866 had delivered three lectures on Lincoln. Hoping to interview Mary, he wrote Robert with a request, but there was one sentence in Herndon's note that worried both mother and son: "I wish to do her justice fully—so that the world will understand things better. You understand me," he said in his melodramatic fashion. Although wary, Mary responded with a flattering, friendly letter agreeing to an interview. But when they met in Springfield in early September 1866—during the time of Lizzy's happy reunion with the Garlands at

Rude's Hill—Mary tried to convince Herndon to leave her out of any biography altogether. "It was not unusual to mention the fact, the history of the wife, in the biography of her husband, further than to say that the two were married at such and such a place," she said.[43]

Herndon, however, did not take the hint. Two months later he delivered his fourth, and most famous, lecture: the tragic "true history" of Lincoln's early love for Ann Rutledge, who died during the couple's engagement, which took place four years before he met Mary Todd. After Ann died, Herndon told his audience, Lincoln "never addressed another woman" with love and affection. This fact, he concluded, dissolved Mary Lincoln's culpability in the well-known difficulties of the marriage. She was not to blame, because Lincoln never loved her.[44]

Robert Lincoln was disgusted. "Mr. William H. Herndon is making an ass of himself," he said when he heard about Herndon's lecture. Mary did not hear of it until a few months later, when she could read the lecture, like everyone else, in broadside form. She was horrified, outraged, and most of all humiliated; but what could she do? In March, she wrote David Davis a series of letters—the only venue open to her—rebutting Herndon's claims: "*Ann Rutledge*, is a myth—for in all his confidential communications, such a romantic name, was never breathed, and concealment could have been no object." As for "the false W.H.," "a hopeless inebriate . . . drudge" with a "vivid imagination . . . I assure you, it will not be *well with him*—if he makes the *least* disagreeable or false allusion in the future. *He* will be closely watched." Two days later, bolstered by a scathing criticism of Herndon in the *Chicago Tribune* that had been written by her former Springfield pastor, she wrote again to Davis: "W H may consider himself a ruined man, in attempting to disgrace others, the vials of wrath, will be poured upon his own head . . . if W.H—utters another word—and is not silent with his infamous falsehoods in the future, *his* life is not worth, living for—I *have* friends. . . . 'Revenge is sweet, especially to womankind but there are some of mankind left, who will wreak it upon him—He is a dirty dog.'"[45]

Herndon's Ann Rutledge lecture came as a terrible blow to the already shattered widow. "It was always, music in my ears, both before & after our marriage," she wrote Mrs. Welles sadly, "when my husband told me, that I was the only one, he had ever thought of, or cared for. It will solace me to my grave." Despondent, Mary wished she were already there. None of her Eastern friends were proving to be trustworthy. Mrs. Cuthbert, her housekeeper, and Mr. Stackpole, the steward she had dismissed, were spreading lies about her. Her blue room friends were "summer friends" after all, and Williamson was a dismal failure, unable to achieve any success in raising funds. Even kind friends like Gideon and Mary Jane Welles had betrayed her by staying faithful to the new administration. "*Her* heart is all right," she said of Mrs. Welles, "yet the desire of some persons to be in office, will cause them to bend the knee—even to treason."[46]

Her forty-eighth birthday, December 13, 1866, had been terribly depressing; she had spent the day thinking about how much she missed her husband—"*if possible*, more than ever and with the exception of my Sons, I felt alone and uncared for in the world." Like the motherless child she basically was, she lamented, "No place is home to me *now*." Indeed, by March 1867, the month of her furious letters to Davis, it had become obvious that she could no longer afford her home but would have to "sell out and secure cheap rooms." She had been there less than a year.[47]

It was in the midst of this ongoing emotional and financial turmoil, reaching a humiliating climax in March, that Mary summoned Elizabeth Keckly: "Now, Lizzie, I want to ask a favor of you. It is imperative that I should do something for my relief, and I want you to meet me in New York, between 30th of August and the 5th of September next, to assist me in disposing of a portion of my wardrobe."[48]

They may have seen each other only once since after the assassination, when Lizzy had visited Chicago about Christmas 1865. (At a charity fair, she had seen a chintz robe she had made for Mrs. Davis before the war exhibited on a wax figure of Jefferson Davis, intended to show what he had been wearing when he was captured.) But nothing could have been more natural in this crisis than that Mary should turn to the Southern woman who had "mothered" her after the assassination, when she had lost her inner and outer bearings, all that essentially had meant "home." She had never forgotten how Lizzy had taken care of her; since then, no one really listened to her anymore, no one did what she wanted. Indeed, looking back, she might have remembered that it was Lizzy who had been there from the very first day she moved into the White House. And it was Lizzy who, over the years, had proven to be her most constant friend and ally.

But there were other reasons to turn to Elizabeth Keckly. Nothing had come of asking Sally Orne to find buyers for her dresses; it is likely that the genteel Mrs. Orne ignored her requests, and so Mary stopped asking. To be sure, Mary would not have been the first needy widow to auction off her belongings. As she told Lizzy, "The Empress of France frequently disposes of her cast-off wardrobe, and publicly, too," without remarks about its propriety. She needed to be doing *something* for herself, and what else could she do? To Williamson she wrote, "You, men have the advantage of us women, in being able to go out, in the world and earning a living." Committed to a hyperfeminized self-image, which she defended with repeated assertions of her "terror of *strong* minded Ladies," Mary could not have carried off her plan to approach brokers to sell her "wardrobe" herself.[49] In making the entrepreneurial African American Elizabeth Keckly her partner, Mary was choosing her one female friend who could range beyond the genteel limitations that society imposed on white women like herself.

Thrifty herself, Lizzy had always felt that in buying expensive dresses beyond her means Mary was "borrowing trouble from the future," but when she read Mary's letter, she decided to help. She knew Mary needed the money, knew she owned "many valuable dresses" she would never wear again, and believed that New York "was the best place to transact a delicate business of the kind." Perhaps Mary's carefully chosen jewels, satins, dresses, and shawls would find appreciative buyers among wealthy, fashion-conscious New Yorkers. Both she and Mary knew New York and felt comfortable there. Finally, Lizzy had another consideration. Mary was the wife of "the man who had done so much for my race," and for this reason, she could not refuse to help her, even though it meant temporarily closing up her business.[50]

The two agreed to meet in mid-September, a year after Mary's interview with Herndon. (Waiting until the fall gave Mary, who was suffering from severe headaches, inflamed eyes, and chills, a chance to go to a spa in Wisconsin during the summer, while Lizzy could finish whatever sewing she had to do.) Lizzy assumed that she would hear from Mrs. Lincoln in September, but before confirming their plans, the impulsive Mary had boarded a train from Chicago and sent Lizzy a note that she would arrive four days later on September 17, expecting to find her friend already there. She also expected Lizzy to reserve rooms at the St. Denis Hotel under the name Mrs. Clarke, the name she had used during the war to travel incognito.

Arriving in New York alone, Mary proceeded to the St. Denis Hotel, which stood on the corner of Eleventh Street and Broadway, opposite the elegant Grace Episcopal Church. Not finding her friend, Mary became frantic. "I am frightened to death, being here alone," she dashed off a desperate letter to Lizzy the following morning. "Come, I pray you, by *next* train . . . *Come, come, come.*"[51]

Back in Washington, Lizzy had received Mary's original instructions, but had stalled. She was leery of a plan that had taken on the aura of an espionage mission, with Mary's disguise and a second-class hotel. She also knew it would be impossible for her as a "colored woman" to reserve rooms for a "Mrs. Clarke," whom the St. Denis would not know. Unable to reach Mary by letter, as she was already en route, and unwilling to risk a telegram, Lizzy had simply waited in Washington, hoping that Mary would change her mind—something the indecisive woman often did. When no letter came by the morning after they were supposed to have met, she sent Mary a telegram that she was on her way and showed up at the St. Denis on the evening of September 18, only hours after Mary had written her urgent note.

The two spent an uncomfortable night sharing a pair of cramped, dingy three-cornered rooms on the servants' attic floor, the only rooms the hotel would offer them together after Lizzy's arrival. The uniformed, "highly perfumed" modern hotel clerk had coldly refused to give the mulatto Lizzy a room on the same floor as the white "Mrs. Clarke," who had demanded that her "friend" be shown "a good room" near her own. "We have no room for her on your floor," the clerk told "Mrs. Clarke" (whom he had already recognized as Mrs. Lincoln); he had a room on the fifth floor. "Well, if she goes to the fifth floor, I shall go too, sir," "Mrs. Clarke" responded.[52] It was perfectly acceptable for a white woman to travel with a nonwhite woman as her servant, but it was intolerable that the two should travel together as equals.

The "miserable" hotel also refused to serve Lizzy dinner in the main dining room. "Are you not Mrs. Clarke's servant?" the steward asked when she presented herself for dinner, while Mary rested upstairs. "I am with Mrs. Clarke," Lizzy said, emphasizing the distinction. It did not matter. "Servants are not allowed to eat in the large dining-room," said the steward, and led her to the servants' hall. "Hungry and humiliated," Lizzy followed, only to discover that the hall was locked for the night. Too proud to stand there any longer, she went back upstairs to Mary's room. When Mary saw Lizzy, who was now close to tears, and heard what had happened, she proposed going out to find a place to eat. "Do you suppose I am going to have you starve, when we can find something to eat on every corner?" But Lizzy refused, counseling caution; "Mrs. Clarke" could not risk raising gossip by going out of the hotel alone at night unescorted, she said.[53]

Not until the next morning, after they had gone out to breakfast, walked up Broadway, and sat down on a bench in Union Square Park, did Mary—from behind the folds of her black veil—reveal to Lizzy all that she had done before her friend arrived. While Lizzy was on the train from Washington,

Mary had paid a visit to W. H. Brady & Co., at 609 Broadway, a diamond broker, whose name she had picked out of the *Herald* over breakfast that morning. At first, the gentlemen of the firm were ready to hurry her out the door, as the prices she asked for her jewelry were outrageous; but they grew suspicious that "Mrs. Clarke" was Mary Lincoln from the name inside one of her rings, and they changed their minds. They were to call at the hotel that very morning.

When the women returned to their hotel, they found Samuel Keyes, William Brady's partner. Mr. Keyes "was much elated to find his surmise was correct," that the mysterious lady *was* Mrs. Lincoln. Before long, he professed to being "an earnest Republican . . . [and] much affected with her story" and outraged at the ingratitude of his Party; moreover, he was delighted by the two trunk loads of dresses, shawls, furs, and jewels that she had lugged from Chicago, ready to sell. Better still, he listened to Mary's complaints seriously, and after hearing "of the treatment she had received at the St. Denis," advised her to move to a better hotel. This was no sooner said than done, and by the afternoon, the two women were settled in the Union Place Hotel.[54]

Before Mary left New York two weeks later, the two women changed address three times and Mary changed her name to "Mrs. Morris," each switch an effort to avoid discovery. At the new hotel, Mary insisted on her disguise, despite Lizzy's suggestion, with Mr. Keyes's support, that she reveal her identity to ensure "the proper respect." However, Mary's shame and purported wish for anonymity kept running afoul of her lifelong need for attention and her demands for deferential treatment. On the sides of her trunks, the words "Mrs. Lincoln, Springfield, Il" remained visible, despite someone's efforts to rub them out. It was like dragging a billboard with her name from place to place.

And yet, posting a billboard conformed to the brokers' idea of the business. Brady and Keyes thought the key to success was in exploiting Mary's fame, not concealing it, and during frequent visits to Mrs. Lincoln, they laid out a plan of action. "Place your affairs in our hands," they assured her, "and we will raise you at least $100,000 in a few weeks. The people will not permit the widow of Abraham Lincoln to suffer." What she needed to do, they advised her, was write "certain letters" about her circumstances that they could take around to "prominent politicians" who had received patronage positions from her husband. These men, Brady argued, "would make heavy advances rather than have it published to the world that Mrs. Lincoln's poverty compelled her to sell her wardrobe." Indeed, as part of the scheme, Mr. Brady would threaten to publish the letters in newspapers if support was not forth-coming.[55]

After one unpleasant carriage ride through Central Park, where they barely escaped an accident, Mary sat down in her hotel and wrote at least five letters addressed to Mr. Brady and dated over the month from Chicago, in order to distance herself from what was basically a scheme of blackmail. "*Urgent necessity,*" she wrote in one letter, was her sole reason for contacting the brokers and sending her "property" to sell. Some of the letters were specifically aimed at Republican officeholders. In one, she referred the brokers to her old blue room friend, the "Hon. Abram Wakeman," who "was largely indebted to me for obtaining the lucrative office" in the Custom House and "would scarcely hesitate to return, in a small manner, the many favors my husband and myself always showered upon him." In another, she expressed fear that hostile "newsmen" might "seize upon the painful circumstances of your having these articles placed in your hands to injure the Republican party politically" in this important off-year election. "Not for the world would I do anything to injure the cause," she protested. But "the necessities of life are upon me, urgent and imperative."[56]

Lizzy was posted at Mary's elbow while she wrote, all the while advising that she use "the mildest language possible." Mary only shrugged off her counsel. As Lizzy realized, Mary had had to borrow $600 from Brady and Keyes for her New York expenses, and probably felt she had nothing to lose. "Never mind, Lizzie, anything to raise the wind. One might as well be killed for a sheep as a lamb," she said, using one of her favorite expressions.[57]

After finishing the letters, the two women decided to look for other ways to dispose of the wardrobe; they figured that the brokers would have success with the letters without having to sell Mary's clothes. Lizzy "hunted up" some secondhand dealers and arranged for them to call on "Mrs. Clarke" at their hotel, but they turned out to be "hard people to drive a bargain with." Next, the women took "a bundle of dresses and shawls" to several stores on Seventh Avenue. Mary "met the dealers squarely," Lizzy recalled with admiration, but "all her tact and shrewdness failed to accomplish much."[58]

Nor did the brokers "accomplish much," and within days admitted failure. The trip was turning into a disaster, ending up costing them money Mary did not have; moreover, she was growing increasingly anxious to return to Chicago. According to Lizzy, Mary was at a point when she would agree to anything. "Money she must have," and she was willing "to play a bolder game." Thus, she gave permission to Mr. Brady to stage a public exhibition for the sale of her wardrobe and to publish her letters in the Democratic *World*, a paper that was always pleased to stir up trouble for Republicans. After making this fateful decision, Mary packed up and left for Chicago, leaving Lizzy behind to manage the rest of the affair and to keep her informed of developments.[59]

Mary Lincoln was on the train to Chicago when her clothing went up in Brady & Co.'s showrooms and the *World* published five plaintive letters from Mrs. Lincoln to Mr. Brady, with an additional story about her "business concerns," a story quickly reprinted in other newspapers. During the ride west, she had the peculiar experience of overhearing two men discussing her affairs while one of them read the *World*. Writing to Lizzy, Mary described the scene, which ended with "my reading man" defending her against the criticism of the other gentleman, a "bluffy individual, doubtless a Republican who had pocketed his many thousands." Later, more bizarrely, she encountered Charles Sumner in the dining car. His sad look made her self-consciously aware of what was happening at "609 Broadway," and she escaped to her car; but he soon reappeared, with gentle looks, to bring her a cup of tea. "When he left me," Mary told Lizzy, "*woman-like* I tossed the cup of tea out of the window, and tucked my head down and shed *bitter tears*." "How much I miss you, tongue cannot tell," Mary concluded this letter, dated October 6. Apparently, the two had had some kind of disagreement before Mary left, for which she wished to apologize. "Forget my fright and nervousness of the evening before. Of course you were as innocent as a child in all you did. I consider you my best living friend, and I am struggling to be enabled some day to repay you."[60] She was eager to smooth things over with the one person she had left in her corner.

This letter to Lizzy was the first of two dozen Mary wrote her friend from Chicago over the next five months, sometimes as frequently as three times a week. In fact, she wrote the next letter "with a broken heart" only hours later. On the evening of her arrival, she told Lizzy, Robert "came up like a maniac, and almost threatening his life, looking like death, because the letters of the *World* were published in yesterday's [Chicago] paper."[61]

This would be only her first shock in the unfolding disaster. Back in New York, the curious came to 609 Broadway to peer at the shawls hanging over the backs of chairs and the dresses piled on a long table, labeled with prices, but no one bought. Some viewers complained about the prices; others noted that the dresses were torn, stained, and too low-cut for wearing. Almost instantly, newspapers everywhere were weighing in on what came to be known as "Mrs. Lincoln's Old Clothes Scandal." "Will not somebody, for very shame sake, go and take away those drygoods the widow of the late Lamented persists in exposing for sale in a Broadway shop window?" one Kentucky paper asked, calling the broker a "Showman Barnum." From Massachusetts came this comment: "That dreadful woman . . . in the open market with her useless finery . . . persists in forcing her repugnant individuality before the world." She was called an "intensely vulgar woman," "unprincipled and avaricious," "a woman of incredible impulses," and worse.[62]

Seated in her rented rooms in the private home into which she and Tad had recently moved (Robert was still on his own at a hotel), Mary read the attacks and relieved her feelings by filling page after impassioned page writing to her "dear Lizzie." Angrily, she commented on what strangers were writing about her. "There is no doubt Mrs. L—*is* deranged," she paraphrased one writer's declaration, "has been for years past, and will end her life in a lunatic asylum. They would doubtless like me to begin it *now*." To modern ears, the criticism smack of misogynistic outrage against a woman who so brazenly violated feminine decorum. As one editor put it, she was "wanting in all the true instincts and delicacy which belong to worthy women." "So much for womanly gentleness and obedience" made the point even more succinctly.[63] But Mary was neither philosophically equipped nor temperamentally inclined to dismiss the attacks as the product of patriarchal bias. And with each verbal assault, she saw her chances of raising even the smallest amount of money dwindling.

In a matter of days, another line of attack appeared. As the November elections approached, Democrats seized on the letters to charge Republicans with having bought favors from the Lincoln White House. In response, Republican newspapers escalated their assaults in their haste to disown the author of the letters. "It appears as if the fiends had let loose, for the Republican papers are tearing me to pieces," she wrote Lizzy on October 9. "If I had committed murder in every city in this *blessed Union*, I could not be more traduced." Republican politico Thurlow Weed used his *Commercial Advertiser* to link Mary's current scandalous behavior to her corruption in the White House, based on his source, old Edward McManus, the doorkeeper Mary had fired before the second inauguration. Other papers seized on the tales. Now everyone could read about the gardener Watt's padded accounts, Napoleon's costly dinner, Lincoln's bartered speech, and how, on leaving the White House, Mary had packed up "all the spoons, gold, forks, etc. to take with her." When she saw the turn of events, Mary assessed the situation accurately.

"They are making a political business of *my clothes*, and not for *my* benefit either," she wrote Lizzy. Thereafter, she blamed "Weed & Co." (which included William Seward and Henry Raymond, editor of the *New York Times*) for wrecking her chances for raising funds.[64]

In New York, Lizzy did what she could to stem the bloodletting. At Mary's suggestion, she gave interviews to the sympathetic New York *Herald*, although the writer of the "Old Clothes" accounts, which ran over several weeks, seems to have been undecided on how to deal with Mrs. Keckly. At first, in an effort to normalize the relationship between the two women in racial terms the *Herald*'s readers could understand, the reporter described the "faithful negro servant Lizzie, the only one who left the luxuries of the White House to follow the fortunes of the President's widow." Yet a later article presented a different view: "When Mrs. Lincoln first conceived of the idea [of the sale] . . . she first consulted her former *modiste*, Mrs. Elizabeth Keckly, upon whose judgment and discretion she had great reliance." By that time, Lizzy was used to shuttling between the two identities—the "faithful Negro servant Lizzie" and Mary's "former *modiste*, Mrs. Elizabeth Keckly"—that explained her existence in white people's minds. However, she had ideas—and a voice—of her own, and she sent a lengthy "correct statement" of the facts to the editors of the New York *Daily News*, which was published in mid-October, at the time Mary was feeling most beleaguered.[65]

Above all, Lizzy used her network of prominent black friends to help Mary. She wrote letters to her friends proposing collections for Mrs. Lincoln be taken up in black churches, an idea that was readily accepted. It was the "colored people's" special "obligation," Frederick Douglass wrote in response to one of her letters, "to aid the widow of the man who broke the fetters of our enslaved people." Lizzy had come to know men like Douglass and Henry Highland Garnet when she organized her contraband association; since the year of Lincoln's death, when she joined the Fifteenth Street Presbyterian Church, where Garnet was pastor, her connections to influential blacks had only strengthened. Douglass and Garnet were especially sincere in their desire to help. When Brady and Keyes proposed sending out circulars advertising Mrs. Lincoln's grave need, Garnet went with Lizzy to see Horace Greeley at his *Tribune* office, but Greeley dismissed the scheme as being in the wrong hands and advised them to put other men in charge.[66]

Meanwhile, at Lizzy's request, Garnet and Douglass agreed to give lectures to raise money, although Douglass, having ample experience with the dangers of putting a black face to any public cause, was dubious as to the effects of featuring himself and Garnet in a lecture series for Mrs. Lincoln: "You should not place me at the head nor at the foot of the list, but sandwich me between, for thus out of the way, it would not give *color* to the idea." Mary Lincoln more than agreed and squelched the idea. "I want neither Douglass nor Garnet to lecture in my behalf," she wrote Lizzy in November. But one week later, when it became public knowledge that Lincoln's estate was suddenly about to be settled and the "papers *raving* over the large income which we are *said* to have," Mary was more eager for these eminent black men's help. "Please see H[enry] Garnet," she wrote; "do urge F.D. to add his name to the circular." She suspected Robert of pushing through the settlement to thwart her New York schemes, after two years of what she regarded as Davis's dawdling, the kind of thought she could share with no one but Lizzy. "R is very spiteful at present, and I think hurries up the division to *cross* my purposes." She now saw "that most of the good feeling regarding my straitened circumstances proceeds from the colored people; in whose cause my noble husband was so largely interested. Whether we are successful or not, Mr. F. Douglass and Mr. Garnet will always have my most grateful thanks. They are very noble men." Learning that Douglass was to lecture in Chicago, she asked Lizzy to tell him to visit her and even expressed her regrets that "if I had been able to retain a house, I should have offered him apartments when he came." However, Mary's initial refusal of aid from their leaders dampened the enthusiasm of potential black supporters and, in the end, Lizzy said, they did nothing.[67]

Lizzy remained the entire fall and winter in New York, where she lived in the houses of various friends and supported herself by sewing. But by November, she was "wretchedly low-spirited" and desperate for money, which Mary could only promise to give her, but not "now." Her growing protests that she needed to go home were met with resistance. "Can you not, dear Lizzie, be employed in sewing for some of your lady friends in New York until December 1st?" Mary implored. After Christmas, Mary offered her the best compensation she could: "Had you not better go with me and share my fortunes, for a year or more?"[68]

It was what Mary really wanted. Feeling frightened, isolated, and assailed on all sides—with even her son working against her—she could not face what was happening without Lizzy Keckly. She was realizing that she was nothing in the eyes of the world of men in which she had thought she could move, in which she had thought she *had* moved. But it was not her inherent importance that had previously protected her. "As *influence* has passed away from me with my husband, my slightest act is misinterpreted," she complained accurately to Lizzy. She resented "the people of this ungrateful country . . . [who] will neither do anything themselves, nor allow me to improve my own condition."[69]

Truly, Lizzy was her "best living friend," as she said; only Lizzy had remained devoted to her cause with nothing but promises to sustain her. In the meantime, her best nonliving friend was her beloved husband, who she believed was "ever retaining" his care of his wife from beyond. "I feel assured his watchful, loving eyes are always watching over us, and he is fully aware of the wrong and injustice" we suffer.[70] Thus, between the two guardians—one maternal, the other paternal—she felt some measure of protection.

But with Lincoln dead, it was the vitally alive Lizzy from whom Mary sought guidance, and she was relying heavily on Lizzy's judgment (as Lizzy had truthfully told the *Herald* reporter). "Write me, my dear friend, your candid opinion about everything," Mary wrote; it was the kind of straightforward plea she could make to no one else. Indeed, only with Lizzy was Mary honest and direct. In contrast, she had been weaving falsehoods for virtually everyone else—for instance, lying to one of her better Washington female friends about the Brady letters: "I was not more astonished than *you* must have been to see my letters, in print."[71]

Early in January, however, Lizzy wrote Mary a letter that thoroughly alarmed her. In a last-ditch effort to wring some money from her clothes, which Mary had begun asking them to return, Brady and Keyes had proposed sending them in a traveling exhibition to begin in Providence, not to sell the wardrobe, but to charge admission to see it, and without consulting Mary, Lizzy had agreed. This was the last straw with Mary for Brady and Keyes. "Why did you not urge them not to take my goods to Providence?" she demanded of Lizzy. "For heaven's sake see K & B when you receive this, and have them immediately returned to me, *with their bill.*"[72]

This was not the only thing Lizzy had done on her own that had ended up vexing Mary. She had also donated her own Lincoln relics—including Mary's bonnet and bloody cloak and Lincoln's glove—to Wilberforce University. No doubt borrowing some of the brokers' methods, Lizzy had decided that an exhibit of the clothes could be used to help rebuild a college building that had burned down the day of Lincoln's assassination; she had sent her idea to Bishop Daniel H. Payne, who had witnessed her pension statement and who now headed Wilberforce. Mary was wild at the thought "that my clothes were to be paraded in Europe—those I gave you—. . . . R[obert] would go *raving distracted* if such a thing was done. . . . How little did I suppose you would do *such a thing*; you cannot imagine how much my overwhelming sorrows would be increased. [Please write the bishop] that it *must* not be done." [73]

By that time, Mary sensed that Lizzy was backing off. Perhaps she was doing something else. Mary had been waiting for weeks for Lizzy to send her a black dress she had promised to make; but that was not all. Lizzy would close up Mary's business with Brady & Co. ("A precious set, truly" was Mary's comment on the pair) and in March would hand them Mary's check for $824, the amount they had received for selling a diamond ring and one or two other items, which they now appropriated "for their expenses." And she would pack up Mary's unsold "goods" and ship them promptly to Chicago. But there had been periods of unwarranted silence—or so Mary thought—when Lizzy failed to write as often as she promised. "Why are you so silent?" Mary wanted to know. At other times, Lizzy had not said what was in her "*heart*. . . . *Why* do you not candidly express yourself to me?"[74]

To be sure, Lizzy could scarcely have kept up with Mary's repeated demands for letters, even if she were not preoccupied with running to 609 Broadway, writing letters to her famous friends seeking help, and trying to earn money sewing on the side. Her Washington business had been virtually shut down and her own need for money by the end of the year was great. Mary had promised her a commission on donations she helped raise, but she "raised nothing and received nothing." She may have expected Mary to relieve her from out of the settlement money, but nothing was ever said about that on either side. What Mary did send her were complaints from "poor me" and more promises for the future.[75]

Lizzy's long-ago nemesis, the schoolmistress Anna Burwell, had once derided the young girls who she said lived on their "expectations" of future income, whether from inheritance or marriage. A woman had to do for herself was Anna Burwell's creed. Mary's insistence on extricating herself from her debts in her own way presented a similarly determined view, however different in aims and means. As a slave, Lizzy had long ago learned what to hope for her "expectations": "As usual with all my expectations, I was disappointed," she had written her mother from Hillsborough. Even if Lizzy's life since slavery had given her more reasons for hope, they never erased her earliest impressions. She could be affectionate and loving, but she kept her distance and she knew to depend on herself.

As it would soon come out, during the fall and winter, while Mary had been opening her heart to Lizzy in her numerous letters, Elizabeth Keckly had been writing a memoir. With fading expectations of ever earning a cent from their joint venture and growing worries about her reputation for the part she had played in the very public "Old Clothes" business, she had determined to do something for herself. (One imagines it was what her literate and proud slave parents, particularly her father, would have wanted her to do.) Her book would begin with her birth and show her remarkable rise from slavery, but mostly, it would tell about her years in the Lincoln White House and end with a detailed account of the past few months. In this last section, she would reveal "the secret history" of Mrs. Lincoln's unsuccessful escapade—that is, the true history of the "Old Clothes Scandal" that only she could tell about the former First Lady's thoughts and actions. In the midst of the uproar, Mary had written her: "If you and I are honest in our motives and intentions, it is no reason *all* the world is so." She now would reveal their "honest . . . motives and intentions." Lizzy presented her memoir as a defense of Mary Lincoln, an attempt "to place Mrs. Lincoln in a better light before the world," by showing the innocent "motives that actuated us."[76]

And that "us" was key. Proud of her reputation for dignity and integrity, Lizzy in fact wanted her book to redeem her own good name as its *primary* motive: "My own character, as well as the character of Mrs. Lincoln, is at stake, since I have been intimately associated with that lady in the most eventful periods of her life. . . . To defend myself I must defend the lady I have served."[77] It was this claim that was particularly bold and that hinted at the more complex, even aggressive motives underlying her writing.

As role models for writing, Lizzy could point to the many former slaves who had written their own stories. In Washington, she was bound to have met Harriet Jacobs, a former slave from North Carolina, whose autobiography of her enslavement and escape had appeared at the beginning of the war. Indeed, her friend Frederick Douglass, a man she admired immensely, had published two popular versions of his autobiography (in 1845 and in 1855; a third would appear in 1893). The Civil War memoir had also already become a widely read genre. And everywhere one looked, people who knew Lincoln were publishing what they knew about his childhood, his New Salem and Springfield years, and his presidency.

Moreover, to make money by authoring a book was a symbolic act for former slaves, who by design had been kept illiterate, invisible, and identified as a possession ("Garland's Lizzy"). Indeed, slavery had doomed its black victims to physical labor; the mental labor of writing a book was for free people only.

For Elizabeth Keckly, who was self-conscious about her lack of education, writing was a daring assertion of self. She had apologized so much to Frederick Douglass about her handwriting that he advised her, "With practice you will not only write legibly but elegantly; so no more apologies for *bad* writing."[78] (This extraordinary self-taught man, who was one of the most brilliant rhetoricians of his day, had earned his slightly condescending tone.)

In New York, Lizzy had been working with a white collaborator and friend of Douglass, a red-haired Scotsman named James Redpath, who would edit her manuscript and get it published. (This was the pattern for publication for other black autobiographers.) A former antislavery journalist and war correspondent for the *Tribune*, Redpath was also an energetic propagandist and promoter, and he must have seen the possibilities for sales in publishing this insider's view of the White House. As an antislavery activist, he also would have appreciated the freedwoman's point of view on the era's political and social revolutions.[79]

At some point during the fall, Lizzy moved to a boardinghouse on Broome Street that was run by Mrs. Bell, a cousin of William Slade, and that was popular with black politicians and activists when they came to New York. Handling Mary's and other business during the day, she apparently wrote in her room at night. In between, in the evenings, she met with Redpath in Mrs. Bell's public parlor to go over the previous night's work. Writing steadily, Lizzy finished the manuscript in March, not two weeks after paying off Brady and Keyes and one year after receiving Mary's initial letter asking her to meet her in New York. Her New York publisher was Carleton & Company, a respectable and successful firm that was known for, among other things, its speed in producing books. By April 1, prepublication advertisements were touting a new book, *Behind the Scenes, or, Thirty Years a Slave, and Four Years in the White House*, which it said was "crowded with incidents of a most romantic as well as tragic interest . . . powerfully and truthfully written." This was typical language for the sentimental literature of the day. Almost immediately, however, Thurlow Weed's *Commercial Advertiser*, scenting Mary Lincoln blood once again, made a more hair-raising pitch. "A Literary Thunderbolt!" it proclaimed, whose author, Mrs. Lincoln's black *modiste*, "has much to say of an interesting, not to say startling nature, in regard to men and things in the White House, Washington, and New York." Soon, Carleton & Co. unveiled a new advertising campaign, featuring *Behind the Scenes—The Great Sensational Disclosure by Mrs. Keckley*.[80] Thus Lizzy's serious, sentimental book became spectacle.

Lizzy's intentions, like the spelling of her name, would thereafter be lost in history. At the age of fifty, she had violated Victorian codes not only of friendship and privacy, but of race, gender, and class. Not surprisingly, the newspapers that attacked Mary Lincoln in the fall, in the spring now leapt to her defense. "Has the American public no word of protest against the assumption that its literary taste is of so low grade as to tolerate the back-stairs gossip of negro servant girls?" asked one New York reviewer. "What family of eminence that employs a negro is safe from such desecration?" an alarmed Washington, D.C., reviewer wanted to know. "Where will it end? What family that has a servant may not, in fact, have its peace and happiness destroyed by such treacherous creatures as the Keckley woman?" Another from Massachusetts argued that the book demonstrated the dangerous consequences of educating the black and Irish working classes—especially women. One can tolerate having a cook who "insists on reading the morning paper while she is getting breakfast" or who borrows "all your pet books" from your library. "All these can be patiently endured in consideration of the many benefits that are supposed to accrue to Bridget and Dinah on account of a smattering of knowledge. But when Bridget and Dinah takes to writing books instead, and select for themes the conversations and events that occur in the privacy of the family circle, we respectfully submit that it is carrying the thing a little too far." This response came from Northern reviewers who felt uncomfortable being confronted with a black seamstress who was obviously more than a "faithful negro servant," who was in fact a free black woman, with autonomy and authority, who moved between a free white and a *free* black middle class. The social threat represented by this black woman's agency also provoked other readers, and someone produced an ugly and viciously racist parody called *Behind the Seams; by a Nigger Woman who took work in from Mrs. Lincoln and Mrs. Davis* and signed with an "X," the mark of "Betsey Kickley (nigger)," denoting its supposed author's illiteracy.[81] Genteel reviewers would not have been so crude, but they shared the parodist's basic sentiments.

Stunned by the reaction, Lizzy wrote a letter in her defense, which her publisher forwarded to the *New York Citizen*, whose editor was one of Carleton & Co.'s best-selling authors. In it, she challenged anyone to read her book alongside "a few choice extracts . . . clipped from the respectable and leading newspapers in the country" that had joined in the "bitter crusade against" Lincoln's widow, and then decide who had in fact scandalized Mrs. Lincoln's name. Was it because "my skin is dark and that I was once a slave" that I am being "denounced?" she asked. "As I was born to servitude, it was not fault of mine that I was a slave; and, as I honestly purchased my freedom, may I not be permitted to express, now and then, an opinion becoming a free woman?"[82]

By June, the sensational headlines about the book had already disappeared. Lizzy gave a reading in Boston, arranged by Redpath, but in the end, the book sold few copies and had little effect on public opinion. Lizzy believed that Robert had managed to suppress its publication; she may have discerned in the various attacks against her Mary's implicit restoration to the special status of white womanhood. Yet, as Lizzy had claimed, nothing she wrote about Mrs. Lincoln was nearly as critical as the newspaper abuse she had endured for months, and much of it was admiring and kind.

Mary read *Behind the Scenes* a few weeks after its publication. She felt thoroughly betrayed by her friend, who had not only published overheard and private conversations, but in an appendix had actually printed twenty-four letters that she had sent to her during the winter and fall. Lizzy's explanation—that she herself had been betrayed by Redpath, who persuaded her to "lend" him the letters, promising not to publish or print anything personal from them—probably never reached Mary. Even so, no explanation would have done any good. Lizzy would also say that Mary knew that she was writing a book, but without evidence to support or refute this statement, we cannot know if this is true or false. In short order, Mary expelled Lizzy from her life, and the closest she ever came in her letters to mentioning her name again was in May, when she dismissed her as "the *colored* historian." In Mary's mind, Lizzy had fallen into the ranks of traitors such as Herndon, who sought to parlay their connections to the famous and the elite into egregious acts of self-aggrandizement. Her color made her immaterial.[83]

In the fall of 1868, one year after her old clothes sale, Mary set sail for Europe with Tad, hoping to recover her health, which had of late gotten worse, and seeking some respite "in a distant land" from her recent sorrows and humiliations at home. Sadly, she would find neither. Nevertheless, in Frankfurt, Germany, she would meet the model dressmaker, a man named Mr. Popp, "who receives many orders from America, and makes for the royal family of Prussia & all nobility . . . [and] Queen Victoria's daughters. . . . He is a very modest man & never speaks of it himself. How different *some* of our boastful Americans, would be."[84] Alone in Germany with her fifteen-year-old son her sole companion, Mary wrote this letter on her fiftieth birthday.

Epilogue

History has not been kind to Mary Lincoln, but it has neglected Elizabeth Keckly altogether. Mary is remembered chiefly as a difficult wife, a heartbroken mother, a manic shopper, and a lunatic. Lizzy is barely mentioned; indeed, her entire existence has been disputed.

After the blowup of their relationship in 1868, the tormented Mary Lincoln spent most of the final fourteen years of her life as a wanderer in this world, waiting for the next. She had once told Lizzy that her "early home was truly at a *boarding* school."[1] Indeed, when she left Springfield for the White House in 1861, with the exception of one year in Chicago, she never again lived in her own home.

After fleeing to Europe following the publication of Lizzy's book, she lived for two and half years among English-speaking expatriates. During that time, she also went touring, seeing parts of Germany, Austria, Scotland, England, France, and Italy as an invalid widow, accompanied variously by her adolescent son, Tad, an occasional friend, or no one, visiting places she had hoped to see as the celebrated wife of a celebrated man.

There were brief respites from misery. In 1870, the honorable Charles Sumner was finally able to steer through a resistant Congress a bill granting her an annual pension of $3,000, which President Ulysses S. Grant signed immediately. That year, she also discovered Elizabeth Stuart Phelps's bestselling spiritualist book *The Gates Ajar*, in which bereaved Civil War wives, mothers, and sisters—Phelps's target audience—could find assurances that the living would be reunited with the dead once they pass through "the gates" between this world and heaven. Helpfully, the novel even gave spiritual explanations for some of the strange physical symptoms that were plaguing Mary, particularly "*all the needles* that are now running through my body," enough for "a handsome *European pincushion*," as she described her experience to a friend. According to Phelps, they were calls from beyond.[2]

Then death again took a wrecking ball to her life. In May 1871 Mary and eighteen-year-old Tad returned to Chicago, where they were reunited with Robert, now a married Chicago attorney and the proud father of a baby girl. Two months later, Tad died of pleurisy (an accumulation of fluid in the pleural sacs surrounding the lungs), with his mother and brother by his side. The death of this son, her "troublesome *sunshine*," she called him, whose young life the unsettled, anxious Mary had virtually claimed for her own, was almost beyond anything she could bear. He was, she said, her "inseparable companion." "As grievous as other bereavements have been, not one great sorrow, ever approached the agony of *this*," she wrote a spiritualist friend. Years later, Robert said that after Tad's death he felt "all used up."[3]

Yet, although she longed to pass "through the gates" to heaven, Mary fought furiously for survival in this world. Dressed gloomily in her widow's weeds, she haunted doctors and spiritualists in a quest for some peace from her mental and bodily sufferings. She visited a health spa on Lake Michigan in Wisconsin that advertised miracle cures for every kind of ailment. At a séance in Moravia, New York, she saw a vision of spirit faces, including Tad's. In Boston, after attending a séance in which her dead husband appeared and put his hand on her shoulder, she had a spirit photographer take a photograph of her, with the President's spirit hovering nearby. She tried to find a "quiet" resort in Canada. Back in Chicago in 1874, where she was living in the Grand Central Hotel, she put herself under the treatment of Dr. Willis Danforth, a respected surgeon, and was taking large doses of chloral hydrate, a sedative and hypnotic, to sleep. She sent despondent notes to her doctor, asking for more medicine. "What is to become of this excessive wakefulness," she wrote, "it is impossible for me to divine." Convinced, or perhaps wishing, that she was about to die, she wrote Robert instructions for her funeral and burial.[4]

Instead, in May 1875, in a glaringly public trial, Robert had his mother declared insane and committed to a mental asylum in Batavia, Illinois, outside Chicago. A parade of unchallenged witnesses, including her nurse, the housekeeper, waiter, and manager of her hotel, salesclerks, Dr. Danforth, and Robert himself, who wept on the stand, gave undisputed testimony about her eccentric behavior. Robert pointed to her mania about money, her uncontrolled spending, and her bizarre spiritualism: her visions and her hearing voices. Even her own physician testified against her, citing her "nervous derangement" and the hallucinatory way she described her symptoms, the "Indian spirit" who was pulling wires from her eyes and sometimes lifting her scalp and replacing it. (No one then knew to link the onset of the acute anxiety, insomnia, and visionary episodes during this period to the tenth anniversary of her husband's murder.) Throughout the trial, Mary was stolid and calm, her only outburst coming during a recess. "Oh, Robert," she cried, "to think that my son would do this to me!" The day after the all-male jury gave its verdict, she tried to commit suicide by overdosing on laudanum and was prevented only by the quick thinking of the hotel druggist, who recognized her and gave her a mixture of burnt sugar and water instead.[5]

Mary thought Robert, who would become rich as a lawyer, banker, and corporate director, had put her away because he had his own plans for her money and, also, mortified by her behavior, wished to hide her from public view. When she managed to secure her own release from the asylum four months later, with the cooperation of sister Elizabeth, who agreed to take her in, she wrote him from Springfield, "You have tried your game of robbery long enough." You have "enemies" in Chicago, she warned him, and I have "friends." Four days before she wrote Robert this letter, in June 1876, the court declared her "restored to reason and . . . capable to manage and control her estate."[6]

She could not remain in Springfield. "I cannot endure to meet my former friends," she told Elizabeth; "they will never cease to regard me as a lunatic, I feel it in their soothing manner. If I should say the moon is made of green cheese they would heartily and smilingly agree."[7] Once more she sought refuge in the boardinghouses of Europe where, alone and far from happy and bad associations, she spent the next four years, mostly in France. She came home in the autumn of 1880, at the age of sixty-two, only because she was now too sick to live alone. She was pleased to lose weight, but arthritis in her spine, limited vision, and fatigue made it dangerous for her to move around. Two falls, one from a ladder while hanging a picture, the other on a flight of stairs, ended her indecision and she prepared to return.

On the uncomfortable, lonely sea voyage home, she was at the top of a stairway when the boat suddenly lurched. A woman standing behind her grabbed her skirt, saving her from hurtling down the stairs. "You might have been killed, madame," said the woman, the actress Sarah Bernhardt. "Yes," Mary answered with what Bernhardt detected was a sigh, "but it was not God's will." After learning the name of the woman she had just saved, Bernhardt reflected that she had "just done this unhappy woman the only service that I ought not to have done her—I had saved her from death."[8]

In July 1881, Mary was again living with the Edwardses, when she heard that the widow of the newly assassinated President James Garfield was to receive an annual pension that was $2,000 greater than her own. Now, "half-paralyzed and half-blind" but "with a frenzy reminiscent of the past," Mary Lincoln engaged in a final campaign to get Congress to increase the amount of her pension.[9]

To strengthen her case, she traveled in the fall to New York, where four doctors examined her, and had them present their report to Congress. The configuration of symptoms in the doctors' report—an inflammation of the spinal cord, connected with "reflex paralysis of the iris of the eye"—suggests these nineteenth-century men may have suspected she was suffering from syphilis. But these symptoms, when combined with others she reported—including her swollen fingers, kidney problems, weight loss, infection, and even the needle-like prickings she described to Dr. Danforth—have pointed recent scholars to a diagnosis of "prolonged and untreated diabetes." In any event, Congress was no longer in the mood to fight her and raised her pension, and even granted her back pay.[10]

However, Mary did not live to savor her victory. After returning to Elizabeth's home in Springfield, she collapsed in her room on July 15, 1882, the anniversary of Tad's death, and died the following morning of a stroke, the anniversary of her father's death. She died surrounded by her overflowing trunks and boxes.

Elizabeth Keckly would outlive Mary Lincoln by a quarter of a century, dying in Washington in her sleep in 1907 at the age of eighty-nine. She had continued sewing, although after her book was published, some of her white customers quietly disappeared. She took in apprentices in dressmaking and became known for her work in training young black seamstresses, many of them freedwomen. In 1890, needing money, the stately, seventy-two-year-old Mrs. Keckly took the Lincoln mementoes she had saved for thirty-five years (after Mary's frightened protest, nothing had gone to Wilberforce University) and sold them through a Washington broker to Charles F. Gunther of Chicago, a candy manufacturer and curio collector. An inventory of "twenty-six articles of Lincoln relics" shows that Gunther paid $250 for the lot. No record exists of how much Lizzy Keckly ultimately received from the transaction. However, among the papers that do remain is a letter to Mr. Gunther, in which the broker's clerk, assuming the usual, misidentifies the elegant Mrs. Keckly as "Mrs. Lincoln's maid." The first item on the list was the " 'Cloak,' worn by Mrs. Lincoln on the night of the assassination wet, with blood stains." Lizzy had signed her name in a barely quavering hand beneath her sworn statement, which appeared at the bottom of the last page, that "every article therein mentioned and delivered is . . . a genuine 'Lincoln Relic.' "[11]

Over the years, Lizzy moved to several different Washington addresses with her friends the Lewises, although she also boarded with two other families. Then, in 1892, at the suggestion of Bishop Daniel Payne, she accepted a position as head of Wilberforce University's Department of Sewing and Domestic Science Arts and moved to Ohio. The next year, when she was seventy-five years old, she organized the dress reform Wilberforce exhibit at the Chicago World's Fair; by the late 1890s, possibly after a slight but career-ending stroke, she returned to Washington. She spent her final years in the National Home for Destitute Colored Women and Children, an institution founded during the war partly with funds contributed by Lizzy's contraband association. When Elizabeth Keckly died, the Reverend Dr. Francis Grimké delivered her eulogy in the Fifteenth Street Presbyterian Church. She was, he said, "a very remarkable woman, and never failed to impress her personality upon all with whom she came in contact. . . . She was a commanding figure, a splendid presence. . . . She was a woman of unusual intelligence, of fine native ability. . . . She was never at a loss for a word, and her words were always well chosen. If she had had the advantages which the young people are having to-day, I feel sure that she would have distinguished herself in some line of literature. . . . She was a woman of remarkable energy and push. . . . She was a woman who thoroughly respected herself."[12]

According to friends who knew her when she was an old and dignified lady, she never got over her falling-out with Mary Lincoln. She made a quilt out of pieces of Mary's dresses, but if she planned to present it to her, she never had the chance. The snobbish, conventional Robert roughly rejected her attempt to apologize to him in person, even though he believed far worse things about his mother than Lizzy ever did. (For his part, Robert tried to collect and destroy his mother's letters, but soon gave up.)[13]

Toward the end, suffering from headaches and crying spells, Lizzy lived a secluded life, not unlike her long-dead friend. A photograph of Mary Lincoln hung in her room. As an old woman, Lizzy told friends that Mary had tried to get in touch with her "in a roundabout way" and that she forgave her. If so, all evidence of this has been erased.

But for her own efforts and those of her friends after she died, history might have erased Elizabeth Keckly as well. In 1935, David Rankin Barbee, a journalist and self-proclaimed "unreconstructed Southerner" and Lincoln hater, declared that not only had Elizabeth Keckly not written the book on whose title page her (misspelled) name appears, but that there was "no such person at all as Elizabeth Keckley." In an Associated Press article entitled "Bizarre Lincoln Story Is Traced," Barbee was reported to have discovered that the Keckly autobiography was a fraud, that it was written by Jane Swisshelm, who had been a Washington correspondent during the Civil War. "This abolitionist sob sister," Barbee argued, "in her utter devotion to the anti-slavery cause, invented an ex-slave who made Mrs. Lincoln's dresses. Jane herself had been a dressmaker."[14]

Unfortunately for Barbee, several readers of newspapers in 1935 had known Mrs. Keckly, and they came forward to testify to her existence. One of these was the Reverend Francis Grimké, Lizzy's pastor and something of a supporter of women writers; his wife was the diarist Charlotte Forten Grimké and his niece the writer Angelina Grimké. Another respondent was John E. Washington, a dentist who had grown up in Washington and was writing a book about the African Americans who served in the White House. One of his subjects was the "intelligent and cultured" Elizabeth Keckly, whom many of those he interviewed remembered well.[15]

Not surprisingly, Barbee felt compelled to clarify his position. What he meant, he wrote to the editor of *The Evening Star* in Washington, was not that no such person as Elizabeth Keckly existed, but that "no such person as Elizabeth Keckley wrote the celebrated Lincoln book."

> Scholars, with whom I cannot class myself, have long been bothered over the authorship of this book. They have not yet found in the Lincoln period another colored woman, reared in slavery, and, therefore, as they assert, naturally unlettered, who had even a knowledge of the alphabet, much less the ability to write as good and vigorous English as was being written in that day. . . . [However,] if Mrs. K. wrote it, that fact blasts one of the very serious indictments ever leveled against the Old South. . . . It would now be a very thrilling discovery if it could be established beyond peradventure that a slave woman had acquired sufficient culture in slavery to write one of the most remarkable books in American literature. I sincerely hope this discovery will be made.[16]

Perhaps the most poignant illustration of the different fates of these two women is found in their final resting places. While Mary Lincoln lies buried in Springfield in a vault with her husband and sons, Elizabeth Keckly's remains have disappeared. In the 1960s, a developer paved over the Harmony Cemetery in Washington where Lizzy was buried, and when the graves were moved to a new cemetery, her unclaimed remains were placed in an unmarked grave—like those of her mother, slave father, and son.[17]

Notes

I spell Elizabeth Keckly's name as she spelled it, without the second "e," but in the notes I keep the spelling of her name "Keckley," as it appears in other sources.

ABBREVIATIONS EMPLOYED IN NOTES

AL   Abraham Lincoln
EK   Elizabeth Keckly
ISHL   Illinois State Historical Library
LC   Library of Congress
LSW   Don E. Fehrenbacher, ed., *Lincoln: Speeches and Writings, 1832–1858* and *Lincoln: Speeches and Writings, 1859–1865* (New York: Library of America, 1989).
ML   Mary Lincoln
RST   Robert Smith Todd
Turner and Turner   Justin G. Turner and Linda Levitt Turner, *Mary Todd Lincoln: Her Life and Letters* (New York: Knopf, 1972).
UKSC   University of Kentucky Special Collections
WHH   William H. Herndon
Wilson and Davis   Douglas L. Wilson and Rodney O. Davis, *Herndon's Informants: Letters, Interviews, and Statements about Abraham Lincoln* (Urbana: University of Illinois Press, 1998).

Prologue

¹ML to EK, Chicago, March [no date] 1867, in Turner and Turner, pp. 417–18.

²ML to EK, Chicago, October 6, 1867, in Turner and Turner, p. 440.

³Mary Clemmer Ames, *Evening Post*, April 18, 1862, p. 1.

⁴See Werner Sollors, *Neither Black nor White yet Both: Thematic Explorations of Interracial Literature* (New York: Oxford University Press, 1997).

⁵ML's biographers only touch on Elizabeth Keckly's character. "She understood [ML], for she was a woman of rare intuition"; she was "more notable than any other who tried to smooth [ML's] pathway";

"Ladylike, she displayed excellent taste, and had survived the importunate demands of her employer" to become "ML's closest friend." Katherine Helm, *The True Story of Mary, Wife of Lincoln. By Her Niece* (New York: Harper & Brothers Publishers, 1928), p. 172; Mary Clemmer Ames, *Ten Years in Washington. Life and Scenes in the National Capital, As a Woman Sees Them* (Hartford, CT: A.D. Worthington, 1876), p. 237; Ishbel Ross, *The President's Wife. Mary Todd Lincoln: A Biography* (New York: G. P. Putnam's Sons, 1973), pp. 108–9.

[6]Proslavery ideologues used the phrase "the family, white and black" to argue that slavery was a benign, paternalistic institution and the master the father to his wife, children, and slaves.

CHAPTER ONE

Readers of Jean H. Baker's *Mary Todd Lincoln: A Biography* (New York: Norton, 1987) will note some discrepancies of fact between that book and mine. I do not identify each case explicitly, but, where there are differences, I try to explain how I arrive at my conclusions.

[1]There is some uncertainty as to whether Levi O. Todd, the first Todd boy, was born the year before or the year after Mary Todd (Baker has argued that Mary came before Levi). His grave in the Todd family lot in Lexington is unmarked, probably the doing of his stepmother, Elizabeth Humphreys Todd. Some of the confusion flows from disagreement over Frances's birth date, which has been given as late as March 1817, making it impossible for Levi to have been born between Frances and Mary. But the deposition in the lawsuit over Robert Smith Todd's estate, in which Eliza Parker's children sued their stepmother and half-siblings, and Frances's tombstone point toward a March 1816 birth date for Frances, making it possible for Levi to have been born between Frances and Mary. Katherine Helm, daughter of Mary's half-sister Emilie, and Alvin S. Keyes, descendant of Levi Todd and owner of a family Bible, put Mary fourth in birth order. Thanks to Dr. Wayne A. Temple of the Illinois State Archives for helping me straighten this out.

The 1810 census lists six slaves in the household of Mrs. Elizabeth Parker; see Baker, *Mary Todd Lincoln*, pp. 17–18. Eliza Todd to "my dear Grandpapa," June 20, 1813, cited in Baker, *Mary Todd Lincoln*, p. 17.

[2]Helm, *Mary, Wife of Lincoln*, p. 103.

[3]Citations in Stephen Aron, *How the West Was Lost: The Transformation of Kentucky from Daniel Boone to Henry Clay* (Baltimore: Johns Hopkins University Press, 1996), pp. 125–26, 72.

[4]Lexington *Herald*, February 7, 1908, quoted in Helm, *Mary, Wife of Lincoln*, p. 12; Catherine Allgor, " 'Queen Dolley' Saves Washington City," *Washington History* 12.1 (spring/summer 2000): 55; Susan Wendel Yandell to her parents, David and Sarah Wendel, November 30, 1825, Yandell Papers, Filson Club, Louisville.

[5]J. Winston Coleman, *Slavery Times in Kentucky* (Chapel Hill: University of North Carolina Press, 1940), p. 5; John E. Kleber, ed., *The Kentucky Encyclopedia* (Lexington: University Press of Kentucky, 1992).

[6]RST to John O'Fallon, April 24, 1812, Todd Papers, Filson Club.

[7]Kleber, *The Kentucky Encylopedia.*

[8]Clay Lancaster, *Vestiges of the Venerable City: A Chronicle of Lexington, Kentucky, Its Architectural Development and Survey of Its Early Streets and Antiquities* (Lexington: Lexington-Fayette County Historic Commission, 1978), p. 11.

[9]Kleber, *The Kentucky Encyclopedia;* Coleman, *Slavery Times in Kentucky,* pp. 14, 81–82; John Logan Account Book, June 30, 1792, Filson Club; Hart cited in Aron, *How the West Was Lost*, pp. 90, 100; percentage of blacks in manufacturers taken from notes in William H. Townsend file, Filson Club.

[10]Not everyone benefited from the system, and in 1803, a suspicious fire consumed the small records office Levi Todd kept in his house, destroying all of the land claims. After that, fireproof offices were installed in the new courthouse on Main Street built in 1806.

[11] Aron, *How the West Was Lost*, p. 122; Levi Todd to John McCulloch, September 24, 1790, cited in Baker, *Mary Todd Lincoln*, p. 5.

[12] Lancaster, *Vestiges of the Venerable City*, pp. 18, 23; J. Winston Coleman, *Stage-Coach Days in the Bluegrass: Being an Account of Stage-Coach Travel and Tavern Days in Lexington and Central Kentucky, 1800–1900* (1935; rpt. Lexington: University of Kentucky Press, 1995), p. 29; Hart quoted in Aron, *How the West Was Lost*, p. 133; Sally Payne Lewis Clay Dudley to Brutus Junius Clay in 1836, quoted in Mary Clay Berry, *Voices from the Century Before: The Odyssey of a 19th-century Kentucky Family* (New York: Arcade Publishing, 1997), p. 8.

[13] Will of Robert Parker, March 1800, Will Book A, Fayette County Courthouse, Lexington.

[14] Robert's estate, valued at more than $14,000 in the 1840s, would have been worth about $244,000 today.

[15] Susan Corlis to John Corlis, Esq., Lexington, August 23, 1821, Corlis Family Papers, Filson Club.

[16] William Clark to John O'Fallon, St. Louis, November 22, 1808, John O'Fallon Collection, Missouri Historical Society, St. Louis. It is unclear if John ever studied with Henry Clay, but he did study with Robert Smith Todd sometime around 1812. Robert apprenticed first in Lexington with Thomas Bodley, Fayette County clerk and a relative of the Parkers by marriage, then in Frankfort with George Bibb, a chief justice of the state appeals court and later a United States senator.

[17] Ann's and Robert's birth dates have caused confusion. I reason from the following: Robert Parker Todd's funeral was July 22, 1822, after his death at fourteen months, placing his birth date in 1821. In *Todd heirs vs. Todd administrators & heirs*, Townsend Collection, UKSC, Ann was said to have been in her nineteenth year when she married in 1846, suggesting a birth date of 1824. George was born July 4, 1825, one day before his mother's death.

[18] By then, opportunities for lawyers had diminished and of his brothers, only Robert remained in Lexington. Three lawyer brothers moved to Missouri; another brother, a doctor, took off for the frontier town of Springfield, Illinois. For sale of Ellerslie, see *The Boarding School of Mary Todd Lincoln: A discussion between C. Frank Dunn and William H. Townsend* (Lexington: Privately published, 1941), p. 33.

[19] *Kentucky Gazette*, July 11, 1825.

[20] "Country women" anecdote in Dr. Lunsford Yandell, "Memoranda for a Life of Lunsford Pitts Yandell," Yandell Papers, Filson Club; Laurel Thatcher Ulrich, *The Midwife's Tale: The Life of Martha Ballard, Based on Her Diary, 1785–1812* (New York: Vintage Books, 1990), pp. 11, 56–57, 170–71, 192; *Anne Powell Burwell's Commonplace Book*, 1745–1839, Virginia Historical Society, Richmond.

[21] At the time, one new mother could be expected to die for every two hundred live births. Charlotte Mentelle, mistress of Mary Todd's boarding school, described childbirth as painful and frightening: "even with the greatest help this moment is always terrible and specially makes me afraid." Charlotte Mentelle, Letters d'Amerique, Lexington, 28 Decembre 1803, UKSC. Thanks to Jean-Louis Ecochard for his translations of the Mentelle letters. Baker, *Mary Todd Lincoln*, p. 21.

[22] On slave beliefs, see Lawrence W. Levine, *Black Culture and Black Consciousness: Afro-American Folk Thought from Slavery to Freedom* (New York: Oxford University Press, 1977), p. 79. Anecdote in Helm, *Mary, Wife of Lincoln*, pp. 25–33. On the phrase "Hide me, oh, my Savior, hide" and other words of prayer used when "imploring mercy at the hands of their oppressors," see William Wells Brown, *Narrative of William W. Brown, A Fugitive Slave* (Boston, 1847), rpt. in Larry Gara, ed., *Four Fugitive Slave Narratives* (Reading, MA: Addison-Wesley., 1969), p. 2.

[23] Sally could have gone to an African American church, for by the 1830s there were three in Lexington, at least two of which had black preachers. Stephen G. Moerland, "Straddling the Fence of Freedom: The Free African-American Community of Antebellum Lexington" (master's thesis, University of Kentucky, 1996), p. 83; Wayne C. Temple, *Abraham Lincoln: From Skeptic to Prophet* (Mahomet, IL: Mayhaven Publishing, 1995), p. 32; Helm, *Mary, Wife of Lincoln*, p. 23.

[24] Coleman, *Slavery Times in Old Kentucky*, p. 104. Court-day slave sales, aimed at the crowds who

flocked into town when the court was in session, were abolished in 1821. In 1847, a special court session decided Lexington needed a bigger whipping post than its old locust one, so they began using a three-pronged poplar tree in the courthouse yard.

[25]Ibid., pp. 105, 148, 145; Coleman, *Lexington's Slave Dealers and their Southern Trade* (Louisville, KY, 1938) rpt. from *The Filson Club Quarterly* 12:1 1938: 1–23.

[26]RST to Elizabeth L. Humphreys, October 9, 1826, RST Papers, ISHL.

[27]Baker, *Mary Todd Lincoln*, p. 12; RST to Elizabeth L. Humphreys, January 13, 1826, RST Papers.

[28]RST to Elizabeth L. Humphreys, February 15, 1826, RST Papers.

[29]Ibid.

[30]Ibid.

[31]RST to Elizabeth L. Humphreys, October 23, 1826, RST Papers.

[32]RST to Elizabeth L. Humphreys, October 25, 1826, RST Papers.

CHAPTER TWO

[1]Edmund Ruffin, *The Farmer's Register*, cited in *Dinwiddie County, "The country of the Apamatica,"* compiled by the Workers of the Writers' Program of the WPA in the State of Virginia, 1942, p. 94. Jefferson, quoted in Wilma King, *Stolen Childhood: Slave Youth in Nineteenth-Century America* (Bloomington: Indiana University Press, 1995), p. 2.

[2]My estimation of the slave women of childbearing age comes from a comparison of the slave births listed in *Anne Powell Burwell Commonplace Book*, 1745–1839, and the 1820 census for the Armistead Burwell household, which lists eleven slave girls to age 14, two slave women to age 26, and three slave women to age 45; also two male slaves between 15 and 26; four to age 43; and two 43 years and older. 1820 Census, Library of Virginia.

[3]Many slave women complied with their master because they knew he had the power to force them anyway. As one woman remembered, "Ma mama said that a nigger 'oman couldn't help herself, fo' she had to do what de marster say. Ef he come to de field whar de woman workin' an' tell gal to come on, she had to go. He would take one down in de woods an' use her all de time he wanted to, den send her on back to work. Times nigger 'omen had chillun for de marster an' his sons and some times it was fo' de ovah seer." In Dorothy Sterling, ed., *We Are Your Sisters: Black Women in the Nineteenth Century* (New York: Norton, 1984), p. 25. The Burwell children were Robert (b. 1802); John (b. 1804); Anne (b. 1805); Lewis (b. 1807); Mary (b. 1809); Armistead Jr. (b. 1811); Benjamin (b. 1813); Frances (b. 1814); Charles (b. 1816, d. 8 days); Charles Blair (b. 1817); William (b. 1819); Nathaniel (b. 1821, d. infancy); Elizabeth (b. 1823).

[4]Colonial and antebellum masters observed higher rates of miscarriage and abortion among slave women than among whites. In 1860, Dr. John S. Morgan of Tennessee reported on a plantation where "every conception was aborted by the fourth month." The master finally learned what was happening; the slave women were taking a "medicine" made from a certain "weed which was their favorite remedy." See Janet Farrell Brodie, *Contraception and Abortion in 19th-Century America* (Ithaca: Cornell University Press, 1994), pp. 52–53, and Sterling, *We Are Your Sisters*, p. 40.

[5]Lucy McCullough cited in Wilma King, " 'Suffer with Them Till Death': Slave Women and Their Children in Nineteenth-Century America," in David Barry Gaspar and Darlene Clark Hine, eds., *More Than Chattel: Black Women and Slavery in the Americas* (Bloomington: Indiana University Press, 1996), p. 159.

[6]Typically, mistresses did not list the father's name along with the mother's name in slave birth inventories. According to the 1815 tax rolls, Armistead Burwell owned about twenty-three slaves: fifteen blacks above age sixteen, one between the ages of twelve and sixteen, and the rest under twelve (the last not considered taxable property). Dinwiddie County Personal Property Tax Lists, Library of Virginia. Between February 1798 and August 1839 nine Burwell slave women gave birth to thirty-two infants, thirteen boys and nineteen girls; *Anne Powell Burwell Commonplace Book*, 1745–1839.

[7]At the height of the African slave trade to Virginia, between 1720 and 1740, a total of 22,940 kidnapped Africans survived the brutal transatlantic crossing. Between 1700 and 1775, when direct imports to the colony stopped, the total number of surviving African immigrants to Virginia ports was 62,450. After that, Virginia's slave population became self-reproducing: whereas in 1700 about 6,500 of the 13,000 slaves in Virginia were Africans, by 1800 only 678 Africans could be counted among 346,000 Virginia slaves. Philip D. Morgan, *Slave Counterpoint: Black Culture in the Eighteenth-Century Chesapeake and Lowcountry* (Chapel Hill: University of North Carolina Press, 1998), pps. 61, 81. One estimate of the total number of slaves imported from Africa into mainland North America is between 500,000 and 600,000. This represents only about 5 percent of the total Atlantic slave trade. Drew Gilpin Faust, "The Slavery Experience," in Edward D. C. Campbell Jr. and Kym S. Rice, eds., *Before Freedom Came: African-American Life in the Antebellum South* (Charlottesville: University of Virginia Press, 1991), pp. 1–20.

[8]The Burwell families owned 26,000 acres of land, centering on the York Peninsula, between the York and James Rivers, from present-day Williamsburg to Yorktown. In the decades before the Civil War, one Burwell slave, Aunt Christian, could remember " 'way back yonder in my mamy time fo' de folks come fum de King's Mill plantation nigh Williamsbu'g. All our black folks done belongs to de Burl fambly uver sence dey come fum Afiky. My granmammy 'member dem times when black folks lan' here stark naked, an' white folks hab to show 'em how to war close. But we all done come fum all dat now, em' I gwine manage my own affa'rs." In Letitia Burwell, *A Girl's Life in Virginia before the War* (New York: Frederick H. Stokes Company, 1895), p. 8.

[9]*Petersburg Intelligencer*, 14 March 1806, cited in Suzanne Lebsock, *The Free Women of Petersburg: Status and Culture in a Southern Town, 1784–1860* (New York: Norton, 1984), p. 5.

[10]John P. Parker, *The Autobiography of John P. Parker, Former Slave and Conductor on the Underground Railroad*, ed. Stuart Seely Sprague (New York: Norton, 1996), pp. 27–28.

[11]Burwell, *A Girl's Life in Virginia before the War*, p. 1. For plantation landscapes, see Lorena S. Walsh, *From Calabar to Carter's Grove: The History of a Virginia Slave Community* (Charlottesville: University of Virginia Press, 1997), introduction; John Michael Vlach, "Plantation Landscapes of the Antebellum South" in Campbell and Rice, *Before Freedom Came*, pp. 21–50.

[12]This was particularly true in the 1830s, a decade of rising abolitionism, inaugurated by the January 1, 1831, publication of William Lloyd Garrison's *Liberator*, a paper devoted to the immediate abolition of slavery. Legislative petitions to Virginia General Assembly, December 11, 1805, cited in Lebsock, *The Free Women of Petersburg*, p. 91. Out of 13,792 inhabitants listed in the 1820 census, 5,373 were whites, 7,751 were slaves, and 668 were free blacks; WPA, *Dinwiddie County*, pp. 93–95.

[13]Frances Trollope, *Domestic Manners of the Americans* (1832; New York: Vintage Books, 1960), p. 192. William Turnbull Burwell to Frances King Burwell, May 16, 1838, Burwell-Catlett Letters, Manuscripts, Swem Library, College of William and Mary.

[14]In 1815, Burwell's estate was valued at $1,265.56. Dinwiddie Country Land Tax Books, 1815–1850, Library of Virginia. Anna Robertson Burwell is the daughter-in-law with the complaint against the family; her story is told in Chapter 4. *Proceedings of the Burwell Family Picnic, held at Burwell Farm, Milford, Ct., August 18, 1870* (Cleveland: G. S. Newcomb & Co., 1870), p. 19. Alfred J. Morison, *The College of Hampden-Sydney, Calendar of Board Minutes, 1776–1876* (Richmond, VA: Heritage Press, 1912), Sept. 26–27, 1821, p. 87.

[15]*Petersburg Intelligencer*, Friday, October 29, 1819.

[16]Elizabeth Keckley, *Behind the Scenes, Or, Thirty Years a Slave, and Four Years in the White House* (1868; rpt. New York: Oxford University Press, 1988), p. 22.

[17]Morison, *Calendar of Board Minutes*, pp. 79, 14; Herbert C. Bradshaw, *History of Hampden-Sydney College* (Privately printed, 1976), pp. 204–5.

[18]Bradshaw, *History of Hampden-Sydney College*, p. 183.

[19]Morison, *Calendar of Board Minutes*, pp. 85–86n.

[20]Keckley, *Behind the Scenes*, p. 19.

[21]Helen Bradley Foster, *"New Raiments of Self":African American Clothing in the Antebellum South* (Oxford: Berg, 1997), pp. 79–80.

[22]Keckley, *Behind the Scenes*, pp. 20–21.

[23]Morgan, *Slave Counterpoint*, p. 334; Eugene D. Genovese, *Roll, Jordan, Roll: The World the Slaves Made* (New York: Vintage Books, 1972), p. 361.

[24]Mary Cole Burwell to Frances King Burwell, Petersburg, June 12, 1844, Burwell-Catlett Papers; Keckley, *Behind the Scenes*, p. 21.

[25]Keckley, *Behind the Scenes*, pp. 23, 27–28. George Hobbs to Agnes Hobbs, September 6, 1833: "I am well satisfied at my living at this place I am a making money for my own benefit and I hope that its to yours also If I live to see Nexet year I shall have my own time from master by giving him 100 and twenty Dollars a year and I thinke I shall be doing good bisness at that and heve something more thean all that. I hope with gods helpe that I may be able to rejoys with you on the earth and In heaven lets meet when will I am determnid to nuver stope praying, not in this earth and I hope to praise god In glory there weel meet to part no more forever. . . . I want Elizabeth to be a good girl and not to thinke that because I am bound so fare that gods not abble to open the way." His last letter to Agnes was dated from Shelbyville, March 1839.

[26]Keckley, *Behind the Scenes*, pp. 24–25.

[27]C. Vann Woodward, *Mary Chesnut's Civil War* (New Haven: Yale University Press, 1981), entry for March 18, 1861, p. 29.

[28]Peter W. Bardaglio, *Reconstructing the Household: Families, Sex, and the Law in the Nineteenth-Century South* (Chapel Hill: University of North Carolina Press, 1995), pp. 48–55.

[29]V. Josiah C. Nott, *Two Lectures on the Natural History of the Caucasian and Negro Races* (1844), rpt. in Drew Gilpin Faust, ed., *The Ideology of Slavery: Proslavery Thought in the Antebellum South* (Baton Rouge: Louisiana State University Press, 1981), pp. 206–38. See also Jennifer Fleischner, *Mastering Slavery: Memory, Family, and Identity in Women's Slave Narratives* (New York: New York University Press, 1996), p. 36. Henry Hughes, *Treatise on Sociology* (1860), quoted in Genovese, *Roll, Jordan, Roll*, p. 218.

[30]Keckley, *Behind the Scenes*, pp. 21, 28–29.

[31]Ibid., p. 30.

CHAPTER THREE

[1]Helm, *Mary, Wife of Lincoln*, pp. 34–35.

[2]See Brodie, *Contraception and Abortion in 19th-century America*.

[3]ML to Eliza Stuart Steele, May 23, 1871, in Turner and Turner, pp. 588–89.

[4]Katherine Helm wrote that as a young girl, Aunt Mary was "a bundle of nervous activity, willful and original in planning mischief, and so the inevitable clashes with her conventional young stepmother" (Helm, *Mary, Wife of Lincoln*, p. 17).

[5]In her retelling of this anecdote (in ibid., pp. 27–30), Helm referred to Mary's wish for a hoop skirt, but hoops were not fashionable when Mary was ten, so it seems likely that the "hoop skirt" came into the story later, by which time Mrs. Lincoln was famous for her hoop skirts. By the late 1850s, when Helm was a young girl, acquiring grown-up hoops was a cause for excitement, worthy of lines in a letter between sisters: "I have a pair of *Hoops* What do you think of that. I sent to Little Rock [Arkansas] for them—and through *flood* and *rain* they reached here safely. . . . I intend to fix Aunt Caroline [a slave] a set so she and I are coming home quite fashionable." Sarah Lane Glasgow to Nannie Glasgow, February 22, 1859, William Carr Lane Papers, Missouri Historical Society. See also Joan Severa, *Dressed for the Photographer: Ordinary American and Fashion, 1840–1900* (Kent, OH: Kent State University Press, 1995).

[6]Helm, *Mary, Wife of Lincoln*, pp. 27–30.

[7]Ibid., pp. 46–48.

[8]Levine, *Black Culture and Black Consciousness*, p. 115.

[9]Helm, *Mary, Wife of Lincoln*, pp. 50–52.

[10]Ibid., pp. 40, 51. Mary's instinctive reach across the color line was, perhaps, a natural consequence of her closeness to Sally. In 1833, she insisted on shaking the hand of William "King Solomon," an impoverished black indentured servant man who, during the cholera epidemic, tirelessly dug graves for Lexington's dead (nearly 10 percent of its population died in three months), when most people were afraid to go near the bodies. Mary's actions scandalized the snobbish Nelson. She was already a teenager, an age when many Southern ladies would have ignored the black man.

[11]Coleman, *Slavery Times in Old Kentucky*, pp. 250–51.

[12]Deposition of George R. C. Todd, October 19, 1852, *Todd heirs vs. Todd administrators & heirs*, Townsend Collection, UKSC.

[13]Helm, *Mary, Wife of Lincoln*, pp. 40, 44, 48. Baker misidentifies Betsey Todd as the source of the "limb of Satan" remark. For African American folktales, see Levine, *Black Culture and Black Consciousness*, p. 112; for discussion of "signifying," see Henry Louis Gates, *The Signifying Monkey: A Theory of African American Literary Criticism* (New York: Oxford University Press, 1988).

[14]Coleman, *Lexington's Slave Dealers*, p. 11. In *Uncle Tom's Cabin, or, Life among the Lowly* (1852), Harriet Beecher Stowe depicted Kentucky slaveholders as aristocratic and relatively lenient and slave traders as lower class, profit-driven, and cruel.

[15]Margaretta Brown to Amelia M. Mason, July 31, 1834, cited in Moerland, "Straddling the Fence for Freedom," p. 38.

[16]The owner of the slave who was shot and killed running out of the dance successfully sued the owner of the school building for the loss of his slave. Moerland, "Straddling the Fence of Freedom," p. 29; Coleman, *Slavery Times in Kentucky*, pp. 102–3, 295–96; Baker, *Mary Todd Lincoln*, p. 68.

[17]Mrs. Humphreys stipulated that "my negro girl, Jane," whom she was leaving to her daughter Elizabeth Todd, was "to be free from all kind of servitude" on Christmas day, 1844. If Jane had any boys before she was free, they were "hereby devised to the said Elizabeth L. Todd" until they were twenty-eight years old, when they should be "free and emancipate from all manner of servitude"; if there were girls, they belonged to Elizabeth Todd until they turned twenty-one, when they were to be set free. Mrs. Humphreys also provided that her slave woman Judy be released on Christmas 1839. Humphreys will in Helm, *Mary, Wife of Lincoln*, pp. 35–38. Elizabeth R. Parker's 1849 will directed Dr. John Parker to emancipate the following slaves from her estate: "Prudence—about 70 years—dark; Ann—about 51 years—dark copper; Cyrus—about 47 years—yellow; Charles—about 46 years—yellow." Mrs. Parker also made provision for John to "pay over to Prudence twelve dollars annually as long as she may live." Helm File, Townsend Papers, UKSC; Baker, *Mary Todd Lincoln*, p. 68. As Robert Smith Todd left no will, his intentions toward his slaves are not known.

[18]Helm, *Mary, Wife of Lincoln*, p. 51. The nonimportation bill was repealed in 1849 after a decade of debates. For nonimportation supporter Robert Wickcliffe, limiting the trade in slaves on Kentucky soil was a matter of honor: If we eliminated "the horrid practice of *driving them like cattle to market . . . a great blot would certainly be wiped off our moral character.*" See Coleman, *Slavery Times in Old Kentucky*, pp. 150, 277; *Lexington Observer and Reporter*, June 12, 13, 1845; June 12, 27, 1849.

[19]Population statistics in Moerland, "Straddling the Fence of Freedom," p. 109.

[20]Samuel A. Oldham Papers, UKSC; Moerland, "Straddling the Fence of Freedom," pp. 15, 65.

[21]Helm, *Mary, Wife of Lincoln*, pp. 1–3, 42–43. Henry Clay ran for President three times: in 1824, 1832, and 1844.

[22]Ibid., p. 43.

[23]Lunsford P. Yandell to Mr. David Wendel, November 17, 1825, Yandell Papers; Helm, *Mary, Wife of Lincoln*, pp. 48–49.

[24]Lunsford P. Yandell to Mr. David Wendel, November 17, 1825, and December 9, 1825, Yandell Papers.

[25]Timothy Flint (1826), cited in Richard L. Bushman, *The Refinement of America: Persons, Houses, Cities* (New York: Vintage Books, 1993), pp. 385–88.

[26]Susan Wendel Yandell to Dr. Wilson Yandell, November 22, 1825, Yandell Papers; Harriet Martineau, *Society in America* (London: Saunders and Otley, 1837), 3:146.

[27]The census of 1840, after Mary Todd left home, lists eleven free whites, three female slaves, two male slaves, and one free colored woman over fifty-five in the Todd household. Fayette County Census Records, Kentucky Historical Society.

[28]*Kentucky Statesmen*, September 14, 1860.

[29]Charlotte Mentelle to her father, Lexington, April 26, 1804, Mentelle Papers, UKSC; translated by Jean-Louis Ecochard.

[30]Dunn and Townsend, *The Boarding School of Mary Todd Lincoln*.

[31]ML to EK, Chicago, October 29, 1867, in Turner and Turner, p. 447. During her first year in the White House, Mary assessed her sisters in a letter to a cousin. Of Ann, she wrote: "Poor *unfortunate* Ann, inasmuch as she possesses such a miserable disposition & so false a tongue—How far . . . are we removed, from such a person. . . . a woman, whom no one respects, whose tongue for so many years, has been considered 'no slander'—and as a child & young girl, could not be outdone in falsehoods—'Truly the Leopard cannot change his spots' . . . I grieve for those, who have to come in contact with her malice, yet even *that*, is so well understood, the object of her *wrath*, generally rises, with good people, in proportion to her *vindictiveness*. . . . Tell Ann for me, to quote her own expression, *She* is becoming still further removed from 'Queen Victoria's Court.'" ML to Elizabeth Todd Grimsley, September 29, 1861, in Turner and Turner, pp. 105–6.

[32]Helm, *Mary, Wife of Lincoln*, p. 45.

[33]Ibid., p. 32.

[34]Elizabeth Todd Edwards interview with WHH, 1865–66, in Wilson and Davis, p. 443.

[35]RST to Ninian Edwards, August 23, 1841, and *Todd heirs vs. Todd administrators*, RST Papers.

[36]Elodie Todd to N. H. P. Dawson, June 12, 1861, cited in Baker, *Mary Todd Lincoln*, p. 57; RST to Ninian W. Edwards, July 12, 1841, RST Papers.

[37]Deposition of Elizabeth P. Edwards, April 6, 1852, in *Todd heirs vs. Todd administrators & heirs*, RST Papers; ML to AL, May 1848, in Turner and Turner, pp. 36–38.

CHAPTER FOUR

[1]Keckley, *Behind the Scenes*, p. 19.

[2]Ibid., p. 32.

[3]Keckley, ibid., pp. 31–32; Burwell, *A Girl's Life in Virginia Before the War*, p. 43. On slaves' status, see Frederick Douglass, *Narrative of the Life of Frederick Douglass An American Slave* (1845; rpt. New York: Library of America, 1994), p. 28.

[4]Robert Burwell to Frances King Burwell, November 19, 1834, Burwell-Catlett Papers; Mary C. Burwell to Miss Fanny K. Burwell, March 14, 1842, Burwell-Catlett Papers.

[5]Robert Burwell to Frances King Burwell, November 19, 1834, Burwell-Catlett Papers.

[6]Unpublished autobiography of John Bott Burwell (1921), The Burwell Family Collection, Resource Room, Burwell School Historic Site, Hillsborough, p. 12.

[7]Thomas Ruffin to Catherine Ruffin, March 5, 1836, in J. G. De Roulhac Hamilton, ed., *The Papers of Thomas Ruffin*, Publications of the North Carolina Historical Commission (Raleigh: Edwards & Broughton Printing Co., 1918), p. 159. The Ruffin daughters described their mother's symptoms "as

palpitations, numbness in tongue and stiffness of jaws, melancholy, and a diseased mind." Town physicians diagnosed her as suffering from hysteria. See Jean Bradley Anderson, *The Kirklands of Ayr Mount* (Chapel Hill: University of North Carolina Press, 1991), p. 66. M. A. Burwell Diary, January 20, 1855, The Burwell Family Collection, Resource Room, Burwell School Historic Site.

[8]Unpublished autobiography of John Bott Burwell; M. A. Burwell Diary, February 2, 1846, The Burwell Family Collection.

[9]Susan Catharine Bott to Margaret Anna Burwell, January 29, 1836, in A. B. Van Zandt, D.D., *"The Lady Elect," A Memoir of Mrs. Susan Catharine Bott of Petersburg, Va.* (Philadelphia: Presbyterian Board of Publication, 1857), p. 156; Margaret Anna Burwell to Frances Burwell, January 5, 1856, The Burwell Family Collection.

[10]Margaret Anna Burwell to Frances Burwell, March 4, 1856, and March 15, 1856; M. A. Burwell Diary, April 10, 1846 and July 10, 1855, The Burwell Family Collection.

[11]Margaret Anna Burwell to Frances Burwell, February 16, 1856; M. A. Burwell Diary, October 12, 1855, and February 11, 1846, The Burwell Family Collection.

[12]Elizabeth Hobbs to Agnes Hobbs, April 10, 1838, in Keckley, *Behind the Scenes*, p. 39. For some reason, Agnes rarely, if ever, wrote back to either her daughter or her husband.

[13]In one particularly dark moment, when "Mr. B is low spirited" too, Anna Burwell wrote in her diary, "it seems to me no one can love me except my young children who do not know me." M. A. Burwell Diary, January 2, 1855, The Burwell Family Collection.

[14]Keckley, *Behind the Scenes*, p. 32.

[15]M. A. Burwell Diary, March 13, 1855, The Burwell Family Collection. Advertisements from the Hillsborough *Recorder* cited in *The Burwell School* pamphlet, The Historic Hillsborough Commission, Hillsborough.

[16]Catherine Ruffin Roulhac to Joseph B. G. Roulhac, August 2, 1837, Ruffin-Roulhac-Hamilton Papers, Wilson Library, University of North Carolina at Chapel Hill.

[17]Cheryl F. Junk, " 'To Become a Power in the Land': The Burwell School and Women's Education in Antebellum North Carolina, 1837–1857," *Hillsborough Historical Society Journal* 2.1 (July 1999): 13–47.

[18]Susan Catharine Bott to Margaret Anna Burwell, December 16, 1835, in Van Zandt, *"The Lady Elect,"* p. 152.

[19]Margaret Anna Burwell to Frances Burwell, January 19, 1856 and January 12, 1856, The Burwell Family Collection.

[20]Jane Clancy to Polly Burke, October 4, 1837, Weissenger Papers, Wilson Library; Anne Webb to Mary W. Burke, November 10, 1837, Weissenger Papers. Mary Webb's graduation certificate, transcript in Burwell School, Resource Room.

[21]Margaret Anna Burwell to Frances Burwell, March 10, 1856, The Burwell Family Collection; Susan Murphy to Mrs. Eliza A. Murphy, July 15, 1848, in Susan Murphy File, Burwell School, Records Room. Homesickness notwithstanding, former students remembered Anna affectionately.

[22]Elizabeth Hobbs to Agnes Hobbs, April 10, 1838, in Keckley, *Behind the Scenes*, p. 42.

[23]Elizabeth Hobbs to Miss Fanny Burwell, Mansfield, April 25, 1842, Burwell-Catlett Papers. Fanny Burwell is Armistead and Mary Burwell's daughter. On May 6, 1969, after previously identifying "Lizzy" as "unknown," P. B. Rogers, the Burwell descendant who transcribed the family letters, added this footnote to the bottom of his transcription: "This day I obtained Elizabeth Keckley's book from the Bucknell University Library and have hardly been able to believe what I have read in it" (Burwell-Catlett Collection).

[24]Margaret Anna Burwell to Frances Burwell, January 25, 1856, and March 10, 1856; John Bott Burwell unpublished autobiography, The Burwell Family Collection.

[25]M. A. Burwell Diary entries: February 24, 1855; February 13, 1855; February 14, 1846; January 24,

1846; July 9, 1855; January 30, 1856; February 12, 1855; December 15, 1855; January 30, 1846; July 9, 1855; January 3, 1855; January 18, 1855, The Burwell Family Collection.

[26]M. A. Burwell Diary, January 30, 1846; February 13, 1855; February 9, 1846; February 16, 1846; December 29, 1855, The Burwell Family Collection.

[27]M. A. Burwell Diary, October 7, October 8, October 10, 1855; December 12, 1855; Margaret Anna Burwell to Frances Burwell, January 12, 1856, The Burwell Family Collection.

[28]Anna's diary and letters from the 1840s and 1850s mention a number of slaves, some of them hired: Hannah, Mary Ann, Julia, Maria, Betsey, Kitty, Aunt Judy, Aunt Ferily, Mitchell, Jacob, Primus, Patsy, Jane, and William. On Kirkland slaves, see Anderson, *The Kirklands of Ayr Mount*, p. 50.

[29]Margaret Anna Burwell to Susan Catharine Bott, February 14, 1851, The Burwell Family Collection.

[30]Mrs. Mary C. Burwell to Miss Fanny K. Burwell, March 14, 1842, Burwell-Catlett Papers.

[31]Keckley, *Behind the Scenes*, p. 32.

[32]Robert J. Curtis, "The Binghams and Classical Education in North Carolina, 1793–1873," *North Carolina Historical Review*, 73.3 (July 1996): 328–77.

[33]Alexander Kirkland to Catherine Ruffin, January 10, 1832, cited in Anderson, *The Kirklands of Ayr Mount*, p. 51. Advertisement in Hillsborough *Recorder*, April 9, 1828.

[34]Keckley, *Behind the Scenes*, pp. 33–38.

[35]As one former slave wrote, "How often did I rejoice that I lived in a town where all the inhabitants knew each other! If I had been on a remote plantation, or lost among the multitude of a crowded city, I should not be a living woman at this day." Harriet Jacobs, *Incidents in the Life of a Slave Girl: Written by Herself*, ed. Lydia Maria Child (1861), rpt. in Jean Fagan Yellin, ed. (Cambridge, MA: Harvard University Press, 1981), p. 35.

[36]Advertisement, July 18, 1838, rpt. in Freddie L. Parker, ed., *Stealing a Little Freedom: Advertisements for Slave Runaways in North Carolina, 1791–1840* (New York: Garland Publishing), p. 682; Douglass, *Narrative of the Life of Frederick Douglass*, p. 34.

[37]Genovese, *Roll, Jordan, Roll*, p. 35; Paul C. Cameron to Thomas Ruffin, December 1, 1835, in Hamilton, *The Ruffin Papers*, pp. 150–51.

[38]Anne Kirkland Ruffin to Thomas Ruffin, February 11, 1835, Thomas Ruffin Papers.

[39]Slaves had a phrase: "Got one mind for the boss to see; got another for what I know is me"; see King, " 'Suffer With Them Till Death,' " pp. 147–68.

[40]Keckley, *Behind the Scenes*, pp. 19–20.

[41]M. J. Taylor to Polly Burke, December 1837, Weissenger Papers; Elizabeth Hobbs to Agnes Hobbs, April 10, 1838, in Keckley, *Behind the Scenes*, pp. 41–42.

[42]At twenty, Lizzy was older than many young slave women who were sexually preyed upon by their masters. In *Incidents in the Life of a Slave Girl*, Harriet Jacobs referred to early adolescence as a "perilous passage" for a slave girl. In her case, her fifty-year-old master "began to whisper foul words in my ear" when she was fifteen (p. 27).

[43]William Alexander Kirkland (1836–1898) and Robert Strange Kirkland (1838–1899) fought on opposing sides during the Civil War. Their mother, Anna, suffered a breakdown, which she dated from "the *fatal* night" of her husband's death, when she was not allowed to visit him because "the physician thought my presence excited him." She spent the rest of her life in an asylum in Raleigh, where she died in 1890. Anna Kirkland to D. Cameron, June 23, 1846, in Anderson, *The Kirklands of Ayr Mount*, pp. 102–3.

[44]Ibid., p. 98.

[45]Catherine Ruffin to Anne K. Ruffin, March 24, 1836, Ruffin-Roulhac-Hamilton Papers.

[46]Catherine Ruffin Roulhac to Joseph Roulhac, September 30, 1839, cited in Anderson, *The Kirklands of Ayr Mount*, p. 99.

47John Kirkland to Mary A. Kirkland, May 10, 1843, cited in ibid., pp. 99–100.

48Thomas Ruffin to Catherine Ruffin Roulhac, May 6, 1843, Ruffin-Roulhac Papers.

49Quotes from Brenda E. Stevenson, "Gender Convention, Ideals, and Identity among Antebellum Virginia Slave Women," in David Barry Gaspar and Darlene Clark Hine, eds., *More Than Chattel: Black Women and Slavery in the Americas* (Bloomington: Indiana University Press, 1996), pp. 169–190.

50Harriet was the great-grandmother and her daughter by lawyer Sidney Smith the grandmother of Pauli Murray, a lawyer, civil rights activist, and deacon in the Episcopal Church. Pauli Murray, *Proud Shoes: The Story of an American Family* (1956, New York: Harper & Row, 1978), p. 47.

51Ibid., p. 33.

CHAPTER FIVE

I rely on the interviews, statements, and letters collected by AL's law partner and biographer, William H. Herndon. I take as my guide the close analysis of the Herndon testimony by scholar Douglas L. Wilson in *Lincoln before Washington: New Perspectives on the Illinois Years* (Urbana: University of Illinois Press, 1997) and *Honor's Voice: The Transformation of Abraham Lincoln* (New York: Knopf, 1998). This testimony is available in Douglas L. Wilson and Rodney O. Davis, *Herndon's Informants: Letters, Interviews, and Statements about Abraham Lincoln* (Urbana: University of Illinois Press, 1998). I am also indebted to Michael Burlingame, *The Inner World of Abraham Lincoln* (Urbana: University of Illinois Press, 1994) and his forthcoming *Abraham Lincoln, Volumes 1 and 2* (Baltimore: Johns Hopkins University Press, 2004). For general information, I use Mark E. Neely Jr., *The Abraham Lincoln Encyclopedia* (New York: Da Capo Press, 1982).

1Paul M. Angle, *"Here I Have Lived": A History of Lincoln's Springfield, 1821–1865* (1935; rpt. Chicago: Abraham Lincoln Bookshop, 1971), pp. 83–89.

2Ibid., pp. 19–21.

3A. Russell to Mrs. Capt. James C. Murray, Kilman by Glasgow, January 30, 1851, Collections, ISHL.

4Simeon Francis, editor of the *Sangamo Journal*, quoted in Angle, *"Here I Have Lived,"* pp. 54–55; Martineau, *Society in America*, p. 84.

5William W. Freehling, *The Reintegration of American History: Slavery and the Civil War* (New York: Oxford University Press, 1994), pp. 22–23.

6John J. Hardin to Robert W. Scott, September 24, 1830, in Helm, *Mary, Wife of Lincoln*, pp. 67–68.

7Ira Berlin, *Slaves Without Masters: The Free Negro in the Antebellum South* (New York: New Press, 1974), p. 167.

8Ohio editor quoted in Angle, *"Here I Have Lived,"* p. 86; Christopher C. Brown, interview, [1865–66], in Wilson and Davis, p. 438.

9Mary Todd to Mercy Ann Levering, July 23, 1840, December [15?], 1840, and June 1841, in Turner and Turner, pp. 14–22, 27.

10James C. Conkling to Mercy Levering, September 21, 1840, Conkling-Levering Papers, ISHL; Elizabeth Todd Edwards, interviews, [1865–66] and July 27, 1887, in Wilson and Davis, pp. 443, 623.

11Mary Todd to Mercy Ann Levering, July 23, 1840, in Turner and Turner, p. 18.

12James C. Conkling to Mercy Levering, [summer 1840], quoted in Angle, *"Here I Have Lived,"* p. 93.

13Wilson, *Honor's Voice*, pp. 201, 213–14.

14James C. Conkling to Mercy Levering, September 21, 1840, Conkling-Levering Papers; Mary Todd to Mercy Ann Levering, December [15?], 1840, in Turner and Turner, p. 21.

15Elizabeth Edwards to Katherine Helm (undated), in Helm, *Mary, Wife of Lincoln*, p. 55.

[16] Elizabeth Todd Edwards, interview, [1865–66], in Wilson and Davis, p. 443; Mrs. ———, interview, Ida Tarbell, Ida Tarbell Collection, Allegheny College. Tarbell's interview notes with Mrs. John T. Stuart (Mary Nash Stuart) read: "Mrs. S. scoffs at the idea that Mr. L. was common or ordinary. Describes him as awkward, badly-dressed, lacked polish, but he was not common" (Ida Tarbell Collection).

[17] Milton Hay, interview with John Nicolay, quoted in Wilson, Honor's Voice, p. 210.

[18] W. H. Herndon to Jesse Weik, January 16, 1886, in Emanuel Hertz, The Hidden Lincoln: From the Letters and Papers of William H. Herndon (New York: Viking Press, 1938), p. 136; Mary Todd to Mercy Ann Levering, Springfield, December [15?], 1840 and June 1841, in Turner and Turner, pp. 19–22, 25–28.

[19] William Jayne to WHH, Springfield, August 17, 1887, in Wilson and Davis, p. 624; Mrs. Benjamin S. Edwards, interview with Ida Tarbell, Ida Tarbell Collection.

[20] Ida Tarbell, "Mary Todd Lincoln: The Wife of Abraham Lincoln," typescript, p. 18, Ida Tarbell Collection; Baker, Mary Todd Lincoln, p. 81; Wilson, Honor's Voice, p. 248.

[21] Milton Hay, interview, [ca. 1883–88], in Wilson and Davis, p. 729; WHH to Ward Hill Lamon, March 6, 1870, in Hertz, The Hidden Lincoln, p. 76.

[22] Joshua F. Speed, written statement, [by 1882], in Wilson and Davis, p. 590. Wilson, Honor's Voice, pp. 171, 92; AL to Mary S. Owens, Springfield, May 7, 1837, in LSW, 1832–1858, pp. 18–19.

[23] David Herbert Donald, Lincoln (New York: Simon & Schuster, 1995), p. 29; Wilson, Honor's Voice, p. 53; Mentor Graham to WHH, May 29, 1865, in Wilson and Davis, p. 11.

[24] Robert L. Wilson to WHH, February 10, 1866, in Wilson and Davis, p. 205; John T. Stuart, interview, [late June 1865], in Wilson and Davis, p. 64; W. H. Herndon, Life of Lincoln (1888; rpt. Cleveland: Fine Editions Press, 1949), p. 126.

[25] Donald, Lincoln, pp. 44–45; Wilson, Honor's Voice, pp. 87–90, 104–5; Henry McHenry, interview, [1866], in Wilson and Davis, p. 534. Stuart interview, [late June 1865], in Wilson and Davis, p. 64.

[26] For analyses of Lincoln's relationships with his father and Mary as well as a chronology of his depressions, see Burlingame, The Inner World, chaps. 2, 5, 9.

[27] Elizabeth Abell to WHH, February 15, 1867, in Wilson and Davis, p. 557; Mentor Graham, interview, April 2, 1866, in Wilson and Davis, p. 243.

[28] Wilson, Honor's Voice, pp. 174–79. Michael Burlingame alerted me to the existence of Lincoln's journalistic satire. AL to Mrs. Orville H. Browning, April 1, 1838, in LSW, 1832–1838, pp. 37–39.

[29] AL to Mary Owens, August 16, 1837, in LSW, 1832–1838, p. 20.

[30] AL to Mrs. Orville H. Browning, April 1, 1838, in ibid., pp. 37–39.

[31] Mary Owens Vineyard to WHH, May 23, 1866 and July 22, 1866, in Wilson and Davis, pp. 255–56, 262–63. On July 22 she wrote, "The last message I ever received from [Lincoln] was about a year after we parted in Illinois. Mrs. Able visited Ky. And he said to her in Springfield, Tell your Sister, that I think she was a great fool, because she did not marry me. Characteristic of the man."

[32] Frances Todd Wallace, quoted in Wilson, Honor's Voice, pp. 180–81; see also pp. 254, 173.

[33] John T. Stuart, interview, [1865–66], in Wilson and Davis, p. 481; Herndon, Life of Lincoln, pp. 150–51.

[34] According to Elizabeth Edwards, Lincoln "was charmed with Mary's wit and fascinated with her quick sagacity—her will—her nature—and Culture—I have happened in the room where they were sitting often & often and Mary led the conversation—Lincoln would listen & gaze on her as if drawn by a Superior power, irresistibly So: listened—never Scarcely Said a word" (interview, [1865–66], in Wilson and Davis, p. 443).

[35] Wilson, Honor's Voice, p. 216; Herndon, Life of Lincoln, p. 166.

[36] See Wilson, Honor's Voice, chaps. 7, 8, 9.

[37] Mary Owens Vineyard to WHH, July 22, 1866, in Wilson and Davis, p. 263.

[38]Quoted in Wilson, *Honor's Voice*, p. 209.

[39]Donald, *Lincoln*, pp. 104–6; Mary Todd to Mercy Ann Levering, July 23, 1840, in Turner and Turner, p. 16.

[40]Mary Todd to Mercy Ann Levering, July 23, 1840, in Turner and Turner, pp. 16–17.

[41]James C. Conkling to Mercy Levering, October 24, 1840, Conkling-Levering Papers.

[42]According to Wilson, Lincoln did not visit Mary in Missouri, as family tradition had it (*Honor's Voice*, p. 218; see also pp. 226–27); Mrs. Benjamin Edwards, interview, Ida Tarbell Collection.

[43]Wilson, *Honor's Voice*, p. 221; Mary Todd to Mercy Ann Levering, December [15?], 1840, in Turner and Turner, p. 22.

[44]Matilda married Newton D. Strong in 1844.

[45]Wilson believes that this special occasion is likely what family would remember as the wedding to which Lincoln never came; see *Honor's Voice*, p. 252. Joshua F. Speed, interview, [1865–66], in Wilson and Davis, p. 474.

[46]Joshua F. Speed, interview, [1865–66], in Wilson and Davis, pp. 474–77.

[47]Mary Todd to Mercy Ann Levering, December [15?], 1840, in Turner and Turner, p. 20.

[48]Wilson, *Honor's Voice*, pp. 225–26.

[49]Mary Todd to Mercy Ann Levering, December [15?], 1840, in Turner and Turner, pp. 20–21.

[50]Ibid., p. 22.

[51]AL to John T. Stuart, January 20, 1841 and January 23, 1841, in *LSW, 1832–1858*, pp. 68–69. Dr. Henry was thought to have persuaded Mary to write Lincoln a formal letter of release, although no letter survives. James C. Conkling to Mercy Ann Levering, January 24, 1841, Conkling-Levering Papers.

[52]Mrs. Jane D. Bell to Ann Bell, January 27, 1841, and Sarah Hardin to John J. Hardin, January 26, 1841, quoted in Wilson, *Honor's Voice*, pp. 236–41.

[53]Mrs. John T. Stuart, interview, Ida Tarbell Collection; Orville Browning quoted in Wilson, *Honor's Voice*, p. 243; Mary Todd to Mercy Ann Levering, June 1841, in Turner and Turner, p. 27. Helen Edwards told Ida Tarbell that she did "not think that Douglas ever courted Mrs. L any more than a number of young men who surrounded her" (Ida Tarbell Collection).

[54]Wilson, *Honor's Voice*, pp. 241–42; Mary Todd to Mercy Ann Levering, June 1841, in Turner and Turner, p. 27.

[55]Elizabeth Edwards, interview, [1865–66], in Wilson and Davis, p. 444; AL to Joshua F. Speed, March 27, 1842, in *LSW, 1832–1858*, p. 93.

[56]AL to Joshua F. Speed, February 25, 1842, in *LSW, 1832–1858*, p. 91.

[57]Lincoln was not forgotten, but he was right about the drift of the friendship after their marriages, though marriage was less the cause than his increasing emotional reserve and their differing politics. AL to Joshua F. Speed, ca. January 1842 and February 25, 1842, in *LSW, 1832–1858*, pp. 76–77, 90–91.

[58]AL to Joshua F. Speed, July 4, 1842, in *LSW, 1832–1858*, p. 95.

[59]For a fuller account of the Shields affair, see Wilson, *Honor's Voice*, pp. 265–83.

[60]AL to Joshua F. Speed, October 5, 1842, in *LSW, 1832–1858*, p. 104.

[61]James Matheny, interview, May 3, 1866, in Wilson and Davis, p. 252; Mrs. B. S. Edwards to Ida Tarbell, October 8, 1895, Ida Tarbell Collection; Mrs. William C. Sherwood [grandniece of Elizabeth Todd Grimsley Brown], statement, Ida Tarbell Collection.

[62]Herndon, *Life of Lincoln*, p. 180n.

[63]Mary Owens Vineyard to WHH, July 22, 1866, in Wilson and Davis, p. 262.

[1]The 1845 inventory lists "Aggy and her child John; Lizzy and her child George" among the slaves. Indenture of trust, October 31, 1845, Dinwiddie Deed Book 4, 1843–45 Library of Virginia.

[2]Anna Burwell to Mary Burwell, September 27, 1842; Mary Burwell to Frances K. Burwell, November 22, 1842; Anne E. Burwell to Frances K. Burwell, July 11, 1843, Burwell-Catlett Letters.

[3]Mary Burwell to Frances K. Burwell, November 22, 1842, Burwell-Catlett Letters.

[4]Ibid.; Mary Burwell to Frances K. Burwell, March 15, 1843; Mary Burwell to Frances K. Burwell, April 15, 1844, Burwell-Catlett Letters.

[5]Mary Burwell to Frances K. Burwell, June 12, 1844, Burwell-Catlett Letters.

[6]Elizabeth Margaret Burwell to Frances K. Burwell, July 6, 1843, Burwell-Catlett Letters.

[7]Elizabeth Hobbs to Frances K. Burwell, April 25, 1842, Burwell-Catlett Letters.

[8]At one time, Garland had political ambitions. He served five years in the Virginia State Legislature and was twice elected clerk of the House of Representatives, where his primary duty was to call the roll. But after he refused to call the names of five newly elected Whigs in a doomed attempt to secure Democratic control of the House (Democrats held one seat more than Whigs), he failed to be re-elected (in the words of a brother-in-law, he was "thrown higher than a Pine"). Charles Blair Burwell to Frances K. Burwell, June 20, 1841, Burwell-Catlett Letters.

[9]Indenture of Trust, October 31, 1845, Dinwiddie Deed Book 4, 1843–45, Library of Virginia; Mary Burwell to Frances Burwell Catlett, January 25, 1847, Burwell-Catlett Letters. At the age of thirty, Fanny married John W. Catlett, a widower with children.

[10]Mary Burwell to Frances K. Burwell, June 12, 1844; Mary Burwell to Frances Burwell Catlett, November 20, 1846, Burwell-Catlett Letters.

[11]Mary Burwell to Frances Burwell Catlett, January 25, 1847, Burwell-Catlett Letters.

[12]Mary Burwell to Frances K. Burwell, June 12, 1844; Mary Burwell to Frances Burwell Catlett, November 20, 1846, Burwell-Catlett Letters.

[13]Anne Burwell Garland to Frances Burwell Catlett, July 19, 1847, Burwell-Catlett Letters.

[14]Lebsock, *The Free Women of Petersburg*, pp. 87–111.

[15]Charles Dickens, *American Notes for General Circulation* (1842; rpt. New York: Penguin Books, 2000), p. 175; Garland's accident reported in Mary Burwell to Fanny Burwell Catlett, January 25, 1847, Burwell-Catlett Letters.

[16]Spotswood Garland to Caroline Garland, June 14, 1847, Garland Family Letters, Virginia Historical Society; Keckley, *Behind the Scenes*, p. 44.

[17]Anthony Trollope cited in Lloyd A. Hunter, "Slavery in St. Louis, 1804–1860," *Missouri Historical Society Bulletin* 30. 4 (July 1974): 233. In St. Louis in the 1850s there was a sharp decrease in the percentage of slaves in the population (p. 236).

[18]Cyprian Clamorgan, *The Colored Aristocracy of St. Louis* (1858), ed. Julie Winch (Columbia: University of Missouri Press, 1999), pp. 45–47, 60. Judy Day and M. James Kedro, "Free Blacks in St. Louis: Antebellum Conditions, Emancipation, and the Postwar Era," *Missouri Historical Society Bulletin* 30.2 (January 1974): 123.

[19]Act of General Assembly and List of Free Negroes Licensed by the County Court of St. Louis County, Dexter Tiffany Collection, Missouri Historical Society. An 1835 Free Negro Code required the licensing of all free blacks.

[20]Day and Kedro, "Free Blacks in St. Louis," pp. 118–19, 124. I have seen no primary evidence of Lizzy secretly teaching black children in St. Louis and she makes no mention of it in her book. Given

her character and situation, it seems unlikely that she would have violated the law and risked her own freedom at this time. Voodoo meetings in William Wells Brown, *My Southern Home: or, The South and Its People* (Boston: A.G. Brown & Co., 1880), p. 69.

[21]Brown, *Narrative of William Wells Brown*, p. 8.

[22]Louis S. Gerteis, *Civil War St. Louis* (Lawrence: University Press of Kansas, 2001), pp. 7–8.

[23]Abraham Lincoln, *Address to the Young Men's Lyceum*, January 27, 1838, in *LSW, 1832–1858*, p. 30.

[24]Gerteis, *Civil War St. Louis*, p. 30.

[25]Mary Burwell to Fanny Burwell Catlett, August 6, 1851, Burwell-Catlett Letters; November 30, 1849, property deed; January 11, 1848, deed selling Albert, St. Louis City, Deed Book, St. Louis Courthouse. Appraisement of Hugh A. Garland's property, Estate Records, St. Louis Courthouse. Census Records of 1850 (Missouri Historical Society) shows ten slaves (five females and five males, all mulatto) and eleven whites in the Garland household. They are Hugh and Anne; Mary with her new husband, Dr. Timothy Papin; Caroline; Fanny; Hugh Jr.; Ann; Margarette; Spottswood [*sic*]; and a newborn, Louis.

[26]ML to Elizabeth Dale Black, September 17, 1853, in Turner and Turner, p. 42.

[27]Solomon Sublette to France Sublette, February 22, 1851, Sublette Papers, Missouri Historical Society.

[28]Wendy Gamber, *The Female Economy: The Millinery and Dressmaking Trades, 1860–1930* (Urbana: University of Illinois Press, 1997), pp. 10, 127–28, 135. Kathryn E. Wilson, "Commodified Craft, Creative Community: Women's Vernacular Dress in Nineteenth-Century Philadelphia," in Barbara Burman, ed., *The Culture of Sewing: Gender, Consumption and Home Dressmaking* (Oxford: Berg, 1999), p. 150.

[29]Receipts in Sublette Papers.

[30]Claudia B. Kidwell, *Cutting a Fashionable Fit: Dressmakers' Drafting Systems in the United States* (Washington, DC: Smithsonian Institution Press, 1979).

[31]Gamber, *The Female Economy*, 129–31.

[32]Severa, *Dressed for the Photographer*, p. 96; Becky Rutberg, *Mary Lincoln's Dressmaker: Elizabeth Keckley's Remarkable Rise from Slave to White House Confidante* (New York: Walker and Company, 1995), pp. 40–41.

[33]Keckley, *Behind the Scenes*, p. 45–6.

[34]Ibid., p. 46.

[35]The Knights of Liberty, known by its members as the Knights of Tabor, was founded by twelve black activists in August 1846. They were active in the Underground Railroad and plotted a revolution against the South for July 1857, but their leader decided that "a higher power was preparing to take a part in the contest between North and South," and he called it off. Moses Dickson, *Manual of the International Order of Twelve of Knights and Daughters of Tabor containing general laws; regulations, ceremonies, drill and landmarks* (1891); rpt. in Herbert Aptheker, ed. *A Documentary History of the Negro People in the United States* (New York: Citadel Press, 1951), pp. 378–79. Edward Bates would become Lincoln's Attorney General and Montgomery Blair would become Dred Scott's attorney and later Lincoln's Postmaster General.

[36]Frederick Douglass, "Is It Right to Buy One's Freedom?" *The Liberator*, January 29, 1847. Original letter written to Henry C. Wright, December 22, 1846.

[37]Keckley, *Behind the Scenes*, p. 47.

[38]Ibid., p. 48.

[39]Ibid., p. 49.

[40]David M. Potter, *The Impending Crisis, 1848–1861* (New York: Harper & Row, 1976), pp. 18–23.

[41]Among the most famous of the famous Senate speeches made during the 1850 session was Daniel

Webster's Seventh of March Address: "I wish to speak to-day, not as a Massachusetts man, nor as a Northern man, but as an American. I speak to-day for the preservation of the Union. Hear me for my cause." Cited in James M. McPherson, *Battle Cry of Freedom* (New York: Ballantine Books, 1998), p. 71.

[42]Potter, *The Impending Crisis*, p. 98.

[43]McPherson, *Battle Cry of Freedom*, pp. 72–73.

[44]Don E. Fehrenbacher, *The Dred Scott Case: Its Significance in American Law and Politics* (New York: Oxford University Press, 1978), p. 177; Len Gougen and Joel Meyerson, eds., *Emerson's Antislavery Writings* (New Haven: Yale University Press, 1995), p. xxxix; "Resolutions by a Committee of Philadelphia Blacks" (October 14, 1850), originally published in *Pennsylvania Freeman*, October 31, 1850, rpt. in C. Peter Ripley et al., eds., *The Black Abolitionist Papers, Vol. 4, 1847–1858* (Chapel Hill: University of North Carolina Press, 1991), pp. 68–70. For descriptions of two early attempts to enforce the Fugitive Slave Law, see Gary Collison, *Shadrach Minkins: From Fugitive Slave to Citizen* (Cambridge, MA: Harvard University Press, 1997).

[45]Hugh A. Garland, *The Life of John Randolphe of Roanoke* (New York: D. Appleton & Company, 1850), 2: 127.

[46]Dred Scott Collection, Missouri State Archives, Washington University Libraries. One specific precedent was the 1837 decision in *Rachel v. Walker*, which established the legal principle in Missouri of "once free, always free" for slaves. See Fehrenbacher, *The Dred Scott Case*, for a full account of the case and its significance.

[47]Keckley, *Behind the Scenes*, p. 49. John F. A. Sanford was the son-in-law of Pierre Choteau, one of Garland's legal clients.

[48]Anne Garland to Frances Burwell Catlett, May 2, 1853, Burwell-Catlett Letters.

[49]Ibid.

[50]Ibid.

[51]Ibid.

[52]Keckley, *Behind the Scenes*, pp. 49.

[53]Ibid., p. 50.

[54]Miss Betty Kleckley Stradford of The National Council for Negro Women in Washington, D.C., a Keckly on both sides, believes that James Keckly may be her paternal great-grandfather. She dates his birth at about 1807–8, says he was white-skinned and that he must have remarried and had children after Elizabeth Keckly left him in 1860. Ann Lieberson, a descendant of free white Kackleys who remained in Virginia, is also interested in James Keckly on the chance that he was owned by and/or related to her ancestors. Family researchers believe that the Kackley/Keckley/Cackley families (and those spellings without an "e" before the "y") are related. I have been unable to locate any primary information on James Keckly.

[55]Anne Garland to Frances Burwell Catlett, January 28, 1854, Burwell-Catlett Letters; Anne Glasgow to Sarah Lane Glasgow, February 20, 1854, Lane Collection, Missouri Historical Society; Keckley, *Behind the Scenes*, p. 50.

[56]Fehrenbacher, *The Dred Scott Case*, p. 276.

[57]Anne P. Garland to Mary Burwell Garland, fragment, late October 1854, Garland Family Papers, Virginia Historical Society. Receipt in Estate of Hugh A. Garland, Esq., October 15, 1854, Estate Records, St. Louis Courthouse.

[58]Armistead Burwell to AL, August 28, 1863, cited in William C. Harris, *With Charity for All: Lincoln and the Restoration of the Union* (Lexington: University of Kentucky Press, 1977), p. 125.

[59]Keckley, *Behind the Scenes*, pp. 50, 56–59.

[60]Ibid., pp. 51–53.

[61]Ibid., pp. 54–55.

[62]Ellen M. Doan is the only other benefactor named. Doan lived with her husband, a dry goods clerk, and their three children and sent Lizzy notes amounting to $100 and $25 in cash. Keckley, *Behind the Scenes*, pp. 56–57; St. Louis City Directory, 1860, Missouri Historical Society.

[63]Ibid., pp. 57–63; Freedom Papers in Missouri Historical Society; Statement of Mrs. Elizabeth Keckly, in application for a War Pension, April 18, 1863, National Archives.

[64]"List of Free Negroes Licensed by the County Court of St. Louis County," Tiffany Collection, Missouri Historical Society.

CHAPTER SEVEN

[1]Judith Peterson, "Secret of an Unhappy Incident," *Illinois Junior Historian* 5 (February 1952): 91. Other contemporaries corroborate Mary's temper and inclination to hurl objects at her husband.

[2]AL to Joshua Speed, Springfield, May 18, 1843, in *LSW, 1832–1858*, pp. 109–111; AL to Richard S. Thomas, February 14, 1843, in *LSW, 1832–1858*, pp. 105–6.

[3]James Conkling to Mercy Levering Conkling, April 18, 1853, Conkling-Levering Papers. Several close friends recalled Lincoln's compulsion for dirty stories, but one example will suffice: "Lincoln had 2 characters—one of *purity*—& the other as it were an insane love in telling dirty and Smutty stories." H. E. Dummer interview with WHH, 1865–66, in Wilson and Davis, pp. 442–43. See also Douglas L. Wilson, "Keeping Lincoln's Secrets," *Atlantic Monthly* 285.5 (May 2000): 78–88.

[4]ML to Sally Orne, October 23, 1869, in Turner and Turner, p. 520; Louis Menand, *The Metaphysical Club* (New York: Farrar, Straus and Giroux, 2001), p. 6.

[5]Robert Smith Todd's gift was over and above the eighty acres of land valued at $400 and annual income of about $120 he gave Mary. See *Todd heirs vs. Todd administrators and heirs*, RST Papers.

[6]Helm, *Mary, Wife of Lincoln*, p. 96; Julia Trumbull to Lyman Trumbull, May 10, 1844, Lyman Trumbull Family Papers, ISHL; Sophie Bledsoe Herrick, "Personal Recollections of My Father and Mr. Lincoln and Mr. Davis," *Methodist Review* (April 1915): 666–79.

[7]The 1850 census records the Edwards household as having "two Irish-born servants, a laborer, and two Kentucky slaves," one of whom was probably Aunt Epsy Smith; see Baker, *Mary Todd Lincoln*, p. 105; "She Worked for Lincoln: Death of a Negress Who Knew Much About Father Abraham," May 10, 1892, unidentified clipping, Michael R. Maîone Files, Ford's Theatre.

[8]Henry B. Stanton, cited in Michael Burlingame, *Life of Lincoln* (Baltimore: Johns Hopkins University Press, forthcoming), chap. 6; I am grateful to Professor Burlingame for making his manuscript available to me. Mary Todd Lincoln interview with WHH, September 1866, in Wilson and Davis, p. 357.

[9]ML to Mary Jane Welles, October 14, 1865, in Turner and Turner, p. 277; on dress, see Bushman, *The Refinement of America*, p. 70; Earl Schenck Miers, ed., *Lincoln Day by Day: A Chronology, 1809–1865*, 1:207; Baker, *Mary Todd Lincoln*, p. 133; Harry Pratt, ed., "The Lincolns Go Shopping," *Illinois State Historical Journal* 47.1 (1955): 66.

[10]Emilie Todd Helm, interview with Jesse Weik, 22 March 1887, in Wilson and Davis, p. 612; James Gourley, interview with WHH, 1865–66, in Wilson and Davis, p. 453.

[11]Harriet Chapman, interview with Jesse Weik, 1886–87, in Wilson and Davis, p. 646. Herndon elaborates on this interview in his *Life of Lincoln*, p. 345. For the view of the Lincoln marriage as "a fountain of misery, of a quality absolutely infernal," which is how Lincoln's closest friends saw it, see Burlingame, *The Inner World*, chap. 9. For an opposing view, see Baker, *Mary Todd Lincoln*; WHH to Jesse Weik, December 1, 1885, in Hertz, *The Hidden Lincoln*, p. 109; Harriet Chapman to WHH, November 21, 1866, in Wilson and Davis, p. 407.

[12]Bushman, *The Refinement of America*, p. 276; Shaw letter, 27 April 1861, cited in Burlingame, *Life of Lincoln*, chap. 6, n. 85. Lincoln's rejection of elements of the male frontier culture is discussed in William Lee Miller, *Lincoln's Virtues: An Ethical Biography* (New York: Knopf, 2002).

[13]Helm, *Mary, Wife of Lincoln*, p. 116.

[14]AL to Joshua Speed, May 18, 1843, in *LSW, 1832–1858*, pp. 109–11; Elizabeth Todd Edwards interview with WHH, in Wilson and Davis, p. 444. Wilson and Davis speculate that "houses" should be "horses."

[15]James H. Matheny interview with WHH, May 3, 1866, in Wilson and Davis, p. 251.

[16]Mary Todd Lincoln interview with WHH, September 1866, in Wilson and Davis, p. 358; ML to Hannah Shearer, June 26, 1859, in Turner and Turner, p. 57.

[17]Herndon, *Life of Lincoln*, p. 215.

[18]Harriet A. Chapman interview with WHH, 1886–87, in Wilson and Davis, p. 646.

[19]Miers, *Lincoln Day by Day*, 1:219–43.

[20]Ibid., 1:250, 257–58, 264–81.

[21]James Conkling and Mercy Levering Conkling to her mother, January 18, 1843, Conkling-Levering Papers; Ida Tarbell, *The Life of Abraham Lincoln* (1895; New York: Macmillan Company, 1917), 1:242; Walter Stevens, *A Reporter's Lincoln*, ed. Michael Burlingame (Lincoln: University of Nebraska Press, 1998), pp. 33–34.

[22]Julia Trumbull to Lyman Trumbull, May 10 and May 13, 1844, Lyman Trumbull Family Papers, ISHL, " 'Took Tea at Mrs. Lincoln's': The Diary of Mrs. William M. Black," *Illinois State Historical Society Journal* 48.1 (1955): 59–64, entries for February 17, 23, and March 29, 1852; James Gourley interview with WHH, 1865–66, in Wilson and Davis, p. 453.

[23]ML to Hannah Shearer, January 1, 1860, in Turner and Turner, p. 62; ML to Mark Delahay, May 25, 1860, in Turner and Turner, p. 64; Ida M. Tarbell, "Mary Todd Lincoln: The Wife of Abraham Lincoln," *Ladies' Home Journal*, February 1828, Ida Tarbell Collection; WHH to Jesse Weik, February 18, 1887, in Hertz, *The Hidden Lincoln*, pp. 176–77.

[24]Elizabeth A. Capps, cited in Burlingame, *The Inner World*, p. 62.

[25]AL to Joshua F. Speed, October 22, 1846, in *LSW, 1832–1858*, p. 145.

[26]Gourley interview with Herndon, 1865–66, in Wilson and Davis, p. 453; Harriet A. Chapman to WHH, November 21, 1866, in Wilson and Davis, p. 407; WHH to Jesse Weik, January 8, 1886, in Hertz, *The Hidden Lincoln*, p. 129.

[27]AL to Joshua F. Speed, October 22, 1846, in *LSW, 1832–1858*, pp. 143–45. Lincoln had just returned from a sad visit to his Indiana home, where his mother and sister were buried, had written a poem inspired by his mournful feelings, and rediscovered his favorite poem, "Why Should the Spirit of Mortal Be Proud?" Eliza Leslie, *Miss Leslie's Directions for Cookery* (1837; new ed. 1851, with new preface; New York: Dover Publications, 1999), p. 7.

[28]David Davis to Sarah Walker Davis, August 8, 1847, David Davis Papers, ISHL.

[29]Lloyd Ostendorf, *The Photographs of Mary Lincoln* (Springfield: Illinois Historic Preservation Agency, 1989), pp. 274–77.

[30]Helm, *Mary, Wife of Lincoln*, pp. 101–2.

[31]Ibid., p. 101; Burlingame, *Life of Lincoln*, chap. 7.

[32]AL to Joshua Speed, August 24, 1855, in *LSW, 1832–1858*, pp. 360–63; Helm, *Mary, Wife of Lincoln*, p. 103.

[33]Burlingame, *Life of Lincoln*, chap. 7; Donald, *Lincoln*, p. 119.

[34]Constance McLaughlin Green, *Washington: Village and Capital, 1800–1878* (Princeton: Princeton University Press, 1962), pp. 150–54; Miers, *Lincoln Day by Day* 1:299, 304; Donald, *Lincoln*, p. 120; Eric Lott, *Love and Theft: Blackface Minstrelsy and the American Working Class* (New York: Oxford University Press, 1995).

[35]Donald, *Lincoln*, p. 120; Green, *Washington*, pp. 150–54; Miers, *Lincoln Day by Day* 1:139, 170.

[36]Donald, *Lincoln*, p. 121; Herndon, *Life of Lincoln*, p. 212; "Spot" Resolutions in *LSW, 1832–1858*, pp. 158–59.

[37]AL to WHH, February 1, 1848, in *LSW, 1832–1858*, pp. 172–73; Baker, *Mary Todd Lincoln*, p. 140; AL to ML, April 16, 1848, in *LSW, 1832–1858*, p. 181.

[38]Baker, *Mary Todd Lincoln*, p. 141; Tarbell, *The Life of Abraham Lincoln*, 1:207–8; Green, *Washington*, p. 155.

[39]Varina Howell Davis to Margaret Howell, January 6, 1850, in Hudson Strode, ed., *Jefferson Davis: Private Letters 1823–1889* (New York: De Capo Press, 1995), p. 59; Donald, *Lincoln*, p. 135. One day after Mary left, three armed men burst into the boardinghouse to arrest the waiter after his master changed his mind about selling him.

[40]Dr. Samuel C. Busey, cited in Tarbell, *The Life of Abraham Lincoln* 1:208; Baker, *Mary Todd Lincoln*, p. 141.

[41]AL to ML, April 16, 1848, in *LSW, 1832–1858*, p. 182.

[42]Ibid.

[43]Ibid.; AL to ML, July 2, 1848, in *LSW, 1832–1858*, p. 203.

[44]AL to ML, April 16, 1848, in *LSW, 1832–1858*, pp. 181–82.

[45]Ibid.

[46]Ibid.

[47]AL to ML, June 12, 1848, in *LSW, 1832–1858*, p. 186; Keckley, *Behind the Scenes*, pp. 235–36; see Burlingame, *The Inner World*, pp. 307–8.

[48]AL to ML, July 2, 1848, in *LSW, 1832–1858*, p. 203. On Lincoln as surrogate father to others besides his wife, see Burlingame, *The Inner World*, pp. 73–91. Burlingame also covers Lincoln's fatherly relation to the childlike Mary (*The Inner World*, pp. 295–96).

[49]ML to AL, May 1848, in Turner and Turner, p. 38; AL to ML, July 2, 1848, in *LSW, 1832–1858*, p. 202.

[50]Neely, *The Abraham Lincoln Encyclopedia*, Hardin entry, pp. 139–40.

[51]Donald, *Lincoln*, p. 135.

[52]AL to C. U. Schlater, January 5, 1849, in *LSW, 1832–1858*, p. 226.

[53]Herndon, *Life of Lincoln*, p. 240.

[54]Ibid., pp. 246–47.

[55]Mrs. John Stuart interview with Ida B. Tarbell, Tarbell Collection; Baker, *Mary Todd Lincoln*, pp. 126–27; ML to Margaret Wickcliffe Preston, July 23, 1853, clipping, ISHL.

[56]Baker, *Mary Todd Lincoln*, pp. 128–29, 270.

[57]ML to Rhoda White, May 2, 1868, in Turner and Turner, pp. 475–77. I am indebted to Dr. Norbert Hirschhorn for the diagnosis of diabetes. See Hirschhorn and Robert G. Feldman, "Mary Lincoln's Final Illness: A Medical and Historical Reappraisal," *Journal of the History of Medicine* 54 (October 1999): 511–42. Baker has reasoned that Mary suffered damage to her urethra during Tad's birth (*Mary Todd Lincoln*, p. 270).

[58]Donald, *Lincoln*, p. 159. Herndon saw Lincoln as "woman-whipped and woman-carved." WHH to Jesse Weik, January 8, 1886. Lincoln pulling the wagon in Herndon to Weik, November 19, 1885.

[59]ML to Emilie Todd Helm, November 23, 1856, in Turner and Turner, p. 47.

[60]ML interview with WHH, September 1866, in Wilson and Davis, pp. 358–61; AL to John D. Johnston, January 12, 1851, in *LSW, 1832–1858*, pp. 255–56.

[61]Herndon, *Life of Lincoln*, p. 238.

[62]Potter, *The Impending Crisis*, p. 165 and chap. 7.

[63]AL to Jesse Fell, December 20, 1859, in *LSW, 1859–1865*, p. 108; AL, "Eulogy on Henry Clay," July 6, 1852, in *LSW, 1859–1865*, p. 267.

[64]John T. Stuart interview with WHH, 1865–66, in Wilson and Davis, p. 482.

[65]Baker, *Mary Todd Lincoln*, p. 146; Donald, *Lincoln*, p. 170.

[66]Frederick Douglass, October 1854 speech, cited in David W. Blight, *Frederick Douglass' Civil War: Keeping Faith in Jubilee* (Baton Rouge: Louisiana State University Press, 1989), p. 46.

[67]William S. McFeely, *Frederick Douglass* (New York: Norton, 1991), p. 188.

[68]Lincoln, Speech on Kansas-Nebraska Act, October 4 and 16, 1864, in *LSW, 1832–1858*, p. 339.

[69]In Blight, *Frederick Douglass' Civil War*, p. 47.

[70]Lincoln-Douglas Debates, Seventh Debate: Lincoln's Reply, October 15, 1858, in *LSW, 1832–1858*, pp. 810–11. See also Burlingame, *The Inner World*, chap 2.

[71]Mrs. B. S. Edwards in interview with Ida Tarbell, undated, Tarbell Collection.

[72]ML to Hannah Shearer, October 2, 1859 and January 1, 1860, in Turner and Turner, pp. 59, 61. Herndon believed that Mary Lincoln was "decidedly pro-slavery in her views. . . . 'If ever my husband dies,' she . . . [said], 'his spirit will never find me living outside the limits of a slave State' " (Herndon, *Life of Lincoln*, p. 343).

[73]ML to Emilie Todd Helm, November 23, 1856, in Turner and Turner, p. 46.

[74]AL to Joshua F. Speed, August 24, 1855, in *LSW, 1832–1858*, p. 363.

[75]Lincoln, October 16, 1854, "Speech on Kansas-Nebraska Act," in ibid., p. 316.

[76]Burwell, *A Girl's Life in Virginia*, pp. 53–54.

[77]Wayne C. Temple, "Ruth Stanton Recalls the Lincolns," *Lincoln Herald* 90 (Fall 1990), pp. 88–92. John S. Goff, *Robert Todd Lincoln: A Man in His Own Right* (Norman: University of Oklahoma Press, 1968), p. 11; Baker, *Mary Todd Lincoln*, p. 107; "Worked for Lincoln; Tells of Home Life: Little Portuguese Woman, Resident Here over Fifty Years, Relates Story," *Springfield Illinois News*, January 23, 1909. Harriet Hanks Chapman interview with Ida Tarbell, October 16, 1914, Ida Tarbell Collection; Wayne Temple, *By Square and Compasses: The Building of Lincoln's Home and Its Saga* (Bloomington, IL: Ashlar Press, 1984), p. 65. Eighteen-year-old Catherine Gordon lived with the Lincolns in 1850.

[78]Mrs. Mary Gaughan in "Lincoln's Domestic Life," *Chicago Herald*, August 30, 1896. Margaret Ryan interview with WHH, October 27, 1886, in Wilson and Davis, pp. 596–97; Elizabeth Todd Edwards interview with WHH, 1865–66, in Wilson and Davis, p. 445.

[79]Donald, *Lincoln*, p. 171.

[80]Baker, *Mary Todd Lincoln*, p. 148; AL to Richard Yates, January 14, 1855, in *LSW, 1832–1858*, p. 354.

[81]AL to Elihu B. Washburne, February 9, 1855, in *LSW, 1832–1858*, p. 355; AL to William H. Henderson, February 21, 1855, in *LSW, 1832–1858*, p. 357.

[82]ML to Hannah Shearer, June 26, 1859, in Turner and Turner, pp. 56–57. Julia Trumbull to Lyman Trumbull, April 14, 1856; Lyman Trumbull to Julia Trumbull, April 25, 1856, Lyman Trumbull Family Papers.

[83]Julia Trumbull to Lyman Trumbull, April 6, 1856, Lyman Trumbull Family Papers.

[84]Mary G. Chandler, *The Elements of Character* (1854; Boston: Crosby, Nichols, and Company, 1856), in University of Illinois Collection; notes and excerpts from Lincoln copy in Tarbell Collection.

[85]ML to Emilie Todd Helm, February 16, 1857, in Turner and Turner, pp. 48–49.

[86]Stephen Whitehurst interview with WHH, 1885–89, in Wilson and Davis, p. 722.

[87]Sarah Sleeper to her mother, June 1865, Sleeper Papers, ISHL; Michael Burlingame alerted me to this letter. Elizabeth Edwards interview with WHH, 1865–66, in Wilson and Davis, p. 444.

[88]*Godey's Lady's Book*, 1844 and 1842, cited in Pamela Herr, *Jessie Benton Fremont: American Woman of the 19th Century* (New York: Franklin Watts, 1987)

[89]ML to Elizabeth Todd Grimsley, September 21, 1861, in Turner and Turner, p. 103.

CHAPTER EIGHT

[1]*The Slavery Code of the District of Columbia* (1862), LC, Law Library, Digital Collection. Two years later, Democratic Mayor Berret would be arrested as a secessionist.

[2]Keckley, *Behind the Scenes*, p. 77.

[3]Green, *Washington*, p. 228.

[4]Julia Taft Bayne, *Tad Lincoln's Father* (1931; Lincoln: University of Nebraska Press, 2001), pp. 22–23. Sixteen years old when the Lincolns came to Washington, Julia Taft was in some ways the daughter the Lincolns never had but wished for.

[5]McPherson, *Battle Cry of Freedom*, pp. 145–53, Sumner cited on 149; David Herbert Donald, *Charles Sumner* (New York: Da Capo Press, 1996), pp. 294–95. Originally 2 vols.: *Charles Sumner and the Coming of the Civil War* (1960) and *Charles Sumner and the Rights of Man* (1970).

[6]McPherson, *Battle Cry*, pp. 150–51, 153.

[7]Miers, *Lincoln Day by Day*, 2:189; McPherson, *Battle Cry*, pp. 158–59.

[8]McPherson, pp. 170–76; "List of Free Negroes," Tiffany Collection, Missouri Historical Society.

[9]Fanny Garland to Fanny Burwell Catlett, August 26, 1858, Burwell-Catlett Letters.

[10]War Pension Application, "Statement of Mrs. Elizabeth Keckley [*sic*]," National Archives; Willard B. Gatewood, *Aristocrats of Color* (Bloomington: Indiana University Press, 1990), p. 251.

[11]ML to Emilie Todd Helm, February 16, 1857, and September 20, 1857, in Turner and Turner, pp. 48–51.

[12]McPherson, *Battle Cry of Freedom*, pp. 178–80; "House Divided" Speech at Springfield, Illinois, June 16, 1856, in *LSW, 1832–1858*, p. 426.

[13]McPherson, *Battle Cry of Freedom*, pp. 182, 188.

[14]Stephen Douglas's Reply, Second Debate, August 27, 1858, in *LSW, 1832–1858*, p. 556; Fourth Debate, September 18, 1858, Douglas's Reply, p. 666; Fourth Debate, Lincoln's Speech, pp. 636–37.

[15]McFeely, *Frederick Douglass*, p. 208; Douglass, "My British Antislavery Friends" (May 26, 1860) and "The Dred Scott Decision," quoted in Blight, *Frederick Douglass' Civil War*, pp. 52–53, 48. See also Maria Diedrich, *Love across the Color Lines: Ottilie Assing and Frederick Douglass* (New York: Hill and Wang, 1999).

[16]McPherson, *Battle Cry of Freedom*, p. 232.

[17]Ibid., pp. 229–30.

[18]Ibid., pp. 209–10.

[19]In Keckly's memoir, Hetzell is misspelled "Hetsill."

[20]W. E. B. Du Bois, *The Souls of Black Folk* (1903; rpt. New York: Library of America, 1986).

[21]Later, Lizzy boarded with Virginia's sister, Mary, and her husband, Robert Booker, a barber. Virginia and Mary's father was the slave of a Secretary of War to Andrew Jackson and their mother was a free woman. The Lewis family is listed as white in the 1870 census. Census data from 1860 census. Constance Green, *The Secret City: A History of Race Relations in the Nation's Capital* (Princeton: Princeton University Press, 1967), p. 50; see also James Borchert, *Alley Life in Washington: Family, Community, Religion, and Folklife in the City, 1850–1970* (Urbana: University of Illinois Press, 1982).

[22]Union Bethel Church Records, Cook Family Papers, Moorland-Spingarn Research Center, Howard University; John E. Washington, *They Knew Lincoln* (New York: Dutton, 1942), p. 47; Mary Logan Hay to Milton Hay, Washington, April 6, 1861, Stuart-Hay Papers, ISHL.

[23]Elizabeth Blair Lee to Samuel Phillips Lee, Silver Spring, December 5, 1860, in Virginia Jean Laas, ed., *Wartime Washington: The Civil War Letters of Elizabeth Blair Lee* (Urbana: University of Illinois Press, 1991), p. 14; Donald, *Lincoln*, p. 256; Green, *Washington*, p. 230; Jefferson Davis to George Lunt, Washington, January 17, 1861, in Lynda Lasswell Crist and Mary Seaton Dix, eds., *The Papers of Jefferson Davis* (Baton Rouge: Louisiana State University Press, 1992), 7:14.

[24]Charles S. Zane statement for WHH, 1865–66, in Wilson and Davis, p. 491; Donald, *Lincoln*, p. 256; Stevens, *A Reporter's Lincoln*, p. 95; Tarbell, *The Life of Abraham Lincoln*, 1:404–5.

[25]E. B. Long with Barbara Long, *The Civil War Day by Day: An Almanac 1861–1865* (New York: Da Capo Press, 1971), p. 28.

[26]Keckley, *Behind the Scenes*, pp. 66–67.

[27]Ibid., pp. 66–68.

[28]Jefferson Davis to Varina Davis, Montgomery, Alabama, February 20, 1861, in Crist and Dix, *The Papers of Jefferson Davis*, 7:53–54.

[29]Horatio N. Taft Diary, entries for January 5, 7, 9, and 11, 1861, LC, Manuscripts Division. John Sellers generously made the Taft diary available to me.

[30]Keckley, *Behind the Scenes*, p. 70; Varina Howell Davis to Jefferson Davis, Washington, November 15, 1860, in Crist and Dix, *The Papers of Jefferson Davis*, 6:371.

[31]Keckley, *Behind the Scenes*, pp. 71–72; Eric Foner and Olivia Mahoney, *A House Divided: America in the Age of Lincoln* (New York: Norton, 1990), p. 74; Elizabeth Blair Lee to Samuel Phillips Lee, Silver Spring, December 5, 1860, in Laas, *Wartime Washington*, p. 14.

[32]Keckley, *Behind the Scenes*, pp. 72–3.

[33][Albert Hale] to [Theron Baldwin], May 31, 1860, in Burlingame, *The Inner World*, p. 278; Mercy Levering Conkling to Clinton Conkling, January 19, 1861, Conkling-Levering Papers.

[34]Robert Todd Lincoln to ML, December 2, 1860, in Helm, *Mary, Wife of Lincoln*, p. 154; *Frank Leslie's Illustrated Newspaper*, January 26, 1861; New York *Tribune*, January 14, 1861.

[35]ML to David Davis, New York, January 17, 1861, in Turner and Turner, p. 71.

[36]Jeannie H. James and Wayne C. Temple, "Mrs. Lincoln's Clothing," *Lincoln Herald* 62.2 (summer 1960): 57.

[37]Interview with J. McDan Davis, Inauguration File, Tarbell Collection; Burlingame, *The Inner World*, p. 282. During the stop in Westfield, New York, Lincoln sought out Grace Bedell, the little girl who wrote him suggesting he grow a beard, and kissed her.

[38]Keckley, *Behind the Scenes*, p. 131.

[39]William Howard Russell, *My Diary North and South* (London: Bradbury & Evans, 1863), 1:46–48.

[40]Keckley, *Behind the Scenes*, chap. 5. Thanks to Susan Greenhagen and to Charles H. Sumner for providing biographical information on Mrs. McLean.

[41]Lizzy Keckly later sold this gown's bodice through W. H. Lowdermilk and Co., a secondhand dealer, to Charles F. Gunther, a Chicago candy manufacturer and collector. The items are now in the Gunther Collection at the Chicago Historical Society.

[42]William Jayne, interview with Ida Tarbell, 1898, Tarbell Collection; Tarbell, *The Life of Abraham Lincoln*, 2:1–3.

[43]Keckley, *Behind the Scenes*, pp. 81–82.

[44]ML to Elizabeth Todd Grimsley, September 29, 1861, in Turner and Turner, p. 104.

[45]"If I cannot be President, I can at least be his hatbearer," the loyal Douglas said. Elizabeth Todd Grimsley, "Six Months in the White House," *Journal of the Illinois State Historical Society* 19:3–4 (October 1926–January 1927): 44.

[46]"Douglass' Monthly," March 1861, in Michael Meyer, ed., *Frederick Douglass: The Narrative and Selected Writings* (New York: Modern Library, 1984), pp. 369–71.

[47]McPherson, *Battle Cry of Freedom*, pp. 262–63; Blight, *Frederick Douglass' Civil War*, pp. 78–79. McPherson argues that contemporaries saw "what they wished or expected to see" in Lincoln's address. Republicans saw firmness, Confederates a declaration of war.

[48]Keckley, *Behind the Scenes*, p. 83.

CHAPTER NINE

[1]Washington, *They Knew Lincoln*, pp. 122–23.

[2]Keckley, *Behind the Scenes*, pp. 83–84.

[3]Virginia Clay, *A Belle of the Fifties: Memoirs of Mrs. Clay of Alabama* (New York, 1904), p. 92.

[4]The first seamstress was probably Mrs. Albina M. Labarthe, the town's leading milliner and dressmaker. ML to Hannah Shearer, April 24, 1859, in Turner and Turner, p. 55; Mrs. Snell anecdote in testimony of H. E. Barker in files of Tarbell Collection. Keckley, *Behind the Scenes*, pp. 84–85.

[5]Mary Brooks Picken, *A Dictionary of Costume and Fashion: Historic and Modern* (1957; rpt. Mineola, NY: Dover Publications, 1999), p. 225.

[6]Interview with Elizabeth Keckly in "Servant of the Lincolns. Aged Negress Once Seamstress at the White House," *Washington Post*, October 14, 1900. Compare with Keckley, *Behind the Scenes*, pp. 83–90. Keckly remembered the levee as being postponed from Friday to the following Tuesday, but according to newspaper reports, Mary looked resplendent in her "Magenta (brilliant red) watered silk" that Friday, and she and the President hosted a formal dinner party on Tuesday, making it unclear which occasion Lizzy meant.

[7]ML to Mary Brayman, June 17, 1861, in Turner and Turner, p. 90; Washington, *They Knew Lincoln*, p. 118.

[8]Gatewood, *Aristocrats of Color*; Green, *The Secret City*, pp. 65–68.

[9]Washington, *They Knew Lincoln*, p. 225. As Pauli Murray's grandmother told her, "Hold your head up high and don't take a back seat to nobody. You got blood in you—folks that counted for something. . . . Aristocrats, that's what they were, going back seven generations right in this state" (Murray, *Proud Shoes*, p. 33).

[10]Washington, *They Knew Lincoln*, pp. 127–29; Neely, *The Abraham Lincoln Encyclopedia*, p. 54; Johnson's annual salary was $600; an army private was paid $13 per month, which came to $676 annually, plus "room" and board.

[11]Helm, *Mary, Wife of Lincoln*, p. 185.

[12]*Harper's Weekly*, March 2, 1861, p. 135; Mark E. Neely Jr., "The Secret Treason of AL's Brother-in-Law," *Journal of the Abraham Lincoln Association* 17.1 (1996); New York *Tribune*, March 28, 1864; John G. Nicolay to General Benjamin F. Butler, April 19, 1864; New York *Tribune*, April 27, 1864. Material on Martha Todd White in William Townsend file, UKSC.

[13]Keckley, *Behind the Scenes*, p. 136.

[14]Mrs. Roger A. Pryor, *Reminiscences of Peace and War* (New York, 1905); Rose O'Neal Greenhow, *My Imprisonment and the First Year of Abolition Rule at Washington* (London: Richard Bentley, 1863), p. 51.

[15]Russell, *My Diary*, p. 61; Keckley, *Behind the Scenes*, 89.

[16]John B. Blake to Harriet Lane, March 11, 1861, in Harriet Lane Papers, LC; Green, *Washington*, pp. 269–70.

[17]Bayne, *Tad Lincoln's Father*, pp. 18–20.

[18]Turner and Turner, p. 114; *Illinois State Register*, October 30, 1864, p. 2. Keckly, like the dressmaker she was, remembered exactly what each lady in the Lincoln party was wearing that night; see *Behind the Scenes*, pp. 88–89.

[19]ML to Hannah Shearer, March 28, 1861, and August 1, 1861, in Turner and Turner, pp. 82, 96.

[20]Grimsley, "Six Months in the White House," p. 48.

[21]In Washington for the inauguration were Mrs. Elizabeth Todd Edwards and daughters Julia Edwards Baker and Elizabeth Edwards; cousin Mrs. Elizabeth Todd Grimsley; her brothers, Lockwood Todd and John B. S. Todd; half-sister Mrs. Margaret Todd Kellogg; brother Levi Todd; half-sister Emilie Helm and her husband, Ben Hardin Helm; brother-in-law Dr. William H. Wallace; and half-sister Martha Todd White. Elizabeth Todd Grimsley to John Stuart, March 20, 1861, and May 24, 1861, in Mrs. Elizabeth Grimsley Files, ISHL.

[22]ML to Hannah Shearer, July 11, 1861, in Turner and Turner, p. 94.

[23]Elizabeth Blair Lee to Samuel Phillip Lee, Silver Spring, July 11, 1861, note added July 15 and December 17, 1860, in Laas, *Wartime Washington*, pp. 61, 18.

[24]McPherson, *Battle Cry of Freedom*, pp. 285–86; Taft Diary, April 22, 1861, LC.

[25]Taft Diary, April 24, 1861; Miers, *Lincoln Day by Day*, 3:37.

[26]Taft Diary, April 25, 1861, May 9, 1861, and May 14, 1861, LC; Green, *Washington*, p. 242; Green, *Secret City*, p. 57.

[27]Tarbell, *Life of Lincoln*, pp. 52–53; Taft Diary, May 24, 1861, LC; Turner and Turner, p. 92; Mary Panzer, *Mathew Brady and the Image of History* (Washington, DC: Smithsonian Institution Press, 1997), pp. 101–2.

[28]Neely, *The Abraham Lincoln Encyclopedia*, p. 88.

[29]"Forward to Richmond" had been the battle cry of Horace Greeley's *Tribune* for over a month (McPherson, *Battle Cry of Freedom*, p. 341). Originally, "John Brown's Body" was not composed for the martyred abolitionist, but for a Sergeant John Brown of Boston, whose regiment improvised words with his name to an old Methodist tune, "Say, Brothers Will You Meet Us?" Irwin Silber, *Songs of the Civil War* (1960; rpt. New York: Dover Publications, 1995), p. 11.

[30]McPherson, *Battle Cry of Freedom*, p. 344.

[31]Keckly interview, "Servant of Lincolns"; Keckley, *Behind the Scenes*, p. 86.

[32]ML to Ruth Harris, November 21, 1861, and May 1862, in Turner and Turner, pp. 115, 126–27.

[33]Washington, *They Knew Lincoln*, p. 77.

[34]Baker, *Mary Todd Lincoln*, p. 182.

[35]Ibid., p. 182.

[36]During the 1860s, Stewart was the wealthiest resident in the city. David B. Sicilia, entry on A. T. Stewart in Kenneth T. Jackson, ed., *The Encyclopedia of New York City* (New Haven: Yale University Press, 1995), pp. 1123–24.

[37]Bayne, *Tad Lincoln's Father*, pp. 20, 14.

[38]Miers, *Lincoln Day by Day*, 3:42–64; Burlingame, *The Inner World*, pp. 298–344; Turner and Turner, pp. 88–89; Baker, *Mary Todd Lincoln*, pp. 185–88; Ernest A. McKay, *The Civil War and New York City* (Syracuse: Syracuse University Press, 1990), p. 9; *New York Commercial Advertiser*, November 16, 1861; ML to Elizabeth Todd Grimsley, September 29, 1861, in Turner and Turner, p. 106.

[39]Miers, *Lincoln Day by Day*, 3:42–64; Burlingame, *The Inner World*, pp. 298–344.

[40]Turner and Turner, p. 88; "The President Talked to by a Strong-Minded Woman," *New York Express*, in *The Crisis* (Columbus, Ohio), October 10, 1861.

[41]Lydia Maria Child to Lucy Searle, October 11, 1861, in Louis P. Masur, *"The Real War Will Never Get in the Books": Selections from Writers During the Civil War* (New York: Oxford University Press, 1993), p. 47.

[42]Keckley, *Behind the Scenes*, p. 149.

[43]Michael Burlingame, "Honest Abe, Dishonest Mary," *Bulletin of the 54th Annual Meeting of The Lincoln Fellowship of Wisconsin*, Racine, WI, Historical Bulletin Number 50, 1994, pp. 11–15; ML to Caleb B. Smith, September 8, 1861, in Turner and Turner, p. 102; ML to John F. Potter, September 13, 1861, in Turner and Turner, p. 104.

[44]Keckley, *Behind the Scenes*, p. 90; "Military Arrests," *National Intelligencer*, August 26, 1861.

[45]Frederick Douglass to Samuel J. May, August 30, 1861, in Masur, *"The Real War,"* p. 106.

[46]ML to Elizabeth Todd Grimsley, September 29, 1861, in Turner and Turner, p. 106.

[47]Taft Diary, September 27, 1861, LC. For a full accounting of Mary's efforts to hide her private spending, see Burlingame, *The Inner World*, pp. 298–304, and Burlingame, "Honest Abe, Dishonest Mary." On the other side, Jean Baker blames Wood, who was in charge of the accounts, for the overspending; local merchants for overcharging the naïve First Lady; critics for holding her "liable for what neither law nor custom gave her control of"; and "Seward's friends [who] gossiped" about her dinner for Napoleon. See Baker, *Mary Todd Lincoln*, pp. 187–89, 199.

[48]B. B. French Diaries, December 14, 1861, B. B. French Journals, LC.

[49]French Diaries, December 16, 1861, LC.

[50]ML to James Gordon Bennet, October 25, 1861, in Turner and Turner, p. 111.

[51]Wikoff told his adventures in *My Courtship and Its Consequences* (1854), *Adventures of a Roving Diplomatist* (1956), and *A New Yorker in the Foreign Office* (1858). "He was very little in America, settled no where, and died of paralysis at Brighton, England, May 3, 1884"; so summed up his biographer. *The National Cyclopedia of American Biography* (New York: James T. White & Co., 1898), 1:316. Mrs. Sickles's lover was the son of Francis Scott Key, composer of "The Star-Spangled Banner."

[52]Burlingame, "Honest Abe, Dishonest Mary," pp. 7, 20–23.

[53]Donald, *Lincoln*, p. 324. Wikoff told his version in the *Herald*, March 3, 1862; ML to Alexander Williamson, December 14, 1866, in Turner and Turner, p. 398.

[54]McPherson, *Battle Cry of Freedom*, pp. 358–65; Long and Long, *The Civil War Day by Day*, pp. 129, 147.

[55]John G. Nicolay to Therena Bates, November 24, 1861, Nicolay Collection, LC; French Diaries, December 22, 1862, LC; *Herald*, December 18, 1861.

[56]Taft Diary, January 2, January 6, and January 11, LC; Bayne, *Tad Lincoln's Father*, p. 43.

[57]Keckley, *Behind the Scenes*, pp. 95–97; Nicolay's Etiquette and Office Intercourse File, Nicolay Collection.

[58]Keckley, *Behind the Scenes*, p. 97.

[59]John G. Nicolay to Therena Bates, February 6, 1862, Nicolay Collection; *Herald*, February 6, 1862; Baker, *Mary Todd Lincoln*, pp. 206–7.

[60]Keckley, *Behind the Scenes*, p. 101; James and Temple, "Mrs. Lincoln's Clothing," p. 60.

[61]Simeon Whiteley to his wife, February 5, 1862, ISHL; Jessie Fremont, "Great Events During the Life of Major General John C. Fremont . . . and of Jessie Benton Fremont," Fremont Papers, The Bancroft Library, University of California, Berkeley, p. 327.

[62]John G. Nicolay to Therena Bates, February 21, 1862, Nicolay Collection.

[63]Keckley, *Behind the Scenes*, pp. 102–3.

[64]Ibid., pp. 103–5.

[65]ML to Julia Ann Spriggs, May 29, 1862, in Turner and Turner, pp. 127–28; ML to Ruth Harris, May 17, 1862 and May, undated, 1862 in Turner and Turner, pp. 125–27.

CHAPTER TEN

[1]Responding to charges after Shiloh that Grant was an incompetent drunkard and a political liability, Lincoln said, "*I can't spare this man; he fights.*" McPherson, *Battle Cry of Freedom*, pp. 402, 413–4.

[2]Quoted in McPherson, *Battle Cry of Freedom*, p. 354.

[3]Henry Mayer, *All On Fire: William Lloyd Garrison and the Abolition of Slavery* (New York: St. Martin's Press, 1998), p. 527; McPherson, *Battle Cry of Freedom*, pp. 355–56.

[4]"Annual Message to Congress," December 3, 1861, in *LSW, 1859–1865*, pp. 291–92; McPherson, *Battle Cry of Freedom*, p. 358.

[5]McPherson, pp. 495–96; Douglass, "Fighting the Rebels with One Hand," January 14, 1862, in Masur, *The Real War*, p. 109.

[6]Frederick Douglass to Charles Sumner, April 8, 1862, in Blight, *Frederick Douglass' Civil War*, p. 108; Douglass's criticism of Lincoln's colonization plan, pp. 122–47. Elizabeth Blair Lee to Samuel Phillips Lee, April 18, 1862, in Laas, *Wartime Washington*, pp. 130–31.

[7]Elizabeth Blair Lee to Samuel Phillips Lee, April 18, 1862, in ibid., pp. 130–31.

[8]Mary Clemmer Ames, *Evening Post*, April 18, 1862, p. 1. On images of slave women in white women's sentimental discourse, see Franny Nudelman, "Harriet Jacobs and the Sentimental Politics of Female Suffering," *ELH* 59 (1992): 939–64; Jean Fagan Yellin, *Women and Sisters: The Antislavery Feminists in American Culture* (New Haven: Yale University Press, 1989); and Fleischner, *Mastering Slavery*, chap. 2.

[9]Elizabeth Edwards to Julia Edwards Baker, March 2 and March 12, 1862, Elizabeth P. Todd Edwards Papers, ISHL; Bayne, *Tad Lincoln's Father*, p. 82; Keckley, *Behind the Scenes*, pp. 116–17; C. P. Weaver, ed., *Thank God My Regiment an African One: The Civil War Diary of Colonel Nathan W. Daniels* (Baton Rouge: Louisiana State University Press, 1998), p. 172; Mrs. Mary Logan Hay to Milton Hay, April 13, 1862, Stuart-Hay Papers; ML to John Hay, ca. May 25, 1862, in Thomas F. Schwartz and Kim M. Bauer, "Unpublished Mary Todd Lincoln," *Journal of the Abraham Lincoln Association* 17.2 (1996): 4. The clipping of the eulogy that Mary saved was written by society journalist N. P. Willis, in whose home Harriet Jacobs was living in the 1850s when she wrote her slave narrative. Jacobs believed that Willis was proslavery and so hid from him the fact that she was writing an abolitionist book.

[10]ML to Elizabeth Grimsley, September 29, 1861, in Turner and Turner, p. 105; Elizabeth Edwards interview with WHH, 1865–66, in Wilson and Davis, p. 445.

[11]Elizabeth Edwards to Julia Edwards Baker, March 12, 1862, Elizabeth P. Todd Edwards Papers, ISHL; Elizabeth Blair Lee to Samuel Phillips Lee, March 1, 1862, in Laas, *Wartime Washington*, p. 104.

[12]Elizabeth Edwards to Julia Edwards Baker, March 2 and March [undated], 1862, Elizabeth P. Todd Edwards Papers.

[13]Elizabeth Edwards to Julia Edwards Baker, April 26, 1862, Elizabeth P. Todd Edwards Paper.

[14]Elizabeth Edwards to Julia Baker Edwards, March [undated], 1862, Elizabeth P. Todd Edwards Papers; Elizabeth Edwards interview with WHH, 1865–66, in Wilson and Davis, pp. 444–45.

[15]Isaac Newton, Commissioner of Agriculture, told John Hay in 1867, "That lady has set here on this here sofy & shed tears by the pint a begging me to pay her debts which was unbeknown to the President." John Hay Diary, February 13, 1867, quoted in Burlingame, "Honest Abe, Mary Dishonest," p. 49.

[16]Whitman quoted in David Blight, *Race and Reunion: The Civil War in American Memory* (Cambridge, MA: Harvard University Press, 2001), p. 21; Green, *Washington*, p. 261; Taft Diary, May 11, 1864, LC.

[17]Ira Berlin, Barbara J. Fields, Stephen F. Miller, Joseph P. Reidy, and Leslie S. Rowland, eds., *Free at*

Last: A Documentary History of Slavery, Freedom, and the Civil War (New York: New Press, 1992), pp. 37–38.

[18] Green, Washington, pp. 276–77.

[19] Jane Stuart Woolsey, Hospital Days: Reminiscence of a Civil War Nurse (Roseville, MN: Edinborough Press, 1996), p. 55.

[20] Ibid., pp. 55–56; Berlin et al., Free at Last, pp. 168–80, 204–8.

[21] Green, Washington, pp. 278–79; Taft Diary, January 6, 1863, LC.

[22] Keckley, Behind the Scenes, pp. 111–12, 140.

[23] Ibid., pp. 139–40.

[24] ML to AL, November 2, 1862, in Turner and Turner, p. 140.

[25] Keckley, Behind the Scenes, pp. 116–17, 104–5.

[26] Burlingame, The Inner World, pp. 296–97; Keckley, Behind the Scenes, pp. 116–17.

[27] Sociologist Orlando Patterson has argued that slavery was a "relation of domination" whose constituent elements were violence, natal alienation, and dishonoring of the slave. These contributed to "the social death" of the slave. See Orlando Patterson, Slavery and Social Death: A Comparative Study (Cambridge, MA: Harvard University Press, 1982).

[28] ML to Mrs. Charles Eames, July 26, 1862, in Turner and Turner, pp. 130–31; Isaac Diller interview, in "Untold History: With a New and Authentic Story about Lincoln and Stanton," St-Louis Post Dispatch, undated clipping in Tarbell Collection.

[29] Long and Long, The Civil War Day by Day, pp. 233–35; AL to George B. McClellan, June 28, 1862, in LSW, 1859–1862, p. 334; Keckley, Behind the Scenes, p. 132.

[30] Howard K. Beale, ed., Gideon Welles Diaries, Vol. 1, 1861–March 1864 (New York: Norton, 1960), p. 70. See abolitionist Lydia Maria Child's favorable response to Lincoln's offer to the border states in Carolyn L. Karcher, The First Woman in the Republic: A Cultural Biography of Lydia Maria Child (Durham, NC: Duke University Press, 1994), p. 441.

[31] AL to Horace Greely, August 22, 1862, in LSW, 1859–1865, pp. 357–58. The colonization scheme collapsed when Honduras and Nicaragua opposed it. A U.S.-sponsored colony of 453 settlers in Haiti in 1863 was decimated by starvation and smallpox, and Lincoln sent a ship to bring the survivors home. This ended official efforts to colonize African Americans. McPherson, Battle Cry of Freedom, p. 509.

[32] "Address on Colonization to a Committee of Colored Men, Washington, D.C.," August 14, 1862, in LSW, 1859–1865, pp. 353–57.

[33] McPherson, Battle Cry of Freedom, pp. 506–10. For a more critical view of Lincoln, see Mayer, All On Fire, 537–39; Blight, Frederick Douglass' Civil War, pp. 138–93; Douglass, "The Black Man's Future in the Southern States," February 5, 1862, quoted in Masur, "The Real War," p. 109.

[34] Keckley, Behind the Scenes, p. 113.

[35] Union Bethel Church Records, Cook Family Papers Moorland-Spingarn Research Center.

[36] "Preliminary Emancipation Proclamation," September 22, 1862, in LSW, 1859–1865, p. 368.

[37] McPherson, Battle Cry of Freedom, pp. 557–58; Mayer, All On Fire, p. 542; Blight, Frederick Douglass' Civil War, p. 108.

[38] Blight, Frederick Douglass' Civil War, p. 115.

[39] Donations: The Sheffield Anti-Slavery Society of England, $24; Aberdeen Ladies' Society, $40; Anti-Slavery Society of Edinburgh, $48; Friends at Bristol, $176; Birmingham Negro's Friend Society, $50; and Birmingham Society, $33, received through Douglass's son, Charles R. Douglass. Keckley, Behind the Scenes, pp. 115–16. Phillip S. Foner and Robert James Branham, Lift

Every Voice: African American Oratory, 1787–1900 (Tuscaloosa: University of Alabama Press, 1998), p. 452.

[40]ML to AL, November 2, 1862, in Turner and Turner, pp. 139–40; ML to James Gordon Bennet, October 4, 1862, in Turner and Turner, p. 138; Keckley, *Behind the Scenes*, pp. 130–31.

[41]ML to Edwin D. Morgan, November 13, 1862, in Turner and Turner, pp. 141–42.

[42]William Quentin Maxwell, *Lincoln's Fifth Wheel: The Political History of the U.S. Sanitary Commission* (New York: Longmans, Green & Co., 1956); Louisa May Alcott, *Hospital Sketches* (1863), in *Alternative Alcott*, ed., Elaine Showalter (New Brunswick: Rutgers University Press, 1988), pp. xviii–xix, 3; Woolsley, *Hospital Days*, pp. 4–5.

[43]Diary of George W. Barbour, May 19, 1864, Bentley Library, University of Michigan; ML to Thomas W. Sweney, April [undated], 1863, in Turner and Turner, 149–50; 145.

[44]ML to AL, November 2, 1862, in Turner and Turner, pp. 140; ML to AL, November 3, 1862, in Turner and Turner, pp. 140–41.

[45]Silber, *Songs of the Civil War*, pp. 10, 21–23; Blight, *Frederick Douglass' Civil War*, p. 112.

CHAPTER ELEVEN

[1]Reverend Jonathan C. Gibbs, *Freedom's Joyful Day*, preached January 1, 1863, printed in the *Christian Recorder*, January 17, 1863, in Foner and Branham, *Lift Every Voice*, pp. 381–83.

[2]Washington, *They Knew Lincoln*, pp. 90–91.

[3]Frederick Douglass, *Life and Times of Frederick Douglass: Written by Himself* (1893; rpt. New York: Library of America, 1994), pp. 790–91.

[4]ML to George Harrington, March 20, 1863, in Turner and Turner, p. 149.

[5]AL to Andrew Johnson, March 26, 1863, in *LSW, 1861–1865*, p. 440; Blight, *Frederick Douglass' Civil War*, p. 148; Taft Diary, June 29, 1863, LC; McPherson, *Battle Cry of Freedom*, p. 687. The 54th Massachusetts led the frontal assault and lost half its men, including Colonel Shaw, who was buried in a mass grave with his fallen soldiers—"with his niggers," one Confederate officer put it.

[6]Keckley, *Behind the Scenes*, pp. 236–37; ML to Charles Sumner, April 5, 1864, in Turner and Turner, p. 174; Keckley Pension papers, Records of the Veterans' Administration, National Archives.

[7]Browning diary entry, cited in Turner and Turner, p. 134.

[8]Noah Brooks, *Washington in Lincoln's Time* (New York: Century, 1895), pp. 64–66. Brooks says he unmasked Colchester as a fraud when, reaching in the dark toward the sounds of thumping, thwanging, and ringing bells, he grasped "the very solid and fleshy hand in which was held a bell that was being thumped on a drum-head."

[9]Barbara Goldsmith, *Other Powers: The Age of Suffrage, Spiritualism, and the Scandalous Victoria Woodhull* (New York: Knopf, 1998), p. 78. Information about spiritualism in these passages is culled from Goldsmith, pp. 27–31, 55; see also Baker, *Mary Todd Lincoln*, pp. 217–20.

[10]Bayne, *Tad Lincoln's Father*, p. 30.

[11]Goldsmith, *Other Powers*, p. 267.

[12]Elizabeth Blair Lee to Samuel Phillips Lee, January 14, 1863, in Laas, *Wartime Washington*, p. 231.

[13]Donald, *Lincoln*, p. 448; *Washington Chronicle*, July 3, 1863; Letter to the Editor, *National Tribune*, November 11, 1920.

[14]Beale, *Diary of Gideon Welles*, June 8, 1863, 1:325, 327.

[15]Ruth Painter Randall, *Lincoln's Sons* (Boston: Little, Brown, 1955), p. 124.

[16]Ibid.

[17]AL to Mary Todd Lincoln, June 9, 1863, in *LSW, 1859–1865* p. 453; Keckley, *Behind the Scenes*, pp. 120–21.

[18]Donald, *Lincoln*, pp. 448–54.

[19]Douglass, *Life and Times*, p. 785; Blight, *Douglass' Civil War*, pp. 168–69.

[20]Keckley, *Behind the Scenes*, pp. 179–81.

[21]Washington, *They Knew Lincoln*, pp. 82–84; Joan D. Hedrick, *Harriet Beecher Stowe: A Life* (New York: Oxford University Press, 1994), pp. 305–6, vii.

[22]Keckley, *Behind the Scenes*, pp. 139–41; W. E. B. Du Bois, *Souls of Black Folk*, pp. 536–46; Nell Irvin Painter, *Sojourner Truth: A Life, a Symbol* (New York: Norton, 1996), p. 215.

[23]ML to Mary Jane Welles, February 1, 1863, in Turner and Turner, p. 147.

[24]AL to ML, September 22, 1863, in Tarbell, *The Life*, p. 386; Miers, *Lincoln Day by Day*, 3:221.

[25]Turner and Turner, *Mary Todd Lincoln*, 154; Randall, *Lincoln's Sons*, p. 124.

[26]Description of Emilie's visit in these passages is in Helm, *Mary, Wife of Lincoln*, pp. 219–33; Emilie Todd Helm to ML, October 30, 1864, Robert Todd Lincoln Papers, LC.

[27]Keckley, *Behind the Scenes*, p. 121.

[28]Ibid., pp. 122–23.

[29]James and Temple, "Mrs. Lincoln's Clothing," pp. 61–62; Donald, *Lincoln*, p. 475.

[30]McPherson, *Battle Cry of Freedom*, pp. 687–88, 698–713.

[31]Taft Diary, December 2, 1863, and December 27, 1863, LC; Green, *Washington*, p. 268. Senator Samuel C. Pomeroy, who had escorted Douglass to the White House in the summer, issued a circular declaring that because Lincoln only went in for "temporary expedients," the "one-term principle" had to be invoked for "a victorious war and a just peace." McPherson, *Battle Cry of Freedom*, p. 714.

[32]Keckley, *Behind the Scenes*, p. 128.

[33]John G. Nicolay to John Hay, January 18, 1864, and January 24, 1864; John G. Nicolay to Therena Bates, December 7, 1862, Nicolay Collection.

[34]Taft Diary, May 25, 1864, LC.

[35]McPherson, *Battle Cry of Freedom*, p. 757; Donald, *Lincoln*, p. 519.

[36]Keckley, *Behind the Scenes*, pp. 119–20.

[37]Ibid., p. 149.

[38]After his sons were no longer welcome in the White House, Horatio Taft soured on Mary Lincoln. His descriptions of her shopping convey the resentment that others shared: "I should rather think that she would have a better chance at the goods if she was to go into the Store but then she *might* get jostled and gazed at and that too would be doing just as the common people do." Taft Diary, December 14, 1864, LC; see also January 2, 1863. ML to A. T. Stewart, April 16, 1864, in Turner and Turner, pp. 174–75; *New York Herald*, May 2, 1864, quoted in Turner and Turner, p. 162; Keckly, *Behind the Scenes*, p. 348; James and Temple, "Mrs. Lincoln's Clothing," p. 64; French Letter Book 14, January 2, 1866, David Rankin Barbee Papers, Georgetown University.

[39]ML to Mercy Levering Conkling, November 19, 1864, in Turner and Turner, p. 187.

[40]ML to Benjamin Butler, January 15, 1864, in Turner and Turner, p. 167; Burlingame, "Honest Abe, Dishonest Mary," p. 11; *Washington Gazette*, January 16, 1887, article attributed to William P. Wood, superintendent of the Old Capitol Prison during the Lincoln administration. In 1866, Stackpole privately borrowed $2,000 for Mary from a Washington financier, which she considered a fair return to her, "as through me," she wrote, "he gained many favors, of my good husband." ML to Alexander Williamson, February 2, 1866, in Turner and Turner, pp. 332–33.

[41]Keckley, *Behind the Scenes*, pp. 147–48.

[42]Ibid., pp. 152–54.

[43]ML to EK, November 2, 1864, in Turner and Turner, p. 182; Elizabeth Keckly to ML, November 19 and November 26, 1864, in National Archives. I am indebted to Michael Burlingame for Keckly's telegrams.

[44]Keckley, *Behind the Scenes*, pp. 127–28.

[45]Ibid., pp. 124–25, 144–45.

[46]Mark E. Neely Jr., "Thurlow Weed, the New York Custom House, and Mrs. Lincoln's 'Treason,'" *Lincoln Lore*, no. 1679 (January 1978): 4. In Wakeman, Mary found a willing vehicle for spreading her rebuttals to the objectionable stories that were regularly appearing in the Democratic *World* about how she used government appropriations to embellish and enrich herself and her family.

[47]ML to Abram Wakeman, September 29, 1864, in Turner and Turner, p. 181; Donald, *Lincoln*, pp. 532–33.

[48]ML to Charles Sumner, March 28, 1864, and April 5, 1864, in Turner and Turner, pp. 172–74; ML to Alexander Williamson, August 19, 1866, in Turner and Turner, p. 382; Donald, *Charles Sumner*, pp. 167–19, 314–20.

[49]Blight, *Frederick Douglass' Civil War*, p. 184.

[50]Nell Irvin Painter finds Colman's version more in keeping with Lincoln's racial attitudes. However, Truth's story is more in keeping with others' accounts of Lincoln's meetings with black people in the White House and with his treatment of people in general. Citations for Truth's visit in Painter, *Sojourner Truth*, pp. 203–7.

[51]McFeely, *Frederick Douglass*, p. 260.

[52]Keckley, *Behind the Scenes*, pp. 92–94.

[53]ML to Abram Wakeman, February 20, 1865, in Turner and Turner, p. 202; Gayle T. Harris, "Mary Lincoln's 1865 Shopping Spree," *The Lincolnian* (May–June 1995): 3; Baker, *Mary Todd Lincoln*, p. 259.

[54]*LSW, 1859–1865*, p. 687.

[55]McPherson, *Battle Cry of Freedom*, pp. 840–41; Keckley, *Behind the Scenes*, pp. 158–60.

[56]Keckley, *Behind the Scenes*, p. 156–57.

[57]Ibid., p. 163.

[58]ML to Abram Wakeman, April 4, 1865, in Turner and Turner, p. 213.

[59]Baker, *Mary Todd Lincoln*, pp. 238–40.

[60]Donald, *Lincoln*, p. 576; ML to AL, April 6, 1865, in Turner and Turner, p. 215.

[61]Keckley, *Behind the Scenes*, p. 241.

[62]Ibid., pp. 164–67.

[63]Ibid., p. 169.

[64]Ibid., 167–73; Miers, *Lincoln Day by Day*, 3:326–27.

[65]Thomas F. Pendel, *Thirty-six Years in the White House* (Washington, DC: Neale Publishing Company, 1902), p. 33.

[66]Keckley, *Behind the Scenes*, pp. 174–78; Baker, *Mary Todd Lincoln*, p. 241.

[67]Donald, *Lincoln*, p. 588.

[1]Keckley, *Behind the Scenes*, pp. 184–86. On the night of the assassination, the powerful and violent Lewis Thornton Powell, better known as Lewis Payne, intent on assassinating Seward, rampaged through Seward's house, leaving five people seriously wounded, including Seward, his sons Frederick and Augustus, a male nurse who had been employed to help Seward recover from a recent carriage accident, and a State Department messenger who happened to be downstairs.

[2]Beale, *Diary of Gideon Welles*, April 15, 1865, 2:290.

[3]Keckley, *Behind the Scenes*, pp. 187–89, 190; French Diaries, April 15, 1865, LC.

[4]Keckley, *Behind the Scenes*, pp. 191–92.

[5]ML to Mrs. James Adams Kasson, January 20, 1866, in Schwartz and Bauer, "Unpublished Mary Todd Lincoln," pp. 10–11.

[6]Elizabeth Blair Lee to Samuel Phillips Lee, April 17, April 19, April 20, and April 22, 1865, in Laas, *Wartime Washington*, pp. 496–99.

[7]French Diaries, April 15, 1865, LC; Elizabeth Blair Lee to Samuel Phillips Lee, April 22, 1865, in Laas, *Wartime Washington*, p. 499; Dr. Anson G. Henry to Mrs. Eliza Dunlap Henry, May 8, 1865, Anson Henry Papers, ISHL.

[8]Keckley, *Behind the Scenes*, p. 196.

[9]Randall, *Lincoln's Sons*, p. 106; Keckley, *Behind the Scenes*, p. 197.

[10]Keckley, *Behind the Scenes*, p. 197; ML to Elizabeth Blair Lee, December 11, 1865, in Turner and Turner, p. 302.

[11]Keckley, *Behind the Scenes*, pp. 196, 219.

[12]Ibid., p. 199.

[13]ML to Simon Cameron, April 6, 1866, in Turner and Turner, p. 351.

[14]Keckley, *Behind the Scenes*, pp. 149, 204; Turner and Turner, *Mary Todd Lincoln*, p. 247. Lizzy said Mary owed $70,000 when she left the White House.

[15]Turner and Turner, *Mary Todd Lincoln*, p. 162; Keckley, *Behind the Scenes*, p. 207; ML to Mrs. James Adams Kasson, January 20, 1866, in Schwartz and Bauer, "Unpublished Mary Todd Lincoln," pp. 10–11; Noah Brooks, "Letter to *Sacramento Daily Union*," dated May 17, 1865, published June 14, 1865.

[16]ML to Charles Sumner, May 9, 1865, in Turner and Turner, pp. 227–28; Keckley, *Behind the Scenes*, pp. 308–11.

[17]I base my dating of Mary's departure on French's dating in his diary. Baker and Turner and Turner date her departure on May 23. French Diaries, May 24, 1865, LC.

[18]Keckley, *Behind the Scenes*, p. 208.

[19]Beale, *Diary of Gideon Welles*, May 23, 1865, p. 310; French Diaries, May 24, 1865, LC.

[20]Quoted in Turner and Turner, p. 235.

[21]Keckley, *Behind the Scenes*, pp. 209–10.

[22]Washington, *They Knew Lincoln*, p. 225.

[23]Keckley, *Behind the Scenes*, p. 214.

[24]ML to Alexander Williamson, December 31, 1865, in Turner and Turner, p. 320.

[25]Keckley, *Behind the Scenes*, pp. 221–22.

[26]Records of the Fifteenth Street Presbyterian Church, Moorland-Spingarn Research Center, Howard University.

[27]Fleischner, *Mastering Slavery*, pp. 117–18.

[28]Keckley, *Behind the Scenes*, p. 241.

[29]Green, *The Secret City*, p. 89.

[30]Keckley, *Behind the Scenes*, p. 253.

[31]Description of Lizzy's visit in ibid., pp. 238–66.

[32]ML to Anson G. Henry, July 17, 1865, in Turner and Turner, p. 260; ML to Charles Sumner, July 4, 1865, in Turner and Turner, p. 255.

[33]ML to David Davis, June 27, 1865, in ibid., p. 254; ML to David Davis, February 24, 1867, in ibid., p. 410; Baker, *Mary Todd Lincoln*, p. 260.

[34]ML to Sally Orne, December 24, 1865, in Turner and Turner, p. 312; Baker, *Mary Todd Lincoln*, p. 260; ML to Oliver S. Halsted Jr., November 11, 1865, in Turner and Turner, p. 279.

[35]ML to Alexander Williamson, November 28, 1865, and February 17, 1866, in Turner and Turner, pp. 288, 337.

[36]Ibid., p. 247; ML to Alexander Williamson, November 19, 1865, and February 17, 1866, in ibid., pp. 286, 336.

[37]ML to Alexander Williamson, January 3, 1866, in ibid., p. 321; ML to Sally Orne, January 4, 1866, in ibid., p. 322.

[38]ML to Sally Orne, August 31, 1865, in ibid., pp. 270–71.

[39]ML to Charles Sumner, May 9, 1865, in ibid., p. 227; ML to Richard J. Oglesby, June 10, 1865, in ibid., p. 244; WHH to Josiah G. Holland, June 8, 1865, in Wilson and Davis, p. xiv.

[40]Robert Todd Lincoln to WHH, December 24, 1866, in Robert Todd Lincoln Collection, Chicago Historical Society.

[41]ML to Sally Orne, December 30, 1865, in Turner and Turner, pp. 318–19.

[42]Ibid., p. 350.

[43]Wilson and Davis, p. 326; ML to WHH, August 28, 1866, in Turner and Turner, p. 384; "Mrs. Lincoln's Denial, and What She Says," printed broadside, ISHL.

[44]WHH, "Lincoln, Ann Rutledge and the Pioneers of New Salem," delivered November 16, 1866, in Springfield, Ill.; printed broadside, ISHL; rpt. Limited edition, Harry Rosecrans Burke, ed. (Herrin, Ill.: Trovillion Private Press, 1945), pp. 5–6.

[45]Goff, *Robert Todd Lincoln*, p. 84; ML to David Davis, March 4, 1867, and March 6, 1867, in Turner and Turner, pp. 414–16.

[46]ML to Charles Sumner, September 10, 1866, in Turner and Turner, p. 386; ML to Alexander Williamson, February 9, 1866, in Turner and Turner, p. 336.

[47]ML to James Smith, December 17, 1866, in ibid., p. 400; ML to EK, March 1867, in ibid., p. 417.

[48]ML to EK, March 1867, in ibid., p. 418.

[49]ML to Alexander Williamson, November 10, 1867, in ibid., p. 452; ML to James Gordon Bennet, October 4, 1862, in ibid., p. 138.

[50]Keckley, *Behind the Scenes*, pp. 269–70.

[51]ML to EK, September, 17, 1867, in Turner and Turner, pp. 433–34.

[52]Keckley, *Behind the Scenes*, p. 275.

[53]Ibid., pp. 280–81.

[54]Ibid., pp. 286–87.

[55]Ibid., p. 288.

[56]ML to W. H. Brady, September 1867, September 14, 1867, and September 22, 1867, in Turner and Turner, pp. 434–36.

[57]Keckley, *Behind the Scenes*, p. 294.

[58]Ibid., p. 289.

[59]Ibid., p. 296.

[60]ML to EK, October 6, 1867, in Turner and Turner, pp. 438–40.

[61]Ibid., p. 440.

[62]New York *Herald*, October 4, 1867; *Louisville Democrat*, October 12 and October 24, 1867; *Springfield Republican*, October 15, 1867; New York *World*, October 6, 1867; *New York Citizen*, October 5 and 19, 1867; *Cincinnati Commercial*, October 13, 1867.

[63]ML to EK, October 13, 1867, in Turner and Turner, pp. 442–43; *Chicago Republican*, October 9, 1867; *Pittsburgh Commercial*, October 29, 1867.

[64]ML to EK, October 9, 1867, November 11, 1867, and November 15, 1867, in Turner and Turner, pp. 441, 448, 453; *Pittsburgh Commercial*, October 29, 1867.

[65]New York *Herald*, October 4 and October 17, 1867.

[66]Keckley, *Behind the Scenes*, pp. 306–20.

[67]Frederick Douglass to EK, October 18, 1867, in ibid., p. 316; ML to EK, November 2, 9, 15, 17, and 24, 1867, in Turner and Turner, pp. 448, 449, 454, 456, 461.

[68]ML to EK, November 21 and 23, and December 27, 1867, in Turner and Turner, pp. 459, 461, 466.

[69]ML to EK, December 27 and October 13, 1867, in ibid., pp. 466, 442.

[70]ML to EK, November 15, 1867, in ibid., p. 454.

[71]ML to EK, October 13, 1867, in ibid., p. 443; ML to Rhoda White, October 18, 1867, in ibid., p. 444.

[72]ML to EK, January 12, 1868, in ibid., p. 468.

[73]Ibid.

[74]ML to EK, January 15, and February 29, 1868, in ibid., pp. 469–70; ML to EK, January 12, 1868, and November 9, 1867, in ibid., pp. 449, 468.

[75]Turner and Turner, p. 471; ML to EK, January 15, 1868, in ibid., p. 469.

[76]ML to EK, November 24, 1867, in ibid., p. 461; Keckley, *Behind the Scenes*, pp. xiv–xv.

[77]Ibid., p. xiv.

[78]Frederick Douglass to EK, November 10, 1867, in ibid., pp. 320–21. Frances Rollin, daughter of a free black elite family in Charleston, read *Behind the Scenes* and sniffed, "It is well written but not by Mrs. K. that's clear." Nor was she impressed by a public reading Keckley gave: "It is too late in the day for her to attempt it especially without a first class teacher." Quoted in Sterling, *We Are Your Sisters*, pp. 459–60.

[79]Redpath, an experienced book editor, had compiled one book of his own articles about the antebellum South and another of other people's speeches and sermons in praise of John Brown. During the war, he published a series of cheap paperbacks of reprints; afterward, he was an organizer of speaking tours for authors.

[80]Washington, *They Knew Lincoln*, pp. 232–36; Frances Smith Foster, ed., introduction to EK, *Behind the Scenes* (Urbana: University of Illinois Press, 2001), pp. lii–lx.

[81]New York *Citizen*, April 18, 1868; *National Intelligencer*, April 25, 1868; *Springfield Republican*, April 22, 1868; *Behind the Scenes; By a Nigger Woman who Took in Work from Mrs. Lincoln and Mrs. Davis*, The National News Co., NY, 1868. Copyright entered by D. Ottolenguel.

[82]New York *Citizen*, April 25, 1868.

[83]ML to Rhoda White, May 2, 1868, in Turner and Turner, p. 476.

[84]ML to Eliza Slataper, December 13, 1868, in Turner and Turner, p. 494.

Epilogue

[1]ML to EK, October 29, 1867, in Turner and Turner, p. 447.

[2]Elizabeth Stuart Phelps, *The Gates Ajar* (Boston: Fields, Osgood & Co., 1868), p. 6; Goldsmith, *Other Powers*, p. 211; ML to Jesse Kilgore Dubois, July 26, 1868, in Schwartz and Bauer, "Unpublished Mary Todd Lincoln," p. 15.

[3]ML to Eliza Slataper, October 4, 1871, in Turner and Turner, p. 596; ML to Elizabeth Emerson Atwater, June 30, 1867, in Turner and Turner, p. 425; ML to David Davis, November 9, 1871, in Turner and Turner, p. 597; Baker, *Mary Todd Lincoln*, p. 308.

[4]"I wish my remains to be clothed in the white silk dress which will be found in the lower drawer of the bureau in my room. I desire that my body shall remain for two days (48) hours, without the *lid* of the coffin being screwed down. On the 3rd day, after my death, Professor Swing, acceding, I wish the coffin taken to the latter's church, he preaching the funeral sermon from the 23rd Psalm. . . . I wish my remains placed beside my dear husband & Taddie's on one side of me." The Reverend Swing was minister at the Westminster Presbyterian Church in Chicago. Mary Lincoln, "For Robert T. Lincoln, Esp. To be opened by him, immediately after my death," August 1874, ISHL; ML to Dr. Willis Danforth, undated, ISHL; Baker, *Mary Todd Lincoln*, pp. 310–13.

[5]Mark E. McNeely Jr. and R. Gerald McMurtry, *The Insanity File: The Case of Mary Todd Lincoln* (Carbondale: Southern Illinois University Press, 1986), pp. 11–17, 34–35; Baker. *Mary Todd Lincoln*, pp. 315–22; Michael Beschloss, "Last of the Lincolns," *New Yorker*, February 28, 1994, p. 55. Recent scholars have argued that her bizarre behavior was caused by post-traumatic stress disorder that was triggered by the anniversary of the assassination. See Norbert Hirschhorn and Robert G. Feldman, "Mary Lincoln's Final Illness: A Medical and Historical Reappraisal," *Journal of the History of Medicine* (October 1999): 525.

[6]ML to Robert Todd Lincoln, June 19, 1876, in Turner and Turner, p. 615.

[7]Helm, *Mary, Wife of Lincoln*, p. 298.

[8]Turner and Turner, p. 704.

[9]Baker, *Mary Todd Lincoln*, pp. 366–67.

[10]Hirschhorn and Feldman, "Mary Lincoln's Final Illness," pp. 535–36.

[11]List of the "Lincoln Relics" and Elizabeth Keckly affidavits, Chicago Historical Society; W. H. Lowdermilk & Co. to Mr. C. F. Gunther, Esq., July 1, 1890, in Gunther Collection, Chicago Historical Society.

[12]Francis J. Grimké, "Mrs. Elizabeth Keckley," Francis J. Grimké Collection, Moorland-Spingarn Research Center.

[13]Washington, *They Knew Lincoln*, pp. 240–41.

[14]*The Evening Star*, November 11, 1935.

[15]*The Evening Star*, November 15, 1935.

[16]"Writer Explains Error in Case of Mrs. Keckley," *The Evening Star*, November 26, 1835.

[17]Rutberg, *Mary Lincoln's Dressmaker*, pp. 157–58.

Acknowledgments

I wish to thank some of the generous people at the libraries and collections my research took me to who went out of their way to help me. They are John Sellers and Clark Evans at the Library of Congress; Kim Bauer, Cheryl Schnirring, and John Stassi at the Illinois State Historical Library; Michael Maione at Ford's Theatre; James Holberg at the Filson Club; Connie Thurson at Allegheny College Library; Cathleen Turner and Ebeth Scott-Sinclair, at the Hillsborough Historical Society; Claire McCann and James Birchfield at the University of Kentucky Library at Lexington; Chuck Hill and Eric Sandweiss at the Missouri Historical Society; Claudia Kidwell at the Smithsonian Institute; Carolyn Goudie at the Virginia State Library and Archives; Janie Morris at the Perkins Library, Duke University; Mary Junta at the National Archives; Joellen P. ElBasheer at the Moorland-Spingarn Research Center, Howard University; Melvina Conley at the Archives of the 22nd Judicial Circuit of Missouri; Gail Redmann at the

Historical Society of Washington, D.C.; and Susan Greenhagen at the SUNY Morrisville College Library.

I also owe thanks to the many people who helped me at the Swem Library, William and Mary College; the Virginia Historical Society; the New York Public Library; the Morgan Library; the Washington, D.C., Public Library; the Bentley Historical Library, University of Michigan; the Southern Historical Collection, University of North Carolina at Chapel Hill; the Hillsborough Public Library; the George Washington University Manuscripts Collection; the Chicago Historical Society; the Hope McCormick Costume Center, Chicago Historical Society; the Kentucky Historical Society; the Hampden-Sydney College Library; the Baker Library, Harvard University.

I was given the opportunity to give talks based on various sections of this book at the Abraham Lincoln Museum; Clark University; Northern Virginia Community College; William and Mary College; Ford's Theatre, sponsored by The Lincoln Forum; the National Archives, sponsored by Abraham Lincoln Institute of the Mid-Atlantic; and City College, CUNY.

I want to thank Steven K. Rogstad, Paul Verduin, Terry Alford, Fred Martin, Charles Hubbard, Gordon Leidner, James Hall, William Lee Miller, and Bill Harris for their special kindness during my travels in Lincoln circles. Neil Scott, Ann Lieberson, Betty Kleckley Stradford, William L. Andrews, Jean Fagan Yellin, and Carla Peterson helped me understand Elizabeth Keckly better. My friends at SUNY Albany supported my stepping out of academia. I am grateful to Joan Severa and Nancy Buenger for setting me straight on historical dress and design; Jean Bradley Anderson for talking to me about the Kirkland family; Virginia Laas for checking for Keckly in Elizabeth Blair Lee's letters; Rita Ostendorf for hunting up that Keckly photo; Barbara Clark Smith for showing me new ways of thinking about Mary Lincoln's wardrobe; Wayne Temple for patiently fielding all my questions; Douglas Wilson for being so very generous with his time and knowledge; Mary Beth Corrigan for opening up the Riggs Bank archives; Norbert Hirschhorn for disabusing me of a few bad medical notions; Joshua Wolf Shenk for talking with me about the Lincolns; Martha Burns for her last-minute help with all the details; Shirley Herscovitch Schaye for her analyses of Todd family dynamics and the word "friendship"; Jean-Louis Ecochard for his translations; Shelley Salamensky for her edits; Chris Bongie, Dagmar Herzog, Michael Staub, Lee Spole Epstein, and Jay Epstein for their hospitality; Karl Kroeber for many lunches; Werner Sollors for keeping the faith; Lil and Erwin Baida for dinner at the A.V.; Diane Cole, Donna Heiland, and Kathy Eden for listening to my woes; and

David Fleischner and Diana Wallerstein for letting me barter my way across the country. I cannot thank Michael Burlingame enough: he helped me enjoy three weeks in Springfield, introduced me to the world of Lincoln scholarship, read sections of my manuscript, and made it all so much fun. Finally, to Alex Schwartz, I owe special thanks for his insights, moral support, and for being so excited for me; and to Annie Schwartz, who kept on top of my daily page production.

Sydelle Kramer gave me wonderful advice; Janet Goldstein got the ball rolling; Ann Campbell read the manuscript with immense care; Jenny Cookson helped make it all work; and Gerry Howard watched over everything. I thank them all.

Index

261–63, 266, 268–71, 275–84; presidential
campaign and election, 1860, 184, 189–90,
193; presidential campaign and election, 1864,
268–70, 275, 279; quip on Todd name, 11;
Richmond, fall of and, 280–81; as "rising
Man," 96–97; Rutledge, Ann, and, 101, 102,
303; St. Louis lynching, speech on, 129;
self-education, 100, 101; Senate candidacy,
178–80, 187–88; speeches, Mary and, 175; in
Springfield, 96–117, 149–60, 168, 170–73;
stepmother and, 101; as surveyor, 99;
Thirteenth Amendment passed, 279–80;
wedding ring inscribed to MTL, 117; women
and, 101, 104–5
Lincoln, Eddie, 157, 161, 169; death of, 169
Lincoln, Mary Todd (MTL): admiration of
husband, 172; agent for, 299–300, 305;
ambitions to marry the President of the U.S.,
57–58, 94; antislavery and changing views on
race, 175–76, 251–53, 292; appearance and
demeanor, 1, 48, 97, 109, 161, 211–12;
attachment to other women, 49–50; as
"child-wife" and "father-husband," 167;
death, 322–23; debts and money problems, 2,
3–4, 290–91, 295, 298–305; emotional
illnesses and grief-stricken behavior, 158,
159–60, 167, 181, 237, 239, 244, 245, 249,
265–66, 272, 288–89, 321; emotional trauma
and losses, 2, 20, 49, 50, 113, 157–58, 171,
230–31, 232, 237, 265–66, 286–89, 320;
employment of free women, 177; final years,
319–23; France and love of things French,
62–63; friends, 93–94, 107, 108, 109, 110,
113, 117, 152, 156, 158, 180, 182, 212–14,
249, 288, 289, 292, 303–4; Germany trip,
318; grave, 325; health problems, 170, 322;
insanity commitment and court release, 321;
intelligence and education, 98–99, 105–6;
media treatment of, 197, 209–11, 221, 227,
301–2, 309–11, 316–17; memory of Lincoln
and papers of, 301–4; pension, 320, 322;
people MTL attracted to, 114; personality
and character, 4, 5, 15, 23, 48–49, 93–94, 96,
97–98, 109–10, 114, 135, 178–79, 180, 193,
208; poetry recitation and love of reading, 63;
politics, love of and ambitions, 93, 105, 106,
115–16, 150, 160, 168, 178–79, 187, 269–70;
premonition, 283; relationship with husband,
149–60, 168–70, 207, 213, 214, 224, 226,
229, 244, 250, 251–52, 265–68, 269–70, 303;
residence, Chicago, 2, 291, 293–95, 298–305,
310; sale of possessions, 300–301, 304,
305–11; sewing ability, 49, 98, 131, 156, 160;
spending habits and fashionable tastes, 3, 17,
19, 45, 47, 49, 98, 131, 167, 197–98, 205–7,

211–12, 217–22, 223–24, 229, 231, 238, 268,
271–72, 274; spiritualism and, 258–60, 288,
320; visions of dead sons, 166
CHILDHOOD AND EARLY YEARS, 8–26; African
American influence, 51; birth 8, 9; complicity
in helping runaway slaves, 52; desolation of
early years, 47, 49, 62; education at Madame
Mentelle's boarding school, 60–62; education
at Mr. Ward's, 58–59, 63; family history, 11,
12–18; family slaves, 10, 22–23, 45–46, 51, 56;
father's favorite, 49, 57–58, 64; half brothers
and sisters, 46, 161, 176; living with sister
Elizabeth Edwards, 63; Mammy, Aunt Sally, 5,
10, 15, 20, 23, 46, 50–52, 53, 55, 252; mother's
death, 21–22, 24; Orchard Springs trips, 47;
siblings, 8, 9, 19, 20–21; social standing of
family, 9–10, 11, 15–18, 60; stepmother and
household under, 25–27, 45–64
AS FIRST LADY: arrival in Washington, 198–99;
assassination of Lincoln, 285–88; assassination
attempt and injury, 260–62; disliked people,
199; dressmaker contacted by, meets EK, 197,
201; fall of Richmond and trip South, 281–82;
New Hampshire trip, 262; image as, 4;
inauguration, 201, 202–3; jealousy of, 275;
Lincoln's reelection and, 269–70; perks,
197–98; photographing of Presidential couple,
4; plea to grant clemency to Mary Real, 251;
political influence of, 197–98, 250, 274,
275–76; power struggles, 270; President's
Mansion, 204–6; refurbishing White House,
3, 218–21, 223–24, 272, 279; rumors about
flirtations, 276; séances in White House, 259;
self-importance, 4; shopping, 196–98, 218–22;
signing of Emancipation Proclamation and,
256; social successes and failures, 211, 213,
214, 225–230; suspicion of, as Southerner,
209–10; task of distracting her husband and
relieving his gloom, 193; vacates White
House, 290–93; war hospitals, help in, 251,
271; White House servants, 208, 218, 273
MRS. KECKLY AND: EK's memoir and betrayal,
318, 319; first meetings, 2, 201–2, 204–7; as
friend and confidante, 3, 5–6, 49, 50, 160,
207, 208, 217–18, 221, 223, 228, 230–31,
232, 239–40, 265, 272–75, 285–95, 313;
kinship with, 6; job recommendation for,
256–57; letters to, 2, 3; meeting, New York
City, 1867, sale of MTL's possessions, and
aftermath, 1–4, 304, 305–15; travel with,
243–44, 249, 281–82
IN SPRINGFIELD, ILLINOIS: absences of
husband, loneliness, growing independence,
155, 157–58; arrival in, 89, 92; child rearing
and, 151, 156, 158–59; compatibility with

Jennifer Fleischner, Ph.D., is the author of *Mastering Slavery: Memory, Family, and Identity in Women's Slave Narratives*. The recipient of a one-year Mellon Faculty Fellowship in Afro-American studies at Harvard, she is currently chair of the English department at Adelphi University.